Indians and Mestizos in the "Lettered City"

Indians and Mestizos in the "Lettered City"

Reshaping Justice, Social Hierarchy, and Political Culture in Colonial Peru

Alcira Dueñas

University Press of Colorado

Published by the University Press of Colorado
5589 Arapahoe Avenue, Suite 206C
Boulder, Colorado 80303

 The University Press of Colorado is a proud member of
the Association of American University Presses.

The University Press of Colorado is a cooperative publishing enterprise supported, in part, by
Adams State College, Colorado State University, Fort Lewis College, Mesa State College, Metro-
politan State College of Denver, University of Colorado, University of Northern Colorado, and
Western State College of Colorado.

∞ The paper used in this publication meets the minimum requirements of the American
National Standard for Information Sciences—Permanence of Paper for Printed Library Materials.
ANSI Z39.48-1992

Library of Congress Cataloging-in-Publication Data

Dueñas, Alcira, 1954–
  Indians and mestizos in the lettered city : reshaping justice, social hierarchy, and political culture
in colonial Peru / Alcira Dueñas.
    p. cm.
Includes bibliographical references and index.
  ISBN 978-1-60732-018-0 (hardcover : alk. paper) — ISBN 978-1-60732-019-7 (electronic book :
alk. paper) 1. Indians of South America—Peru—Politics and government. 2. Mestizos—Peru—
Politics and government. 3. Indian authors—Peru—History. 4. Peruvian literature—Indian
authors—History and criticism. 5. Learning and scholarship—Peru—History. 6. Anti-imperialist
movements—Peru—History. 7. Social justice—Peru—History. 8. Political culture—Peru—
History. 9. Peru—Ethnic relations. 10. Peru—Intellectual life. I. Title.
  F3429.3.P65D84 2010
  985'.01—dc22
                          2010015105
Design by Daniel Pratt

19 18 17 16 15 14 13 12 11 10   10 9 8 7 6 5 4 3 2 1

In the spirit of the known and unknown thinkers of the Andes, and to Lucas, Mateo, and Christopher Javier for coming into my life.

CONTENTS

Illustrations

ACKNOWLEDGMENTS

IN THE YEARS SINCE THE INCEPTION OF THIS BOOK, many people have kindly contributed to its completion, beyond what I can possibly acknowledge here. This book was made financially possible by grants from the Ohio State University–Newark and the Ohio State College of Arts and Sciences. Special thanks to Kenneth Andrien and Joanne Rappaport, who meticulously read my work more than once and provided meaningful criticism and constant support. David Garrett, Daniel Reff, Fernando Unzueta, and Maureen Ahern read and offered significant comments on one or several chapters. Sinclair Thomson deserves special gratitude for his meticulous reading of this book and his valuable suggestions. The book's final shape was greatly improved by the constructive criticism and wise suggestions of two anonymous reviewers selected by the University Press of Colorado. I express gratitude to Darrin Pratt, my editor, for his efficiency, flexibility, and unyielding interest in my work. The helpfulness and time spent on my requests by the staffs of the Archivo General de la Nación (Lima), the Biblioteca Nacional (Lima), the Archivo Departamental del Cuzco, the Archivo Arzobispal del Cuzco, the Biblioteca del Palacio Real (Madrid), the Archivum Romanum Societatis Iesu (Rome), and the Lilly Library (Bloomington, Indiana) were instrumental to the successful completion of this book. Finally, a special thank-you to Jesús Alcántara for his crucial help in Sevilla and Madrid; to my student research assistant, Meghan Hensley, for her tireless work and patience; and to Mateo Zabala, graphic designer, for his contribution.

Indians and Mestizos in the "Lettered City"

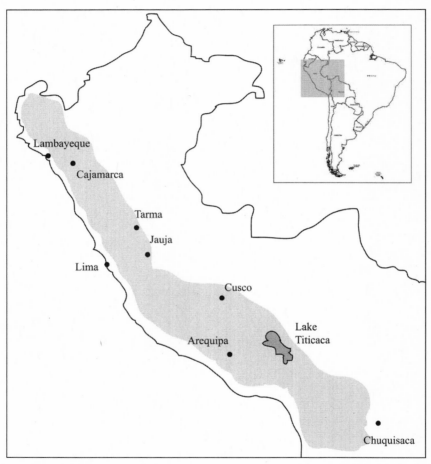

Figure 0.1 Colonial Andean Writers' Places of Origin. Illustration by Mateo Zabala.

INTRODUCTION

THE WORLD OF LETTERS in colonial Spanish America was a terrain of cultural interaction and contention. With important antecedents in the late sixteenth and early seventeenth centuries, Peruvian indigenous and mestizo writers continued to make inroads into the world of the literate while attempting to achieve social change during the mid- and late colonial period. During these years, literate Andeans crossed the Atlantic, showing up in metropolitan seats of power with their writings, their demands, and their representatives and fundamentally complicating our reflections on the nature and variety of responses to Spanish colonial impositions.

This book tells the story of a group of Andean writers and their scholarly works rarely acknowledged in studies of political or cultural resistance to colonial rule in the Andes. It shows that the production of Andean critical renditions of colonialism and efforts to reform society continued and developed broadly from the mid-1600s through the late 1700s, far beyond the well-known pioneering works of writers such as Santacruz Pachacuti Yamki Salcamaigua, Titu Cusi Yupanqui, Inca Garcilaso de la Vega, and Felipe Guamán Poma de Ayala. Later writers developed intellectual and social activism, engaging themselves and their fellow collaborators in political projects that revealed their continually evolving consciousness and unstated effort to challenge the definition of Andeans as "Indians."[1]

Andean scholars and activists contributed a significant colonial critique and carried out lengthy campaigns to reposition themselves as an autonomous "Indian nation" in an increasingly demeaning colonial world. They expressed their wish for ethnic autonomy in their struggles to have native and mestizo Andean women and men admitted to religious orders, to allow Andean men to enroll in schools and universities and to hold positions of power in ecclesiastic and civil administrations, and to create their own honorific symbols and organizations.

The reconstruction of this intellectual and political history is crucial for contemporary understanding of the major late-colonial upheavals in Cusco and La Paz, since the Andean writings under question reveal that issues such as the elimination of the *mita* (labor draft) system and the abolition of *corregidores*—raised by leaders of the Great Rebellion in 1780–1783—had been articulated earlier by the scholars under examination. This points to a preexisting discursive tradition of scholarly resistance to Spanish rule by Andeans. The notion that Spanish colonialism remained essentially unchallenged for over two centuries following the military defeat of the Inca at Vilcabamba (1572) has been widely accepted in narratives of Andean history. Studies of resistance to Spanish rule in the Peruvian Andes have remained focused largely on the dramatic political upheavals that swept through the area in the eighteenth century, with even greater concentration on the major pan-Andean rebellions led by Tomás Katari in Chayanta, Túpac Amaru in Cusco, and Túpac Katari in the area of La Paz (contemporary Bolivia) (1780–1783).[2] The complex texture of resistance in any colonial situation, however, can involve layers of thought, action, and negotiation far more subtle than the armed confrontation of a political regime.

In seventeenth- and eighteenth-century Peru, educated indigenous and mestizo subjects utilized the discursive strategies and theological knowledge available to them to question the legal and religious grounds of colonial power. The impetus for their oppositional politics was rooted in their changing daily experiences as colonized ethnic elites and their exposure to new European forms of knowledge and communication. As Andeans attempted to negotiate rights with the Spanish monarchs, they also resignified the preexisting Andean tradition of *mañay*. This age-old tradition, crucial during the formation of the Inca empire, sought a political and religious compromise through reciprocal agreements—not necessarily equal agreements—between victors (who demanded "favors") and the colonized (who "cooperated," expecting to secure the conditions for their social and cultural reproduction). The religious compromise replicated the one between humans and the supernatural to secure continual renewal of the life force.[3]

From the mid-1600s through the 1700s, a strong thematic pattern in Andean writing becomes increasingly apparent: discussions of the legal and imagined relationship between the king and his Indian subjects to foreground the inconsistency between the legal discourses of the crown and the everyday practices of its representatives in the Indian villages, rural areas, and colonial cities of the viceroyalty. Such discrepancies were particularly evident in the practices of provincial magistrates (*corregidores*), the regular and secular churches, and the regional high courts (*audiencias*)—especially during the social crises that ensued after the major overhauls of the Toledan reforms and during the Bourbon era, the two major social and political conjunctures demarcating the time span of this study.

The presence of Andean writers and their associated texts and discourses[4] in the *audiencias* and the royal court in Spain prompts a reconsideration of Angel Rama's notion of the "lettered city," or *ciudad letrada*, as the exclusive province of an elite class of state and ecclesiastic functionaries who both controlled the written word and wielded their power to define the terms of order within the empire.[5] The realm of the colonial lettered world, however, was hardly an uncontested space in which only the state and the church functionaries, or *letrados*, found expression. The Andeans studied in this work and dozens of other Indian authorities and their representatives who visited the royal courts in Spain and the Americas, bringing petitions (*memoriales*) and critical renditions of the state of things (*representaciones*), fought their way into the *ciudad letrada*; their texts were produced in contentious loci and originated from colonial cities and rural areas alike before making their way to centers of imperial power and discourse. As Rolena Adorno has pointed out, Andean voices of protest unveil the flexibility and power of writing as a sign and reveal the *ciudad letrada* to be not only a field of power relationships but also one of internal and external collaborations.[6] Andean scholars worked in collaboration, and their texts and activism circulated through trans-Atlantic networks of diverse supporters.

In this book I use the term "Andean" in a broader cultural sense rather than a strictly geographic one.[7] I use the term to refer to the entire group of natives and their mestizo descendants, with whom they shared a common pre-Columbian past and a colonial present of similar subordinate status; the term also encompasses those generations of mestizos who shared with their indigenous kin spaces, linguistic and social practices, and scholarly and social activism in both the colonial urban centers and the countryside. Rather than remain semantically confined to the geographic area of the mountains and valleys of the Peruvian Andes, the term "Andean" refers to a shared and changing culture that predated Spanish colonialism—a culture composed of the peoples native to those coastal and rainforest regions where pre-colonial civilizations had expanded and the region that constituted the geopolitical space that came to be known as the Viceroyalty of

Peru in the sixteenth century. Following Alberto Flores Galindo's understanding of the word, I also think "Andean" is a useful term to avoid the racist connotations of the Spanish-imposed "Indian."[8] In a more political sense, the term
"Andean" can also be applied to creoles who shared common local cultures with,
and supported agendas favorable to, Andeans. The Oruro rebellion is a case in
point (Chapter 5).

For more than two decades, Andeanists have accepted in one way or another
the idea that Andean protest writing under colonial rule disappeared after the
well-known works by indigenous and mestizo chroniclers of the late sixteenth
and early seventeenth centuries.[9] Even though scholars have yet to "discover"
texts similar in length and linguistic complexity, it has been readily assumed that
this literary and political tradition virtually disappeared from the Andes soon
thereafter.[10] The present study holds that this intellectual Andean tradition continued in a new guise during the seventeenth and eighteenth centuries, particularly during periods of social unrest and upheaval. In their writings, later Andean
authors articulated the mental state of a collective of scholars and supporters of
the cause for Indian justice, which complicated and expanded the meaning of
writing in the earlier texts. The later native and mestizo intellectuals developed a
sustained and somewhat coordinated legal activism and attempted systematically
to directly negotiate their demands with the Spanish king, a practice that had
appeared incipiently even earlier than the Andean chroniclers at the turn of the
seventeenth century. Following the early Andean chroniclers, writing became a
locus of sustained power contestation broader than the texts themselves. As such,
it involved collective action, trans-Atlantic travel, and networking by Indian
agents and supporters, as well as discursive construction and lobbying and negotiating with authorities—from the local and viceregal levels to the royal court in
Spain.

This book examines the mid- and late-colonial scholarly practices of educated Andeans and explores the roles these intellectuals played in social movements and the emerging public life of the mature colonial period. Andean scholarship under Spanish rule was inherently a political practice that sought to free
Andeans from the constraints of the colonial society. As ethnic Andeans were
turned into "Indians" by colonial legal definitions and social and political practices, Andean intellectuals attempted systematically to reshape their identities as
free and mature subjects, thereby undoing the stereotypes of minors, neophytes,
and the culturally inferior built by colonial law, the church, and the colonialists
themselves.

A painstaking textual analysis is conducted to establish the nature of Andean
discourses of justice and power, which both resembled and departed from earlier analogous traditions. By focusing on Andean writings as cultural texts, we
are able to discern the political culture of the writers involved, the historical and

social production of their narratives, their strategies for reshaping identities, and the politics of Andean religion—all of which mirror the struggles to redefine Andean scholars' cultural and political positions in a colonial situation.[11]

The discourse analysis of Andean texts reveals the historical deconstruction of the category "Indian" by colonial Andean intellectuals themselves as they utilized knowledge from their own religious education, cultural experience, long travels, and critical reflections to write political tracts that reframed their identities as mature and progressive subjects willing to move away from the subordinate positions to which colonialism relegated them. They did this not necessarily by rebelling against the king but instead by writing, negotiating diplomatically, and advocating justice for themselves. The texts under study make apparent early notions of "Indian nation" in the mid-colonial Andes as a political construct aimed at erasing social and cultural differences among Andean elites so they could present themselves as a "united front" in an effort to respond to the systematic loss of political authority and growing disregard for the status of the Indian nobility during the late colonial period. Thus, this book contributes to a more refined understanding of the intellectual world of Andeans at the outset of a postcolonial era not easily seen in studies of the rebellions themselves.[12]

During the period of study, the tradition of Andean scholarship was interrelated with other forms of thought and political discourse that circulated simultaneously in Peru. Andean scholars voiced a critique against Spanish "tyranny" and mistreatment of Indians, also found in creole patriotic discourses.[13] But unlike creole patriots, who ultimately struggled for their own political power, Andeans advocated an agenda of ethnic autonomy that challenged colonial hierarchies and ethnic discrimination. Such a sense of autonomy overlaps with the tone and chronology of the "Andean utopian" and Inca messianic projects of the late 1600s and the 1700s.[14] Unlike these projects, however, the Andean scholarship under examination renounced association with the Inca past and the return to Inca ways and only claimed Inca descent to access noble privileges important within colonial society as validation of political authority.

Most of the writers studied here were comparatively obscure figures in Andean history who went unnoticed by most colonial officials, although probably less so by members of the local church. These scholars and their texts exemplify a political culture grounded in the discursive history of intellectual Andean resistance to colonial power that inflects the more familiar narratives of political resistance and violence. These educated Andeans emerged from a segment of colonial society that formed shortly after the Spanish conquest, commonly designated *indios ladinos,*[15] individuals who stood at the threshold between the indigenous and Spanish societies and played crucial roles as Indian representatives before the colonial authorities. These figures functioned as cultural brokers who learned to manipulate and negotiate the signs and symbols of Spanish and

Andean cultures. While attempting to translate one culture in terms of the other, they maintained a difficult balance at best, striving to convey Andean views and concerns to an interlocutor who remained distantly, almost unreachably, located at the top of the colonial body politic and the Catholic Church.

These cultural brokers challenge the idea that mestizos sought to distinguish themselves from their Indian ancestors and that Indian and mestizo worlds tended to separate as colonialism progressed. Their scholarship forces us to reconceptualize the relationships between Indians and mestizos. Particularly from the late seventeenth century onward, intellectual Andeans appeared to advocate for the rights of both groups together; even more intriguing, the mestizo relatives of the Indian nobility appear to have been included as important members of the "Indian nation," to whom the broad opportunities demanded also applied. Thus, Andean texts contribute to the problematization of the ethnic ascriptions of the colonial society beyond legally established definitions to the actual resignification of such categories by Andeans themselves.

Among the earliest and most significant Andean intellectuals in mid-colonial times to engage in this practice was the Indian noble Don Jerónimo Lorenzo Limaylla, who claimed to be a chieftain, or *cacique*, from the Luringuanca *repartimiento* in Jauja Province. Among other writings, Limaylla presented the king with the "Memorial Dado a la Majestad del Sr. Don Carlos II" (ca. 1677) and the "Representación hecha al Sr. Rey Dn. Carlos Segundo" (ca. 1667).[16] Contemporary with Limaylla's influential work, Juan de Cuevas Herrera, a mestizo parish priest from the province of Charcas, wrote the extensive "Cinco memoriales" (ca. 1650) to the king.[17] In 1691, Juan Núñez Vela de Rivera, a mestizo presbyter and prebendary (*racionero*) from the Arequipa cathedral, composed an important *memorial* to King Charles II in which he defended a range of comprehensive rights of indigenous and mestizo nobles.[18] This group of writers responded in different ways to the devastating impact of the Toledan reforms in Peru and to the collateral effects of the campaign of extirpation of idolatry.

In the eighteenth century, the newly imposed *repartimiento de comercio* (forced distribution of goods among native communities, also known as *repartos*), attempts by the Bourbons to assign mestizos to the status of tributaries, new exactions to the population across the board, and increasing attempts by the Bourbons to limit Indian authority exacerbated the preexisting unrest and prompted further development of the Andean tradition of writing to protest injustice. Efforts emerged to substantiate abuses and resort to more systematic legal expedients to criticize colonial law and justice, as well as to develop a more elaborate and comprehensive set of reforms. Vicente Morachimo, the legal representative of Indians, or *procurador de naturales* and *kuraka* (Andean lord) from Chica y Chimo, Saña Province, presented the king with his "Manifiesto de agravios y vejaciones" (1732),[19] as well as numerous letters that contained allegations involving a variety of local community issues during the 1720s and 1730s. Slightly better known than his predecessors, Fray Calixto de San José Túpac Inca, a mestizo and Franciscan lay brother from Tarma Province, was the leading figure behind the lengthy and perhaps most important late-colonial Andean text, the "Representación verdadera" (ca. 1749–1750), which he delivered to the king in 1750.[20] A very similar anonymous text entitled "Planctus indorum" was written around 1751 and was addressed to the pope.[21] As with many other shorter pieces of writing from a larger group of *caciques* and other Indian authorities filing complaints and petitions, these Andean authors addressed their manuscripts to the king; some delivered them in person to either the monarch or the Council of the Indies in Spain.

At the close of the eighteenth century, the views of elite Andeans became intriguingly juxtaposed in the writings of members of the Inca and Cusco elites, prompted by the Great Rebellion of 1780–1783. An array of Túpac Amaru's edicts and letters (1780–1781) and the eighty-seven-page panegyric "Estado del Perú," dedicated to the bishop of Cusco, Juan Manuel Moscoso, by the Inca noble José Rafael Sahuaraura (1784), give intriguing nuances to, and new understanding of, the mental state of intellectual Andeans in the late years of colonial rule in Peru.

This varied group of Andean thinkers and social leaders expressed a unique and complex Andean political culture that highlighted engagement to achieve justice and redefine ethnicity as a collective, seamless "Indian nation." The work of these seventeenth- and eighteenth-century authors brings to light a more subtle struggle for ethnic autonomy in the face of increasing colonial discrimination against Andeans, a struggle they advanced at times in which their cultural and social differences were increasingly blurred by the institutional efforts to incorporate them into the colonial apparatus as "Indians."

ANDEAN TRADITION OF TEXTUAL PRODUCTION

Andeans' discursive production in written texts is nearly as old as Spanish colonialism in Peru itself. Alphabetical writing made its way to the New World as Europeans and their institutions arrived in Peru in 1532. The cultural and political world of Indian officials and other native elites almost immediately began to incorporate European forms of communication, mostly as a result of the new functions assigned to Indian authorities as intermediaries between the Spanish government and Amerindian commoners. Oral tradition, as a form of communicating ideas, experiences, and feelings—itself predating the advent of alphabetic writing in the Andes—continued to permeate Andean written texts, in some cases more visibly than others.[22] The writing tradition of the Andean scholars studied in this book retains subtle traits of orality—such as narration in the first person, plural voice, and the circular reiteration of subjects that appears in texts such as the "Representación verdadera" and the "Cinco memoriales."[23]

Writing by *kurakas* and Inca lords appeared early as a response to the drastic changes that ensued with the Spanish conquest and, more particularly, following implementation of the Toledan reforms, which gave more definite form to a colonial system in the Andes.[24] In an attempt to counter colonial control over *cacicazgos* (office of the *cacique*), Andean authors systematically criticized the system's failure to enforce early royal decrees that endorsed Indian authorities' hereditary rights to nobility and political office. In so doing, *kurakas* from different Andean regions also produced writing that appeared to incorporate colonial values and Christian discourses to argue for their own recognition as both nobles and legitimate Indian authorities in the new society.[25] They not only wrote to the king to challenge the Toledan imposition of alien methods of succession on native chiefdoms, but they also fought the *encomienda* system (grants of Indian labor and taxes awarded to Spanish conquistadors). In 1560, in the midst of the movement to abolish the *encomienda*, Dominicans such as Fray Bartolomé de las Casas (Bishop of Chiapas) and Fray Domingo de Santo Tomás (Bishop of Charcas), representing a group of *kurakas* from the Huarochirí and Titicaca areas at the court of Madrid, conveyed the *kurakas'* offer to purchase *encomiendas* in perpetuity.[26] While hoping to get rid of abuses by *encomenderos* (*encomienda* holders), these *kurakas* were also trying to avoid colonial intermediaries by rendering their tribute directly to the crown.[27]

These were only some of the pioneers who developed distinctly Andean writing practices in the post-conquest years. They began with meetings of *kurakas*, credible ecclesiastics, and prominent judges, in which *kurakas* provided input on the composition of particular pieces of writing, discussed their problems and petitions, and gave signed powers of attorney to clergymen and judges who would represent Amerindian elites before the king. These authorized representatives eventually drafted documents on behalf of Andean lords to negotiate with higher authorities the terms of their mutual relationships. As Andeans tried to adjust to the new colonial demands and simultaneously maintain their political power, social organizations, and cultures, this practice continued and expanded in various forms throughout the nearly three centuries of colonial rule in the Andes.

The prolific Indian and mestizo literary production that followed in the late sixteenth and early seventeenth centuries is well documented in the field of Andean studies.[28] The intellectual expression of colonized peoples in the Andes left an impressive body of texts that not only recorded valuable information on pre-colonial Andean religion, societies, and cultures but also revealed the emerging Andean writing tradition that ensued from the trans-cultural encounter between Europe and the Amerindian worlds. Rather than representing a brief phenomenon of protest, however, this discursive culture continued to develop—

particularly during the social upheavals provoked by the *mita* and the *composiciones de tierras* (amendments of land titles for a fee) in the late sixteenth and the seventeenth centuries and later in the eighteenth century as preexisting conflicts became exacerbated by the *repartimiento de comercio* and the Bourbon reforms, as explained in Chapter 2.

Mid- and late-colonial Andean writing continued the cultural legacy of Don Felipe Guamán Poma de Ayala, not only in his view of the Spanish conquest and his critique of colonial rule but also in his belief in writing as a means of denouncing social injustice and finding relief from colonial chaos and injustice.[29] While Andean litigants and petitioners won a number of significant legal battles, enforcement of those achievements proved difficult and gave Andeans a motive for subsequent petitions and criticism of the colonial judicial system, a history reconstructed in Chapter 6. More clearly, the writers under study also show how Inca Garcilaso de la Vega's work was received by his mid- and late-colonial Andean counterparts. Both Juan de Cuevas Herrera and Fray Calixto de San José Túpac Inca drew on de la Vega's *Comentarios reales* to defend the "Christian" nature of Inca religion and to reassert their own claims to Indian nobility. More generally, his work contributed largely to the creation and re-creation of memories of the Inca past among posterior Andean intellectuals.

The Andean practice of composing *memoriales* and *representaciones* had its roots in the institutionalized practice of reporting on the state of the colonies, as Spanish rule began to consolidate in the Andes in the late sixteenth century.[30] As tools of imperial hegemony, *representaciones* and *probanzas de méritos* (proofs of merit that were prerequisites for royal rewards) were templates of Spanish administrative writing designed to verify the imperial subjects' compliance with colonial mandates and goals and to build political legitimacy through a system of rewards, or *mercedes*, given by the crown in return for its subjects' loyalty. The texts examined here conform in various ways to this genre of Spanish administrative writing. Although *representaciones* and *probanzas* were mostly at the disposition of nobles and government functionaries, whose writings usually legitimized colonial royal policies, Andean writers seized these discursive spaces to "inform" the king about matters in Peru, questioning colonial justice and state administrators to emphasize the need for their own political participation in social change.

In colonial times, alphabetically written texts utilized European theological and rhetorical devices and were usually discussed and diffused through oral and written means among Andeans' social networks. Thus, they are complex, transcultural, and political in nature. They emerged from a kind of cultural "contact zone,"[31] a space in which colonial impositions and Andeans' expectations of reciprocity and justice clashed; and they generated textual, legal, and social battles over the redefinition of Andeans' place in the colonial world. Their scholarship appropriated the terms of colonial political and religious discourses to produce

Andeans' own truths. Overall, Andean intellectuals demonstrated the practical impossibility of achieving social harmony as promised by and imagined in the Habsburg legal discourse of the first two centuries of colonialism in America, as well as the fallacies inherent in Christian discourses of spiritual equality as preached and implemented by the colonial church. Andean scholars selected tenets from European theologies to convey to the crown and eventually to the church in Peru the urgent need for social change to forestall political upheaval and social unrest. An important part of this scholarly work by Andeans was the construction of new discourses of social justice and reform, which enabled these writers to create and sustain a systematic critique of the colonial system in the Andes and argue for a kind of social change that would ultimately secure ethnic autonomy.

Andeans' mid- and late-colonial writing bridged the intellectual, social, and cultural gaps that set them outside the exclusionary world of the *ciudad letrada*. For Angel Rama, the judicial and political space of the *ciudad letrada* was inhabited exclusively by powerful peninsular and creole officials, who controlled literacy, information, and knowledge central to the implementation of the Spanish imperial project.[32] In reality, the colonial *ciudad letrada* was also populated by voices from nonwhite "neighborhoods," where thinkers of indigenous, mestizo, and African descent contested dominant views and articulated their own.[33] In so doing, the Andeans' scholarship and activism also bridged the world of the Spanish and Indian republics, contributing to the demise of this concept and its functionality as an analytical category for historians. Instead, this book demonstrates the ways Andean intellectuals were significant actors in the creation and transformation of the colonial culture, which emerged as Spaniards, Indians, and their mestizo descendants contended for the creation of cultural and social meaning in the narrow streets of the *ciudad letrada*.

In their texts, educated Andeans endeavored to move beyond being characterized by their official status as "Indians." To deliver their arguments to the power spheres of the colonial world, they sought to place themselves in social and political spaces usually reserved for Spanish subjects, becoming both trans-Atlantic and provincial travelers. While acting as lobbyists and advocates for Andean causes in the royal courts, they generated an informal trans-Atlantic network of Indian nobles and non-Indian collaborators who worked together from Peru to Spain to advance petitions, lawsuits, and a broader platform for Andean autonomy in the royal court. In a secular guise, they became advocates for a project aimed at a rather modernizing education for Andeans (in "sciences and letters"), which, in their eyes, was consistent with their reclaimed status as noble subjects of an imperial king.

To grasp the complexity of the political and scholarly culture of mid- and late-colonial Andeans, it is necessary to look back to alternative forms of political expression by the colonized through their writings and anti-colonial discourse, which are more subtle than mass protest and armed resistance. Andean critical writing did, however, remain linked in some form to social protest and eventually to widespread rebellion. This became another pattern of Indian political culture under Spanish rule: the use of combined patterns of writing and judicial action as the primary means to attain justice, but also the willingness to resort to rebellion when legal struggles proved ineffective.

The history of late-colonial protest and rebellions exemplifies the combination of legal and violent means to attain justice.[34] The consolidation of writing as a political practice by elite Indian and mestizo ladinos was grounded in a long-standing tradition of legal action by Indian authorities, who seized opportunities created by law to obtain justice.[35] Royal legislation defined the limits of colonial officials' authority and enabled *caciques* to address the *audiencias* directly with their grievances, while *corregidores* were expected to provide justice for Indians at the provincial level and Andeans were to be represented by *protectores de naturales*. In his discussion of Andeans' use of the colonial justice system, Steve Stern argued that they consistently utilized the judicial system and won some valuable small victories in the courts. Instances in which justice was obtained within the parameters of colonial law helped soften the blow of colonial restructurings and probably slowed their pace, but they inevitably strengthened the colonial juridical system, the perception of the king as the supreme authority, and Spanish institutions as a whole. Andeans came to depend on the king and his courts to settle not only their internal disputes but also legal disputes that introduced rifts within their communities. Ultimately, Andeans' resort to the colonial justice system strengthened the hegemony of both the crown and the colonial system.[36] Andean scholars from the mid-seventeenth century onward pursued legal action through critical writings that discussed the contradictions inherent in the legal system and used them as a reason to support and further their agenda for social autonomy.

THE QUESTION OF ANDEAN AUTHORSHIP

For native Andean intellectuals and other Indian leaders, writing was one point within a spectrum of political resources deployed to contest detrimental colonial policies. Andeans wrote in the midst of conflicts between community and state, but they were not professional writers in the modern sense of the word and did not compose their texts as intellectuals detached from the realities of their fellow Indians. Their writings emerged from their daily experiences as subordinate colonial subjects, and their scholarship was embedded within the context of their efforts to negotiate the terms of colonial rules that were imposed upon them and that regulated relationships between Indian subjects and the empire. Their textual production combined diverse elements, ranging from knowledge and discussion of colonial law, utilization of material from religious education, literacy, and acquaintance with the colonial administrative and legal culture to social and political activism that flowed through more institutional channels, such as the local Indian *cabildos* (town councils) and the intervention of *protectores de naturales*.[37]

Because some of the more complex Andean writings emerged in times of social unrest or impending rebellion, when activists feared persecution, some writers filed their manuscripts anonymously for protection. Contemporary historians must confront this practice as one of many issues that complicate the idea of authorship and textual production by colonial subordinate subjects. Although Andean texts such as the seventeenth-century "Representación hecha al Sr. Rey Dn. Carlos Segundo" and the "Memorial Dado a la Majestad" were filed and claimed by the Jauja Indian noble Don Jerónimo Lorenzo Limaylla, supporting the idea that he was the author, the origin of these texts is being challenged (Chapter 2). The eighteenth-century "Representación verdadera," more commonly associated with Fray Calixto de San José Túpac Inca, seems also to have been filed anonymously—copies extant in the archival repositories bear no signatures or self-attribution (Chapter 3). The choice of anonymity seems to make sense, given the harsh criticism of the church and the Spanish elites' exclusionary policies and attitudes toward Andean elites leveled by a mestizo member of the lower clergy.

I argue that given the cross-ethnic and cross-cultural interaction that took place in the colonial environment, Andean writing usually surpassed the boundaries of individual expression and literary creation and became a collective undertaking. The line separating the individual composer of final drafts from those whose ideas, aspirations, grievances, and struggles formed the core of the manuscripts became increasingly diffused. The texts at hand not only reflect the collective nature of the issues at stake, the concerns and interests of Indian authorities and intellectuals who began to speak on behalf of the "Indian nation," but they also mirror more clearly the cross-cultural collaboration that transpired in the writing of *memoriales* and *representaciones* bound to the Spanish king. Andean leaders certainly provided input to identify the issues at stake and the necessary proposals; perhaps clerical supporters, judges, lawyers,[38] or educated Andeans drafted and edited the manuscripts. As social activists, both Indians and mestizos participated in different capacities (e.g., messengers, *escribanos*, printers) in the wider political project of achieving social inclusion and redress for the injustice of the *mita*, restitution of *cacicazgos*, *repartimiento de comercio*, *composiciones de tierras*, and others. Their texts became a form of collective, "combative scholarship"—a trans-cultural expression in itself—that Andean intellectuals developed over decades of colonial rule and exposure to religious education, European literature, and interaction with Spanish subjects.[39]

Today's notions of individual authorship seem inadequate to understand Andeans' roles in the colonial lettered world. The notion of collective authorship more appropriately defines the scholarly interaction among educated Andeans, their clerical mentors and supporters, *caciques*, and other Indian authorities who worked together to produce texts within the trans-cultural space of the "contact zones." In the process of conceiving, composing, and circulating their texts, members of the Indian elite made inroads into the colonial world of letters.

The world of elite Indians was also closely connected to the ecclesiastical realm of parish priests, missionaries, and clerical teachers who mentored virtually all of the Andean scholars considered in this book. While these groups of individuals were drawn together and linked by complex power relationships, a vibrant process of trans-culturation transpired. Pastoral writings (sermons, manuals, epistles, prayers) aimed at fostering conversion circulated among clerics and the literate Indian and mestizo elites, shaping their writings in unexpected ways. Through this literature and preaching, clerics urged *caciques* to instill Catholic values in their constituencies; priests intervened in conflict resolutions and also contributed to creating political tension in Indian communities. Yet mid- and late-colonial Andean writers further expanded such cultural and political "contact zones," as—by becoming new actors in the colonial "republic of letters"— they also redefined and negotiated cultural identity, notions of Christianity, and political participation with Spanish authorities (Chapters 7, 8).[40]

Paradoxically, although these writings used Christian discourses to construct Andean identity, an anti-clerical and anti-colonial tone generally underlies them, as the writers also criticized the colonial practices of the church and state authorities. Priests and members of religious orders, either genuine supporters of Indian causes or with other stakes in helping to mobilize indigenous and mestizo groups against the colonial authorities, may have collaborated with Andeans in composing the texts. The Franciscans who supported both Jerónimo Lorenzo Limaylla and Fray Calixto de San José, for example, were instrumental in helping them cross the Atlantic clandestinely and also offered them shelter and support in Spain, as the Andeans remained in the Iberian Peninsula for long periods. Ecclesiastics, in their role as protectors and mentors of Andeans, as well as other mestizo and creole agents immersed in the colonial literate world, likely intervened in unanticipated and untraceable ways in the final versions of Andean texts.[41]

Nevertheless, the texts remain Andean insofar as Andean scholars brought to bear their own experiential knowledge and criticism as colonial subordinates. The crisis of their societies lay at the center of these texts, and lettered Andeans made their own choices in selecting and rethinking the specific theological frameworks they deemed most effective to persuasively convey their political views and authorize their demands. Collective authorship becomes apparent in the contributions of the social networks of Indian authorities and mestizo supporters that were behind each single petition or more complex treaty, as spelled out in Chapters 2 and 3. Thus, in attempting to ascribe the texts solely to one or even a few individual authors, we lose the full cultural complexity and literary richness of Andean texts and scholarship. Seeing the texts as collectively authored allows us to identify the frequently overlooked bridges between the Indian and Spanish republics, as well as the inroads Andeans had been making in the streets of the *ciudad letrada*. Viewing these texts as isolated pieces, detached from the context of the collective political and intellectual projects of which they were a part, drastically simplifies them. The texts must be understood fully within the social, cultural, and political contexts behind their production and later reception.

In discussing the discursive production of Andean elites in the colonial context, Peruvian literary critic Carlos García-Bedoya has maintained that it was the organic relationship between the writing and the social group of the indigenous nobility who sponsored and consumed it, rather than the ethnic ascription of its authors, that characterized Andean discursive production. Such a group becomes a single emergent "social subject," whose links to a common ancestry allowed it to represent the "republic of Indians" and whose cohesion stemmed from shared ideas about the pre-Hispanic past, the Spanish conquest, and the colonial order.[42]

A neat cohesiveness of Andean thinking and the homogeneousness of Andean elites as a "social subject" are difficult to establish. In accounting for their different time periods and specific social roles, however, the few writers studied in this book reflect somewhat similar criticisms of the colonial authorities; a general concern with justice, reciprocity, and political autonomy under colonial rule; and a shared view of Spanish colonialism as an inherently unfair, corrupt, and anti-Christian system (Chapters 5, 6). For García-Bedoya, the texts could have been written by elite Indians, creole priests, or mestizos. The point of this book is, instead, to argue that members of all three groups contributed in different capacities to the preparation, composition, and dissemination of the writings. These practices were inextricably connected with both social activism among Indian authorities and communities and the negotiation of proposals directly with the king and the Council of the Indies in Spain.

This intellectual interaction has been represented as the relationship between Indian communities and a kind of specialized intellectual external to those communities. Literary critic Martin Lienhard has maintained that the first Andean written testimonies were produced by literate outsiders, non-community members, who would compose texts on behalf of the *común* when the community had no literate member. He added that "some testimonial texts seem to be the result of a more or less authentic cooperation between a group of Indians and an external literate agent."[43] What Lienhard means by "authentic cooperation" between two such parties is unclear, but in the texts analyzed in the present book there is no clear-cut line of separation among the writers, the writing itself, and the intellectual and social activism that accompanied it, since a variety of actors participated in the discussion, composition, and distribution of the texts. These roles will become clearer in Chapters 2 and 3 in the particular contexts that preceded the discussion of authorship for Limaylla's texts and for the "Representación verdadera," respectively. The individuals who functioned as composers were connected in a variety of ways with the community of *kurakas* who sought to negotiate privileges and a softening of colonial demands with the king; possible contributors included educated Indians and their mestizo descendants, priests, lawyers, Indian *escribanos*, and other sympathizers. The *kurakas* were ambassadors to the crown and played active roles as mediators between the communities and local authorities as well.[44]

MENTORSHIP AND EDUCATION OF INDIGENOUS ELITES

We can ask, how did Andeans become writers and scholars, and what factors influenced their thought and their texts? Soon after the Spanish conquest, the church and the crown endeavored to incorporate indigenous authorities in advancing the spiritual conquest. These institutions collaborated in a pedagogical strategy for indigenous religious transformation, establishing Jesuit-led *colegios de caciques* (schools for *caciques*). While the *colegios* were somewhat unstable, members of the Andean elite—including most of the writers considered in this book—also developed scholarly skills through direct, individual mentorship by Franciscans, Jesuits, and other clergy.

Felipe Guamán Poma de Ayala was likely one of the earliest and best-known Andeans educated in this fashion by a mestizo religious man, Martin de Ayala, also apparently his half-brother.[45] The Andean mestizo Juan de Cuevas Herrera from La Plata received his education at the Lima Jesuit seminary school starting in 1610. Jerónimo Lorenzo Limaylla from Jauja joined the school of *caciques* in El Cercado in 1648 and was also mentored by the Franciscan missionaries of the Jauja area. Fray Calixto de San José Túpac Inca from Tarma received most of his religious education at the Franciscan seminary in Valencia (Spain) in 1750–1753, having also been mentored by Franciscan missionaries in Tarma, Lima, and Cusco in the period 1727–1749. Juan Santos Atahualpa and Túpac Amaru II are said to have studied at the San Borja Jesuit school in Cusco.[46] Typically, clergymen would "adopt" indigenous boys as protégés, servants, or both and would endeavor to teach them the Castilian language and Christian doctrine and to change their customs while using them for household labor. Occasionally, noble Indians also had access to the seminary schools of religious orders (*colegios mayores*), such as the Jesuit college of San Pablo.[47]

During the post-conquest years, the church targeted native authorities as key agents for religious conversion, with the goals of transforming Andean cultures at large according to the European model of Christianity, implementing a civilizing agenda, and instilling "good customs" into Amerindians' behavior.[48] Over time, however, the educated Andeans who were mentored in this way and with whom this study is concerned challenged these functions of literacy and religious education through critical writing and activism.

The project of native schooling was consistent with the goals of religious purification campaigns known as the "extirpation of idolatry," centered in the Archbishopric of Lima in roughly 1608–1629, 1641–1671, and 1724–1730.[49] A champion of the early 1609 campaigns, the Jesuit Francisco de Avila, recommended the creation of *colegios* for *caciques* as the best strategy for destroying native religions.[50] Up to 1552, the goal of this pedagogical policy was to mentor a group of native preachers who would supply the needs of *curas doctrineros* (parish priests), by then very scarce.[51] They would lead the religious transformation of indigenous societies from the top, down to the *ayllus* (communities of common-ancestry and blood-related members). At the inception of the project, the crown even seemed to believe that following this schooling, Andean elites should attend a university.[52] These purposes seemed to have changed by 1576, however, when Viceroy Francisco de Toledo promoted the foundation of the schools only to indoctrinate *caciques* and change their customs.[53]

A long history of tension between Viceroy Toledo and both the Lima archbishop and the Jesuits, combined with systematic opposition by other colonial elites, explains the delay in enforcing existing rulings for the foundation of the *colegios*.[54] The Cusco Inca lords, aware of the potential of the existing legislation, began to petition in 1601 for the creation of *colegios* "for the *Ingas principales* [Inca authorities] from Cusco and other *kurakas* of this kingdom, where they may learn the things of our faith and all *policia* [urbanity] and Christianity so that our children and descendants *can teach it to their subjects*"[55] (emphasis added). The *Ingas principales* of Cusco were aware of these early mandates and pressured the colonial state to enforce them, seeing an opportunity to better their lot in society. While they seemed to share the spirit of such royal decrees, they also made clear a desire to install native teachers to educate Andean generations to come.

It was not until July 1618 that King Philip III founded the first school of *caciques*, the Colegio de Caciques El Cercado, called "El Principe," in the indigenous town of El Cercado on the outskirts of Lima. Concomitantly, a jail for Indian dogmatizers, known as the "Casa de Santacruz," a house of sorcerers and idolaters (*casa de hechiceros e idólatras*), was founded in an adjacent building. Inmates were confined for religious "reeducation" through physical punishment, torture, and systematic indoctrination. A second seminary school for *caciques*, San Francisco de Borja (known as San Borja), was founded in Cusco in 1621. The *colegios* in Lima and Cusco functioned somewhat intermittently for most of the seventeenth and eighteenth centuries, a period in which more than 500 children of *curacas* were enrolled, although many only briefly. Among those enrolled in this school in 1648 were Jauja Andean noble Jerónimo Lorenzo Limaylla and his political rival from the Luringuanca *repartimiento* in Jauja, Don Bernardino Mangoguala Limaylla.[56] Late-colonial Inca rebels such as Juan Santos Atahualpa and Túpac Amaru are also said to have enrolled in San Borja. The expulsion of the Jesuits in 1767 deepened the schools' decline. As part of the Bourbons' systematic attack against the Cusco Indian nobility in the aftermath of the Great Rebellion, a royal decree eliminated San Borja in 1785.[57]

Some uncertainty surrounds the philosophical teachings imparted in the *colegios*. In 1583 the Jesuits planned to teach "science, grammar, rhetoric, philosophy, and logic."[58] The *colegios* functioned as a tool for the indoctrination and linguistic change of Andean authorities under colonial rule; consequently, faculty emphasized Castilian grammar, alphabetic writing, and reading. In addition, the *colegios* sought to instill Christian practices and beliefs in native elite students through daily scheduled sermons and the reading of catechisms in Castilian. Apparently, the *colegios* also contributed to the dissemination of Inca Garcilaso de la Vega's *Comentarios reales de los Incas* in the classrooms.[59] Evidence suggests that paintings of Inca nobles covered the walls of San Borja, while theatrical representations of the Inca past and other visual images strengthened the native students' sense of Inca identity.[60] This exposure to the culture and symbols of the Inca past would have defined San Borja and El Cercado as centers that recast the variety of ethnic identities of the native students, who came from various regions under the homogenizing symbols of "Inca" and "Christian."[61]

Literacy, however, proved a highly controversial tool for empire building and social control within these schools. Although Spanish literacy enabled missionaries to promote Indian conversion and Hispanicization, native students used that literacy in unanticipated ways. The educated Andeans studied in this work, aside from other *caciques* mentored individually or in religious colleges and schools for *caciques*, directed their literate skills to compose manuscripts that spoke in opposition to the crown. Literacy would soon be perceived as a dangerous tool in the hands of colonized Andeans, who quickly learned how to sue unjust officials and engaged in litigation and critiques of *corregidores* and other Spaniards—to the point that missionaries and government officials came to fear and distrust lettered Andeans.

Perhaps one of the earliest examples of Indios ladinos who acted as representatives of other Andeans was Felipe Guamán Poma de Ayala, who endeavored to teach other Andeans literacy and how to craft and file *pleitos* (lawsuits) against *corregidores*. He was aware of the consequences this use of literacy posed for Indians in small towns such as Lucanas, where one of his disciples, Don Cristobal de León, was put to the gallows for suing the *corregidor*. Nevertheless, among his many recommendations for "good government," Ayala deemed it necessary to have at least one lettered functionary and two protectors, two *procuradores*, one interpreter, and another bilingual person who knew how to draft *memoriales* and file them with the lettered functionary so Indians could attain justice.[62] Spaniards perceived litigating *caciques* as traitors and "spies" who pretended to have no knowledge of the Spanish language so they could gather valuable information to be used against Spaniards.[63] Andeans' skills as litigants and negotiators of new royal decrees required knowledge of Spanish law and the ability to craft petitions and properly file complaints. Such legal knowledge came from contact with lawyers, study of Spanish laws, and access to juridical literature—particularly Juan de Solórzano's *Política Indiana*. Andean authorities also learned from interaction with *escribanos* and their manuals, such as Gabriel Monterroso y Alvarado's *Práctica Civil y Criminal e Instrucción de Escribanos*, known among Andeans as "the Monterroso."[64]

Colonial efforts to mentor Andean elites seem to have produced mixed and often ambiguous results, and colonial officials continued to see a relationship among educated Indians, litigants, and rebels. The Andean writers under discussion denounced overexploitation, challenged *mita* quotas against Indians in the Potosí mines and the corruption of *curas doctrineros*, and pursued long-lasting lawsuits for the retention of *cacicazgos* while in Madrid seeking resolution of their petitions. Historian Alaperrine-Bouyer established that alumnae *caciques* of El Cercado school were persecuted for suing abusive *curas* (priests) and officials and for signing letters defending their communities and protesting injustice. For essentially the same reasons, a number of other students were later accused of idolatry and occasionally singled out as instigators of uprisings. Among those in the first group were alumnae Don Rodrigo Flores Guainamallque from Santo Domingo de Ocros (Cajatambo), who enrolled in El Cercado in 1621; Don Juan Picho from the Luringuanca *repartimiento* (Jauja), enrolled in 1650; and Don Rodrigo Rupaychagua from Guamantanga, enrolled in 1634. Specifically accused of instigating protests against *obrajes* (textile workshops) and practicing idolatry was Francisco Gamarra (1653). Listed as filing *capítulos* (demands) against ecclesiastical authorities in particular were Gabriel Camaguacho (1627), Francisco Chavín Palpa (1638), and Cristóbal Pariona (1645). Among those accused of idolatry were Don Sebastián Quispe Nina (1651), Gómez Poma Chagua (1656), Juan de los Ríos (1621), and Francisco Pizarro (1627).[65]

In different political conjunctures of indigenous unrest and upheaval during the eighteenth century, colonial officials grumbled bitterly about the failure of the native schools. Perhaps the most intriguing pattern that emerged is the involvement of several educated Indian leaders in the century's major anti-colonial upheavals. Even if only a few cases of educated rebels can be documented, the initial goal of turning native elites into good Christians and loyal subjects was seriously undermined, as even the few leaders involved were sufficient to pose a serious threat to the colonial order. Juan Santos Atahualpa and José Gabriel Condorcanqui Túpac Amaru II, the leaders of two rebellions to challenge the missionary project and the political stability of Spanish colonialism, are said to have emerged from the San Borja school for *caciques* in Cusco.[66] Juan Santos Atahualpa openly praised the Jesuits as educators and included them in his future plans to rule the Andes. A group of Christian *kurakas* educated in the Franciscan mission schools of Santa Rosa de Ocopa (Jauja Province) supported him and played leading roles in the rebellion.[67] Túpac Amaru II also attended classes in arts and theology at the University of San Marcos in Lima. His brothers and young supporters were classmates at San Borja, years before the rebellion.[68]

But a similar pattern of educated Indians who backed the status quo was also found. Former students at San Borja were also among the Inca elite who actively opposed the Túpac Amaru Rebellion. Among them was a powerful *kuraka* from Chincheros (Cusco area), Mateo García Pumacahua, who later became lieutenant general of the national army and fought Spain in the 1814 Peruvian campaign for independence. García Pumacahua had fought fiercely against Túpac Amaru II's insurrectional forces in 1781 and was instrumental in their defeat, as a result of which he received a royal appointment with a handsome salary.[69] Another alumnus of San Borja, José Rafael Sahuaraura, wrote a panegyrical defense of the Cusco bishop Juan Manuel Moscoso in 1784, reviewed in Chapter 3.[70] Members of the two Inca lineages were rewarded with the few posts granted to Andeans as *curas doctrineros* after the upheaval, and several members of their families successfully joined the priesthood. Furthermore, according to some accounts, the Cercado school for *caciques* "produced many Indians famous in the pulpit and in the forum," like Francisco Patiño, who became a Jesuit priest and was instrumental in the foundation of the *cofradia* (brotherhood) of Indian *oficiales* (city workers) in Cusco circa 1690.[71]

This study demonstrates, however, that educated Andeans could also question Spanish rule in ways less visible than leading and opposing armed struggles. By using literacy, rhetoric, Latin, and political theology, along with their experiential knowledge as subordinated colonial subjects, they constructed critical views of the colonial order to empower their own political agendas, reformulating the religious philosophical tenets they learned as part of their education. Ultimately, the Scholastic and Neo-Scholastic ideas taught in the seminary schools of Jesuits, Franciscans, and Dominicans and perhaps also disseminated through individual mentorship of the Indian nobility actually legitimized Andean rebellions, as the discourses of Túpac Amaru II as well as rebels in Huarochirí, Oruro, and other areas demonstrated. Perhaps the most salient impact of Andeans' exposure to education was the formation of a group of intellectuals who functioned as significant political actors and cultural mediators between the Indian and Spanish worlds. Some of them became critical anti-colonial thinkers and writers who left an important paper trail that allows contemporary historians to understand their political culture, their use of identity and religion, their relationships with the church and the state, and their understanding of, and place within, colonialism.

The selection of Andean texts studied in this book broadly reflects the regional patterns of social unrest and rebellion that swept through the Andean world in the seventeenth and eighteenth centuries.[72] These regional patterns largely followed the colonial economic geography, with its central focus on mining (Potosí) and its gravitating orbits of regional commerce, haciendas, and *obrajes* along the Potosí-Lima axis: Potosí, La Paz, Cusco, Huancavelica, and Lima. Linked to this extensive economic axis and participating in market activities to a lesser degree were smaller agricultural and manufacturing areas such as Chuquisaca, Arequipa, Cochabamba, Oruro, Puno, Huamanga, Jauja, Huarochirí, and provinces to the north of Lima such as Trujillo and Saña. The binding force of the colonial *mita* from Potosí and Huancavelica linked these areas and largely accounted for regional patterns of protest and unrest. Even the rebellion of Juan Santos Atahualpa, which erupted in the Amazon frontiers of the Viceroyalty of Peru, was largely a protest against *mitas* and *obrajes*. The growing pressure of the *repartimiento de comercio* and the fiscal policies of the Bourbons added motive for the rebellions and turmoil in the specified regions, as well as in other Andean areas farther north into the Province of Quito and the Viceroyalty of New Granada (discussed in Chapter 3).

Rather than proceed strictly from every region of the viceroyalty, the texts in this study tend to reflect the social conflicts and political concerns of Andean representatives from only some of the indicated regions. The additional supportive documents of Indian activism come from *kurakas* from different areas, who also had the opportunity to meet and interact in Lima when they traveled to advance their business interests in the *audiencia* capital. The texts considered in this book circulated primarily in the royal courts of Madrid, Lima, and surrounding provinces; and this urban environment of consultations, discussions, and negotiation shaped the form and discourse of the documents. A large number of *kurakas* and other educated Amerindian elites gathered in Lima, the viceregal capital and seat of the *audiencia*, to advance their cases in court, which facilitated the emergence of networks for social and legal activism.[73] Cusco was another crucial point of Andean discourse production because the province likely contained the largest concentration of literate Inca descendants who had validated their nobility status through writing, painting, and performance of nobility. The book's core documentary basis reflects this regionalism and consists of texts that members of the Andean elite from the Provinces of Charcas, Jauja, Tarma, Trujillo, La Paz,

Arequipa, and Cusco composed during times of social unrest, open rebellion, or both and that currently rest in major colonial archives in Spain, since most of the documents were originally directed to the Spanish king.

This book also relies on archival documentation pertaining to social movements from regional and local archives in Peru to capture issues of identity formation, as well as the religious and political views of elite and a few non-elite members of Andean societies. Extensive documentation from the Jesuit archives and the Peruvian national and regional archives has provided evidence for discussions of Amerindian education, rebellions, church mandates, viceregal policies, Indians in the church, and similar topics.

The corpus of Andean scholarship in mid- and late-colonial Peru is introduced in Chapters 2 and 3, respectively. These chapters conceptualize the times and present the writers' backgrounds and writings, with links to social and political issues. The reception of the texts and their political implications are also discussed.

The chapters that follow develop a discursive analysis of the major Andean texts, guided by their more salient themes. In Chapter 4 I discuss the European background of Andean discourses. I reveal the extent to which the writers drew on medieval political theologies of "natural right," "common good," and "tyranny" to justify the rights of Indian lords to retain their chiefdoms and seek redress for the dispossession of their lands and resources by the Spanish invaders. I argue that intellectual Andeans altered the purpose of these notions by attempting to adapt them to a colonial situation, highlighting the chaos introduced by the arrival of the Spanish and their institutions in the Andes.

In Chapter 5 I review Andean critiques of Spanish colonialism, which focused on its judicial institutions, the Catholic Church, and the Potosí *mita*. I argue that Andean narratives of social justice were a reformulation of early Lascasian and Franciscan models of criticism, which Andean elites selected and redeployed to legitimize their claims for inclusion in the state and the church. Cross-referencing Andean scholarship with other non-Andean critiques of colonialism in Peru, I demonstrate that prominent creoles, "enlightened" officials, and ecclesiastics likewise used critiques of colonial justice to strengthen other disparate agendas of evangelization, state reform, and militarization of the empire.

In Chapter 6 I reconstruct the history of Andean intellectuals' advocacy for the admission of indigenous elites into prestigious social institutions, from the 1650s through the 1780s. This is a rarely acknowledged history within colonial Andean political culture, in which these lettered Andeans sought full membership in the church for their noble counterparts—asserting their ability to perform as priests, missionaries, bishops, and officers of the state while also demanding access to a kind of secular education in schools and universities and pursuing social distinctions as a way out of their historical subordination. Thus, while seeking avenues of social inclusion, Andean intellectuals challenged the power relationships between the two "republics" and redefined their own place within the changing world of colonial Peru. Their critical discourses capitalized on the gap between the potentially favorable mandates of the monarch and the systematic disregard of such laws by the colonial church and Peruvian authorities. Over time, the campaigns for social inclusion yielded a more comprehensive social and political platform, which took shape in mid–eighteenth-century Lima amid an insurrectionary conjuncture. Later in the chapter I examine these approaches to reform informed by aspirations of ethnic autonomy. The mental state of the late-colonial Andean writers reveals them to have been incipient modern subjects, carving out spaces in which to intervene in the changes to the justice system so they could resolve the protracted unenforcement of laws fought for by other Andean scholars since the late seventeenth century.

The cultural changes in Andeans' views of themselves and their colonial others, as well as changes in their religiosity at the outset of the modern era, are discussed in Chapter 7. How did Andean intellectuals question their identity as "Indians," and, as a result, how did they describe themselves? In addition, how did they view the Spanish and other subordinated groups? Andeans constructed their own identities in a relational and oppositional manner, which inadvertently conveyed the politics of identity formation. While presenting themselves as true Christians, they constructed the identity of the colonizers as non-Christian; while they perceived themselves as noble subjects, they critically demanded from the Spanish nobility the payment of tribute usually expected from commoners. Even as they advocated strategically for their own rights, Andean elites contributed to the formation of identities of other subordinated subjects through internalized colonial prejudices, and they exhibited ambivalent views toward Christianity and the role of the church.

The religious identities and views of Andean scholars and their use of Christian rhetoric stand out as central issues of identity formation in their writing. I problematize Andeans' Christian identity based on their own language and self-proclamations. While intellectual Andeans were invested in outward expressions of piety and devotional language, their religious discourse reveals a highly political interpretation of Christianity. Their redefinition of notions such as "divine justice," "sin," "love," and "Christian behavior" de-legitimized Spanish authorities by portraying them as immoral rulers and, more broadly, by questioning the power relationships between the "republic of Indians" and the "republic of Spaniards." Christian love became a political tool that condemned exclusionary divisions among equals and qualified colonialism as a "sin." Elite Andeans' desire and willingness to become priests were supported largely on political and social grounds. They viewed obtaining positions in the church as a means to break

Spaniards' monopoly within the religious institution that controlled the sanctioned forms of spirituality in colonial society rather than seeing it as a path to spiritual perfection.

NOTES

1. In the twenty-first century, increasing scholarly interest has emerged regarding the study of Indians and mestizos, or ladinos, as transformative agents in colonial culture, from different perspectives: as lower church officials, interpreters of law and canonical texts, and creators of meaning (Charles, *Indios Ladinos*; Durston, *Pastoral Quechua*); as trans-Atlantic activists and writers (Dueñas, *Andean Scholarship and Rebellion*); as Indian town officials strategizing to defend local self-rule (Yannanakis, *The Art of Being In-Between*); and as fighters for chiefdom power (Alaperrine-Bouyer, "Enseignements et Enjeux"; Puente Luna, *What's in a Name*).

2. For comprehensive studies of late-colonial Andean rebellions, see O'Phelan, *La gran rebelión*; Cornblit, *Power and Violence*; Stern, ed., *Resistance, Rebellion, and Consciousness*; Stavig, *The World of Túpac Amaru*; Robins, *Genocide and Millennialism in Upper Peru*; Serulnikov, *Subverting Colonial Authority*; Thomson, *We Alone Rule*; Glave, "The 'Republic of Indians' in Revolt."

3. Millones, *Historia y poder en los Andes*, 134–135; Pease, *Perú Hombre e Historia*; Stavig, *The World of Túpac Amaru*.

4. In this book I use the term "discourse" to stress the ways institutions, individuals, and groups use language to construct ideas, identities, and agendas in a particular social and cultural milieu, mostly with regard to the Andeans under study and other related colonial institutions and subjects. The notion of discourse, however, supersedes the boundaries of written texts and includes all nonverbal expression. Institutional discourses in particular shape people's thinking and put limits on what can be expressed. I assume, however, that looking at Andean discourses also allows one to identify their creative power and intellectual agency. For more specific definitions of discourse, see Foucault, *Archeology of Knowledge*.

5. Rama, *La ciudad letrada*.

6. Adorno, "La 'ciudad letrada' y los discursos coloniales," 23.

7. It is important to clarify, however, that in this work I only include Andeans from what was known as the Viceroyalty of Peru. In general usage, the term "Andean" cannot be restricted to this region, since a vast array of Andean groups and cultures existed north and south of the viceroyalty's colonial limits.

8. Flores Galindo, *Buscando un Inca*, 15–16.

9. The most important works of this period include Don Diego de Castro Titu Cusi Yupanqui, *Instrucción al licenciado Don Lope García de Castro*; the Huarochirí Manuscript, anonymous text compiled and edited by Jesuit Father Francisco de Avila; Inca Garcilaso de la Vega, *Comentarios reales de los Incas*; Juan de Santacruz Pachacuti Yamqui Salcamaygua, *Relación de antigüedades deste reyno del Piru*; Felipe Guamán Poma de Ayala, *Nueva corónica y buen gobierno*. For comprehensive studies of these works, see Adorno, *From Oral to Written Expression* and *Cronista y príncipe*; Chang-Rodríguez, "Peruvian History and the Relación of Titu Cussi Yupanki"; Castro-Klaren, "El orden del

sujeto en Guaman Poma"; Zamora, *Language and Authority*; Salomon, "Chronicles of the Impossible"; Brading, "The Inca and the Renaissance"; Spalding, *Royal Commentaries of the Incas*; Yupanqui, *History of How the Spaniards Arrived in Peru.*

10. Adorno, *Cronista y príncipe*, 229; also in "La 'ciudad letrada' y los discursos coloniales," 7–8. Following Lienhard, Adorno maintains that the growing obliteration of Indian elites contributed to the end of Indian and mestizo writing production after 1620. The Andean critical writings studied here appeared in the following decades and continued through the late-colonial years and even to the present (see Epilogue).

11. In its attempt to understand the overall impact of colonial Andean writing on the transformation of Andean and colonial culture, this book has benefited from the postcolonial studies discussion and scholarly production of the past twenty years, which have foregrounded the crucial role of language and textual analysis in the study of subordinate groups in colonial societies that otherwise would be invisible in the historical record. Equally important is the recognition that these subjects produced knowledge that empowered them to intervene in the shaping of their own destiny, a trans-cultural way of thinking produced in contentious loci. Among other pertinent contributions, see Seed, "Colonial and Postcolonial Discourse"; Mignolo, "Colonial and Postcolonial Discourse" and *Local Histories/Global Designs*; Rappaport, *Politics of Memory* and "Object and Alphabet," 271–292.

12. This study also builds upon foundational works in Andean ethnohistory, which focus on indigenous peoples under Spanish rule and particularly on the roles of *kurakas* and their cultural, political, and religious responses to colonialism, as well as upon those that have problematized existent interpretations of Andean religion, political culture, and native identity. Among others, these studies include Stern, *Peru's Indian Peoples*; Spalding, *Huarochirí*; Pease, *Kurakas, Reciprocidad y Riqueza*; Glave, *Trajinantes*; Ramírez, *The World Upside Down*; Mills, *Idolatry and Its Enemies*; McCormack, *Religion in the Andes*; Thomson, *We Alone Rule*; Serulnikov, *Subverting Colonial Authority.*

13. Brading, *First America*, chapters 14–15.

14. Flores Galindo, *Buscando un Inca* and "La nación como utopía"; Burga, *El nacimiento de un autopía*; Szemiński, *La utopía tupamarista* and "The Last Time the Inca Came Back."

15. The figure of the *indio ladino* (a converted Amerindian proficient in Spanish, who had adopted Spanish customs) was established in the Andes and Spanish America as cultural interaction between the Spanish and Amerindian worlds increased in the colonial society. Rolena Adorno has studied the images, experiences, and roles of *indios ladinos* as they emerged in colonial Peru during the late sixteenth and early seventeenth centuries. By becoming literate in Castilian, Adorno maintains, *indios ladinos* functioned as cultural intermediaries, serving in various capacities as *lenguas* (translators, interpreters, scribes), church officers, *alguaciles* (policemen), and *fiscales* (overseers of Indian converts' behavior, sacristans, and coadjutors) and playing such roles as messianic leaders, litigants, and, ultimately, writers. Adorno, "Nosotros somos los kurakakuna." In this book, I include lettered mestizos in the category of ladinos, particularly when dealing with the mestizo relatives of Indian-elite ladinos.

16. BRP, Sign. II/2848, 204–210v, hereafter cited as Limaylla, "Memorial," and BRP, Sign. II/2848, 211–247v, hereafter cited as Limaylla, "Representación."

17. BRP, Sign. II/2819, 218–269v, hereafter cited as Cuevas, "Cinco memoriales."

18. AGI, Indiferente General, 648.

19. AGI, Lima, 422, 1–13v, hereafter cited as Morachimo, "Manifiesto."

20. BRP, Madrid, Sign. II/2823, 118–169v, hereafter cited as "Representación verdadera."

21. Navarro, *Una denuncia profética desde el Perú a mediados del siglo XVIII*. The full title of the manuscript is "Planctus indorum christianorum in America peruntina."

22. For an examination of the role of oral tradition in early Andean texts of the colonial period, see Adorno, *From Oral to Written Expression*.

23. Although the subject remains almost unexplored in Andean history, the figure and tradition of the Andean intellectual seem to have existed in ancient Andean and Inca societies. Szemiński, "The Last Time the Inca Came Back," 281. Szemiński holds that this tradition became diffused and simplified with the homogenizing efforts of evangelization in the colonial period. If this is the case, then the intellectual complexities embodied by colonial Andean scholars may, in fact, be an analog for an ancient tradition in the Andes.

24. Inspired by the vision of jurist and entrepreneur Juan de Matienzo in 1567, the Toledan reforms (1569–1582) aimed to establish political stability and secure a steady flow of wealth from Peru to Spain. They included these central policies: a large-scale relocation of Andeans to tighten control over their labor and political structures and to facilitate evangelization; such resettlement of otherwise scattered and dangerously autonomous Indian communities (*ayllus*) into Indian towns (*reducciones,* or reservations) included a parallel structure of Indian government; a reassessment of tribute, *mita*, and other labor quotas; redistribution of lands; and the subordination of indigenous communities and authorities to the political control of the colonial state through Spanish *corregidores* and *cabildos*. Indigenous *cabildos* would be staffed by Indian officials, such as *alcaldes* (top *cabildo* authorities) and *regidores* (aldermen). Indians would be appointed to lower church offices as *fiscales* and cantors. Stern, *Peru's Indian Peoples*, 72–73. See the corresponding laws in Lohmann Villena and Sarabia Viejo, *Francisco de Toledo*, 1: 1–120.

25. The Guacra Paucar, *kurakas* from Jauja during the years 1555–1570, for example, claimed to have supplied Pizarro's soldiers with goods during the battles against the Inca and petitioned for noble privileges, using the Iberian principles of *pureza de sangre* (purity of blood) and "good services" rendered to enhance Spanish imperial goals. In 1555 they expected to be reimbursed for expenses and losses they had incurred in these early conflicts, a practice also interpreted as an Andean approach to the colonizers on the basis of reciprocity. Pease, *Perú Hombre e Historia,* 311. Simultaneously, though, they also seem to have been implicated in subversive activities that were part of a larger pan-Andean insurrection against the Spanish conquest of the Andes. Ibid. Later in the 1580s, Felipe Guacra Paucar, his brother Francisco Guacra Paucar, and Francisco Tisy Canga Guacra—members of a noble Indian family from the Jauja Valley—disputed in court what they saw as a denial of their legitimate right to succession to the Luringuanca *kurakazgo* (chiefdom) of the Jauja Valley, challenging the legitimacy of the Limaylla lineage to the chiefdom's succession. Box 5, Peru, Noviembre 18–Enero 22, 1600, Lilly Library, Bloomington, Indiana. Andean *probanzas de nobleza* can be counted by the thousands in colonial archives. This practice continued throughout the colonial period until the Bourbons launched their attack on the Cusco Inca nobility in the aftermath of the Túpac Amaru Rebellion.

26. Pease, *Perú Hombre e Historia*, 312. Both ecclesiastics championed the campaigns against the *encomienda* system in Mexico, the Caribbean, and Peru. Las Casas in particular had been denouncing abuses by Spanish conquistadors since the early years of the conquest and was instrumental in the promulgation of the New Laws in 1542, which curtailed the power of *encomenderos*.

27. One of the signers of these powers of attorney was Carlos Limaylla, *cacique principal* from Luringuanca (Jauja Valley) and grandfather of Jerónimo Lorenzo Limaylla, one of the Andean writers discussed in this book. Pease, *Kurakas, Reciprocidad y Riqueza*, 152–153, 155–156.

28. See some of the most important texts of this period and the most comprehensive studies about them in note 9.

29. Quispe-Agnoli, *La fé andina en la escritura*.

30. Initially an obligation of *protectores de naturales* and most other government officials, sending reports on the general state of things in the colonies with suggested remedies for existing problems, became part of these officials' administrative duties. In Spanish America, this tradition began almost with the conquest itself. Andean representatives, *procuradores de indios*, intellectuals, *caciques*, and native priests—who had been exposed to colonial administrative culture in a variety of capacities—seized this institutional opportunity to question the everyday functioning of colonialism and to participate in shaping and reforming society.

31. Pratt, *Imperial Eyes*, 4. Mary Louise Pratt defined "contact zones" as contentious spaces created in colonial situations where struggles between cultures take place, often in the context of power relationships between colonizers and the colonized. The well-known work of Felipe Guamán Poma de Ayala (*Nueva corónica y buen gobierno*) exemplifies an early type of Andean writing from within a "contact zone."

32. Rama, *La ciudad letrada*.

33. On the participation of African descendants in the lettered culture of mid-colonial Lima, see Jouve Martín, *Esclavos de la ciudad letrada*. For the first decades of the 1800s in Uruguay, see Acree, "Jacinto Ventura de Molina."

34. See Rowe, "Movimiento Nacional Inca del siglo XVIII," 2; Serulnikov, *Subverting Colonial Authority*.

35. This tradition started in the Andes around the 1540s, when Andean *kurakas* engaged in the campaigns against the *encomienda* system referred to earlier and supported the actions of Fray Domingo de Santo Tomás and Fray Bartolomé de las Casas to obtain laws that curtailed the power of *encomenderos*.

36. Stern, *Peru's Indian Peoples*, 114–138.

37. Concomitant with these forms of communication, *kurakas* apparently used *quipus* (Andean knotted cords) to communicate with each other, particularly in preparation for insurrections. Szemiński, "The Last Time the Inca Came Back," 291. Even though *quipus* had been burned and prohibited after the extirpation of idolatries, they survived probably unnoticed by colonial authorities and circulated restrictively among native authorities. AGN, Lima, Escribanía, Siglo XVIII. Protocolo no. 187, Años 1790–1818, 213, 396, 298v.

38. Individual Spanish judges and *procuradores de naturales* occasionally supported the cause of social justice for Indians. For an examination of a few significant cases from

the late sixteenth century, see Glave, *De Rosa y espinas*, 27–68.

39. Dueñas, *Andean Scholarship and Rebellion*, 140.

40. An intriguing case of cross-cultural collaboration and perhaps an alternative approximation of the idea of collective authorship, however unacknowledged, emerged in the late–eighteenth-century natural history and political economy conceived by the enlightened Bishop of Trujillo, Baltazar Martínez Compañón. Emily Berquist has demonstrated that the bishop convoked anonymous Indian and mestizo teams of painters, artisans, and informants, who not only provided artistic skills for 1,327 drawings but also rendered crucial observations and local knowledge for the bishop's intellectual and enlightened project of creating an orderly and prosperous Trujillo. Through this "collaboration with Indigenous informants," the "Hispanic science of empire" expanded botanical knowledge in the New World. See Berquist, *Science of Empire*, 117–127.

41. Letters and *representaciones* that judges presented to higher authorities on behalf of Andeans, for example, had been preceded by letters, visits, and petitions by Andean authorities and writers to these prominent members of the state. Before composing his "Cinco memoriales," Juan de Cuevas Herrera had sent an extensive *memorial* to the minister of the Audiencia de Charcas, Juan de Palacios, who died before he could deliver his promise to forward it to the king and the pope. Cuevas, "Cinco memoriales," 220v.

42. García-Bedoya, "Discurso criollo y discurso andino en la literatura peruana colonial," 190–192.

43. Lienhard, *La voz y su huella*, xxvi. Lienhard transcribed and commented briefly on a series of writings by or about indigenous intellectuals from the Spanish conquest to the twentieth century. His introduction focuses on the communicative process of the epistolary genre, which unveils a kind of "Indian textuality" (written, dictated, and uttered texts) oriented mostly toward negotiation with colonial authorities, a kind of "diplomatic" text.

44. For the practical needs of this book, individual names of authors are used, given that the names of those who contributed in different capacities went unrecorded. It is to be understood, however, that these individuals were only the more visible end of a collective supporting the writings and the causes they articulated.

45. Adorno, "Felipe Guaman Poma de Ayala," 146.

46. Eguiguren, *Diccionario histórico cronológico*, 41, 874.

47. Martín, *Intellectual Conquest of Peru*, 17, 36.

48. Duviols, *La destrucción de las religiones andinas*. In 1512–1513, the Laws of Burgos ordered *encomenderos* to teach Castilian literacy to Amerindians. In 1535, another *real cédula* (royal decree) made the education of elite Indians mandatory. In 1540 and 1563, King Charles I commanded friars to teach "good customs" to native elites, whereas in *reales cédulas* from 1569 and 1573, King Philip II had commanded Viceroy Francisco de Toledo to establish seminary schools for Indian nobles in all cities of Peru. *Recopilación de Leyes de Indias* (Libro VI, Título 1, 1.18; Libro 1, Título 13, 1.5), at http://www.congreso.gob.pe/ntley/LeyIndiaP.htm.

49. The extirpation campaigns were well under way in 1565, following the *Taki Onkoy* (dance sickness)—a public demonstration of Amerindian rejection of Catholicism through endless dancing and display of ancestral *huacas,* or holy objects—and a general call to return to ancestral worship (1564–1565). The campaigns attempted to purify

Catholicism and to uproot all vestiges of native religious traditions. The extirpating efforts also sought to discipline and civilize Indians who had relapsed into their former religious practices after being baptized and ostensibly converted. Following a judicial process that involved denunciation, investigation, sentence, and chastisement, Andean "dogmatists" were rendered powerless, and their traditional ability to mediate between the human and supernatural worlds was seriously compromised. Griffiths, *The Cross and the Serpent*; Mills, *Idolatry and Its Enemies*.

50. Even as late as 1660, Don Diego León Pinelo, the legal defender of Indians, or *protector de naturales,* in Lima, maintained that the main reason to maintain the Cercado school of *caciques* was to uproot Indian idolatry. Marzal, *La transformación religiosa peruana*, 141.

51. Alaperrine-Bouyer, *La educación de las élites*, 47.

52. Morachimo, "Manifesto," 337.

53. The new goals become clear in the words of a Jesuit mentor, cited without proper name or date in Eguiguren, *Diccionario histórico cronológico*, 523: "*to instill in natives good customs and to separate them from their parents, so that they do not replicate the bad example their parents set with the superstition of their old religion.* Later on, when they return to their towns, they will teach their subjects what they learned. And it will be of great avail, because Indios principales command great authority among their subjects" (original emphasis). From a vacant *encomienda,* Toledo designated 1,000 pesos for the Lima school of *caciques* and 800 for the one to be founded in Cusco, but none of the schools was founded during his term in office. *Inca,* "Colegio de Caciques," 780; Alaperrine-Bouyer, *La educación de las élites*, 48–49.

54. In explaining the reasons for this delay, Monique Alaperrine-Bouyer argued that the Jesuits were initially reluctant to support the schools for *caciques.* Allied with the majority of members of the Audiencia of Lima, the Jesuits managed to redirect the funds available from both donations and the endowment set up by Toledo for founding schools for creoles. Alaperrine-Bouyer, *La educación de las élites*, 50–71. The reader may find useful Alaperrine-Bouyer's detailed discussion of the politics of the creation of the schools for *caciques,* including the financing and the ensuing political tensions among *encomenderos,* the crown, and the Jesuits, as well as the local alliances against the schools. Alaperrine-Bouyer, "Esbozo de una historia del Colegio de San Francisco de Borja de Cuzco," 44–53; O'Phelan, *La gran rebelión*, 53.

55. AGI, Patronato, 171.

56. *Inca,* "Colegio de Caciques," 800–829. For a history of some of the *caciques* who studied in El Cercado and San Borja and for details on the limitations of the rosters published in *Inca,* see Alaperrine-Bouyer, *La educación de las élites*, chapters 5 and 7: 123–178, 207–222.

57. Alaperrine-Bouyer, "Esbozo de una historia del Colegio de San Francisco de Borja de Cuzco," 54.

58. Osorio, *Clamor de los Indios Americanos*, 29.

59. Lorandi, *De quimeras rebeliones y utopías*, 109.

60. Flores Galindo, *Buscando un Inca*, 69.

61. Dean, *Inca Bodies and the Body of Christ*, 112–113. Dean argues that in the rebirth of the Inca past through the efforts of Indian nobles, the Jesuits were a sort of

"midwife." They strengthened the native students' sense of nobility; in fact, they "joined" the Inca nobility, as Martin de Loyola, Ignacio de Loyola's nephew, married Ñusta Beatriz. Dean also considers the Jesuit educational project a work of comprehensive trans-culturation of the Inca elite.

62. Guamán Poma de Ayala, *Nueva corónica*, 460–463, 495[499]–498[502], 453, 484[488]. A 1683 royal decree prohibited the teaching of Latin, rhetoric, and logic to native students for fear they would arrive at heretic conclusions; the measure was temporary, however. Duviols, *La destrucción de las religiones andinas*, 335. Following Guamán Poma's advocacy of Indian authorities' command of Spanish, Bruce Mannheim has maintained that Spanish literacy was crucial for a colonial *cacique* to be able to defend his charges in court. While the colonial government encouraged *caciques* to learn Spanish, attacks on the Jesuit schools of *caciques* for turning Indians into litigants came from different fronts. Mannheim, *Language of the Inca since the European Invasion*, 65, 76.

63. Bartolomé Alvarez denounced Indios ladinos for having visited the English captain Francis Drake following his clandestine arrival at the southern Pacific coast of the Viceroyalty of Peru in 1579. He also accused *kurakas* from the Province of Pacasas of having sent Drake a letter addressed to "the Magnificent Lutheran Lords" and supposedly of having killed Spaniards in the Machaca *repartimiento* (Charcas). Alvarez, *De las costumbres*, 267–268.

64. Ibid., 268. On the interaction between *escribanos* and Indian nobles in the production of notarial documents and truth more generally, see Burns, "Notaries, Truth, and Consequences."

65. Alaperrine-Bouyer, *La educación de las élites*, 207–222.

66. Although the San Borja school records extant today are rather scant and fragmentary and no direct evidence is available that documents the enrollment of Juan Santos Atahualpa and Túpac Amaru II, historians claim they did attend the school. Eguiguren, *Diccionario histórico cronológico*, 41, 874. For comprehensive studies of eighteenth-century rebellions, see sources cited in note 2.

67. According to Fray Bernardino de Izaguirre's account of the rebellion, Juan Santos gained the support of *kurakas* from the area, including Santabangori from the town of Quisopongo in the Central Sierra; Siabar, the *kuraka* of the Cunibo nation, who headed an insurrection in 1737; Mateo de Assia, a Christian *cacique* from Metraro, who was a lieutenant in the service of Juan Santos; and an Indian captain of the Cunibo nation named Perote, who contributed to the mythical accounts around Juan Santos's disappearance, declaring that his body vanished in smoke in front of the Indians. Izaguirre, *Historia de las misiones Franciscanas*.

68. Eguiguren, *Diccionario histórico cronológico*, 41, 874.

69. García Pumacahua was an outstanding entrepreneur, well-known in the Cusco area for his wealth and lavish demonstrations of loyalty to the king. Stavig, *The World of Túpac Amaru*, 251, 259.

70. Sahuaraura Tito Arauchi, "Estado del Perú."

71. Figuera, *La formación del clero indígena*, 384 (quotation); ARSI, Peru 17, ca. 1690, 130; Saignes, "Algún día todo se andará," 438.

72. O'Phelan, *Un siglo de rebeliones anticoloniales*, 110–111. For the eighteenth century, O'Phelan found that both the rebellions from the Castelfuerte era (1724–1736)

and those that erupted later, in the 1750s and 1780s, took place along the colonial economic axis that extended from Potosí to Lima. These areas proved more prone to social protest, with the commercial and economic circuit from Potosí playing a transitional or articulating role between Upper and Lower Peruvian provinces, both politically and economically.

73. In 1996, Nuria Sala I Vila noticed aspects of a network from Lima, which she identified as dating from 1783. Sala I Vila, "La rebelion de Huarochirí en 1783." She briefly described this network as a group of middlemen residents of Lima who helped convey information from the plaintiffs to the viceregal authorities of the Audiencia of Lima and disseminated laws among the indigenous communities. The Indian networks described in this book, however, encompass a larger group of people acting in different regions, which fundamentally incorporated elite Indian and mestizo scholars, creole clerics, lawyers, and a few sympathetic Spanish judges in provinces and colonial centers of Peru. Very important, though, such networks also connected with other Indian and non-Indian supporters in the royal court and reached out to the king. These networks began to function early in the post-conquest years, but they became more visible in the first half of the seventeenth century, when the campaign against the *mita* was in full sway, discussed further in Chapter 2.

✢ 2 ✢

FOUNDATIONS OF SEVENTEENTH-
CENTURY ANDEAN SCHOLARSHIP

T HE PRODUCTION OF CRITICAL REPRESENTATIONS of the social state of affairs in the seventeenth century was embedded in the major transformations Spanish colonialism brought to the Andes.[1] This chapter offers an overview of Andean scholarship, introducing the most critical issues of the time, the writers, their texts, and the social practices associated with Andean writing during that century. The production of fairly complex social critiques and reform programs by literate mestizos and Indians was part and parcel of a wider complex of political and cultural practices developed during, and prompted by, the cycles of social unrest brought about by the implementation of the Toledan reforms. The composers of these tracts/texts created informal networks of Indian authorities and supporters to advance their struggles against the impact of the reforms and used writing as a strategy for negotiating social change with viceregal and royal authorities on both sides of the Atlantic.

The key issues affecting indigenous communities in the seventeenth century and their links to Andean writing introduce the chapter. The social background and political roles of the period's writers guide the reader through the circumstances that led these figures to engage in the practices that characterized their scholarly culture.[2] Their texts are introduced next, highlighting their genesis, thrust, and impact. Since some Andean texts raised ongoing issues that prompted more radical responses, the relevant insurrectionary contexts and the place of the writings in those contexts are presented as well, when pertinent. The group of writers identified here includes a by no means exhaustive list of the numerous *kurakas*, their mestizo relatives, sympathetic clergy, and others who likely intervened in the texts' composition and whose names went unrecorded.

NETWORKS OF ANDEAN CONTESTATION: CAMPAIGNING AGAINST THE TOLEDAN REFORMS

The imposition of colonial institutions in the Andes following the Spanish conquest brought tremendous social upheaval to the native communities. Indian authorities moved in different ways to address the initial and subsequent shocks as early colonial impositions were more systematically attempted after implementation of the reforms of Viceroy Francisco de Toledo (1569–1582).[3] The most destabilizing changes for indigenous groups included demographic devastation and the *encomienda* system, coupled with the loss of communal lands and the obliterating effects of the later compulsory mining draft. The harshness of the *mita* obligation forced Andeans to flee their communities, making it increasingly difficult for *caciques* to comply with the colonial state's *mita* quotas and tribute demands. Adding to these pressing factors, Andeans from the large jurisdiction of the Archdioceses of Lima underwent various cycles of ecclesiastical campaigns known as the extirpation of idolatry (1609–1626, 1641–1671, 1724–1730). The campaigns not only obliterated the cultural texture of Andean communities but also left them impoverished and divided; in addition, they created an opportunity for further abuse of native women and men by corrupt and incompetent clerics. Widespread official corruption and the unchecked power of local elites in the seventeenth century increasingly undermined the possibilities of justice for Andeans.[4] All of these circumstances reverberate in the background of the Andean writings introduced later in this chapter, whose antecedents can be traced back to the earliest campaigns against the institutions of colonial rule.

In one of the earliest efforts to address the havoc created by the Spanish colonizers, Fray Bartolomé de las Casas proposed eliminating the *encomiendas* in his 1542 writings and advocated the end of Indian slavery, the restitution of Indian lands to their legitimate owners, and consideration of Indians as free subjects under the protection of the king.[5] In 1582, twenty-four *caciques* from the Province of Charcas (Qaraqaras, Chichas, Chuyes, and Charkas Indian nations), led by the *kuraka* Don Fernando Ayavire from the Sacacas *repartimiento* (Province of Chayanta), engaged in a campaign to abolish the mita—advancing *memoriales* and signing powers of attorney to have Ayavire represent their greater number of grievances and demands before the king in Spain. In a *memorial* known as the "Memorial de Charcas" (the Charcas memorial), they indicted Viceroy Francisco de Toledo for the dispossession of the ethnic lords of the four Indian nations, the imposition of the *mita*, the reassessment of tribute quotas, and sequels of his reforms in the Province of Charcas more generally. The *caciques* offered suggestions to the king, similar in nature to some of those made by Jerónimo Lorenzo Limaylla, about how to deal with this legacy and condensed the major aspects of the Andean political and social crisis in the early seventeenth century into fifty-two short chapters.[6] The "Memorial de Charcas" became a sort of model of writing and social activism by *kurakas* and their social networks to confront the impact of Toledo's reforms, which also relied on groups of lawyers, judges, and clergy for support and likely for help in crafting the *memoriales* to the king.

In the aftermath of the epidemics in the late sixteenth and first half of the seventeenth century, the *composiciones de tierras* gave new impetus to the movement for restitution. In his *El primer nueva corónica y buen gobierno*, Andean scholar Felipe Guamán Poma de Ayala supported the restitution of Amerindian lands, defending Andeans' "natural right" to their lands and denouncing the *composiciones de tierras* endorsed by the king because he was not the rightful owner of those lands.[7] Guamán Poma de Ayala questioned the overexploitation of Indians in the mines of Huancavelica, Potosí, and others and attributed these abuses to a lack of royal control over the miners. He recommended a series of institutionalized checks and balances designed to monitor the activities of miners and *azogueros* (owner of a silver mine, a silver amalgamation mill, or both) through periodic *visitas* (inspections).[8]

During the seventeenth century, as the *mita* system increasingly replaced the *encomiendas*, Indian authorities and groups of relatives and supporters responded to these challenges with a combination of judicial, political, and intellectual strategies. *Caciques* organized social networks to campaign against the *mita* system in the Audiencias of Lima and Charcas and the royal court in Spain and continued to advance the movement for land restitution. Judges and clergy also participated in the efforts, which occasionally were led by viceroys such as Conde de Lemos in the 1660s. Dozens of *caciques* crossed the Atlantic during the seventeenth century to defend their causes in Madrid, where they also helped advance the petitions of other Andeans from different regions of Peru, acting as their legally empowered representatives in Madrid. Writing, usually in the form of critical *representaciones* accompanied by concrete petitions, was central to empower the negotiations of Indian authorities and representatives with the top authorities of the realm. In the seventeenth century these leaders sought to ease the burden of the *mita* and ultimately called for its abolition. They also fought for invalidation of fraudulent *composiciones* and the corresponding restitution of lands.[9]

As *kurakas* from different Andean areas systematically complained about the *agravios y vejaciones* (abuses and vexations), they created a trope of protest grounded in the injustice and suffering of Indians under the *mita* and denounced the hardships of personal service that continued to be forced upon them in the seventeenth century, long after the crown had prohibited such service.[10] Their efforts to fight the *mita* system through incipient networks of writing and social activism were exemplified early by the "Memorial de Charcas," backed by the action and signatures of the twenty-four *kurakas* in the Province of Charcas, and the "Memorial Dado a la Majestad del Sr. Rey Don Carlos Segundo" (ca. 1677) and "Representación hecha al Sr. Rey Don Carlos Segundo" (ca. 1667) by Jerónimo Lorenzo Limaylla, supported by his Franciscan mentors in Jauja, among other writings.

A clearer legal and social activism developed during this conjuncture that surrounded the fight for abolition of the *mita*. Indian authorities also pursued negotiations with the *audiencias* and the king to temporarily waive the draft so they could attain a *renumeración,* or a new assessment of the Indian population (also known as a *revisita*), that reflected the demographic change following the major epidemics of the 1620s and 1630s—years before Viceroy Conde de Lemos proposed doing so in 1669.[11] In addition, the campaigners demanded restoration of the lands communities had lost as a result of the growing number of *composiciones de tierrras,* as many Indian lands were quickly assumed to be available or abandoned. *Kurakas* thus presented petitions to the *audiencias* to control the local *corregidores'* and *hacendados'* (estate owners') power. *Corregidores* were accused of retaining Indians in their private businesses, thereby obstructing the fulfillment of the *mita*.[12] Indian campaigners also filed lawsuits against individual *azogueros* and miners in an effort to explore every legal possibility to circumvent forced labor policies in the Andes. When these efforts proved insufficient, Indian insurrections were attempted as an extreme tactic in the search for justice.

Since the early seventeenth century, the Andean campaign against the *mita* system and for the restitution of lands had prompted Indian authorities to cross the Atlantic systematically in pursuit of a solution to these protracted social crises. Either directly or through the *protectores de naturales, caciques* and *gobernadores* desperately petitioned for government action—including one from the communities of the Angaraes *repartimiento,* in the central highlands, in 1625. They petitioned for the first time for exemption of the *mita* service in the Huancavelica mines, which the crown granted for a renewed ten-year period. Later, in 1646, Don Christobal Cuycapusca, Don Pedro Cuycapusca, and Don Juan de Yanamisa—*caciques principales* from the same *repartimiento*—sent *memoriales* to the king explaining the new crisis created by a recent earthquake and asked for a ten-year prorogation of the exemption to *mita* service in the Huancavelica mines.

They were granted a new eight-year extension of the waiver as a result of the last petition.[13]

That same year, the court received a visit and a *memorial* from yet another Andean who identified himself as Don Juan Lorenzo Ayllón, "Indian from the Provinces of Peru," who claimed to be a noble descendant of the *caciques* of Luringuanca in Jauja Province. Ayllón had traveled clandestinely to meet the king and denounce the fact that, since the beginning of the colonial *mita*, about 1 million Indians had perished as a result of the lethal dust they inhaled, combined with mortal diseases, in the mines. After reminding the king of the Jauja Indians' financial and military cooperation with Spain in earlier times of Inca rebellion, Ayllón demanded that the Indians working in Huancavelica be exempt from the *mita* for a period of twenty or thirty years so they could rest, return to the Indian towns they had abandoned, and resume their indoctrination.[14] In 1666 the *cacique principal* from San Pedro Pillao (Tarma), Don Diego Sánchez Macario, traveled to Madrid to ask for an exemption of his *repartimiento* Indians from *mitas* and personal service, which had caused many tributaries to abandon their towns and made his duty as tax collector and organizer of the *mita* impossible to fulfill.[15]

Kurakas from the coastal zones subject to the Huancavelica and Potosí mines were also among the Andean leaders who traveled to meet with the king and the Council of the Indies to negotiate alleviation of the *mita* burden for their communities.[16] On March 14, 1647, King Philip IV received a visit from Don Andrés de Ortega Lluncón, *cacique* and *pachaca* (local native lord of 100 households) *principal* of Lambayeque in the Saña *corregimiento*, who demanded resolution of several lawsuits he had filed years before that had remained stuck in Madrid. Don Andrés complained bitterly of the *agravios y vejaciones* inflicted on his Indians by Viceroy Marqués de Mancera, who had disregarded previous calls for justice from the *kuraka*. Don Andrés's previous *memoriales* had been sitting in the viceroy's office since the early years of his predecessor, Conde de Chinchón. Don Andrés voiced his frustration with the current viceroy's political influence, which slowed the resolution of his petitions. As a result, he went to the court to ask explicitly that Viceroy Marqués de Mancera be removed.[17]

Another Indian noble visitor to the court in Madrid, Don Carlos Chimo, also from the town of Lambayeque (Saña *corregimiento*), addressed the king in 1647 to denounce additional *agravios* concerning his Indians, particularly conflicts resulting from the *composiciones de tierras* and the abuses by judges in charge of them. Don Carlos produced a *memorial* with support letters written by other *caciques* from the area, voicing general discontent regarding the illegal behavior of the *corregidores* from Saña and Chiclayo and of an *audiencia* judge, Pedro de Meneses, who had sold community lands and struck a *composición de tierras* that had harmed the communities. When he first approached the Council of the Indies, Don Carlos Chimo had been prompted to leave Spain, but he disobeyed and searched for the king in Zaragoza, where he ultimately found him. Carlos Chimo obtained a copy of the 1646 royal mandates to Viceroy Marqués de Mancera for the creation of a junta (in this case, a committee of judges and clerics) to investigate and resolve these and similar complaints previously leveled by others. As was usually the response in such cases, the king remitted the case to the Council of the Indies for consultation, and the process of justice stagnated as the council prompted the petitioner to leave Madrid so his behavior would not be imitated.[18] The investigation took nearly two years, at the end of which the *alcalde del crimen* (*audiencia* judge who specialized in criminal cases) from the Lima Real Audiencia, Don Bernardo de Iturrizarra, exonerated his fellow *audiencia* judge Pedro de Meneses, stating that he had sold no lands in the town of Lambayeque.[19]

The campaigns incorporated petitions for the restitution of communal lands, the number of which had increased by the 1660s. The petitioners described different modalities of what they considered fraudulent *composiciones de tierras* and mismanagement by judges colluding with *corregidores, escribanos, encomenderos, curas,* and *protectores de naturales.* The *caciques principales* from the bishopric of La Paz—Don Cristóbal Nina, Don Juan Quispe, and Don Pedro Larua, members of a large social network of native authorities in southern Peru—exposed the minutia of the illegal *composiciones,* providing the names of the colluding officials and details about the location and magnitude of their mismanagement, as well as the violence involved in the process. They presented their allegations to the *real audiencia's fiscal,* Don Pedro Vásquez de Velazco, also the judge in the previous viceroy Marqués de Mancera's *residencia* (review), which was being conducted at the time. The *caciques* denounced judges and other petty judicial officials for confiscating the original land titles exhibited by Indian litigants to prevent continuation of due process and thus prevent the restitution of lands to their legitimate owners.[20]

One of the most actively engaged Indian authorities in Upper Peru during this period, the *cacique* and *gobernador principal* of Jesús de Machaca (Pacajes Province), Don Gabriel Fernández Guarache, filed a comprehensive set of *capítulos* (accusations) that emphasized the decadence within the region, the detrimental effects of escapism,[21] and the necessity of a *revisita*; he also asked the *audiencia* to put an end to the corruption and injustice. Another prominent *cacique,* Don Bartolomé Topa Hallicalla from Asillo (Azángaro), also stood out during the campaigns. A writer of *memoriales* and a relentless litigant, he, along with Fernández Guarache, devoted handsome amounts of money to advance litigation against the region's mine owners. The two men led a network of *caciques* that operated in the region southwest of Lake Titicaca. Hallicalla held several noble titles and allied with the colonial authorities, when necessary, to suppress the Laicacota uprising and diminish the power of mine owners. He was a principal campaigner against the *mita* in the Peruvian Andes, fighting for laws against the *mita de faltriquera* (*mita* rendered in cash) during the time of Conde de Lemos; he was also an active entrepreneur in the areas of mining, *estancias* (ranches), mills, and trade for many years.[22] These two diligent *kurakas* offered Conde de Lemos persuasive evidence to pursue the abolition of the *mita* system. Fernández Guarache explained in his *memoriales* that he had to assume financial responsibility for the missing *mitayos* of Pacajes and petitioned the viceroy to reduce the number of *mitayos* from his area and suspend the practice of holding *kurakas* responsible for the *mita* of an entire province. Fernández Guarache was vocal in demanding substantial reforms to the *mita*; he advocated a system of two break weeks combined with one work-week and the suspension of day and night shifts.[23]

Although the *mita* was not formally abolished in their time, the *kurakas'* campaign was partially successful, since ordinances prohibiting the *mita de faltri-quera* were issued in 1657. Hallicalla obtained generous noble privileges in com-pensation for his support of the viceregal army in the uprising in Laicacota against local miners and *azogueros*. Fernández Guarache and Hallicalla helped persuade Viceroy Conde de Lemos to call for the abolition of the *mita*.[24] Fernández Guarache's petitions and allegations in particular were discussed by the interim viceregal government of the Audiencia of Lima and later reached the Council of the Indies, which decided in 1668 to command Conde de Lemos to act against the abuses denounced in Fernández Guarache's *memoriales*.[25]

As denunciations increased, the king received multiple visits from Indian ambassadors, each of whom represented a regional network of Andean authori-ties in Peru. In 1664, as a final example, the Cajamarca *cacique* Don Antonio Collatopa, who claimed to be a descendant of the Incan ruler Huayna Capac, per-sonally delivered his *memorial* to King Philip IV, in which he leveled accusations of abuses and mistreatment against governors and parish priests in the northern sierra. The grievances were associated with the hardships Indians experienced in the Huancavelica and Potosí *mitas*. His denunciations were supported by the Augustinian Fray Juan de la Madre de Dios.[26] Don Antonio appeared to lead one of the networks of *caciques* from different regions of Peru who sent petitions against the *mita* system to the royal court and their own *memoriales* and Indian representatives to the king. Among those supporting Don Antonio Collatopa's actions in Madrid were Don Joséph Mayta Capac Tito Atauche, Don Nicolás Noyo Chumbi, Don Francisco Pilco Guaraz, Don Melchor Atauche Túpacusi Rimache Inga, Don Francisco Rodríguez Pilco, Don Bartolomé Xulca Poma, Don Juan Curi, and Don Francisco Nina Lingon.[27]

These cases of Indian legal activism demonstrate that Indian authorities were at the forefront of the struggles against the *mita*, in which the writing of *memo-riales* asking for reform of the system and the collective effort of informal Indian networks played a significant role. These Andeans' endeavors were fostered by the search for a direct dialogue and negotiation of policies with the king and his advisory council in Madrid. They expressed the fact that seventeenth-century Andean writing and activism were another facet of the larger trans-Atlantic exchange derived from the colonial relationship, which was prompted and shaped by the disruption Spanish colonialism generated in the Andes. The countless *memoriales* from groups of *caciques* seeking justice and denouncing the ineffectiveness of the early royal policies issued to alleviate the burden of the *mita* and the factual dispossession of Indian communal lands attest to the internal contradictions of a colonial system that used Christianity and social harmony at the level of colonial discourse but could only deliver non-enforced protective laws. Even the 1660 royal decree—put in place after a long campaign by Andeans, ecclesiastics, colonial judges, and viceroys—remained ineffective as of 1622, making evident the depth of the general crisis of the colonial state in the Viceroyalty of Peru.[28] The active responses to such crisis are more vividly expressed in the social practices and texts of the Andean intellectuals introduced in the sections that follow.

JUAN DE CUEVAS HERRERA

One of the most striking features of Andean critical scholarship is the fact that some of the writers were members of the church and made the ecclesiastical institution the target of their criticism (Figure 2.1). For more than twenty years, the Andean Juan de Cuevas Herrera was a *cura doctrinero* in Carancas and other Indian towns in the Province of Charcas. Born in Chuquisaca (or La Plata, Charcas) sometime around 1590, Cuevas presented himself as a mestizo descendant of the Inca Cristobal Paullu, son of Huayna Capac and brother of Huascar. Cuevas joined the Jesuit seminary in Lima as a brother of the order on November 21, 1610. He studied arts and law for a year before taking vows as a priest.[29] In 1616, the young Cuevas Herrera was working for the Cusco bishop Dr. Fernando de Mendoza, apparently helping him sort out books for censorship.[30] As did Felipe Guamán Poma de Ayala, Cuevas assisted the Jesuits in the extirpation campaigns in the Province of Huarochirí in 1620.[31]

Cuevas Herrera's long career as a traveling parish priest allowed him to witness firsthand the relationships between Andean Indians and parish priests, *corregidores*, their lieutenants, miners, and *caciques*; he learned the minutia of everyday life in small parishes, where he mediated in conflicts between indigenous commoners and Spaniards as Andeans called on him for help. Cuevas Herrera traveled extensively throughout the Viceroyalty of Peru before he wrote to the king, likely at an advanced age, while he was a *cura beneficiado* (curate) in the parish of Andamarca and Hurinoca (Carangas, west of Lake Titicaca). He incorporated his experiential knowledge in his *memoriales* to the king, "reporting" on

✠

CINCO MEMORIALES

en que breve, y sucintamente se dà noticia de los mayores impedimentos
que hay para que estos Indios del
Perú no acaben, de entrar en la Ley
y costumbres Evangelicas, dirigidos al Rey nuestro Señor
por el Lizenziado Juan
de Cuebas Herrera Cura
Beneficiado de los Pueblos
de Andamarca, y Huri-
noca en la Provincia
de los Carangas, natu-
ral de la Ciudad dela
Plata en los Carchas

Prologo.

R. eparte Dios sus dones, como es venido allj
aquex vexmo scientis.º ynos se apuxan, por predican, otros
tienen por felicidad una Lectura: providencia de Dios, que
sino hubiera diversas inclinaciones, pereciera la vanidad,
que tanto nermove el Universo, assi en lo natural, como en lo político. Vací con natural compasion à estos
miserables Yndios, creció con la Edad, y la Experiencia

Figure 2.1 "Cinco memoriales" by Juan de Cuevas Herrera. BRP, Sign. II/2819, folio 218.

the religious state and social ills of rural areas in Upper Peru (Bolivia). Cuevas Herrera's narrative was empowered by the fact that he had witnessed the events he questioned, and he presented himself as an honest priest: "A priest I am ... and I will speak as a witness, since I have been a curate for twenty years and today I am poorer than the first day."[32]

Cuevas Herrera addressed the king with his extensive manuscript entitled "Cinco memoriales,"[33] a testimonial rendition of the erroneous practices of colonial functionaries and priests, which the writer claimed to have experienced directly or known from someone who had witnessed them firsthand. Rhetorically speaking, Cuevas Herrera crafted his "Cinco memoriales" in the format of pastoral visitation reports, which provided full accounts of the state of religious, social, and personal matters in the provinces. Even though substantially less extensive than Guamán Poma's *Nueva corónica*, the "Cinco memoriales" follows a similar model of pastoral rhetoric and devastating criticism of colonial officials' corruption, which included priests, prelates, and *caciques*. Both men, however, purportedly supported the evangelization process. As a Jesuit *cura doctrinero*, Cuevas must have been exposed to the ecclesiastical literature available for training preachers. A large genre of pastoral letters, manuals, sermons, and treaties was produced during the formative period of the Peruvian church (1548–1585) that was available for instructing *doctrineros* in matters of faith and that also assessed the spiritual state of the Indians and the obstacles to their full conversion. Juan de Cuevas Herrera partook in the rhetoric of the pastoral genre in his "Cinco memoriales," as he set out to render an account in which he "briefly and succinctly made known the major impediments for the complete entrance of these Indians from Peru to the Christian law and customs."[34]

In the aftermath of the extirpation campaigns in the Archbishopric of Lima, which proved unable to eradicate native religious practices, Cuevas Herrera represented the view of those who believed Indians were poorly indoctrinated as a result of the incompetence of the secular clergy. Moreover, natives ran away from mission towns because of the violent treatment parish priests inflicted upon them. More specifically, the "Cinco memoriales" focused on the obstacles that prevented the full conversion of Andeans to Christianity in the seventeenth century, after more than a century of missionary activity in the Province of Charcas. He presented a detailed discussion of the parish priests' failure to reach out to indigenous communities and provided firsthand accounts of the wide variety of abuses *curas doctrineros* committed against poor Andean women, men, and children. The Andean *doctrinero* was vocal in describing the incompetence of *curas beneficiados* in the Aymara language and critically exposed the larger realities of evangelization in his region.[35] For him, the overall obliteration of Andean societies by Spaniards was what prompted Andeans to run away to the mountains where they could live on the margins of Christianity, a major hurdle to the success of evangelization. He also denounced the corrupt practices of *corregidores* at all levels and the actions of abusive and illegitimate *caciques*. Cuevas Herrera concluded each *memorial* with proposed policies to alleviate the situations he discussed.

The "Cinco memoriales" also offers a testimonial account of life in the mines. The author claims to have lived for a time as a miner in Potosí, where he witnessed the plight of Andean *mitayos* from the sixteen provinces ascribed to the mine— an experience he felt enabled him to write an authoritative, critical account of the *mita* system. He also documented different forms of personal service Andeans were forced to perform for Spanish colonists in haciendas and Spanish towns.

Juan de Cuevas Herrera's *memoriales*, however, also reveal his deep admiration for the Jesuits and his endorsement of their missionary agenda.[36] Echoing a similar sentiment in Guamán Poma's work, Cuevas Herrera advocates a more central role for Jesuits in evangelization, asking that all Indian towns in the Province of Charcas be given to the Jesuits. In this, he also echoed similar proposals made by other members of the civil government, such as the Audiencia of Lima's judge Juan de Padilla in 1657 when he raised his own *memorial* to the king, denouncing the poor state of evangelization in Peru as an alternative to the extirpation campaigns.[37] More likely, however, the text echoed the debates of the mid-seventeenth century that began to question the effectiveness of the extirpation campaign.[38]

Prior to his "Cinco memoriales," Cuevas Herrera had apparently written several similar manuscripts, which he sent to the *real audiencia* of Charcas's minister Don Juan de Palacio to deliver to the king. Palacio died before he could accomplish the task. Cuevas Herrera found inspiration for his writings in a treatise by the Franciscan father Juan de Silir and in those of other ecclesiastics who had written in favor of justice for Andeans.[39] Following his previous unsuccessful attempts to reach the king through Spanish officials, Cuevas composed his "Cinco memoriales" sometime in the second half of the seventeenth century. Although there is no clear indication that Cuevas Herrera traveled to the royal court, the document must have reached the king at some point, since it rests today in the library of the royal palace in Madrid.

Like other Andean scholars of the colonial period, Juan de Cuevas Herrera found himself in an ambiguous position. As a Catholic *cura doctrinero*, his role was to advance Indian Christianization and support the state policies of colonialism, while as a mestizo of Incan descent, he may have been more sensitive to the social plight of his fellow Andeans. In the "Cinco memoriales," the parish priest constantly negotiates his roles between endorsing evangelization and condemning the behavior of colonial authorities and colonialists vis-à-vis Andeans. His *memoriales* represent both a reformulation of colonial Christianity and a frontal attack on the church for failing to fulfill the promise of full inclusion of Andeans after more than a century of evangelization in the Charcas Province. The Andean parish priest's text bears witness to the conflicting perceptions of religion by colonizers and the colonized and the ways Andean intellectuals managed to explain idolatry while struggling to reconcile their roles with the goals of colonial indoctrination.[40] Cuevas Herrera wrote this *memorial* in his later years, when he was seeking to obtain a prelateship as ecclesiastical *visitador* (pastoral inspector) in his province in the hope of overcoming poverty at the end of his life. By then, other indigenous scholars from central Peru were using writing and litigation in search of their own place within their native political sphere.

DON JERÓNIMO LORENZO LIMAYLLA

The efforts of Andean scholars such as Cuevas Herrera within the church lead us to those of his counterparts who also struggled for power positions of a different kind, namely, the *cacicazgos* of the Indian communities. Originally from the Luringuanca *repartimiento* (*encomienda* district) of the Mantaro Valley (Jauja Province), the elite Andean Don Jerónimo Lorenzo Limaylla belonged to one of the valley's oldest and most powerful *kuraka* lineages. The Limayllas' ability to dominate the *cacicazgo* over the centuries and their matrimonial alliances with members of other prominent Mantaro Valley families allowed them to amass a considerable fortune. They managed community lands and labor and participated in the local spiritual economy through the management of *cofradías'* assets, generous donations, and other *obras pías* (pious works). They also developed a close relationship with the Franciscans of the local parishes and with local colonial administrators.[41]

The Mantaro Valley was perhaps the wealthiest area in the central highlands of Peru, where one of the first Spanish settlements was established in the town of Jauja sometime around 1533. The location was privileged, close to the Pacific and at the crossroads of Cusco Province and the central rainforest. The Indian population of Jauja, around 100,000, was among the largest in Peru at the time of the Spanish conquest. The region experienced major deterioration under Spanish rule, as Jauja became one of the fourteen provinces within the orbit of the Huancavelica *mita*. The Indian population, including the seven *repartimientos* of the Jauja *corregimiento*, quickly declined; by 1570 it only amounted to 50,000.[42]

Internal rifts and lengthy legal disputes over the newly imposed *caciques* plagued the indigenous communities of the Mantaro Valley following implementation of the Toledan reforms, as traditional norms of succession were replaced by Spanish ones. Ambiguity involving succession methods was common, however, leaving space for negotiation. Starting in the 1580s, *kurakas* from Jauja Province had been engaged in legal disputes over their right to area chiefdoms. The Guacra Paucars (Felipe Guacra Paucar, his brother Francisco Guacra Paucar, and Francisco Tisy Canga Guacra) and the Limayllas were allies at times, but they also became rival lineages as they disputed in court over their right to succession of the Luringuanca *kurakazgo* (*cacicazgo*, or chiefdom).[43]

The struggle to access this *kurakazgo* in the mid-seventeenth century generated a lengthy lawsuit (1655–1671) that pitted Jerónimo Lorenzo Limaylla against his distant cousin Bernardino Mangoguala Limaylla, after the latter had been officially recognized as the successor of the last legitimate *kuraka*, Don Jerónimo Valentin Limaylla. Jerónimo Lorenzo Limaylla was an illegitimate child of Don Jerónimo Valentin Limaylla, a condition that proved detrimental to his aspirations to power in the Luringuanca *kurakazgo*. Both Jerónimo Lorenzo Limaylla and his cousin had enrolled in the Colegio de Caciques, El Príncipe, in El Cercado, the Indian town of Lima, in 1648.[44] Jerónimo Lorenzo Limaylla was also mentored by Franciscan *curas doctrineros* from Jauja, who likely immersed him in Christian teachings and taught him to write in Castilian.

In 1655, the year the *audiencia* confirmed his cousin in the Luringuanca *cacicazgo*, Jerónimo Lorenzo Limaylla initiated the lawsuit but still introduced himself as an Indian *cacique principal* and *gobernador* of the Luringuanca *cacicazgo*, a direct heir of the region's main ethnic lords, and a descendant of the Inca Pachacuti (the ninth Inca king), a grandson of Viracocha (the eighth Inca king), and a great-grandson of Yaguarhuacas (the seventh Inca king). To advance his *pleito*, the Jauja noble traveled frequently to Lima and the Spanish court in Madrid, where he busied himself writing letters and petitions. His two major pieces of writing come from the lawsuit and stand out as rather sophisticated renditions of native identity and anticolonial critiques (Figures 2.2 and 2.3), which played an important role in his entire campaign to be recognized as a noble political authority. In his "Representación," he also presented himself as a legitimate representative of the Jauja native lords, who allegedly entrusted him to advance their petitions to the king.[45]

Limaylla's texts incorporated elements of the discourses of social justice, common in the writings that had sustained the campaign against the *mita* service in Andean Peru since the early seventeenth century, and were part and parcel of the long-standing tradition of collective protest and action exemplified in the "Memorial de Charcas," introduced earlier. Limaylla seized every possible opportunity to retain his lineage's hold over the political and social structures within the Mantaro Valley. He was a Christian Andean who had a solid knowledge of Spanish law and theology. In addition, he had experience dealing with the Audiencia of Lima, and later in the 1660s he was exposed to the workings of the Council of the Indies in Spain. His strategy to become head of the Luringuanca *kurakazgo* entailed a combination of advancing lawsuits against *kurakas* he perceived as illegitimate, writing representations and petitions to the king in search of noble recognition and related privileges, traveling to the royal court to advance his and other *caciques*' petitions, and, ultimately, joining most *kurakas* of the

✠

MEMORIAL,

QVE PONE A LOS REALES PIES
de nuestro gran Monarca Carlos Se-
gundo, Rey de España, y de
la América,

DON GERONIMO LORENZO LIMAYLLA, INDIO
Çazique Principal, y Governador en la Provincia del Valle de
Xauxa, del Repartimiento de Luringuanca, en
el Reyno del Perù.

PARA QVE SV MAGESTAD SEA SESVIDO DE
mandar inftituir, para los Indios Nobles, en quienes concurran las ca-
lidades expreffadas en èl, vna Cavalleria, ù Orden, à femejança de
las Militares, con que fe obviaràn los inconveniêtes graves, que oy fe ex-
perimentan, y ferà de alivio, honra, y perpetuo reconocimiento para
aquellas Naciones, y de gran confequencia en vtil de los Reales ave-
res, por las circunftaucias que fe reconoceràn en èl.

SEÑOR:

DON Geronimo Lorenço Limaylla, Indio Cazique Principal de la Provincia de Xauxa, Repartimiento de Luringuanca, de la Corona Real de fu Mageftad, Reyno del Perù, hijo
vnico de Don Lorenço Valentin de Limaylla, vltimo Cazique
Principal, y Governador que fue de dicha Provincia, y Repartimiento, nieto de Don Bernardo Guacra Paucar Limaylla, viz-
nieto de Don Geronimo Guacra Paucar Limaylla, y reviznieto
de Don Carlos Limaylla, a quienes por accion natural, y civil, les
perteneciò fer Caziques, y por lo inmemorial fe confirma; y afsi-
mifmo defcendiente de los Reyes que fueron de aquel tan dila-

A   tado

Figure 2.2 "Memorial" by Jerónimo Lorenzo Limaylla. AGI, Indiferente, 640, folios 1–4.

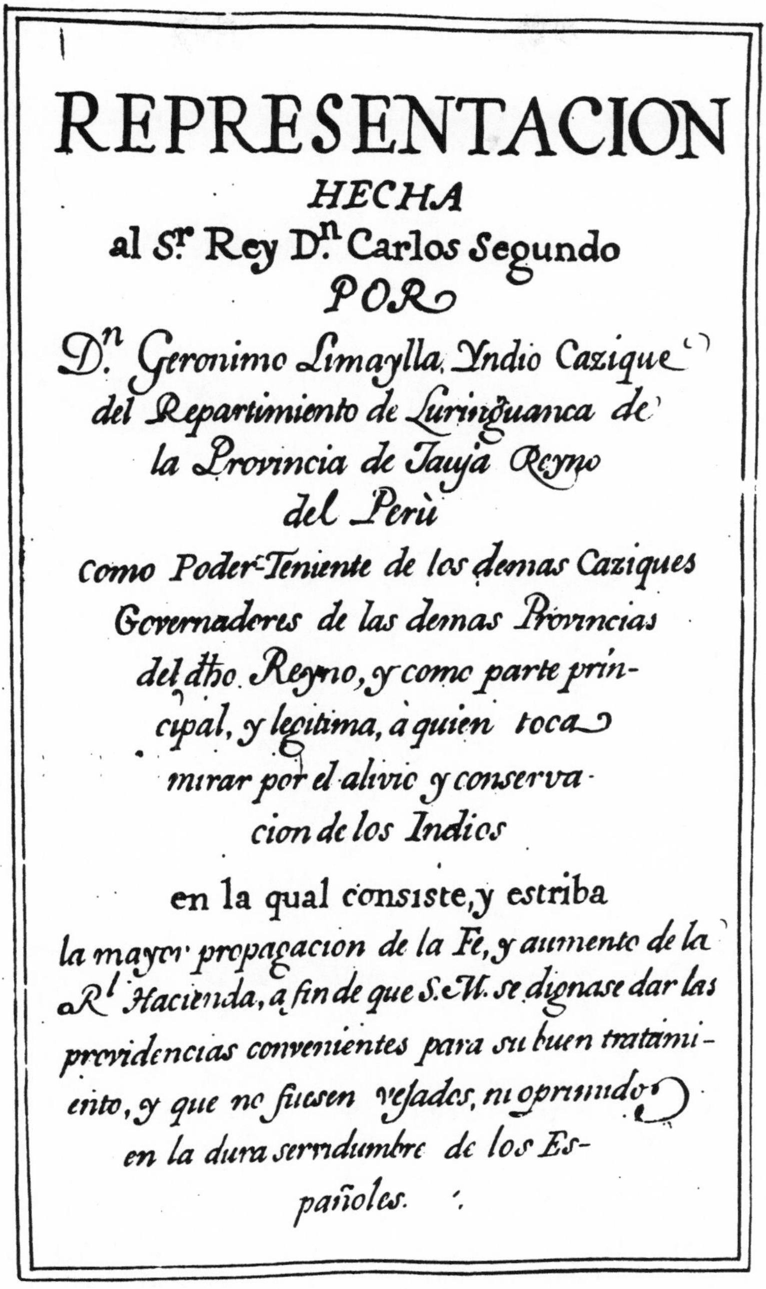

REPRESENTACION

HECHA
al Sr Rey Dn. Carlos Segundo
POR

Dn. Geronimo Limaylla, Yndio Cazique
del Repartimiento de Luringuanca de
la Provincia de Tauja Reyno
del Perù
como Poder-Teniente de los demas Caziques
Governadores de las demas Provincias
del dho. Reyno, y como parte principal, y legitima, à quien toca
mirar por el alivio y conserva-
cion de los Indios

en la qual consiste, y estriba
la mayor propagacion de la Fe, y aumento de la
Rl Hacienda, à fin de que S. M. se dignase dar las
providencias convenientes para su buen tratamiento, y que no fuesen vejados, ni oprimidos
en la dura servidumbre de los Españoles.

Figure 2.3 "Representación" by Jerónimo Lorenzo Limaylla. BRP, Sign. II/2848, folio 211.

Andean provinces liable to the *mita* service and the region's Franciscan mission-aries in denouncing violations of colonial laws and the excesses of officials in the *mitas* and *obrajes*.[46]

These practices reflect the negotiation of multiple roles by Andean elites, which must be considered within the wider context of *kurakas'* social activism as a whole.[47] Limaylla's representations unveil a political practice that superseded the mere concern for noble privilege and reached the level of cultural resistance through a lettered critique of colonial practices of justice. Limaylla's texts disputed the fabricated identities of Indian subjects as "irrational beings" in the colonial dis-course and, in turn, constructed the colonizers as "anti-Christian."[48] The language used in his "Memorial" and the "Representación" also bears witness to the extir-pation campaigns in the Jauja area, as reiterations and contestations of Andeans' "idolatrous" behavior resonate in the background of Limaylla's writings.

Limaylla reformulated colonial hierarchies by proposing social equality for Amerindian elites and noble Spaniards, thereby validating Andean elites' rights to privileges. On this basis, he requested the creation of a knightly order for noble Andeans and proposed that Spaniards pay tribute and render personal service as well. While he appeared to endorse both *pureza de sangre* as the basis of the Andean elite's nobility and Indian authorities' duty to render "good service" to the crown, he criticized Andeans' social and moral debasement at length to high-light the king's failure to fulfill his reciprocal duties to his indigenous subjects.

Most of the complaints and denunciations in the texts relate to the oppres-sive conditions of work in the Potosí silver mines and the Huancavelica mercury mines and to the tax pressures on native communities that ensued as a result of the demographic decline. The manuscripts discuss the negligence of colonial officials in enforcing the pope's and the king's mandates on the *mita* service, a long-lasting "anomaly" that spoke to the poor state of justice and the legal rights of Andeans as free subjects under colonial rule. The "Representación" recounted unenforced royal mandates since the time of the conquest and discussed "natu-ral" and "divine law" to demonstrate Spanish rule's lack of legitimacy in the colo-nial Andes. Limaylla argued for the Andean right of self-rule by reformulating Scholastic notions of "common good" and "natural right" (see Chapter 4). The link between social harmony and social justice for the Amerindian subjects of the Spanish empire appears natural for Limaylla. The two manuscripts share simi-larities with the narrative style of Guamán Poma's *Nueva corónica*, with its run-on sentences, little or no punctuation, and inconsistent spellings and sentence construction. The style does resemble the textual features of many archival docu-ments of the seventeenth century and, less frequently, the eighteenth century—documents such as administrative reports, letters, accounts, *representaciones*, and *memoriales* such as Fray Calixto's "Representación verdadera."[49] Limaylla's writ-ings appear less mediated, perhaps reflecting a transitory stage in the process of accommodating Andean oral traditions with the demands of Spanish administrative and legal writing.

The royal authorities largely dismissed Limaylla's petition and underestimated his ability to compose complex texts. The petition Jerónimo Lorenzo Limaylla raised to King Charles II in his "Memorial" from around 1677 was denied because the Council of the Indies considered a knightly order for Indian nobles "inconvenient," since it would encourage the preservation of Inca and Aztec memories and thereby instill in them an undesirable sense of nobility that would divert them from work and provoke them to riot and flee to the "mountains." More clearly, the royal councilors believed Limaylla was incapable of producing the kind of writing he submitted. They presumed that a clergyman must have written the "Representación" and simply reiterated the previous decrees ordering investigations of denounced abuses.[50] Even today, Limaylla's ability to compose such texts has been questioned anew, albeit in a different form.

Historian José Carlos de la Puente Luna has challenged Jerónimo Lorenzo Limaylla's identity as the subject behind the long dispute over the Luringuanca *cacicazgo* (1655–1671), thereby opening the door to questions about the authorship of the two texts traditionally ascribed to Limaylla. Following the line of argument advanced by the appointed *cacique* Bernardino Mangoguala Limaylla, Puente Luna argues that the true claimant of the *cacicazgo* was not the actual Jerónimo Lorenzo Limaylla but an impostor. An Indian commoner from Reque (Trujillo) named Lorenzo Ayún Chifo allegedly passed himself off as Jerónimo Lorenzo Limaylla, who Bernardino claimed had died at age eight (no death certificate available). Ayún Chifo was an Indio ladino and a Christian who, according to Puente Luna, emulated the Franciscan ideal of sanctity and also coveted the Luringuanca *cacicazgo*.

Puente Luna did not study the documents under discussion, but he dismissed the possibility that the *memoriales* addressed to the king were written by *kurakas* or, more concretely, by Jerónimo Lorenzo Limaylla.[51] Several historians have hitherto acknowledged Limaylla as the author of the "Representación" and the "Memorial."[52] Monique Allaperrine-Bouyer rejected the hypothesis of the "impostor" introduced by Bernardino, basing her discussion on the proceedings of the legal case, focusing on the background information of the two parties involved in the lawsuit, and assessing their arguments against each other. She concluded that Jerónimo Lorenzo Limaylla was the most legitimate candidate to inherit the *cacicazgo* but was displaced by an unworthy individual more suitable to the Spanish authorities; for her, Limaylla represents the plight of *curacas* without a chiefdom.[53] Allaperrine-Bouyer, however, did not analyze Limaylla's texts in detail and did not discuss authorship.

Whereas Puente Luna regarded Ayún Chifo as a typical "social climber" and an Indian emulate of the Franciscans, the actual *memoriales* to the king with which I am concerned in this book reveal the Andean writers as agents of intel-lectual resistance.[54] As opposed to simply "acculturated" Indians and "emulates" of Franciscan Christianity, the individual(s) behind these texts criticized colonial practices and contributed to a vision of social change for Andeans using their own redefinitions of Christianity. To understand fully the notion of authorship in these texts, one must account for the relationship of mentorship between Andean nobles and the clergy, which usually took place in the schools for *caci-ques*, seminary schools, or individually.

At an early age, Jerónimo Lorenzo Limaylla was entrusted to the Franciscan Fray Andrés de la Cuesta for mentorship,[55] and in 1648 Jerónimo Lorenzo enrolled in the Jesuit school of *caciques*, El Príncipe, in El Cercado, Lima.[56] Andeans mentored individually by religious men were probably exposed to much the same literature as those who attended more formal seminary schools, where the Jesuits exposed students to the teachings of Spanish theologians such as Francisco de Vitoria and Francisco Suárez, the latter of whom questioned the legitimacy of Spanish rule in the Americas. A true seventeenth-century heir of Lascasian discourses of social justice, the Jesuit Diego de Avendaño's *Thesaurus indicum* circulated widely among Andeans mentored by clerics. Avendaño wrote in favor of natives and condemned abusive Spanish officials and black and Indian slavery in colonial Peru. In the first volume of the *Thesaurus*, he listed forty-two accusations against miners and the mining system in Peru, some of which under-lie Limaylla's texts. Against Aristotle's justification of slavery, Avendaño argued that the true natural law was freedom and the right to life.[57]

Andeans mentored by Franciscans must have been familiar with critical works by other influential Franciscans, such as Fray Jerónimo de Mendieta (1526–1604), a mystic missionary who saw in the Americas the advent of the "millennial kingdom" and counteracted Aristotelian justifications of native slavery with the Christian principle of equality of all men before God.[58] Inspired by Mendieta, Fray Buenaventura de Salinas y Córdoba led the criticism of the Potosí *mita* sys-tem and advocated Indian causes in colonial Peru.[59] These are just a few works within a wider genre of non-Andean discourse that supported Indian interests and criticized colonial justice in Peru throughout the colonial period.[60]

To what extent the clergymen intervened in the writing of Limaylla's *memo-riales* to the king is difficult to ascertain. What is more relevant is that the Andean texts under discussion are infused with the Scholastic and Neo-Scholastic politi-cal theologies contained in the ecclesiastical discourses of the Franciscans and the Jesuits as much as they speak to the Andean experience of colonial subordination. Texts such as Jerónimo Lorenzo's formed part of a larger Andean political strat-egy to gain access to indigenous power positions at a time when Spanish norms of political succession and other colonial demands on Indian labor were being imposed on Andean peoples by the Toledan reforms, beginning in the 1560s.

Along with their writing, Andean ladinos like Jerónimo Lorenzo Limaylla combined extensive litigation with trans-Atlantic travel to meet the king and present their demands and with occasional participation in rebellions when other means failed.[61] The Franciscans supported Limaylla's trans-Atlantic endeavors. A 1667 letter from the Franciscan Fray Alonso Zurbano, a preacher in the town of Mataguasi (Jauja Valley), that elaborated on the suffering of natives at the hands of the Jauja *corregidores*—the "false Christians"—was filed along with Limaylla's two main manuscripts.[62] In letters written in 1656 to the rebel Bartolomé Mendoza from Huancavelica, Limaylla appears to acknowledge his collaboration with the Franciscans.[63] Limaylla thus interacted not only with native lords, Franciscan missionaries, and Jesuit teachers—from whom he learned Christian notions of justice—but perhaps also with local leaders such as Mendoza, who were engaged in insurrectionary approaches. Limaylla's texts in a way legitimated struggles against the *mita* and for the *cacicazgo* by appealing to theologies of common good, the natural right, and the legitimacy of fighting tyranny. This principle is the link between Andean intellectuals and the rebels of the time, since Limaylla felt struggles against the injustice of the *mita* were legitimate forms of fighting tyranny within the highly tense atmosphere that prevailed.

Parallel to the peaceful attempts to reverse the problematic *mita* system, social unrest and plans for massive insurrections were made in the face of delayed legal solutions. Aside from the general unrest generated by the *mita*, the first six decades of the seventeenth century saw scattered uprisings against Spanish *obrajes* and increasing tributes in different regions of the Viceroyalty of Peru.[64] A pan-Andean insurrectionary conspiracy led by *kurakas* from Charcas, Cusco, Moquegua, the Mantaro Valley, Huancavelica, Cajamarca, and Trujillo—regions liable to the *mita* system—was under way in 1666. Although the rebels attacked the *mita* system, *obrajes*, and tributes in their incendiary papers, it seems that Indian nobles' early claims for access to the priesthood were also raised in this insurrectionary conjuncture.[65]

Kurakas such as Don Antonio Collatopa and members of his network from Cajamarca, along with Gabriel Fernández Guarache and Bartolomé Topa Hallicalla and their network from Charcas, were involved in the conspiracy, which spread out from the viceregal capital on December 17, 1666. Diego Lobo, a Cajamarca leader, apparently wrote a document that contained the rebels' propositions, and the 1664 *memorial* Collatopa took to Spain to negotiate *mita* exemptions was attributed to Don Carlos Apoalaya.[66] Two Indian captains of the Lima Compañía de Naturales (Indian militia) who participated, Don Juan Ordoñez and the Indian cobbler and captain Don Andrés de Arenas, wrote papers documenting the proceedings of meetings they had held. Two leaders who had been executed were actively engaged in writing *memoriales* to the king and had sent two other Indians to the royal court along with Don Juan Cornejo, royal *visitador* from the Audiencia of Lima.[67] Although the texts of these writings did not survive, it seems they raised similar issues to those contested in the legal battles of the *kuraka* leadership, delineated previously.[68]

Don Jerónimo Lorenzo Limaylla, like Hallicalla, advocated justice for *mitayos* and sought noble privileges for himself and other Indian authorities. Simultaneously, he was being investigated in connection with the 1666 rebellion as an associate of one of the apprehended Andean leaders. As indicated earlier, authorities had intercepted letters from 1656 that Limaylla wrote to Bartolomé de Mendoza, *alcalde* of the Huancavelica parish and a main leader of the rebellion, in which Limaylla also indicated his close alliance with the Franciscans to attain his political objectives.[69] Limaylla's "Representación" was also written to contribute to the *kurakas'* overarching struggle against abusive personal service. The text was written around 1667, when rumors about a possible increase in the demands of personal service spread to the Jauja area, prompting *kurakas* to hasten their petitions and reiterate their demands for the abolition of the *mita* system. Limaylla's "Representación" echoes this concern, as the author traced the history of royal decrees prohibiting Indian slavery back to 1501 in an effort to persuade the king of the need to eliminate the *mita* service.[70]

Limaylla's legal activism in Peru and Madrid and his use of Christian theology were only incipient antecedents to the roles of other Andeans such as Juan Núñez Vela de Rivera, who at the end of the seventeenth century developed these techniques to attain a more comprehensive set of privileges for nobles of a redefined "Indian nation" of elite Indians and mestizos.

JUAN NÚÑEZ VELA DE RIVERA

The world of noble Indians and that of their mestizo relatives and acquaintances in Peru were at times indistinguishable. This cultural and social proximity was embodied in the mestizo presbyter and *racionero* (prebendary) from the Arequipa cathedral, Juan Núñez Vela de Rivera, another Andean writer, lobbyist, and trans-Atlantic traveler in the late seventeenth century. He was probably best known in Spain for his campaign in support of noble recognition and social inclusion for elite Andeans and their mestizo descendants. Núñez resided in Madrid from 1691 through 1695, where he elevated petitions in conjunction with *caciques* from Peru who had been working collectively to advance the admission of Andeans to secular positions and ecclesiastical institutions and to allow them to partake in symbolic practices of sanctity—including the canonization of the mestizo Don Nicolás Ayllón, best known as Nicolás de Dios.[71] This social and cultural movement strove to redefine Andeans as full Christians, reworking old Iberian notions of *pureza de sangre* to access spheres of social privilege to which they felt entitled as nobles of the Indian republic.[72]

As a result of Núñez's writings and leadership in Spain, the king issued a *real cédula* on April 16, 1693, making Indians and mestizos eligible for positions in the Holy Office Tribunal.[73] For Andean activists fighting for social inclusion within the church, this *cédula* represented a step forward in overcoming their long-standing exclusionary status as "neophytes"—commonly held against them when they applied for ecclesiastical positions—and an advancement of their recognition as full Christians. In response to the 1693 *cédula*, Núñez suggested to the *caciques* from Lima that they adorn the Copacabana Chapel with a "good painting as a token of our gratitude and duty,"[74] specifying details that later allowed for the creation of iconographic expressions by others who supported Núñez's agenda. Thus, it seems plausible that, aside from writing and social activism in Peru and Spain, the intellectual Andean movement studied in this book also involved deployments of iconographic representations of Inca nobility related "ethnically" to the king. These representations empowered Indian and mestizo elites and could possibly constitute an expression of the newly self-fashioned "Indian nation."

Núñez's best-known writing is a *memorial* written in 1691 to King Charles II, requesting that the king grant honors to elite Indians and mestizos, as well as eligibility to serve in secular and ecclesiastical positions. He petitioned the king for a canonship for himself in the Lima Cathedral as well.[75] In 1695 Núñez returned to Lima, where he continued his activism in the proceedings for canonization of Nicolás Ayllón; he was also appointed chaplain of the Copacabana Chapel and *beaterio* (house of *beatas,* or religious women not bound by vows) in the Indian town of El Cercado.[76] In response to Núñez's 1691 *memorial*, King Charles II finally issued a royal decree in 1697, commonly known as the *cédula de honores*, according nobility and privileges—access to ecclesiastical and secular positions—to elite Indians and their descendants equal to those granted to noble Spaniards, which usually required proof of *pureza de sangre*. The decree extended to mestizo women the right to profess as nuns and join monasteries.[77] This ruling proved instrumental in Andeans' subsequent legal campaigns for racial equality and ethnic autonomy in Peru.

CONCLUSION

The seventeenth-century manuscripts by Juan de Cuevas Herrera, Jerónimo Lorenzo Limaylla, Juan Núñez Vela de Rivera, and dozens of *kurakas* who included complaints and petitions in their letters and *memoriales* were instrumental in social and political activism to fight the social distress unleashed by the Toledan effort to consolidate Spanish rule in the Andes. The writings prominently featured the erosion of ethnic lords' political power, the oppressive conditions of work in the silver mines, and the tax pressures on native communities—all of which worsened both the impact of the Indian demographic decline initiated in the preceding century and the failure of evangelization after the campaigns of extirpation.[78] In the midst of this social crisis, however, Andean authors and activists sought to intervene positively to restore social balance and justice by networking and writing critical tracts, proposing new legislation, demanding new social spaces, and, ultimately, coming together as a collective of Indian authorities and ecclesiastical mestizo allies to denounce and negotiate the colonial impositions. In the process, they became a more cosmopolitan elite of trans-Atlantic travelers and lobbyists seeking the enforcement of justice directly from the king.

In the eighteenth century, the Indian struggles against colonial oppression would continue and intensify as the Bourbons attempted to regain control and revitalize the trans-Atlantic economy, thereby exacerbating preexisting social and political tensions. The work of the Indian networks based in Lima and southern Peru became more visible as the campaign against the *mita* system continued. Andeans also expanded their agenda for justice into other, larger social and political arenas, in which their overall agenda for ethnic autonomy took on new ramifications. The social and economic realities of the eighteenth century presented new challenges and opportunities for Andean scholars, in the forms described in Chapter 3.

NOTES

1. The chronological division of Chapter 2 (writers from the seventeenth century) and Chapter 3 (writers from the eighteenth century) is only a practical one and does not reflect a clear-cut historical difference.

2. For the seventeenth century the focus is on writings produced after the appearance of Andeans' major works, such as Vega, *Comentarios reales de los Incas*, and Guamán Poma de Ayala, *Nueva corónica*. In Chapters 2 and 3, disparities in the amount of background information provided for the Andean writers under study reflect the current state of archival information available. For that reason, in Chapter 3 a more complete context is provided for Fray Calixto de San José Túpac Inca and the "Representación verdadera" than for the other writers and texts.

3. See Chapter 1, note 21.

4. For comprehensive studies of the impact of Spanish colonialism on Andean life, see Stern, *Peru's Indian Peoples*; Spalding, *Huarochirí*; Pease, *Kurakas, Reciprocidad y Riqueza*; Glave, *Trajinantes*; Ramírez, *World Upside Down*. For studies of the campaigns of extirpation, see Mills, *Idolatry and Its Enemies*, "An Evil Lost to View," and "Bad Christians in Colonial Peru"; Duviols, *La destrucción*. On the problem of official corruption, see Andrien, *Crisis and Decline*.

5. Casas, *Brevísima relación de la destrucción de las Indias*.

6. Among others, the *caciques* and signatories demanded a new *retasa* (reassessment of tribute rates, or *tasas*) and *revisita* to adjust tribute rates and *mita* quotas to reflect the demographic decline in their areas, to recognize the status of hidalgos and privileges for *caciques* and *principales* but especially for the natural lords who ruled over lordships

of 10,000 vassals during Inca times, and to put an end to the *composiciones de tierras* in Charcas. AGI, Charcas, 45, Ayavire et al., ca. 1582, 1v–12. Waldemar Espinosa Serrano published this document and dated the memorial in 1582, based on accompanying documents dated in November of that year. Espinosa Serrano, "El memorial de Charcas," 1. In chapter 52, however, the text mentions the Cercado school for *caciques* in Lima, which was founded in 1618, suggesting that the document or parts of it were written later in the seventeenth century. In a 2006 reproduction of "El memorial de Charcas," revised by John V. Murra, there is indication that the document was either written or filed in 1600. Platt, Bouysse-Cassagne, and Harris, *Qaraqara-Charka*, 828. A wide variety of Andean letters written since the sixteenth century in the Province of Charcas are also reproduced in this compilation.

7. Guamán Poma de Ayala, *El primer nueva corónica*, 858, 915[929].

8. Ibid., 489–491, 526[530]–528[532].

9. For studies of the *mita* system in Peru, see Brading and Cross, *Colonial Silver Mining*; Bakewell, *Miners of the Red Mountain*; Cole, "Abolitionism Born of Frustration" and *Potosí Mita*. For a legal perspective, see Zavala, *El servicio personal de los indios en el Perú*.

10. *Recopilación de leyes de las Indias*, Libro VI, Título VI, "Del Servicio Personal."

11. Cole, "Abolitionism Born of Frustration," 320.

12. Such cases had begun to occur soon after implementation of the Toledan reforms. Those who addressed the Audiencia of La Plata in search of government control included Don Francisco de Michaca from Porco, in 1608; Don Pedro Uychu from Porco, 1610; and Don Gabriel Fernández Guarache from Pacajes, in 1634. Ibid., 307–333, 310.

13. AGI, Lima, 7, Madrid, Septiembre 1, 1646. Reproduced in Konetzke, *Colección de documentos*, vol. 2, 407–409.

14. AGI, Lima, 15, Abril 4, 1646.

15. AGI, Lima, 10, Madrid, September 18, 1666.

16. The impact of epidemics and demographic decline in the coastal zones of Peru seemed to have been harsher than it was in the highlands, and even Spaniards complained about the decimation of the Indian coastal population. As a result, a large proportion of Indians from the coast migrated to Lima or became *forasteros* (*ayllus* resident aliens, liable to lower tribute than originary residents) in other regions. Cook, *Demographic Collapse*, 154, 210.

17. Reproduced in Konetzke, *Colección de documentos*, vol. 2, 415–416.

18. AGI, Lima, 15, Madrid, Junio 13, 1647; Madrid, Julio 23, 1647. Transcribed in ibid., 420–422.

19. AGI, Indiferente General, 1660, Lima, Marzo 8, 1649.

20. AGI, Indiferente General, Marzo 30, 1650.

21. AGI, Charcas, 56, Escribanía 868a.

22. Glave, *Trajinantes*, 202–203.

23. Cole, "Abolitionism Born of Frustration," 321.

24. Glave, *Trajinantes*, 209–212, 296; AGI, Charcas, 463, Cuaderno no. 13.

25. Cole, "Abolitionism Born of Frustration," 322.

26. AGI, Lima, 15, Junio 27, 1663. Fray Juan sent his own *memoriales* to the royal court, exposing the realities of Indian exploitation by priests in *obrajes*, and he was astonished when he traveled to entire areas where "idolatry" was widely practiced and few

spoke Castilian. He joined those asking for prohibition of *obrajes* and supported severe punishments for *corregidores, curas,* and *caciques* who did not speak both Castilian and Quechua—which for him was the cause of Indians' rampant ignorance of Christianity. Such assessments echoed Juan de Cuevas Herrera's contemporary critique of the poor state of evangelization in Charcas Province.

27. The king reiterated his command that the special junta he had designated in 1660 should meet more frequently and hear and address the problems Indians raised. AGI, Lima, 574, Libro 26, f. 243. In Konetzke, *Colección de documentos,* vol. 2, 519–523; AGI, Lima, 17, Mayo 17, 1663.

28. AGI, Lima, 15, Noviembre 29, 1662.

29. ARSI, Catálogo Público de la Provincia del Perú, No. 89, Enero 1, 1613, page 9.

30. Cuevas Herrera, "Cinco memoriales," 222v.

31. Eguiguren, *Diccionario histórico cronológico,* 523.

32. Cuevas Herrera, "Cinco memoriales," 221.

33. The full title of the manuscript is "Five memorials, informing briefly and summarily about the major impediments for the Peruvian Indians to fully Enter the Evangelical Law and Customs. They are directed to the King Our Lord by the Licenciado Juan de Cuevas Herrera, Parish Priest from the Andamarca and Huarinoca Towns in the Carangas Province, and a native from La Plata City in the [Charcas]." Cuevas Herrera [ca. 1650], BPR, Sign. II/2819, 218–269v. See the original Spanish titles of this and the other Andean manuscripts under study in the Bibliography.

34. Ibid., 218v. The phrase corresponds to the first part of the manuscript's subtitle. Among other important writings of the pastoral genre in Spanish, these were the best-known: the Jesuit José de Acosta's *De procuranda Indorum salute*; parish priest Pedro de Quiroga's *Coloquios de la verdad*; Joseph de Arriaga's *La extirpación de la idolatría en el Pirú*; Archbishop Pedro de Villagómez's *Carta pastoral de instrucción y exhortación*; and Alonso de la Peña Montenegro's *Itinerario para párrocos de indios.*

35. Cuevas Herrera, "Cinco memoriales," 220v, 222v.

36. Ibid., 220v, 222v, 239, 252, 255.

37. Ibid., 222v, 255; García Cabrera, *Ofensas a Dios pleitos e injurias,* 57–59: "May God put in the heart of Y.M. the desire to fill this kingdom and its churches with the pastors of the Company of Jesus, and this new Christendom, which is Y.M.'s responsibility, would have a different face."

38. García Cabrera, *Ofensas a Dios pleitos e injurias.*

39. Cuevas Herrera, "Cinco memoriales," 118v.

40. Such perceptions and strategies are addressed in Chapter 7.

41. Lorandi, *De quimeras rebeliones y utopías,* 94.

42. Cook, *Demographic Collapse,* 200–201. Cook discusses the disparity of the figures in different sources and seems to accept the estimates of the *Relaciones Geográficas* (1582), which recognized a total of only 27,000 war Indians. The demographic decline was serious in the Luringuanca *repartimiento,* the birthplace of Jerónimo Lorenzo Limaylla: from 3,374 Indians in 1575, the tributary population shrank to 799 in 1630, with the rate of decline accelerating more rapidly from 1617 to 1630.

43. Latin American Manuscripts, Peru, Box 5, Noviembre 18–Enero 22, 1600, Lilly Library, Bloomington, Indiana.

44. Inca, "Colegio de Caciques," 805.

45. In 1670 the *cacique* Rodrigo Rupaychagua and others from the Arequipa, Angaraes, Canta, Pillaos and Chinchero, Huamalies, and Guayaquil *repartimientos* entrusted Limaylla to deliver to the king and the Council of the Indies a letter in support of Viceroy Conde de Lemos. Alaperrine-Bouyer, "Enseignements et Enjeux," 115.

46. AGI, Lima, 15, Noviembre 28, 1662. Jerónimo Limaylla appears signing a collective petition to the king and supporting the actions of Don Juan de Padilla against injustice and the Andeans' poor indoctrination. Other *caciques* of this network who signed the petition include Don Carlos Apoalaya from Jauja, Don Joséph Mayta from Omasuyo, Don Cristóbal Yamke from Vilcashuaman, Don Melchor Atauche Topacusi Rimauche Inga from Arequipa, Don Jacinto Ninagualpa from Vilcashuaman, and a *cacique* from the town of Oropesa (Cusco). Franciscan Buenaventura de Salinas y Córdoba had been active in the Jauja region in the 1640s along with other Franciscan *doctrineros* who joined him in the campaigns against the *mita*.

47. For discussions of the multiple roles played by Andean *kurakas*, see Glave, *Trajinantes*, 281; Pease, *Kurakas, Reciprocidad y Riqueza* and *Perú Hombre e Historia*.

48. See Chapter 7 for analyses of identity in Limaylla's texts.

49. A discursive analysis of these themes in Limaylla's texts is presented in Chapters 4, 5, and 7.

50. AGI, Lima, 12. According to Konetzke, *Colección de documentos,* vol. 2, 656–657, "[I]t is obvious that such a memorial could not be written by Don Jerónimo (even though it is printed in his name) but by a clergyman that took the voice of this Indian to digress at length on this matter."

51. Puente Luna, *What's in a Name.* Two pieces of evidence Puente Luna used, however, beg for further discussion, as they question his own argument. First, Bernardino sent two letters (in 1660 and 1661, respectively) to Jerónimo, who was in Lima at the time, immediately after the *audiencia* had denied his claims and reconfirmed Bernardino in the *cacicazgo*. Puente Luna, *What's in a Name*, 133. Those letters make it clear that Bernardino is using Jerónimo Lorenzo as his legal representative in Lima; he calls him "nephew" and "relative" and thanks him for his support because "in the end, as the saying goes, blood ties are stronger and make one acknowledge one's relatives" (ibid.). Although the motives of the letter are unclear and the incoming letters from Jerónimo Lorenzo are not available, one wonders why Bernardino would entrust his personal businesses in Lima to an "impostor" who had long been his political rival. If Jerónimo Lorenzo had died at an early age, and if Ayún was an impostor, as Bernardino claimed and Puente Luna agrees, why would Bernardino address letters to a Jerónimo Lorenzo Limaylla in 1660? Second, according to the rosters of the Cercado school for *caciques*, both Jerónimo Lorenzo and his cousin Bernardino were enrolled in 1648, which implies that Jerónimo Lorenzo must have been alive at least at age twelve or older, seven years before the start of the dispute in 1655. *Inca,* "Colegio de Caciques," 779–883. Puente Luna has yet to make a convincing case concerning the identity of the claimant of the Luringuanca *cacicazgo* and the authorship of the manuscripts in question. Nevertheless, both Ayún and Jerónimo Lorenzo responded to a similar category of Indios ladinos seeking to advance their social positions in colonial society. For the practical purpose of designating authorship of the texts in this book, I continue to use the name Jerónimo Lorenzo Limaylla as it appears on the cover page of

the manuscript copies in the Biblioteca Real del Palacio in Madrid and in the documents of the lawsuit extant in AGI, Escribanía, 514C, unless new research sheds more indisputable light on the issue.

52. Pease, *Kurakas, Reciprocidad y Riqueza*; Lorandi, *Spanish King of the Incas*; Alaperrine-Bouyer, "Enseignements et Enjeux," 114–116.

53. Alperrine-Bouyer, "Enseignements et Enjeux."

54. For studies of Andeans as "social climbers," see Spalding, *Huarochirí*, 209–238, and "Social Climbers"; Stern, *Peru's Indian Peoples*, 158–183.

55. Alaperrine-Bouyer, "Enseignements et Enjeux," 114.

56. Inca, "Colegio de Caciques," 865.

57. Avendaño and García, *Thesaurus indicum*.

58. Mendieta, Izcabalceta, and García, *Historia eclesiástica Indiana*.

59. Salinas y Córdoba, *Memorial de las historias del Nuevo Mundo Pirú*.

60. Other creole writers who supported Indian causes were Don Juan de Padilla ("Memorial de Julio," 1657); Don Diego León Pinelo, judge of the Audiencia of Lima and *protector de naturales* in the late 1650s; and Juan Vélez de Córdoba, rebel leader and author of the Oruro "Manifiesto" in 1739, whose textual analysis is developed in Chapter 5.

61. For the Andean combination of judicial strategies and rebellion in the late eighteenth century, see Serulnikov, *Subverting Colonial Authority*.

62. AGI, Indiferente General, 640, Fray Alonso Zurbano, Febrero 1667. Zurbano's letter was apparently requested by another Franciscan supporter of Limaylla's in Spain.

63. Pease, *Kurakas, Reciprocidad y Riqueza*, 165.

64. Saignes, "Algún día todo se andará," 431–432; Pease, *Perú Hombre e Historia*, 318; Glave, *Trajinantes*.

65. Alaperrine-Bouyer, "Enseignements et Enjeux," 122.

66. AGI, Lima, 15, Carta de Don Cristóbal Laredo a la Reina regente Mariana de Austria, Lima, Febrero 16, 1667. Colonial authorities deliberately minimized the importance of this movement, but, in reality, the Indian leaders had been preparing the insurrection for five years, and the Audiencia of Lima was aware of some happenings in the years preceding 1666. Glave, *Trajinantes*, 200. The *audiencia* recognized in its report to the regent Queen Mariana that the contentions raised by the conspirators had been reiterated in previous years. In 1663, Indians from Cajactambo had set fires to local *obrajes* and attacked the *audiencia's alcalde del crimen* Fernando de Velasco y Gamboa, in charge of investigations in the area. The accused declared that they had serious plans for a general insurrection in various provinces. The *audiencia* recognized the depth of exploitation and mistreatment of Indians by *corregidores*, *azogueros*, and *curas*. AGI, Lima, 15, Reporte de la Real Audiencia de Lima a la Reina Regente Mariana de Austria sobre la conspiración de 1666. Lima, Febrero 16, 1667.

67. AGI, Lima, 15, Carta de Don Cristóbal Laredo a la Reina Regente Mariana de Austria, Lima, Febrero 16, 1667.

68. One of the more likely links between legal and rebellious struggles at that time was Don Bartolomé Topa Hallicalla, the wealthy *kuraka* from the town of Asillo (Azángaro *corregimiento*), introduced earlier. During the years 1647–1678, while engaged in legal battles against the *mita*, he wove multifarious alliances with local authorities according

to his personal interests. As a result of the investigations into the 1666 Lima conspiracy, he was summoned to court, but his participation could not be clearly established at that time. Testimonies implicating Hallicalla came to be known at a later date, however. Glave, *Trajinantes,* 297–298. Glave cites testimony by Hallicalla's nephew and the town's scribe that implicated the *cacique* as one of the organizers of the frustrated 1666 Lima rebellion.

69. Pease, *Kurakas, Reciprocidad y Riqueza,* 165.

70. The Calchaquíes, indigenous peoples from the southeastern frontier area, Tucuman Province, also rose up in rebellion in 1658; in 1659 they proclaimed the Spanish wanderer Don Pedro Bohorques as their "*inga.*" Bohorques was later condemned to prison in Lima. But when the 1666 conspiracy was discovered, the *audiencia* became wary about rumors that the Lima rebels also intended to proclaim him as their *inga*; he was sentenced to death and decapitated in 1667. AGI, Lima, 16, 1666. For a comprehensive history of the rebellion of the Calchaquíes and Don Pedro Bohorques, see Lorandi, *De quimeras rebeliones y utopías.*

71. Estenssoro Fuchs, *Del paganismo a la santidad,* 468–498.

72. In the early sixteenth century the Iberian notion of "purity of blood" was based on the assumption that only those descending from "old Christians" on both maternal and paternal lines of ancestors were considered "pure" and therefore entitled to privileges and opportunities denied to converts with either Jewish or Muslim mixed blood. Martínez, *Genealogical Fictions.*

73. Estenssoro Fuchs, *Del paganismo a la santidad,* 495. Estenssoro Fuchs stressed the importance of this disposition for advancement of the Indian struggles for recognition as full Christians of "pure blood," part of which was intended to question the inquisitorial *fueros* (immunity) for Indians—a tacit reaffirmation of their neophytism.

74. Buntix and Wufffarden, "Incas y reyes españoles," 165–167. Seeking legitimacy from Spanish and Andean perspectives, Núñez was adamant that the Spanish kings in the painting should be designated as "*ingas*" and be added subsequently to the list of the "Ingas gentiles, natural lords of the bountiful Peruvian Kingdom," which he also provided in the letter. Likewise, Núñez specified that the names of the inquisitors who supported the ruling be listed under that of "our Inga," Charles II. According to Buntix and Wufffarden, the iconographic project of the creole cleric from Lima, Fray Alonso de la Cueva, was based on the political ideas expressed in the 1690s' textual work of Núñez. Alonso de la Cueva is considered the intellectual author of an engraving from around 1725 featuring effigies of a genealogical "succession" of Inca and Spanish rulers up to the second rule of Philip V. Pictorial copies of this engraving circulated in Lima and El Cercado in the 1720s and, later, elsewhere in Peru and Upper Peru. Gisbert, *Iconografía y mitos indígenas en el arte,* 130.

75. Buntix and Wufffarden, "Incas y reyes españoles," 164.

76. Estenssoro Fuchs, *Del paganismo a la santidad,* 497.

77. AGI, Madrid, Real cédula, 26 de Marzo de 1697. In Konetzke, *Colección de documentos,* vol. 3, part 1, 66–69. A comprehensive analysis of this *cédula* and its significance for Andean social movements is developed in Chapter 6.

78. For a comprehensive understanding of this social and economic crisis, see Cole, *Potosí Mita*; Bakewell, *Miners of the Red Mountain*; Cook, *Demographic Collapse*; Andrien, *Crisis and Decline*; Glave, *Trajinantes.*

❋ 3 ❋

ANDEAN SCHOLARSHIP IN THE EIGHTEENTH CENTURY

Writers, Networks, and Texts

T HE EIGHTEENTH-CENTURY COUNTERPARTS OF Juan de Cuevas Herrera, Jerónimo Lorenzo Limaylla, and Juan Núñez Vela de Rivera lived and wrote in a different social milieu. Preexisting conflicts deepened in the 1700s and new ones appeared, prompting the creation of more comprehensive agendas and forms of legal activism that shed light on the politics of the "Indian nation" and its historical construction through a more sophisticated discourse, *cabildo* politics, and Andean lobbying in the core of the Spanish empire. The networks of scholarly and activist collaboration expanded and their issues diversified as Andean intellectuals and leaders in Spain struggled to obtain socially empowering royal decrees. This chapter explains the new elements of this social milieu and introduces the most visible writers of the eighteenth century, identifying their roles as Andean leaders within such a context and in connection with the collective circuits of knowledge, logistics, and activism they developed. Their texts are described and contextualized, and issues of authorship of anonymous texts are discussed.

The 1700s witnessed escalating social unrest and reform of the empire. The introduction of the *repartimiento de comercio* in the late seventeenth century created further havoc in communities in the following decades, which worsened in the 1720s as Viceroy Castelfuerte attempted economic revival. His infamous *numeraciones* (censuses) increased the number of tribute payers and *mitayos* following a severe cholera epidemic and displaced mestizos to tributary status after they became liable for tithes and other ecclesiastical contributions, all of which unleashed revolts in the 1730s.[1] In the last years of the 1600s and at the start of the 1700s, ecclesiastics seem to have enjoyed greater support from the government, as several archbishops rose to the viceregal office, albeit some of them temporarily. Local priests exerted stronger personal authority in their parishes; the increasing number of Andeans' complaints about excessive demands by *curas* and conflicts between *curas* and *corregidores* over the *repartos* further charged an already tense social atmosphere.[2]

The Bourbons intended to address the empire's inherited and new problems through administrative, secular, and fiscal reforms that ended up triggering an upsurge of discontent, lettered criticism, protest, and rebellions—all of which found expression in the Andean writings of the period. The reformers sought to centralize the government and augment royal revenue by increasing fiscal demands on a wide section of the population. They tightened demands on Indian labor and legalized the hated *repartos* in 1756, something Castelfuerte had favored since 1724. Progressively, the "enlightened" reformers attempted to curtail the autonomy of the church by secularizing parishes run by the regular orders (1753), confiscating ecclesiastical property, and ultimately expelling the Jesuits from the Spanish empire.[3] These anti-clerical policies stirred up criticism of the viceregal authorities among the regular orders, particularly the Franciscans who enthusiastically supported Andean critical writings and trips to Spain in 1749.[4]

Criticism of the deepening official corruption that had begun in the 1600s was prominent in the new century's Andean texts. Writers particularly criticized the way corruption impacted the effectiveness of the legal system in matters pertaining to the enforcement of the *cédula de honores* and the redress to continued excesses against Amerindians and mestizos by colonial political, ecclesiastical, and economic agents. In the late 1740s, while the "Representación verdadera" was being prepared, problems with the *repartimiento* were being debated in Lima. Viceroy Conde de Superunda was expected to regulate the *repartimiento* quotas and curtail corruption; he introduced a new *arancel* (quota) that amounted to de facto legalization of this unpopular practice.[5]

In the 1700s the Andean tradition from Cusco of using Inca memory to support Indian claims of nobility spread to other areas of the viceroyalty and expanded into a utopian ideology that aimed to restore Inca traditions and rule.[6] This tradition expressed itself through writing, heraldry, iconographic art, dress, and ceremonial life. Utopian ideologies, however, coexisted in unpredictable ways with different Andean agendas based on both the age-old tradition of Andean criticism and reform efforts and the Bourbons' newer criticism of long-standing Habsburg administrative practices (Chapters 5 and 6).

The writers and social activists in the first half of the 1700s, including Don Vicente Morachimo and the Franciscan Fray Calixto de San José Túpac Inca, reflected on these issues and shared common ground with their earlier counterparts in directing their critiques toward the webs of corrupt *corregidores*, judges, priests, and *caciques*. They also used their writing as part of a wider social activism through Andean social networks operating on both sides of the Atlantic. The new scholars, however, incorporated a broader set of concerns, proposals, and denunciations and, particularly in the case of Fray Calixto, simultaneously engaged the different powers of colonial society (e.g., the king, the church, the *audiencias*, miners, *hacendados*, merchants) in debates about colonial justice, social exclusion, and political participation. The writings of Andeans evolved as the tensions grew unsustainable, mirroring the upheavals of the late eighteenth century as rebels such as Don José Gabriel Condorcanqui Túpac Amaru II sought to address—often violently—some of the issues raised in earlier decades by Andean intellectuals and social leaders.

Although the legal campaigns for abolition of the *mita* system did not succeed in the 1600s, Andean leaders continued to test the strength of the colonial judicial system in the Bourbon era, expanding their presence in the public spaces of *audiencias* and the king's court. Through discussions in meetings, traveling between provinces and to the viceregal capital, and crossing the Atlantic Ocean from Lima to the royal court, the networks of writers and litigants grew larger in the eighteenth century and connected Indian authorities from areas as remote as Chachapoyas, in the Peruvian Amazon; Cusco, the central Andean zone of the Mantaro Valley (including the mining area of Huancavelica); Lima; and beyond to the northern coastal provinces. With agents in Lima and Spain also connected to Indian nobles from Mexico, these networks incorporated noble Indians and mestizos, legal advisers, Indian priests, Spanish and creole ecclesiastics, Indian and mestizo *escribanos*, sympathetic *procuradores de naturales*, and a few *audiencia* judges. These agents helped structure, draft, print, disseminate, and properly file *memoriales* in the regional *audiencias* and the royal court in Spain. Designated *caciques* or their representatives conducted the "diplomatic" strategy, traveling to the royal court with their writings and negotiating new decrees that responded to the demands presented.

In Madrid, Indian noble residents at the court met and worked with sojourning Andean envoys from Peru, sharing information and helping deliver the petitions to the appropriate destinations.[7] One of the best-known Indian residents at the royal court in Madrid was Don Juan de Bustamante Carlos Inga, an Indian noble from Cusco. Bustamante used his access to the king to help Fray Calixto de San José Túpac Inca and the *caciques* from El Cercado advance petitions for

Indians' free passage to Spain.[8] In 1754 another prominent member of this network who was traveling in Madrid, the Tlaxcalan Indian noble and *presbítero* (presbyter) Don Julián Cirilo y Castilla, gave a speech before the Council of the Indies in defense of autonomous education for Indians.[9] By the 1720s the Lima network of Indian activists had widened the scope of its work, adopting causes of Andeans from various areas of the viceroyalty who were not in a position to travel to Lima to seek justice in the *real audiencia*.[10] It was in the royal courts of the Audiencia of Lima and Madrid during this era where legal advocates for Indian justice such as Don Vicente Morachimo focused their work and found the cases that substantiated their legal discourses.

DON VICENTE MORACHIMO

The more prominent Indian networks of colonial Peru were centered in Lima and on the indigenous town council in El Cercado; they worked in conjunction with Indian officials who served in the colonial state. A prominent member of this network in the 1720s and 1730s, Don Vicente Morachimo, claimed to be a descendant of the ancient Chimu lords of coastal Peru and introduced himself as *diputado general* and *procurador de naturales* from the town of Lambayeque (Saña Province) in 1722. As a *diputado general* and *procurador de naturales*, Morachimo was literate and knowledgeable about Spanish law and judicial procedures; he became the steward of the legal rights of the *caciques* and communities under the jurisdiction of the Audiencia of Lima.[11] As a *procurador de naturales*, Morachimo operated mostly in Lima and Madrid, but his writings reflect the colonial experience of communities throughout the viceroyalty of Peru—particularly those located in the coastal zones to the north of Lima in the Provinces of Saña and Trujillo, where he had been a *cacique* in several towns of the Chicama and Chimo valleys.

Morachimo was one of the earliest Andean nobles to visit the royal court in the eighteenth century, when Viceroy (and Archbishop of Lima) Diego Morcillo Rubio de Auñón granted him permission to travel to Spain and present his complaints against the land surveyor Don Pedro de Alsamora directly to the king in 1721.[12] Morachimo received power of attorney from various *caciques* to advance their causes in the Audiencia of Lima and in Spain. His visits to the Spanish court as an Indian legal representative gave him the legal knowledge and experience necessary to fulfill his duties and establish himself as an intermediary between the upper officials and the Indian elites and communities under the jurisdiction of the Audiencia of Lima.

The position of *diputado general de Indios* not only entailed knowledge of the Spanish legal codes but also required a substantial amount of writing, typically judicial *memoriales*, lawsuits, and reports to the king. Morachimo composed *memoriales* to the king in 1722, 1724, 1727, 1729, and 1732 and remained in Spain for several years lobbying for their implementation and awaiting responses from the Council of the Indies and the king. The bulk of his denunciations against colonial justice delved into the colluding networks of *corregidores, audiencia* judges, and viceroys. During those years, Morachimo approached the Council of the Indies and King Philip V to expose the social unrest in the northern coastal zone of Lambayeque: the hardships of the *mita* system, loss of communal lands, and abuses of *corregidores*. He advocated the abolition of the *mita* institution, opposed abusive land surveys and illegal *composiciones de tierras*, and supported the restitution of lands to the dispossessed and allotments to landless indigenous groups. He also fought against the excesses of the *corregidores' repartimiento de mercancías* and the *numeraciones* and ultimately denounced the imprisonment of *caciques* who complained against the *corregidores* and called for their removal from office. In response, King Louis I issued another *real cédula* on January 21, 1724, prohibiting further land inspections and surveys and commanding the restitution of lands to those affected.

The escalating tensions resulting from such situations and the growing number of *memoriales* with complaints from *caciques* prompted Morachimo to compose his best-known writing, the "Manifiesto de agravios y vejaciones" (Figure 3.1). He visited the royal court again in 1732 to expose the systematic failure of the king's protective policies and to file the "Manifiesto" with the Council of the Indies.[13] In addition to substantiating the aforementioned issues, in the "Manifiesto" Morachimo voiced his concern that officials' irregularities had prompted Indians to run away to the mountains, thus fomenting idolatry and hampering evangelization, and he warned the crown about the threat such an irregularity represented to the stability of the kingdom. Morachimo also committed to support the legal campaigns of native elites' defense of their right to nobility, a continuing political struggle since the late seventeenth century. Morachimo demanded enforcement of the 1697 *cédula de honores*, which granted Andeans the right to enjoy secular and ecclesiastical positions and extended noble privileges to Indians. A royal decree dated January 21, 1725, restated the purposes of the previous ruling in response to Morachimo's demands. These were crucial legal weapons in the struggle for social equality by Andean elites for nearly the next forty-five years. A long list of legal transgressions of previous royal policies designed to protect Indian commoners also substantiated Morachimo's critical assessment of the state of justice in late-colonial Peru.[14]

The "Manifiesto" remains an important document for the study of Andean legal culture and discursive formation. Copies circulated widely in Madrid and Spanish Peru, since the Bourbon court supported its printing and distribution; the denunciations of corruption and social unrest also justified the Bourbon agenda of administrative reform. It seems that the manuscript was utilized in 1749

✠

MANIFIESTO
DE LOS AGRAVIOS,
BEXACIONES, Y MOLESTIAS,
QUE PADECEN LOS INDIOS DEL REYNO DEL PERU.

DEDICADO
A LOS SEÑORES DE EL REAL,
y Supremo Confejo, y Camara
de Indias.

POR EL PROCURADOR, Y DIPUTADO GENERAL
de dichos Indios.

SEÑOR.

ON TEMOR TOMARA LA PLUMA EN
efte aſſumpto, recelandome de paſſar por la
Aduana de ſer mortificado, como lo fueron
todos los de mi claſſe, en aquellas Provincias
(lo que harè patente) à no reconocer la benig-
nidad, con que V. M. mira por los pobres In-
dios; pero conociendo lo juſtificado de V. M. cobrè alientos
para poner en ſu Real conſideracion los agravios que experi-
mentan: Efto, Señor, no es fabula, ni iluſion, ſi una verdad
defuuda, sòlida, y ſin baño; y en fin, un breve diſeño.

Se conſidera, que el verſe aniquilados los Indios, ha re-
ſultado de el rigor con que ſon tratados; lo principal por los
Corregidores, por componerſe los mas de perſonas, que toda
ſu vida eftàn exercitados en tratar, comerciar, y manejar cre-
cidos caudales; de lo que reſulta, el que no ay Corregidor, que

A   no

Figure 3.1 "Manifiesto de los agravios y vejaciones" by Vicente Morachimo. AGI, Lima, 422, 1732, folio 1.

to substantiate the critical reports of Spanish visitors Jorge Juan and Antonio de Ulloa (the *Noticias Secretas de América*) about the social disorder in late-colonial Peru.[15] Morachimo's "Manifiesto" also played a role as a blueprint for the uprisings in the late 1730s and indirectly for those in the 1750s.

The text spelled out the many abuses and broken laws that eventually culminated in the initial uprisings of the eighteenth century. The motifs of these movements coincided with the evils voiced in the "Manifiesto," specifically the abusive *mita* system, which the Bourbons attempted to expand to mestizos; the illicit practices of *corregidores* and their *repartimiento de comercio*; and rejection of the personal service demanded of Indians and allegedly of mestizos as well. These factors played a part in the movement of Andahuaylas in 1726 and the rebellions of the 1730s in Cochabamba (Charcas) and Cotabambas (Cusco), where Andeans demanded the removal of Spanish *corregidores* and the replacement of Spanish *alcaldes* by creoles and in which Spanish authorities were killed and rebels brutally executed. In 1739 Juan Vélez de Córdoba rose up in arms, reiterating Morachimo's complaints against the Bourbons' attempts to assimilate mestizos to the status of *tributarios* and to demand the end of tributes, *mitas*, and *repartos*.[16]

The "Manifiesto" thus helped shape other writings of the period as it circulated among rebels, providing a legal foundation others could use to demonstrate the legitimacy of rebellion as a means to achieve justice when the colonial legal system failed to redress Indian subjects. Morachimo died at age fifty in the San Lorenzo Hospital in Madrid.[17] While in Madrid, where he traveled many times to represent the legal causes of Andeans in Peru, Morachimo met another Peruvian and mestizo lay brother who became instrumental in the movement for the social empowerment of Andeans and who is discussed next.

FRAY CALIXTO DE SAN JOSÉ TÚPAC INCA

A key figure of the social and intellectual leadership in mid–eighteenth-century Andean Peru was the Franciscan and mestizo lay brother Fray Calixto de San José Túpac Inca. He represented a sophisticated type of Andean scholar that emerged in the mid-eighteenth century when winds of rebellion swept through the viceregal center. Originally from Tarma (in the Peruvian north-central Andes) and born sometime around 1710, he claimed to be the son of Doña Dominga Estefanía Túpac Inca, a member of the Inca elite, and Don Pedro Montes, possibly a Spaniard or a mestizo. Fray Calixto professed to be a "descendant of the eleventh Inca King named Túpac Inga Yupanqui."[18]

This Andean scholar's intellectual evolution was largely informed by his relationship with the Franciscan order starting in young adulthood. Fray Calixto joined the Franciscan convent of his town as a *donado* (servant allowed to wear the habit) in 1727, later becoming an ecclesiastical official in the Province of

Lima where he served for about nine years as the procurator of the Holy House of Jerusalem, managing donations for the Franciscan missions. For two years he served as the procurator for the Santa Rosa de Viterbo *beaterio*.[19] During these years he met Franciscan Fray Antonio Garro, a creole priest and teacher of Quechua at the Convento Grande de Jesús in Lima, who supported the cause of Indian justice and perhaps contributed to the writing of Andean *representaciones*.

Under the orders of Fray José Gil Muñoz, later the commissary of Franciscan missions in Peru, Fray Calixto was bound to the Holy Land in 1744. The weather in the Atlantic kept him from completing the trip, however, and he had to return from Guatemala to the Province of Charcas, where Gil Muñoz assigned him to the Quillabamba Valley missions. These were the years of the rebellion by Juan Santos Atahualpa in the central *selva*, a region neighboring the missions of Quillabamba.[20] As a missionary in the Charcas and Cusco provinces after 1744, Fray Calixto came in close contact with Fray Isidoro de Cala, with whom he eventually traveled to Spain to deliver the "Representación verdadera." Cala, a peninsular and Franciscan missionary in the Cerro de la Sal area, was another sympathizer with the Andeans' cause and worked toward rebuilding the Franciscan conversion of the Viceroyalty of Peru's Amazon frontier. Cala was a preacher and taught theology at the Franciscan convent in Lima; he later became the commissary of the Apostolic Province of San Antonio de Charcas. He was assigned to the Cusco missions of Quillabamba, where Fray Calixto joined him in 1744. Cala directly supported Calixto's activities and was one of various Franciscans who wrote recommendation letters to the king on behalf of Fray Calixto, certifying his credentials as a Franciscan functionary and missionary. Calixto was also recommended by Fray Juan de San Antonio, a Franciscan attorney of the Cerro de la Sal conversions and vice commissary of the Franciscan mission, who was in Spain in 1751 recruiting missionaries to rebuild the Cerro de la Sal missions. While Fray Calixto was residing in the Franciscan convents in Madrid and Valencia (1750–1753), he was in contact with Fray San Antonio and obtained reference letters he attached to support the "Representación verdadera."[21]

The mestizo friar also built connections with *kurakas* from regions beyond his native Tarma, including Jauja, Huarochirí, Lima, and Cusco.[22] This probably occurred because he was aiding Franciscan missionaries in various provinces and because he lived in Lima in the 1730s, where he related with the *cabildo* in Santiago del Cercado, a convergence point for network members living in and visiting Lima.[23] The authorities within El Cercado's *cabildo* empowered Fray Calixto to represent them in Rome and Madrid and to deliver manifestos to both the pope and the king. Calixto's fluency in Quechua, Spanish, and Latin, as well as his cultural proximity to native Andeans and mestizos, enabled him not only as an author but also as an Indian representative and helped him advance Andeans' interests—particularly the concerns of the nobility of Inca descendants.[24]

In 1748 Fray Calixto returned to Lima, meeting with El Cercado *cabildo,* preparing the "Representación verdadera," and getting ready for his trip to Europe. After drafting the manuscript, Calixto consulted the *caciques* of El Cercado and the Franciscans from Lima about the final version before he traveled to Jauja in August 1748. In November he proceeded to Cusco to share the manuscript with the *caciques* of the Indian *cabildo,* who were hesitant to sign for fear of reprisal even though they supported the content. Accompanied by Isidoro de Cala and with little financial support, Fray Calixto finally departed clandestinely from Cusco to Buenos Aires on September 25, 1749, on the way to Spain to deliver the "Representación verdadera."[25]

Through old and new acquaintances, Fray Calixto helped to connect and expand the network from Lima to Spain, finding allies who shared a common agenda for the social repositioning of elite Indians and mestizos. In Madrid, Calixto contacted noble Incas from Cusco, such as Don Juan de Bustamante Carlos Inga, who resided at the court and joined the efforts of the network of El Cercado to seek justice directly from the king.[26] The network of Indian allies in Spain eventually extended to noble Indians from Mexico, including the Tlaxcalan Cirilo y Castilla, who had been in contact with Don Felipe Tacuri Mena— another trans-Atlantic traveler from El Cercado *cabildo.*[27] The Tlaxcalan noble campaigned in Madrid for autonomous schools for Indians in Mexico, inspiring Don Felipe, who, in turn, encouraged El Cercado *caciques* to petition for native schools with Indian teachers.[28]

As described, the work of the eighteenth-century Indian network centered in Lima was also supported by Franciscan missionary authorities and priests, including Fray José Gil Muñoz, Fray Antonio Garro, and Fray Isidoro de Cala. They provided assistance to the writers and disseminators of the "Representación verdadera," logistical support for their trans-Atlantic travel, and educational opportunities in Spain. Members of the Jesuit order also contributed at different stages, offering advice and assistance; for example, Fray Calixto consulted with the Jesuits from the San Borja school of *caciques* in Cusco in 1749 and sought their support for his journey to Spain. Although the Jesuits apparently offered no financial support, it seems they did persuade the friar to proceed with the undertaking. As the priest of El Cercado in 1750, the Jesuit Father Felipe de Mantilla sent *memoriales* to the king in Spain, supporting the Indians.[29]

While in Spain, Fray Calixto joined the seminary school in the Franciscan convent of Saint Spirit in Valencia (Spain) in 1752, where he was trained and ordained as a lay brother.[30] He returned from Spain to the missions of Charcas in 1754 and was back in Lima in 1756, apparently organizing clandestine protest activities with the Indians of El Cercado native *cabildo.* Viceroy Conde de Superunda accused the friar of instigating new Indian conspiracies in 1756 and, in January 1757, ordered his imprisonment and expulsion to Spain, where Fray

Calixto remained secluded in the Recolection of the Adamuz Desert, a Franciscan outpost in the Province of Granada.[31]

THE "REPRESENTACIÓN VERDADERA"

Following the festivities celebrating the coronation of King Ferdinand VI in Lima in February 1748, *caciques* from El Cercado Province and other Indian and mestizo leaders discussed the need to address the problems related to their social exclusion, the injustice of the *repartimiento de comercio*, and other unresolved social issues from past decades. The *caciques* set up a council of twelve *caciques principales* who were to organize the movement. They entrusted Fray Calixto with writing a manifesto that would be resubmitted to the *caciques* for final scrutiny before delivery to the king in Spain.[32] The "Representación verdadera" was finished in early 1749 and was printed soon thereafter (Figure 3.2).[33] The council entrusted Fray Antonio Garro to compose in Latin a *memorial* to the pope, which came to be known as the "Planctus indorum" (Indian Lamentation). The two texts were written anonymously and printed clandestinely in Lima.[34] The "Representación verdadera" was written around 1749, and the "Planctus indorum" was perhaps composed in late 1750 and early 1751.[35] Fray Calixto de San José and Fray Isidoro de Cala brought the two texts and many other supporting documents to Europe. They handed the "Representación verdadera" to the king on August 23, 1750.[36]

As with many other indigenous texts of the colonial era, Andean writers sought to present their manuscripts in a language and a format that appealed to the king or to their addressees.[37] Enveloped in the language of the biblical lamentation of the Prophet Jeremiah, the "Representación verdadera" is a treatise that combines theological and political debates on Indian priesthood and denounces a variety of abuses against native Andeans by *corregidores*, parish priests, and judges in colonial Peru. The central argument is that Amerindian and mestizos are entitled to join religious orders, to hold ecclesiastical and secular positions, and to receive a more secular education in "science and letters."

More important, the manuscript introduces a discussion of the Andeans' notion of social justice under colonialism (see Chapter 5), a theological and historical defense of Amerindians' and mestizos' right to become Catholic priests, and a proposal for social and administrative reform (see Chapter 6). The manuscript ultimately argues that colonial subjection of indigenous peoples in *obrajes*, mines, and *mitas* prompted them to run away from Christianity and ultimately to rebel, thus rendering impossible the completion of the Spanish empire's religious and economic project. The text argues that for centuries, colonial authorities and ultimately the king had neglected Andeans' plight by failing to enforce the royal protective laws that granted them participation in opportunities for social

Figure 3.2 "Representación verdadera." Facsimile reproduced in José Toribio Medina, *La Imprenta en Lima (1584–1824)* (Santiago, Chile: Impreso y grabado en casa del autor, 1905), 541.

ascent and civil service. The only way out of such chaos would be to provide for an Indian priesthood and inclusion of Indian administrators in the colonial state to replace corrupt Spanish officials.

The manuscript is structured in long narrative blocks glossed with Latin headings taken from chapter 5 of Jeremiah's "Lamentations." The subtitles seek to associate the grievances the prophet Jeremiah raised to Jehovah with the complaints Andeans addressed to Ferdinand VI. The *Book of Jeremiah* was a compendium of sermons, oracles, autobiographical sketches, and history. The Hebrew prophet served as a minister in Judah in the last forty years of its existence as an independent state, before falling captive to the Babylonians.[38] The "Lamentations" in particular was a poem of yearning and grief over the decadence of the nation of Judah following the siege of Jerusalem (the Holy Land) in 586 BC. Although Jeremiah expressed his sadness as a personal sorrow, present in the background is a "national suffering" over the demise of the independent state of Israel.[39] Hebrew prophets incorporated satire in their preaching, and their narrative strategy consisted of subtly questioning someone or something without openly confronting the reader. They looked for agreement between audience and speaker about the "undesirability of the object of criticism."[40] Likewise, the "Representación verdadera" incisively interrogates the reader and uses exclamations to vividly convey the "Indian lament" in order to move the reader to act upon the anomalous situation that begs for an immediate solution.

The critique of Spanish officials in Fray Calixto's "Representación verdadera" appears enveloped in the sophisticated rhetoric style of the Hebrew prophet Jeremiah, a rhetoric with widespread ecclesiastical use in the Andes. In chapter 5 of Jeremiah's "Lamentations," the prophet reminded God of the oppression the Hebrews experienced under the foreign rule of the Chaldeans: "Remember, O Jehovah, what is come upon us: behold and see our reproach. Our inheritance is turned unto strangers, our houses into aliens. We are orphans and fatherless."[41] Likewise the "Representación verdadera" rephrased Jeremiah's "Lamentations," lamenting the state of Andeans under Spanish rule while advancing point-by-point denunciations of social injustice.

According to the biblical book Exodus, to "remember" something alludes to "doing" something immediately to resolve an anomalous situation.[42] Just as Jeremiah prompted Jehovah to save his people, the Andeans speaking in the "Representación verdadera" urged the king to restore justice in the Andes. Jeremiah acknowledged the sin of his forefathers as the cause of the Hebrews' enslavement by Egyptians and Assyrians and hoped Jehovah's eternal kingdom would rescue the Hebrews from slavery. The poem finishes with a somber tone: "But thou hast utterly rejected us; Thou are very wroth against us."[43] In a similar fashion, the "Representación verdadera" paraphrases this statement: "Despreciándonos nos arrojásteis y os airásteis grandemente contra nosotros."[44]

Ultimately, Fray Calixto 's narrative empowered Andeans as the "chosen people," transposing the Hebrews to Andeans and thus bringing Jeremiah's metaphor to the Andean present as a way of equating the legitimacy of the Andean people's struggles against Spanish oppression with the Hebrews' struggles against their own slavery in the book of Exodus.

THE QUESTION OF COLLECTIVE AUTHORSHIP OF THE "REPRESENTACIÓN VERDADERA"

In the wake of an Indian conspiracy to assassinate the viceroy in Lima in June 1750 and the Huarochirí rebellion that followed on July 29, the king ordered Viceroy Conde de Superunda to investigate and to explain the irregularities and complaints detailed in the "Representación verdadera." Reporting on the events in Lima, the viceroy described the links between the text and the recent conspiracy and the Huarochirí rebellion. Superunda initially accused the Franciscan Fray Antonio Garro, one of Fray Calixto's Franciscan collaborators, but he exonerated him when he realized that Fray Calixto was one of the main figures behind the production of the text.[45] Nevertheless, one must not dismiss the possibility that Garro and others, such as the peninsular Franciscan Fray Isidoro de Cala, may have collaborated with Fray Calixto in composing the text because there was a previous relationship among the men, as explained earlier.

Superunda's initial accusation of Garro as having written the text has misled some historians about the key role Fray Calixto played in the composition and diffusion of the manifesto and in the activism inextricably linked to it.[46] It later became evident that even Superunda considered Fray Calixto one of the key architects of the manifesto, and he was also convinced that in 1756 Fray Calixto was planning and directing another conspiracy:

> [W]hen he [Fray Calixto] arrived in the city, [he] started to spread his old ideas, creating unrest and raising hopes in the Indians, protesting the capital punishment applied to the conspirators of 1750. . . . [H]is prelates then put him in tight seclusion, depriving him from communicating with other indians [*sic*]. . . . Because it was imperative to find out how far the thoughts of the indians [*sic*] had gone and what plans resulted from the meetings so cautiously organized and directed by the lay Fray Calixto, I decided to delegate the investigation to Audiencia Judge Don Pedro Bravo del Rivero. . . . In the middle of the investigation, it has transpired, and rumors have spread, that they were planning another conspiracy.[47]

As discussed earlier, Fray Calixto maintained correspondence with other Indian nobles and advocates of Indian education and ethnic autonomy in Spain. Following the coronation festivities of Ferdinand VI in Lima, the twelve *caciques* from El Cercado entrusted Fray Calixto with composing a manifesto to the king

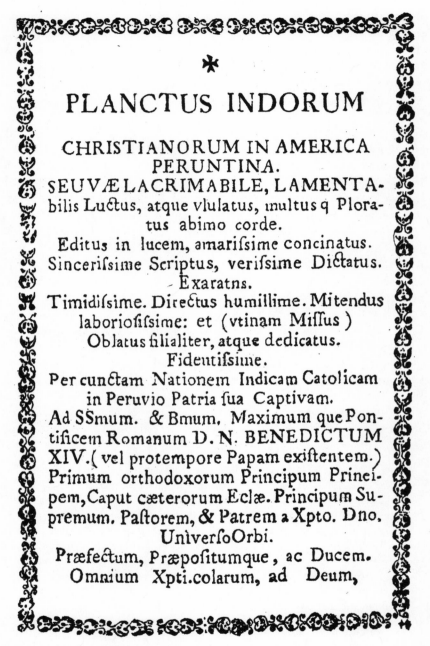

PLANCTUS INDORUM

CHRISTIANORUM IN AMERICA
PERUNTINA.
SEUVÆ LACRIMABILE, LAMENTA-
bilis Luctus, atque vlulatus, multus q Plora-
tus abimo corde.
Editus in lucem, amarifsime concinatus.
Sincerifsime Scriptus, verifsime Dictatus.
- Exaratns.
Timidifsime. Directus humillime. Mitendus
laboriofifsime: et (vtinam Miffus)
Oblatus filialiter, atque dedicatus.
Fidentifsime.
Per cunctam Nationem Indicam Catolicam
in Peruvio Patria fua Captivam.
Ad SSmum. & Bmum. Maximum que Pon-
tificem Romanum D. N. BENEDICTUM
XIV.(vel protempore Papam exiftentem.)
Primum orthodoxorum Principum Prinei-
pem, Caput cæterorum Eclæ. Principum Su-
premum. Paftorem, & Patrem a Xpto. Dno.
UnìverfoOrbi.
Præfectum, Præpofitumque, ac Ducem.
Omnium Xpti.colarum, ad Deum,

Figure 3.3 "Planctus indorum." Facsimile reproduced in José Toribio Medina, *La Imprenta en Lima (1584–1824)* (Santiago, Chile: Impreso y grabado en casa del autor, 1905), insert before page 541.

and Garro with writing the "Planctus indorum" to the pope (Figure 3.3). Since the two texts bear a thematic and rhetorical resemblance, Calixto and Garro likely at least discussed the issues to be addressed and collaborated in the composition.

The "Representación verdadera" in particular was a key piece within an entire political and intellectual agenda designed to reposition Andeans in late-colonial society. The project involved collective writing, social and political activism, exchange of legal information and ideas, circulation of manifestos, and ultimately participation in rebellions, whether directly or indirectly. The notion of authorship in this case would deviate from the current idea of individual authorship. The manuscript's final version is a product of Andean collective authorship and social activism: the voices of various *kurakas* and *cabildo* members remain in the background of the text, as some of them defined during *cabildo* meetings the issues to be addressed in the manifesto. Later, other regional *kurakas* were consulted about a draft, and they provided insights and revisions. In a letter from Madrid dated November 14, 1750, and addressed to the Indian *cabildo* in Lima asking for economic support, Fray Calixto stated:

> The time has come to manifest in favor of my beloved brothers, as I expressed
> . . . in all the meetings and consultations we held after the royal celebrations
> of the coronation of our King and Lord Don Ferdinand VI. . . . With such
> purpose, I went to the Jauja Valley in mid August 1748, and the same year,
> in early November, I went to the great city of Cuzco with the manifesto or
> "Exclamation" to share it with our relatives the caciques and nobles of that city
> and its provinces.[48]

Andean collective authorship includes the contributions of known and unknown *caciques* to the discussion, composition, and diffusion of the manuscripts, as well as their participation in the informal networks discussed earlier—such contributions both preceded and followed the final drafting of the text. Also, Calixto, Garro, Cala, and other contributors and sympathizers with the movement who composed similar documents acted in different capacities as mediators between Andeans and the Spanish authorities. Fray Calixto's role as cultural and social mediator originated in his activities as a missionary in Cerro de la Sal and the Province of Cusco in the early 1740s, where he was able to placate native protestors on the verge of rebellion.[49]

The ideas in the text express the viewpoints and expectations of various *caciques* and other Indian and mestizo leaders, many of whose names, backgrounds, and specific contributions went unrecorded, as mentioned earlier. Apparently, Indian leaders of the 1750 Lima conspiracy, including Antonio Cobo and Julián de Ayala, were present during the 1748 meeting and may have participated in the discussions that led to the composition of the manuscript and later revisions of the final draft. Cobo was an alumnus of El Principe school of *caciques* and used a prophecy by Santa Rosa to raise consciousness and gain supporters for the rebellion.[50] Indian *cabildo* members in 1748—including Don Santiago de la Vega, Don Pedro Condor Anchay, Don Martin Guaman, Don Isidro Colqui y Pruna, and Don Francisco Jordán—may also have participated in the discussion meetings, since they were convened at the suggestion of the *cabildo*. Fray Calixto referred to them, and to the practice of discussing and collectively approving the contents of the manuscript, in the aforementioned letter.[51]

The entire manuscript was written in the first-person plural "we," perhaps suggesting the writing project's collective character. In a collective undertaking such as this, the "author" is actually a network of social and intellectual leaders who, beyond their literacy and theological and philosophical backgrounds, are actively engaged in defending the interests of Indian authorities and their communities—a defense that takes a particular expression in the written text. In these circumstances, writing and discursive battles are one among a variety of political tools in the Indians' struggle for ethnic self-assertion and racial equality. These networks supported the rebels and social movements in Lima and Huarochirí in 1750, although the topic is not openly raised in the manuscript.[52]

The literate Indians who wrote and filed *memoriales*, either in connection with networks or by themselves, used credited sources to improve both their writing skills according to colonial administrative standards and their legal knowledge.[53] Andean scholars such as Juan de Cuevas Herrera, Jerónimo Lorenzo Limaylla, Juan Núñez Vela de Rivera, Vicente Morachimo, Fray Calixto de San José, and dozens of other *kurakas* who filed lawsuits against Spaniards based their legal claims on knowledge acquired from the *Política Indiana,* written by the Spanish jurist Juan de Solórzano.

Although it is probably the richest expression of the hybrid Andean cultures in the late colonial period, the "Representación verdadera" has remained largely unstudied as a social and cultural text in its own right. In spite of the manuscript's recognized centrality in both the so-called Inca nationalist movement and the Inca renaissance of the eighteenth century, very little attention has been paid to the literary, political, and religious complexity of the text itself. Ironically, all the scholars[54] who have devoted any attention to it, with one exception,[55] have used an abbreviated version of the manuscript, which Francisco Loayza (1948) and Jorge Bernales Ballesteros (1969) edited and published. The most important political and theological elaboration of late-colonial Andean religion—a sixty-folio section titled "Breve y compendiosa satisfacción"—is missing in the edited version most commonly used. Loayza and Bernales Ballesteros advanced the notion of an indigenous nationalism in the colonial Andes as a precursor of the modern Peruvian nation and presented the "Representación verdadera" as an emblem of past Peruvian nationalist movements and a *"reformista"* (reformist) and *"fidelista"* (royalist) document.

In 1954, historian John Rowe placed the "Representación verdadera" and the role of Fray Calixto within the context of a *movimiento nacional Inca* (Inca nationalist movement), which he broadly defined as a series of both peaceful campaigns to redress Indians from the abuses of the colonial system, without modifying the system, and rebellions during the 1700s in which elite Andeans attempted to restore the Inca dynasty by creating a completely independent Inca state—a monarchy in the Spanish style, but with indigenous leaders. The Inca nationalists allegedly upheld the Catholic religion by proposing the formation of an Inca Catholic Church in correspondence with the Spanish Catholic Church. In turn, the independent Inca state envisioned would follow the "ideal state [Inca] Garcilaso [de la Vega] depicted when trying to reform the Spanish administration."[56] Such attributions of nationalism to late-colonial Andeans led some scholars to see this text and the Túpac Amaru Rebellion as antecedents of the independence movement.[57] The textual analysis in subsequent chapters demonstrates that as opposed to an imagined Inca nationalism and beyond Fray Calixto having an Inca surname, the critique of Spanish colonialism and the proposals for social change in the "Representación verdadera" envisioned Andeans participating as equals with Spaniards and mestizos in the judicial and political administration of the colonial state and denied late-colonial Indian elites' ethnic affiliations to their Inca forefathers.[58]

The chapters that follow show that the "Representación verdadera" not only formed a part of but also distanced itself from the Scholastic tradition, as it subverted the content of such ideas to both de-legitimize the imperial rule of Spain in the Americas and grant political power to natives and mestizos. The textual analysis is necessary to elucidate the mental world of Andean subjects in the late colonial period, particularly the themes of Andean political autonomy as expressed in writing and the intellectual struggles for social inclusion and racial equality. The various voices and discourses the text articulates, the subtle meanings and turns Andeans gave to the dominant colonial notions of religion and identity, their understanding of social justice, and their philosophical and political views anticipated the Túpac Amaru Rebellion and help us reassess the roles of Andean intellectuals and protest writings in the rebellions in mid– and late–eighteenth-century Peru. Fray Calixto also understood the institutional climate of reform in the Bourbon era and seized the opportunity to propose a program of changes. But the manuscript was also produced in the midst of a pre-insurrectionary conjuncture in the viceregal capital and circulated among rebels in 1750, as Fray Calixto arrived in Madrid to advance the comprehensive set of reforms contained in the manifesto.

The widespread and abusive practice of *repartimiento de comercio* long remained, in part because of the relaxation of the justice system, fueled by the auctioning of *audiencia* and *corregidor* posts since the seventeenth century.

Unrest increased with the new *arancel* introduced by the viceroy during the following years. The situation worsened with the royal attempts to degrade mestizos, and the systematic exclusion of Andeans from colonial social institutions deepened. In this arena of conflict, the Bourbons' mounting fiscal demands triggered a wave of Indian rebellions and conspiracies in eighteenth-century Andean Peru, beginning approximately in the 1730s. Located at the center of colonial power, Indians and mestizos had been planning a massive insurrection since 1748, which eventually came to fruition in 1750. The movement began in the viceregal capital and continued in adjacent regions, such as Huarochirí. Led by Andeans Antonio Cobo, Francisco Jiménez Inga, the mestizo scribe and military chief Miguel Surichac, his lieutenant Pedro Santos, and the scribe Julián de Ayala, the rebellion broke out in Huarochirí on July 25, 1750—less than a month after the plans for the rebellion in Lima, to have taken place on June 29, 1750, were discovered.[59]

Aware of the circulation of the "Representación verdadera" among the insurrectionists, Viceroy Conde de Superunda declared that the rebels were protesting "the mistreatment they receive from corregidores, judges and curas.... [B]ut [the Indians have] mainly become exasperated for not being largely admitted in the priesthood and the secular positions of government and the ecclesiastical dignities that Spaniards customarily occupy," in spite of the fact that their lifestyles and social interactions gave them a sense of belonging to the Spanish world.[60] These were the core concerns and revindications of the "Representación verdadera." Later in 1757, the viceroy confirmed the circulation of Andean writings during the upheavals: "[The rebels] destroyed bridges, and wrote letters ... promoting rebellion in the towns and rural areas."[61] Superunda was referring more directly to the impact of the "Representación verdadera," which, along with the 1739 Oruro "Manifiesto" by Juan Vélez de Córdoba, circulated widely in mid–eighteenth-century Peru and inspired native self-assertiveness and rebellion.[62]

In his statement, Superunda was also alluding to an anonymous manifesto—possibly written by the Amerindian leader Francisco Jiménez Inga, the mestizo Miguel Surichac, or both, and in part copied and rephrased from the "Representación verdadera"—which was confiscated from one of the *cabezas del motín* (main leaders) executed in August 1750.[63] This manifesto is a paraphrase of the "Representación verdadera," written in the biblical style of Jeremiah. The work equates Andeans with the Hebrews struggling for liberation under the guidance of Moses and evokes the Holy Trinity as "the radiant torch, the sweet medicine of the divine religion, the secure foundation of our salvation."[64] The proclamation denounces the oppression commoners and Indian nobles, indigenous women and children, and mestizos ("our relatives, sons of *caciques*") suffered in the colonial *obrajes* and mines, as well as the lack of education and impediments to entering monasteries. The manifesto calls for prompt action:

God has its time limited, and for us, it's been two hundred years since we are being purged for [the faults of] our progenitors. Remember, fellows, and be aware of the narrow account we will give before God's tribunal. He who does not love his fellow-creatures cannot possibly love God. It is stated in the Holy Commandments.... [And] since [God] sees [his] law so infringed ... we must stand for our honor ... for how much longer must we live in this lethargy and ignorance? ... God is with us in this, and he propitiates that we elect a Captain General as the Hebrews elected Moses to deliver them from their captivity.[65]

The rhetorical format and specifically the denunciations of the Andeans' exclusion from education and the priesthood detailed in this rebel blueprint had been articulated similarly in the "Representación verdadera." The redefinition of an Andean identity separate from that of their ancestors paraphrased the rhetorical strategies of Andean scholars in the text, when they rejected stereotypes of idolatry by disassociating current generations of Andeans from their Inca ancestors (see Chapter 7).

Although Fray Calixto did not participate directly in the 1750 rebellion because he was in Lisbon on his way to deliver the "Representación verdadera" in Madrid, he participated in the inception of the rebellion: the 1748 meetings with the Lima *caciques* and other *kurakas* and possibly even clerics such as Fray Antonio Garro, where the rebellion was initially discussed. The group planned the composition of the texts for the king and the pope and approved Fray Calixto's trip to Europe to deliver them and negotiate a solution to the issues raised. A committee of twelve *kurakas* would lead the rebellion if Fray Calixto's efforts in Spain failed.[66]

The "Representación verdadera" voiced the concerns of Andean elites from Lima and other Andean provinces who were conscious of more sophisticated forms of social exclusion; it also denounced the exploitation of *mitayos*, the abuses of the *repartimiento de comercio*, and the more general mistreatment of Indian women and men in most Andean regions—all of which were triggering factors in the contemporary rebellions. Fray Calixto was particularly adamant about the ubiquitous discrimination against mestizos by Spaniards and the Bourbon attempts to assimilate them into the status of "Indians."

The text also voiced the realities underlying the rebellions in the frontier areas that were only indirectly connected to the Potosí-Lima axis and possibly more connected to the rebellion in Huarochirí and the social unrest in the frontiers of Cusco Province, where other educated Andeans, including Juan Santos Atahualpa, voiced protest discourses while leading a massive insurrection (1742–1753). Little is known about a possible connection between Fray Calixto and Santos Atahualpa. Among Franciscan missionaries, Fray Calixto was known for mediating in dispute resolutions during his missionary work in Tarma and the Quillabamba missions, both neighboring areas of the rebel territories.[67] But more clearly, in the "Representación verdadera" Fray Calixto avoided any possible implication regarding the rebellion—diminishing its importance and referring to it as a simple "noise," limited in geographic scope, that occurred because Indians were harassed by *corregidores* and missionaries.[68] Fray Calixto presented the rebellion as a deliberate exaggeration by Spanish authorities who sought to justify disproportionate official expenditures. Even against the accounts of his superiors concerning the widespread support Indians, mestizos, and blacks lent to Santos Atahualpa, he strove to deny indigenous participation in the insurrection.[69] Instead of plainly rejecting the anti-clerical (more specifically, anti-Franciscan) rebellion by Juan Santos Atahualpa as emphatically as his superiors did, Fray Calixto held Spanish officials responsible for the violence because of the ill treatment they inflicted upon the indigenous peoples of the area.

Like Fray Calixto, Santos Atahualpa allegedly supported the idea of an Indian priesthood, admitting that Indians could get along without Spanish missionaries. He was said to have stated that if the missionaries were unwilling to preach to the jungle Indians without having to bring black soldiers with them, he would bring the Bishop of Cusco to ordain priests in the jungle.[70] Santos Atahualpa would only accept Jesuit clerics in his would-be "kingdom."[71] The sources that recorded Santos Atahualpa's background and actions, however, are mostly second- and thirdhand accounts whose veracity is difficult to establish. Nearly thirty years later, in 1781, another massive insurrection—this one in a central area of the viceroyalty—erupted, bringing to the surface the ideas, writings, and political activism of an Andean rebel much better known in the historical record that reveal the connections between the earlier ideas and discourses of Andean intellectuals and those of Túpac Amaru.

JOSÉ GABRIEL CONDORCANQUI TÚPAC AMARU II

The tense atmosphere in the Andes in the late eighteenth century led to the eruption of rebellions, which, like the Great Rebellion of 1780–1783, resulted from an exacerbation of the social unrest generated by the Bourbon legalization of the abusive *repartos* and the increase of fiscal exactions. These rebellions, however, were simultaneously the reiteration and culmination of a long-standing criticism and legal reform efforts by Andean intellectuals and social activists, such as those introduced in this and the previous chapter.[72] In contrast, the later leaders Túpac Amaru II and Julián Apasa Túpac Katari more clearly became political activists and insurrectionists in the 1780s. Their writing was contingent upon the needs of the rebellion; it was a writing of insurgency and emergency. Nevertheless, their texts conveyed their complex political and religious imaginaries, and their rebellion gave voice and political strength to reform issues proposed by the Andean scholars introduced previously and by earlier rebels. Their depositions, although filtered by judicial scribes and other officials, still allow a glimpse of their religious views, identities, and perceptions of colonialism.

A disciple of the Jesuits in the San Borja school of *caciques* in Cusco, Túpac Amaru II produced a large number of letters, edicts, and *pasquines* (pasquinades) suitable for interpreting the political, religious, and cultural mind-sets of Andean leaders in the late eighteenth century. Although he wrote at a different historical conjuncture, Túpac Amaru's discourse was embedded in a long-lasting religious and political framework familiar to earlier scholars, including Juan de Cuevas Herrera, Jerónimo Lorenzo Limaylla, Fray Calixto de San José Túpac Inca, and others preceding the Great Rebellion. The resort to biblical discourses and images to represent colonial oppression, the use of Scholastic notions of "common good," and the understanding that fighting tyrannical regimes was a legitimate cause were common thematic threads among these writers, and some key items of Túpac Amaru's political programs had been proposed earlier.

In the second half of the 1600s, over a century after the imposition of Spanish *corregidores* in the provincial government, the Andean scholar Juan de Cuevas Herrera had proposed replacing *corregidores* with an Indian equivalent to the Spanish *alcaldes ordinarios*.[73] Less than a century later, as the hated *repartimiento de comercio* produced further havoc within Andean societies, Fray Calixto de San José Túpac Inca introduced the idea of replacing Spanish with Indian *corregidores* in 1748.[74] Túpac Amaru reinstated this demand as exchanging the *corregidor* for an *alcalde mayor* from the "Indian nation" or from among other people of "good conscience," with a moderate salary and whose function was to administer justice and provide for the "policía cristiana" of Indians and others.[75] Further, he demanded that a new *audiencia* be created in Cusco to facilitate Andeans' access to justice. Earlier, rioters in different regions of Spanish America had called for the suspension of the *alcabala* (sales tax) prior to the Great Rebellion.[76] As in previous proposals for administrative reform made by earlier Andean intellectuals, the leaders of the Great Rebellion chose not to challenge the authority of the king.

The potency of Túpac Amaru's discourses of power rested in his ability to combine a rhetorical strategy of justice with programs previously voiced and with political imaginaries shared in the lettered world of Peru and to place them at the center of a massive rebellion, where they would gain political strength. Túpac Amaru's discourses were buttressed with the power of his actions and his weapons. The rebel leader took on roles of power unprecedented among previous Andean leaders. His approach to carrying out justice included giving orders through edicts, which emulated the power of royal decrees and viceregal ordinances; supplanting the king's judicial functionaries; claiming that he was executing the king's *reales cédulas*; mobilizing troops to kill Spanish authorities; and ultimately proclaiming himself as an Inca king and an envoy of God, the ultimate expressions of power and social order in this late-colonial Andean vision.

Túpac Amaru's discourses also represented a culmination of previously available utopian discourses that called for the establishment of an Inca king to restore social harmony in the realm in chaotic times, when Spanish rule proved ineffectual in imparting its own form of justice through laws designed to bring about social harmony.[77] With antecedents in the rebellion of the Calchaquíes in the 1650s, during which a "Spanish Inca" king was "crowned," Inca utopian discourses had become stronger in the eighteenth century. The Andeans behind the frustrated 1739 insurrection in Oruro planned to depose the viceroy and empower an Inca king, just as Juan Santos Atahualpa had apparently attempted to do in the montaña central in the years 1742–1753.[78]

The rebel leader from Upper Peru, Túpac Katari, embodied perhaps a deeper sense of Andean political autonomy even before the start of the rebellion, as a tradition of Andean self-rule was prevalent in earlier movements in La Paz.[79] During the upheaval he also carried out radical acts of power appropriation, supplanting colonial authorities during the rebellion in his area. Túpac Katari acknowledged having appointed *caciques*, captains, *mandones* (authorities), and *oidores* (judges). The judicial authorities, however, charged him with also having appointed a president, *corregidores*, *justicias mayores* (magistrates), colonels, accountants, *alcaldes*, and *regidores* (*cabildo* officials) in the new provinces.[80] In the rebel provinces under Túpac Katari's leadership, commanders of the rebellion were called *oidores* by the Indians. Katari's wife, Bartolina Sisa, was called "Viceregn" by the commoners. In his absence, she substituted for Katari as a commander, and it seems that the rebels obeyed her commands.[81]

Although Túpac Amaru's "decrees" have a rather fixed format, they reveal his professed identities, political ideas, and expectations. Their introductions always present his self-proclamation as a descendant of the Incas of "the royal blood," following a long tradition in colonial Andean writing that had been used earlier by the first *kurakas* who wrote to the king after the conquest; by Andean scholars such as Garcilaso de la Vega, Guamán Poma, Limaylla, Cuevas Herrera, and Fray Calixto; and by creoles such as Juan Vélez de Córdoba and Spaniards such as Don Pedro Bohorques. As Fray Calixto professed in the "Representación verdadera" in 1749–1750, José Gabriel Condorcanqui Túpac Amaru II claimed he had acted on behalf of his fellow Andeans in response to their "clamor" for help in finding a "*remedio*" (remedy) for the "*abusos y vejaciones*" they suffered at the hands of the European *corregidores*.

In his edicts, the leader strove to make it clear that rebellion was a last resort after Andeans had sought legal redress of their grievances for lengthy periods by filing complaints in the tribunals but "*no hallaban remedio*" (to no avail). In practice, his unique acts of power and defiance of the colonial establishment—

such as commanding the imprisonment and killing of *corregidores*, calling for the confiscation of their assets, and abolishing *mitas, alcabalas*, and *repartimientos*— constituted the rebel leader's approach to the enforcement of the royal laws that had long been disregarded by colonial authorities. Túpac Amaru's pursuit was one of social justice for Andeans, informed by a long legacy of Andean writing and political culture under Spanish rule. The writers studied in this work, as well as their manuscripts, represent the utmost expression of the Andean tradition of resorting to justice through the judicial opportunities granted by the system—a political practice whose frustrating results exacerbated the capacity for subtle resistance by Andeans, which erupted in the late eighteenth century in rebellious discourses and insurrection.

Túpac Amaru's discourses of rebellion specifically provide a window into the changes and continuities in Andean critiques of colonialism in the late eighteenth century. Echoing the Andean writings of preceding decades, his edicts and letters revealed that Túpac Amaru's rendition of colonialism shared Scholastic ideas of "common good" and Spanish Neo-Scholastic political theories that justified rebellion against tyrannical rulers. Unlike the other Andean intellectuals' discourses analyzed in later chapters, however, Túpac Amaru's discourses of rebellion openly defied the colonial order by advocating the use of violence against colonial authorities. In some particular conjunctures, however, the frontier between subtle and radical resistance to colonialism by Andean thinkers was difficult to distinguish. Andean scholars and social activists such as Jerónimo Lorenzo Limaylla, Gabriel Fernández Guarache, Bartolomé Topa Hallicalla, and Fray Calixto de San José managed to advocate social change by coupling the writing of complex texts with support for more radical struggles, including the frustrated rebellions in Lima in 1666 and 1750 and the Huarochirí rebellion in 1750.

While the rebellion produced its own kind of insurrectionary writing, in the aftermath of the insurrection the Andeans who had opposed it also used the written word to express their views by attacking the rebels in a counter-discourse that endorsed the colonial status quo. José Rafael Sahuaraura Tito Atauche, a member of one of the most prominent lineages in the Cusco area, wrote an eighty-seven-page eulogy of the Bishop of Cusco, Don Juan Manuel Moscoso y Peralta, in 1784, known as the "Estado del Perú," in which he also offered his enraged condemnation of the Great Rebellion.[82] This text reveals Andean writing and discursive production as highly contested at the onset of Spanish colonialism in Peru.

CONCLUSION

This introductory journey in Chapters 2 and 3 has examined the lives, times, and texts of Andean scholars in the seventeenth and eighteenth centuries who continued the intellectual tradition of writing colonial critiques and renditions of their understanding of the world before and after the Spanish conquest begun by their earlier counterparts Tito Cusi Yupanqui, Santacruz Pachacuti Yamki, Felipe Guamán Poma de Ayala, and Inca Garcilaso de la Vega. Like their earlier counterparts, the later Andean scholars engaged in intellectual work that reflected the transformation of Andean societies under Spanish rule and contributed in their own ways to shape the views of their contemporaries.

Unlike the early Andean scholars, however, the new Andean intellectuals contributed to the formation of social networks across the Atlantic built informally by Indian authorities, scholars, clerics, and other supporters in an attempt to shape the impact of colonialism on Andean societies and to advance a political project of ethnic autonomy in a collective manner. The roles of these Andean networks and scholarship intersected at different conjunctures with the rebellions—successful or not—Andeans organized in 1666, 1750, and 1780–1782 to confront the upheaval Spanish colonialism had brought to their societies. This convergence expressed—both in scholarship and during rebellions—what intellectual and political leaders perceived as a protracted weakness of the colonial system of justice, which failed to address the sources of social discontent and the general decline of their societies.

As Indian nobles and their mestizo descendants, *curas doctrineros*, prebendaries, lay brothers, and *protectores de naturales*, the Andean ladinos studied in this work accomplished both social and intellectual tasks, leaving a record of social leadership and complex writings that reveal their exposure to the colonial lettered world and their willingness to partake in it. These intellectuals were in a liminal and problematic position, at the threshold between the disparate worlds that came into conflicting contact following the European invasion of the Americas. The Toledan reforms prompted seventeenth-century Indian and mestizo leaders to engage in a complex intellectual activism so they could retain/recover their political status and search for social balance in times of drastic change. The writers paint a picture of the variety of political, religious, and social issues that constituted the substance of Andean scholarship in the seventeenth century. The struggles of Jauja nobles to retain their *cacicazgos*, expressed in the writings of Jerónimo Lorenzo Limaylla; the social damage caused by the oppressive *mita* in the Provinces of Charcas and Jauja, voiced in both Limaylla's and Juan de Cuevas Herrera's *memoriales*; Cuevas Herrera's debates over the obstacles to successful evangelization of Andeans when the extirpation campaigns were in full sway; and the early stages of organized movements for social inclusion of Andean nobles, voiced by Juan Núñez Vela de Rivera, closed the seventeenth century with an unfinished project that would slowly develop in the following decades.

Eighteenth-century Andean scholars mobilized their intellectual weapons and social activism because they not only inherited the long-standing injustices unleashed during the previous century but also faced new challenges to their social standing, as well as further exactions and fiscal pressure, as the Bourbon reforms attempted to modernize the empire and strengthen it politically. Procurador General Vicente Morachimo exposed the critical role of legal discourses in fighting injustice as pressing hardships—old and new—swept the Provinces of Saña and Trujillo, where the *mita*, the *repartimiento de comercio*, and land disputes presented renewed opportunities for the illegal practices of the *corregidores, audiencia* judges, and viceroys. Mid– and late–eighteenth-century scholars and social activists, such as Fray Calixto de San José and José Gabriel Condorcanqui Túpac Amaru II, stood at the threshold between reform and rebellion at times of heightened social conflict in Lima and Cusco, respectively—crucial areas for colonial economic and political interests and regions deeply affected by the Bourbons' reform efforts. They offered the most complex forms of resistance to colonial domination, combining, to different degrees, rhetorical and real weapons to defy the power of the state and church authorities. As the colonial order was shaken off by the Great Rebellion in 1780–1783, Andean scholarship also reflected the positions of the Cusco Inca elites who supported the colonial regime during and in the aftermath of the upheaval.

In the midst of social and cultural interaction and conflict, the intellectual practices of Indios ladinos took on unique forms, defying conventional ideas of authorship and scholarship. Present-day notions of individual authorship are insufficient and even oversimplistic when applied to Andean writing, as Limaylla's seventeenth-century "Memorial" and "Representación" and the eighteenth-century "Representación verdadera" demonstrate. Unlike European writers, who usually practiced individually, colonial Andeans tended to work collectively in the production of their manuscripts. In addition, they relied on informal systems of interconnected agents—both Andeans and non-Andeans—for the collection of information, identification and discussion of content, composition of the final text, diffusion, and ultimately the advancement of their petitions. Authorship in this context surpasses the work of the individual who might sign or edit a draft of the text and becomes a more complex collective endeavor that reflects more than the challenges of colonial Andean intellectuals and those they sought to represent. This collective endeavor also brings to the surface the intense cultural, political, and intellectual interaction among Indian and mestizo Andeans, Spaniards, and creoles on both sides of the Atlantic.

Andeans' participation in the pursuit of justice through the Spanish legal system also put them in close contact with the lettered world of jurists, lawyers, judges, and clergy. They were engaged in the book culture of their time through religious literature, Spanish and Andean chronicles, manuals for *escribanos*, Spanish laws, and juridical texts. As authors and litigants, they found themselves struggling to access the exclusionary colonial world of letters and its circuits and striving to come to terms with the culture of the Spanish and creole *letrados*.

The next stage of this journey explores the European background of Andean writings to begin to discern the nature of the scholarship and discourses crafted by lettered Andean ladinos. The philosophical and theological notions that traveled to the Andes with Spanish clergy, scholars, and writers, and the change such notions underwent in the new settings, become more apparent as a textual analysis of the writings under study is developed.

NOTES

1. O'Phelan, *Rebellions and Revolts*, 58–74.

2. Ibid., 53. The rebellions of the era in Cotabambas (Cusco, 1730), Cochabamba (Charcas, 1730), and Oruro (1739) expressed the social unrest these policies created. For more information on these rebellions, see ibid.

3. For studies of the Bourbon policies, see Stern, *Resistance, Rebellion, and Consciousness*; O'Phelan, *Un siglo de rebeliones anticoloniales* and *La gran rebelión en los Andes*; Stavig, *The World of Túpac Amaru*; Fisher, Kuethe, and McFarlane, *Reform and Insurrection*; Garrett, *Shadows of Empire*.

4. These policies had begun early in the century with royal decrees limiting the expansion of convents and organizations run by the regular orders. The ecclesiastical patronage by the king, in the 1753 Concordat, ultimately gave power to the crown to control the size of the regular clergy. Andrien, "Coming of Enlightened Reform in Bourbon Peru," 6–7, 9.

5. For detailed studies of the *repartimiento de mercancías*, see Nölte, *Repartos y rebeliones*; Moreno Cebrián, *El corregidor de indios*.

6. See pertinent references in Chapter 1, note 14.

7. Lienhard, *Testimonios, cartas y manifiestos indígenas*, xxvi. Lienhard first qualified Indian writings as "diplomatic texts," a variety of manuscripts intended for negotiation with the colonial authorities.

8. Don Juan de Bustamante Carlos Inga was a descendant of Don Melchor Carlos Inga, who had received an *encomienda* in 1582 and held the titles of count and marquiz in 1599. These titles were denied to Bustamante in the eighteenth century; he only attained the lesser distinction of "Gentilhombre de Boca" and a substantial pension. BNM, Manuscrito 20193, "Ascendencia de Carlos Inga." See also Cahill, "Liminal Nobility," 182–184. Bustamante also received petitions for help in Madrid from Francisco Zevallos, Antonio Chaigua Cassamusa, and other participants in the Huarochirí rebellion. Members of the Uchu Inga lineage from Cusco also appeared as permanent residents at the royal court in Madrid in the second half of the 1700s, enjoying substantial patronage. O'Phelan, "Linaje e Ilustración," 841, 849–850.

9. Tacuri Mena, 1755, in Loayza, *Fray Calixto Túpac Inca*, 81–82. According to Tacuri Mena, "Don Julián Cirilo y Castilla seeks the foundation of a school for kids of our nation to be governed by presbyters of our nation. . . . On Santa Rosa's day in 1754, Don Julián preached a sermon to the Council of the Indies which has been amply applauded by nobles of both sexes." Ibid., 82.

10. One of the most visible leaders of the Lima network in 1726 was Don Francisco Saba Capac Inga, *cacique principal* from Pachacama, Lurin, and its ports. These Indian

authorities supported collective petitions he led: Don Bartolomé Cristobal Chumbingo, *gobernador* of Santiago del Surco; Don Juan Bautista Arteaga, captain of Huamanga; Don Juan Ignacio Quipulivia, *segunda persona* (*cacique* of the lower moiety) of the Partido de Chaucarima; Don Santiago Calixto, *procurador* of the town of La Magdalena; Don Lorenzo Beltrán, *alcalde* of the Changuay Port; and Don Juan de Dios Aldave, *cacique principal* of Charapopto. AGI, Audiencia de Lima, 495, Lima, Junio 6, 1726.

11. Although during the sixteenth and seventeenth centuries the terms "protector" and "*procurador de naturales*" were often interchangeable (*Recopilación*, Libro VI, Título VI); by the eighteenth century the terms were clearly differentiated. The *procurador de indios*, also known as *diputado general de indios* (Indians' general deputy), was clearly a legal representative of an indigenous corporate body, hired to move along legal cases at both the royal court in Spain and the *audiencias*.

12. Rowe, "Movimiento Nacional Inca del siglo XVIII," 3–33, esp. 17.

13. AGI, Lima, 422, Letter from the Council of the Indies to the Viceroy of Peru, Marqués de Castelfuerte, March 5, 1733. The manifesto's complete title is "Manifesto of aggravations and vexations suffered by the Indians from the Kingdom of Peru, dedicated to the Lords of the Royal and Supreme Council of the Indies by the General Deputy and Attorney of the said Indians." Although Vicente Morachimo filed the "Manifiesto" with the Council of the Indies in September 1732, the council only acknowledged receipt on March 5, 1733. In 1735 the king issued a decree reminding Viceroy Marqués de Castelfuerte about the *real cédula* from February 21, 1725, stating his concern about justice for Indians.

14. AGI, Lima, 422, 1–13v; Morachimo, "Manifiesto," 1732.

15. Andrien, "*Noticias secretas de América.*"

16. O'Phelan, *Un siglo de rebeliones anticoloniales*, 94–102. *Caciques* from seventeen provinces in southern Peru were implicated in planning a massive movement to take place in November 1737. *Audiencia* authorities targeted the *cacique* Don Andres Cacma Condori from Azángaro as the head of the movement; he was also accused of associating with the *cacique* Don José Orcoguaranca from the San Blas parish (Cusco). Rowe, "Movimiento Nacional Inca del siglo XVIII," 18. The 1739 Oruro uprising was one of the first attempts to depose the Spanish king and crown an Inca monarch in the eighteenth century. The leader, Juan Vélez de Córdoba, a creole from Moquegua who claimed to be the grandson of an Inca king, led a cross-ethnic movement to reestablish the Inca empire, which would have resulted in him being crowned the new emperor. Fifteen *caciques* from Moquegua and Cochabamba were allegedly involved. O'Phelan, *Un siglo de rebeliones anticoloniales*, 106; Cornblit, *Power and Violence in the Colonial City,* 103. The most important aspects of this aborted movement and of the Andean tradition of writing are represented in Juan Vélez de Córdoba's "Manifiesto" (best known as the "Manifiesto de Oruro"), written in 1739, which advances a series of petitions and complaints similar in nature to those found in most Indian and mestizo writings of the 1700s studied in this book (AGI, Charcas, 363). A textual analysis of the "Manifiesto" is developed in Chapter 5, in the context of the intertextual relationship between Andean and creole writings. For a complete discussion of the social movements of the 1730s, see O'Phelan, *Un siglo de rebeliones anticoloniales*; Cornblit, *Power and Violence in the Colonial City.*

17. O'Phelan, "Linaje e Ilustración," 842.

18. Loayza, *Fray Calixto Túpac Inca*, 65, 69. The eleventh Inca king, Inga Yupanqui, was actually Pachacuti (the tenth Inca), to whose name Garcilaso de la Vega added the "Inga Yupanqui" in the succession of Inca kings presented in his *Comentarios Reales de los Incas*. Rowe, "Movimiento Nacional Inca del siglo XVIII," 12.

19. Loayza, *Fray Calixto Túpac Inca*, 69–70.

20. During these years, the Franciscans were confronting the destruction of their mission towns in the Cerro de la Sal, initiated in 1742 by Juan Santos Atahualpa and his rebels. By 1747 the Franciscans were building new missions in the Quillabamba Valley. Ibid., 72–74; Vargas Ugarte, *Historia del Perú virreinato*, 243. The rebellion broke out in 1742, also affecting the Franciscan missions of Quillabamba. John Rowe maintained that the movement was led by Pablo Chapi, an Indian the Franciscan missionaries identified with Juan Santos. Rowe apparently saw them as two different persons. Rowe, "Movimiento Nacional Inca del siglo XVIII," 19. For studies of the Juan Santos insurrection, see Varesse, *La sal de los cerros*; Zarzar, *"Apu Cachauaina Jesús sacramentado"*; Loaiza, *Juan Santos el invencible*. The manuscript's complete title is "A Truthful Representation and Lamentable Exclamation Rendered by the Whole Indian Nation to the Majesty of the Lord King of the Spains [*sic*] and Emperor of the Indies, Lord Don Ferdinand VI, Begging His Attention and Help in Redeeming Them from the Outrageous Affront and Dishonor They Suffer Since More than Two Hundred Years Ago. Exclamation from the American Indians, Using the Same Lamentation that the Prophet Jeremiah elevated to God in Chapter 5 and Last of His Lamentations."

21. Fray Pedro Juan de Molina, a general minister of the Franciscan Order of Minors in Madrid, supported the promotion of Fray Calixto from *donado* to lay brother and authorized the guardian of the Saint Spirit convent in Valencia to conduct his novitiate and profession of vows. Loayza, *Fray Calixto Túpac Inca*, 69–70, 72–76.

22. Viceroy Conde de Superunda reported that letters from Indians from "different parts of the kingdom" were confiscated from Fray Calixto after his imprisonment, including powers given to him to legally represent Indians and a letter from Spain from the Andean Don Felipe Tacuri Mena, written on July 30, 1755, encouraging Fray Calixto and the Indian *cabildo* to fight for autonomous Indian schools. Ibid., 89–90.

23. The *cabildo* officials facilitated Fray Calixto's role as their representative in Spain, collecting the original documentation that proved his Inca descent. Indian authorities in 1749 included Don Santiago de la Vega, Don Pedro Condor Anchay, Don Martin Guaman, Don Isidro Colqui y Pruna, and Don Francisco Jordan. Cala, May 7, 1751, and Fray Juan de San Antonio, May 17, 1751, both in ibid., 72–74. Don Antonio Chaiguaca appeared to have been an Indian legal adviser of the *cabildo* in 1749. Ibid., 61.

24. His role as intermediary was made difficult, however, by limited financial resources, which proved detrimental in his journey to Spain. The friar complained to the Indian *cabildo* of a lack of financial support and asked for money and official power of attorney to advance other petitions the *kurakas* had presented in court through Spanish representatives, with little effect. Ibid., 54.

25. Ibid., 50–53.

26. Letter from Fray Calixto de San José Túpac Inca to El Cercado *cabildo*, Noviembre 14, 1750. Reproduced in Loayza, *Fray Calixto Túpac Inca*, 57–58. At Fray Calixto's

request, Bustamante agreed to write a *memorial* demanding Indians' freedom of passage to Spain to King Ferdinand VI in 1750. Bustamante presented the petition to the king "on behalf of the noble caciques and military Indians who reside in this city." The king denied general permission but accepted that license to pass to Spain should be granted to those who could justify the reason for their trip before the viceroy. He further commanded that help should be provided for them. "Real Cédula, Enero 19, 1751," in Polo, "Un libro Raro," 632–633.

27. Cirilo y Castilla had moved to Madrid sometime around 1754 and lived in Spain for thirty-five years, during which time he obtained recognition as a presbyter; Don Felipe Tacuri Mena had been sojourning in Spain in 1754–1755. Loayza, *Fray Calixto Túpac Inca,* 80.

28. Don Felipe Tacuri Mena, Julio 30, 1755, "A los señores mis Amantes y Speriores del Cabildo," reproduced in ibid., 80–83.

29. Fray Calixto de San José Túpac Inca, November 14, 1750, in Medina, *La Imprenta en Lima,* 549; also Loayza, *Fray Calixto Túpac Inca,* 49–62.

30. AGI, Lima, 988. Letter from Brother Calixto de San José to the president of the Council of the Indies, reproduced in Loayza, *Fray Calixto Túpac Inca,* 66–68; Vargas Ugarte, *Historia general del Perú,* 243. In the letter, Fray Calixto expressed his personal interest in obtaining a position as a lay priest.

31. Carta del Conde de Superunda al Rey, Lima, Enero 30, 1759, in Loayza, *Fray Calixto Túpac Inca,* 92–94. Upon his imprisonment, members of El Cercado *cabildo* expressed solidarity with and recognition of Fray Calixto as their representative and fully supported him in Lima in November 1756. According to members of El Cercado indigenous *cabildo,* "Fray Calixto has conducted [our] matters with 'divine hands,' with competence and religious resignation." Bandin Hermo, "Un descendiente de los Incas," 90.

32. Rowe, "Movimiento Nacional Inca del siglo XVIII," 20.

33. Ibid., 33. Rowe proposed 1748 as the printing date. That date is disputed by the manuscript itself, however, which refers to 1749 as the "current year" at the moment the manuscript was being completed: "Since those years when the Admiral Christopher Columbus discovered the Hispaniola Island until the current one of 1749, there have been 257 years of affronts." "Representación verdadera," 165. After their ordeals traveling under cover to Spain, Fray Calixto and his companion, the Franciscan Fray Isidoro de Cala, sneaked into the crowd during a royal hunting excursion and handed the "Representación verdadera" to the Bourbon king Ferdinand VI. Loayza, *Fray Calixto Túpac Inca,* 93.

34. Rowe, "Movimiento Nacional Inca del siglo XVIII," 33.

35. There is also the possibility that these texts were written in stages or rewritten for different occasions. The first reference to a Latin text composed for the pope comes from 1744, when Fray Calixto was first given legal power to represent Indian authorities from El Cercado and to deliver the document to the pope, something he could not accomplish. Don Francisco Zevallos was also sent later with a letter to the pope, in the frustrated journey discussed earlier. The tentative dates were given previously for the "Planctus indorum" in its latest form, since it incorporates references to the Huarochirí rebellion in July 1750. "Planctus indorum," 19[109], 20[118], 20[122], in Navarro, *Una denuncia profética desde el Perú,* 427–428, 458–459, 469.

36. Loayza, *Fray Calixto Túpac Inca*, 53, 93. Uncertainty still exists about the second document addressed to the pope, which the friars brought to Europe in 1750. It might be an early version of the "Planctus indorum," which they sent to the pope through a banker they met in Lisbon, along with a letter or petition in Latin written by Fray Isidoro de Cala. The other possibility, which is more likely, is that only the letter was sent to the pope at that time because the version of the "Planctus indorum" that survives today refers to the events of the Huarochirí rebellion in July 1750, when the two friars were arriving in Lisbon. Ibid., 52.

37. Lienhard, *Testimonios, cartas y manifiestos indígenas*, xxix. According to Lienhard, native writers "adjusted to the cultural horizon of the interlocutor . . . a sort of superficial 'concession' to the addressee."

38. Holbrook, *Jeremiah: Faith amid Apostasy*.

39. Ibid., 119.

40. Adorno, *Writing and Resistance in Colonial Peru*, 123.

41. Saphier, *Book of Jeremiah*, 207.

42. Holbrook, *Jeremiah: Faith amid Apostasy*, 126.

43. Saphier, *Book of Jeremiah*, 5:1–3.

44. "Representación verdadera," f. 32v.

45. Loayza, *Fray Calixto Túpac Inca*, 88.

46. Bernales Ballesteros, "Fray Calixto de San José Túpac Inca," 15, relied on the viceroy's initial indictment and assumed that the author was Fray Antonio Garro. In turn, historians from recent decades who use only Bernales Ballesteros's incomplete version of the "Representación verdadera" and his introductory essay are similarly misled.

47. Loayza, *Fray Calixto Túpac Inca*, 88–89.

48. Ibid., 49; Bandin Hermo, "Un descendiente de los Incas." Bandin maintained that the printed manuscript, or "Exclamación," was given to Fray Calixto by the *caciques* from Lima in 1749.

49. At the meetings in El Cercado in 1748, where the *caciques* and other Indian leaders were planning an insurrection, the friars and *caciques* agreed to postpone the rebellion until the "Representación verdadera" was delivered to the king, perhaps believing Fray Calixto's mediation would produce the needed reforms and make the violent rebellion unnecessary. AGI, Lima, 597, Madrid, Marzo 29, 1751, in Konetzke, *Colección de documentos*, vol. 3, 25; Bandin Hermo, "Un descendiente de los Incas," 91. In addition to entrusting Fray Calixto with the task of delivering the printed manuscript to the king and the Council of the Indies, they gave him an older *representación* from 1744 to deliver to the pope. Andeans appealed to the pope because they probably knew that back in 1586, Pope Gregorio XIII had granted mestizos the right to be ordained as priests, provided they were competent and legitimate children; the last requirement was dispensed for mestizos. To support their claims, the *caciques* had clearly instructed Fray Calixto to secure sufficient copies of the papal bulls issued on their behalf. Bandin Hermo, "Un descendiente de los Incas," 91.

50. Osorio, *Clamor de los Indios Americanos*, 17. Saint Rose of Lima was said to have prophesied the return of the Inca empire to Peru in 1750 and to have proclaimed the end of Spanish rule in the Andes.

51. For practical purposes, when referring to the authors of the "Representación verdadera" I use the singular name Fray Calixto, although the plural is meant. Regarding the

final version of the "Representación verdadera," Fray Calixto crafted it possibly in association with Fray Antonio Garro and Fray Isidoro de Cala.

52. These networks of Andean scholars, social activists, rebels, lawyers, clerics, and others sympathetic to the movement operated in variable, informal, and efficient ways. The Cercado *cabildo* maintained permanent communication with members of these networks in Spain and meticulously instructed all participants on what needed to be accomplished. For example, regarding the power of attorney the *cabildo* issued to Fray Calixto in 1744, the *cabildo* clearly instructed Calixto that the goal of his mission was to obtain "*providencias* [mandates] from the king to improve the condition of Indian nobles." The second power of attorney, given to him on October 30, 1756, spelled out that the friar must obtain copies of all testimonies given at court, as well as briefings, papal bulls, letters and apostolic dispatches, and royal decrees (in triplicate). He was instructed to send such documents immediately to the *cabildo* in Lima. On the other hand, in 1756 the *cabildo* was adamant that Fray Calixto should conform in every way to the instructions given; regarding future actions, he should wait for new instructions to come in later letters. Bandin Hermo, "Un descendiente de los Incas," 94.

53. Alvarez, *De las costumbres y conversión de los indios del Perú*, 268–269. In the town of Andamarca, Province of Carangas, for example, Andeans used Spanish manuals, such as the popular *Monterroso*, with instructions to *escribanos* regarding their practice in civil and criminal legal cases. In the town of Corquemarca, other Indians acquired the *Siete Partidas*, a comprehensive legal code compiled in Spain by King Alfonso X.

54. Loayza, *Fray Calixto Túpac Inca*; Bernales Ballesteros, "Fray Calixto de San José Túpak Inca"; Peralta, "Tiranía o buen gobierno"; Rowe, "Movimiento Nacional Inca del siglo XVIII"; Lienhard, *Testimonios, cartas y manifiestos indígenas* and "Writing from Within"; Estenssoro Fuchs, *Del paganismo a la santidad*.

55. Osorio, *Clamor de los Indios Americanos*.

56. Rowe, "Movimiento Nacional Inca del siglo XVIII," 14.

57. Loayza, *Juan Santos el invencible*, 84.

58. The text has also been interpreted as a "hybrid text," wrapped in European forms but based on Andean sources and narratives. Lienhard, "Writing from Within," 177. Others see it as a mere product of the Franciscans' Scholastic tradition and an attempt to gain the king's favor in an effort to counterbalance the power of the Jesuits at the local level. Peralta, "Tiranía o buen gobierno," 67–68.

59. Valcárcel, *Rebeliones coloniales sudamericanas*, 59–60. For a comprehensive understanding of the Huarochirí rebellion and the Lima conspiracy, see BRP, Sign. 59-5-26; Spalding, *Huarochirí*; O'Phelan, *Un siglo de rebeliones anticoloniales*; Valcárcel, *Rebeliones coloniales sudamericanas*.

60. Conde de Superunda, Lima, 24 de Septiembre de 1750, in Loayza, *Juan Santos el invencible*, 163, and *Fray Calixto Túpac Inca*, 85.

61. Moreno Cebrián, *Relación y documentos de gobierno del virrey del Perú*, 248.

62. O'Phelan, *Un siglo de rebeliones anticoloniales*, 115.

63. Valcárcel, *Rebeliones coloniales sudamericanas*, 60. Valcárcel attributed the insurgents' proclamation to a participant with the last name Ayala, cited previously. He was probably referring to Julián de Ayala, one of the organizers of the rebellions to take place in Lima and Huarochirí.

64. BRP, Sign. 59-5-26, 10.

65. Ibid., 11.

66. Rowe, "Movimiento Nacional Inca del siglo XVIII," 20.

67. Cala 1751, in Loayza, *Fray Calixto Túpac Inca*, 69–70.

68. "They resisted and ultimately killed some and then hid themselves in the deepest forests … where undoubtedly they will die." "Representación verdadera," 124. In reality, both the "Representación verdadera" (123v–124) and the "Planctus indorum" (Navarro, *Una denuncia profética desde el Perú* [02.8], 169–171) deny that a rebellion in its own right actually occurred, but they admit to a massive runaway from "the tyranny and frequent robbery perpetrated by a corregidor who harassed the Indians." Ibid., 169.

69. "[T]here was not a single Indian, among the millions of Indians and mestizos living in the kingdom and the highlands, who have raised even a finger to support this rebellion, not one absentee, nor a single one has gone to follow the [r]ebel." "Representación verdadera," 124–124v. Viceroy Conde de Superunda suspected that Fray Calixto had been corresponding with the rebel leader Juan Santos Atahualpa in the Cerro de la Sal, but further empirical evidence is needed to prove this. As a missionary in the Quillabamba missions from 1744 to 1748, Fray Calixto traveled close to the rebel areas.

70. Varesse, *La sal de los Cerros*, 110.

71. Amich, *Historia de las misiones*, 182–183.

72. Since the Great Rebellion is likely one of the most studied episodes in colonial Andean history, only a general reference to its relationship to Andean writing appears in this section. A more detailed analysis of the rebel leaders' religious and political imaginary is presented in Chapter 7. For more comprehensive studies of the rebellion itself, see references in Chapter 1, note 2.

73. Cuevas Herrera, "Cinco memoriales," ca. 1650, 147v, 151v. Spanish *alcaldes ordinarios* were usually the mayors of Spanish towns or senior council aldermen with civic and policing duties. Prior to Cuevas, in Charcas in 1609 a creole clergyman, Pedro Serrano, had suggested the convenience of removing *corregidores*.

74. "Representación verdadera," 167v.

75. Even in the midst of the insurrection, Túpac Amaru asked Bishop Moscoso to send "good clergymen" to indoctrinate native Andeans in the regions he controlled. O'Phelan, *Un siglo de rebeliones anticoloniales*, 304. Interestingly, in 1750–1751 the "Planctus indorum" attributed the same demand to Juan Santos Atahualpa in the midst of his 1742 uprising; "Planctus indorum" [02.8], in Navarro, *Una denuncia profética desde el Perú*, 168–170.

76. O'Phelan, *Un siglo de rebeliones anticoloniales*, 304–305.

77. See further elaboration on Túpac Amaru's utopian ideas, the language of the rebellion, and other aspects of the Great Rebellion in Walker, *Smoldering Ashes*, chapter 1; Flores Galindo, *Buscando un Inca*; Campbell, "Ideology and Factionalismo."

78. Durand, *Colección documental de la independencia del Perú*, 229–233. In other instances, rumors spread by the Indian Juan de Dios Orcoguaranca (Paucartambo) about the breakout of a general Indian insurrection in 1777 would lead to the crowning of an Indian king, and a similar account was known about another Indian rebellion planned to start in Huarochirí and Camaná in 1777. The Indians had prepared a document calling

upon different provinces to participate in the uprising, which would return the kingdom to its "legitimate Indian" owners.

79. For a thorough analysis of Túpac Katari's political ideas, political and spiritual practices, and roles in the Great Rebellion, see Thomson, *We Alone Rule*; Valle de Siles, *Historia de la rebelión de Tupac Catari*.

80. Valcárcel, *Rebeliones coloniales sudamericanas*, 175–176.

81. Ibid.

82. AGI, Lima, 76; Sahuaraura Tito Arauchi, "Estado del Perú." José Rafael's father, Don Nicolás Jiménez de Cisneros Sahuaraura, allegedly a descendant of Pachacuti Inga Yupanqui and Topa Inga Yupanqui, had been the hereditary *cacique* of the Santiago parish in Cusco and was very active in its Indian sodality. Don Nicolás had reached the positions of lieutenant captain and general commissary of cavalry in the Indian militia, distinctions earlier enjoyed by his grandfather, Don Asencio Ramos Atauche, and his uncle, Don José Ramos Atauche. AGI, Lima, 76; Sahuaraura Tito Arauchi, "Estado del Perú"; Durand, *Colección documental de la independencia del Perú*, 243.

❧ 4 ❧

THE EUROPEAN BACKGROUND OF ANDEAN SCHOLARSHIP

C OLONIAL ANDEAN WRITING REMAINS A KEY EXAMPLE of the trans-culturation of early-modern European forms of communication, areas of knowledge, and categories of thought that made their way to the Americas with the Spanish invasion, which became transformed during the process of colonialization. This chapter builds on the notion of trans-culturation, which Cuban sociologist Fernando Ortiz first introduced in 1940, to counteract oversimpli-fied and racist notions of the "acculturation" and "de-culturation" of indigenous peoples under Spanish colonialism. In the transition from one culture to another, Ortiz maintained, a process of cultural creation occurs that expresses not only the acquisition of the new culture but also the loss of the previous one. The new culture that emerges is unique, incorporating something of both cultures while remaining a new creation that is different from the previous two.[1] This notion of trans-culturation was later redefined as the ways subordinated groups in colonial settings chose and reworked the cultural messages implanted by the predominant culture, an idea that describes even more precisely the nature of colonial Andean writing.[2] Inasmuch as the colonizers imposed values and practices on the colo-nized, however, they could not control Andeans' ability to make "something else out of them," not necessarily by rejecting the colonial culture but by "subverting it from within."[3]

The identification of the intellectual roots of, and theoretical justifications for, Andean discourses of protest and power constitutes the purpose of this chapter. In building a scholarly interpretation of the post-conquest state of the indigenous peoples and formulating a theoretical legitimation of ethnic autonomy, Andean writers used European philosophies and political theologies in ways that questioned the primacy of Spanish authority over Andean self-rule. Andean scholarly production in mid- and late-colonial Peru thus bore witness to the ongoing trans-culturation of European intellectual currents from the late-medieval and early-modern periods into colonial Andean worldviews.

During the seventeenth and eighteenth centuries, Andean intellectuals participated in political and theological discussions that revealed their awareness of the major intellectual trends of the day on both sides of the Atlantic. This chapter begins by outlining these contemporary intellectual currents and demonstrating their influence on the construction of Andean texts. The subsequent sections examine the most salient discussions in which European intellectual roots are visible and show the ways Andean authors modified their sources. Andean scholars discussed the nature of the Spanish empire in Peru and the relationships between the king and his Amerindian subjects through renewed debates over the legitimacy of the Spanish conquest and colonial rule. They also discussed at length their legitimate right to self-rule as their political structures were challenged during the Toledan era.

PHILOSOPHY AND POLITICAL THEOLOGY

As representatives of various religious orders arrived in the Americas, they brought philosophies and political theories prevalent in early-modern Spain. Missionaries also introduced a Christian theology of justice to sustain their mission of evangelization. These principles were diffused from pulpits and classrooms attended by children of the native elite. Educated in this European tradition, native and mestizo intellectuals in colonial Peru drew upon streams of European thought that reached back to the Scholastic tenets of Thomas Aquinas in the thirteenth century and their reformulation by Renaissance Spanish scholars in the sixteenth century.[4] Aquinas's understanding of a ruler's political legitimacy underlies most of the *memoriales* and *representaciones* the Andean native scholars discussed in this study brought to the king. According to Aquinas, the king's authority comes from his subjects, as do the powers of justice and the law: "The multitude or the public persona has this coercive power, which pertains to the exacting of punishments. . . . Therefore, it pertains to it alone to make laws." Aquinas advocated incorporating reforms to limit the king's power. He believed the people should rise in rebellion to depose their king only as a last resort against persistent tyranny and obstruction of the common good; even then, rebellion should be initiated only through public consent.[5]

A recurring interest in Andean scholarship, from Felipe Guamán Poma de Ayala onward, was to propose changes that would limit the power of the king's representatives in Peru. After Guamán Poma, Andean leaders addressed these suggestions in their writings and followed them up with trans-Atlantic visits to the king, which became almost a ceremonial act of delivering the manuscripts in person to the Council of the Indies—the last instance of justice that advised the king—and eventually to the king himself.

The notion of natural law constituted a cornerstone of medieval Augustinian and late-medieval Thomist Scholasticism. Saint Augustine reformulated the traditional Greek and Roman definitions of natural law as reason or the law of nature, proposing instead that natural law was a set of moral principles based on the "divine will" and "divine law" that govern social life. In the view of late-medieval Christian philosophers, such as Aquinas, natural law fundamentally defines all social relationships and aims for the common good; "felicity and happiness are the ultimate end of human life. Hence . . . it is necessary that law properly looks to the order of the common happiness."[6] Natural law was a key concept in medieval Christianity, used to lay a foundation of what was morally right and wrong and to establish standards of ethics that defined who belonged in a community and how interactions between communities or nations should be conducted.

Aquinas defined human laws as laws that derive from divine laws and are understood by human reason: "From the precepts of natural law, as from some common and non-demonstrable principles, human reason must proceed to dispose of more particular matters . . . discovered by human reason, [which] are called human laws."[7] This is an important step because, later, Neo-Scholastic scholars would separate the two forms of law and allow for human capability to undo human laws, thus opening the possibility for political action and social change. This principle would empower Andean scholars, such as Fray Calixto de San José Túpac Inca, who were convinced that useless royal decrees could and should be changed. Their proposals for social reform showed they were aware of the people's ability to make and change laws or at least to engage rulers' power through reform.

Dominican and Jesuit theologians in Spain undertook a revival of Scholasticism in the sixteenth century. They incorporated the new political and legal concepts of tyrannicide and the right to depose a ruler, initiating what came to be known as Neo-Scholasticism. To be sure, this was just one aspect of a new trend of conservative thought that enabled the Catholic Church to contest the Reformation and the more humanist emphasis of the Renaissance.[8]

In Spanish America, some of the best-known exponents of Neo-Scholasticism were Francisco de Vitoria, an Aristotelian from the University of Salamanca; his disciple, Francisco Suárez; and Juan de Mariana. These Jesuit scholars took a leading role in preserving the dominance of the Catholic Church in the face of the Reformation and the humanist challenge of Renaissance scholars, who diverted from theological explanations of phenomena and events and focused more on the study of the individual. However, the introduction of these scholars' rethinking of Thomist political theories of law and society, themselves reformulations of Aristotelian notions of society, laid out the theoretical groundwork that would evolve into more radical theories of social and political change. In this sense, Spanish Neo-Scholasticism played a mediating role between medieval theology and modern ideas of the state and society.

In the debate over the legitimacy of Spanish rule in America and the new legal status of indigenous peoples, Vitoria's ideas carried significant weight in colonial Andean writings. Vitoria defended non-Christian natives as rational people who he thought were "infidels" only because they had not been instructed in the colonizers' new religion.[9] He also supported the property rights of indigenous subjects, comparing their status to that of Hebrews and Muslims who had traditionally been allowed to keep their property while subjected to foreign rule. Following Vitoria, Fray Bartolomé de las Casas and Domingo de Soto defended the rights of native Andeans to own possessions and to retain the *señorío* (lordship) of their communities.

In line with the Thomist notion of civil societies, in the mid-eighteenth century Fray Calixto struggled to prove that Andeans were rational people, or *gente de razón*, and to assert that they had natural rights and were fully capable of governing themselves, which amounted to questioning Indians' legal definition as perpetual minors.[10] To support late-colonial Andeans' advocacy of Indian priesthood, education, and civil service, he maintained that Indian subjects were "rational" and "old Christians," no longer subject to royal or spiritual tutelage. Fray Calixto constructed native Andeans as *gente de razón* "[b]ecause what, otherwise, prevents [these] reduced Indians and old Christians, inhabitants of cities, villages and places in the mountains, who live urban political lives, from becoming competent to serve in the religious priesthood, and in honorable positions, both secular and ecclesiastical?"[11]

Both Fray Calixto and Juan de Cuevas Herrera contested accusations of native idolatry by, in turn, accusing the Spaniards of inducing idolatrous behavior in Indians through their unjust and negligent actions. They sought to shake off the negative connotations of the term "barbarian," which had become synonymous with the terms "idolater" and "infidel" in sixteenth-century Scholastic debates. Being labeled infidels, idolaters, or barbarians automatically excluded Amerindian societies from the Aristotelian and Thomist category of civil societies. Such a construction accorded indigenous societies a pre-social status and therefore made them legally subject to foreign rule and thus to political and social disenfranchisement.

In one of his main reformulations of Thomism, Francisco Suárez disputed the idea that civil law was derived from natural law. Suárez postulated that positive law was added for the government of humankind and was not derived from natural law. Thus, he de-emphasized the normative character of natural law in civil matters, separating human law from divine law. Suárez also defined the perfect community or potential state, regulated by civil law, as a community capable of possessing an independent political government, following Aristotle. Concomitantly, Suárez shared the Thomist idea that kings derive their power from the people, based on a general pact by which society subjects itself to a ruler. Since this is a human compact and not a divine design, this pact belongs to the realm of human law, and the ruler has no natural or divine right to rule. Subjects can withdraw their allegiance to kings according to the conditions of the compact. Suárez defined tyrannical rule as existing either when power is seized without just title or when a legitimate ruler abuses power and allows corruption, thereby neglecting the common good. In either case, the right to rebel or to depose a tyrannical king would be legitimate. The decision to dethrone or to kill a king, even a foreign king, could be taken by the council of the commonwealth.[12]

Perhaps one of the most consistent patterns in colonial Andean writings was the denunciation of the fact that royal laws favoring indigenous peoples had remained systematically unenforced for most of the colonial era, largely because of the neglect of church and state officials. Andeans tried to make the king aware of infringements of his laws by colonial officials. After their attempts failed, not surprisingly, the rebels in Huarochirí in 1750 and Túpac Amaru in 1781, among others, spoke openly and identified tyrannical rulers who ignored just laws as factors that triggered their rebellions.

The corpus of Scholastic and Neo-Scholastic ideas outlined earlier underlies Andean texts in several ways. A common theme in these texts is that the king allowed corruption and obstruction of the common good; then, the colonial system is construed as exemplifying tyrannical rule. The notions of common good and tyrannical rule appeared explicitly in the writings of the Jauja noble Jerónimo Lorenzo Limaylla, in the "Cinco memoriales" of the *cura doctrinero* Juan de Cuevas Herrera, and in the "Representación verdadera." These Andean scholars reformulated the idea of the common good as a form of social justice, an end to Andeans' marginalized position in colonial society, which they defined as the restitution of *cacicazgos* and lands to their original owners and relief from the *mita* in their seventeenth-century texts. Placing greater emphasis on noble Andeans' access to religious, political, and social institutions, writings in the eighteenth century saw justice in relief from the *repartimiento de comercio*, the abolition of *corregidores*, and reform of the justice system itself (see Chapter 6).

With the exception of the discourses of power articulated by Túpac Amaru and Juan Santos Atahualpa, the right to rebel or to depose the king was not explicitly formulated in the other Andean texts under study—although Amerindian thinkers were widely invested in substantiating tyranny at the level of colonial everyday life, expressing their desire to put an end to such tyranny. They felt entitled to participate in certain levels of government and assumed they had the right to seek the replacement of corrupt and negligent officials and to change laws they considered harmful or useless. More than direct rebellion, Andean writing advocated reform of the colonial justice system. Some Andean scholars, however, not only clandestinely supported specific rebellions but also spurred rebellion by others through their writings. Their overall goal was to attain a measure of ethnic autonomy in the face of their people's irretrievable loss of political authority. Within this framework, some core discussions gravitated around the justice and legitimacy of the first act of Spanish presence: the conquest and Spanish rule. To understand the ways Andeans partook in this discussion by utilizing and reformulating Scholastic and Neo-Scholastic tenets, a review of the debate on this matter, initiated by Fray Bartolomé de las Casas, is offered subsequently.

Beginning in the second half of the sixteenth century, the ideas of Vitoria, Suárez, and Casas were taught in the theology classes at Lima's University of San Marcos, mainly by Jesuits and Dominicans. Also at that university, Fray Domingo de Santo Tomás was an enthusiastic disseminator of Casas's ideas, while the Franciscan Jerónimo Valera from Chapapoyas introduced the Scholastic philosophy of Duns Scotus when he held the first chair of theology at San Marcos starting in 1701. Thus, the various positions within the Scholastic debate over the Spanish conquest were represented both at the University of San Marcos and in the *colegios mayores*. The Suaristas and Thomist approaches ultimately prevailed, as the Jesuits and Dominicans dominated the academic colonial environment.[13] At the same time, members of the indigenous and mestizo nobility were exposed to these teachings, as described in Chapter 1.

THE LEGITIMACY OF SPANISH RULE: THE DEBATE AMONG SPANISH THEOLOGIANS

Since the conquest years, the Spanish crown had been concerned with asserting and legitimizing its sovereignty in America, particularly after Casas's campaign against the *encomienda* system began. For the Catholic kings and many Spanish clerics and jurists in the conquest era, the legitimacy of the Spanish presence in the Americas rested on the 1493 bull by Pope Alexander VI, which granted the newly "discovered" territories to Spain and authorized the crown to conduct and control the evangelization effort.

Along with Father Antonio de Montesinos, Casas raised an indictment of the early colonizers' cruel exploitation of native Andeans, aware of the threat these practices represented for the success of evangelization. Casas's challenge stirred a trans-Atlantic debate over the crown's right to take over Indians' lands, resources, and political structures.[14] Sharing a view that gained support among some Spanish scholars in the late fourteenth century, medieval political philosophers believed "barbarians" (the "other") who did not live in "civil societies" were subject to the dominium, or *señorío*, of foreign rulers, who could make claims to sovereignty and property rights over their lands and other assets. Furthermore, a Christian sovereign could legitimately wage a "just war" if the subjects refused to acknowledge Christ or the papal authority.

Despite challenging Spanish conquistadors and advocating for the protection of Indians, Fray Bartolomé de las Casas was one of the first Europeans to introduce the discriminatory term "barbarian" to the New World and to apply it to indigenous peoples. In fact, in his *Apologética Historia Sumaria*, Casas classified barbarians into five categories: (1) those who demonstrated irrational behavior, unclear thinking, and degenerate customs; (2) those who could not articulate in their own languages theological or intellectual categories that existed in Latin; (3) those who lacked forms of government based on states and laws; (4) those who did not possess any of these qualifications but who were not Christian (infidels); and (5) those who, though not falling into any or all of the previous four categories, were invested in destroying Christianity (*barbarie contraria*). He decided that Amerindians belonged in the fourth category.[15] As a result, their freedom should be preserved and protected through "persuasive" methods of evangelization so they would become fully civilized and true Christians. According to the sixteenth-century Scholastics, *dominium*, as a right of possession, referred not only to property rights but also to control over people's actions, bodies, and liberty.[16] When it became clear that the Incas and the Aztecs had actually developed complex political societies, the Spanish right to *dominium* began to fall under scrutiny—although not until forty-seven years after the 1493 papal bull granted Spain rights of *dominium* over indigenous lands and polities and entrusted the crown with the conversion enterprise.

The situation took an interesting turn with the interjections of Francisco de Vitoria, who questioned the pope's authority to rule in temporal matters, raising doubts about the power of the 1493 bull to grant Spain sovereignty and property rights in America. Furthermore, according to Vitoria, even if native peoples refused to accept Christ and ignored the pope's authority, it was illegal to wage war on them and seize their property.[17] As long as Europeans viewed natives as irrational, the notion that only rational individuals and societies were entitled to the right of *dominium* defined the debate in favor of Spain's right of *dominium*. Rational beings were defined as those with full mental capacity to understand and do practical things, but Vitoria conceded that Native Americans, although "semi-animal," had "certain" rational characteristics. They were able to live in cities (polities), marry, and organize their own form of government. Because Amerindians had the rudiments of rationality, Vitoria maintained, all they needed was education to become "fully rational." They were not "natural slaves" but more like minors who, although totally entitled to *dominium*, were unable to exercise it fully for the time being. Therefore, the crown could legitimately exercise tutelage of native Andeans until they metaphorically came of age and attained their full status as rational beings. As part of its protective role, then, the crown would be entitled to retain them as subjects and to retain their assets in its possession.[18] Before the arrival of the Spaniards, Vitoria argued, Indians had been the true lords of the land and owners of their assets, both public and private. He concluded that even if the emperor had power over the entire world, he did not have the power to occupy the barbarians' territory, depose their lords, impose new ones, and subject them to tribute.[19]

The fact remained, however, that tutelage could not be preceded by conquest because tutelage is an act of charity, inconsistent with coercion. On the other hand, Vitoria defended Spaniards' right to travel overseas and to teach their religion; if not allowed to do so, he acknowledged, they were entitled to wage a just war against a tyrant to avenge the offense and defend innocents. Although it remained to be proven that Amerindians had offended the Spaniards and that the Spaniards had come in peace, Vitoria argued that waging war was illegal, that Native Americans were free subjects, and that the crown had rights of tutelage and sovereignty over them but no property rights whatsoever.[20]

Jerónimo de Mendieta, the Franciscan missionary and mystic who was convinced that the Americas were the place where the millennial kingdom of God would take place, was one of the foundational thinkers and writers in favor of justice for Indians. He most greatly influenced the thoughts of the Franciscan missionaries in Mexico, but he had great influence in Peru as well. Mendieta was a visceral critic of the *repartimiento* in Mexico, which violated precepts of both divine law and natural law, since native Andeans had surrendered peacefully to the "yoke" of Christianity. He defended the rights of Indians to hold private property and to succeed their ancestors in their *cacicazgos*.[21] Others, including Juan Ginés de Sepúlveda, maintained that the right of *dominium* only applied to those who had one king and a structured political organization, as well as to those who did not worship many gods and were familiar with natural laws. For them, native Andeans were "barbarians" and "natural slaves" who had been justly defeated in the conquest war. Sepúlveda in particular held that native Andeans' organizations were not truly political but only represented a blind adhesion to tyrants and, as such, were far from true republics. Therefore, it was legitimate to depose such rulers as Atahualpa and the Aztec emperor Montezuma, who allegedly did not seek the common good but rather only their personal good, thus losing their right to *dominium*. Their lands and resources, therefore, were lawfully seizable.[22] Among those who shared and disseminated Francisco de Vitoria's ideas in Peru were Fray Bartolomé de las Casas, Fray Domingo de Santo Tomás, and the Spanish lawyer Francisco Falcón.

Casas was best known for his critical views of conquistadors and his engagement in a debate with Sepúlveda over Indian slavery, which he advanced by pressing the crown to create the necessary laws to establish justice for Indians and restrain the power of *encomenderos* in America. The New Laws of 1542, forbidding Indian slavery and curtailing *encomenderos'* privileges, sought to progressively end the *encomienda* system. Although not completely effective, the New Laws were the king's response to the Lascasian indictments. Casas supported Vitoria's idea that even infidels had the right to possess land and other assets and the right to *señorío* over their own peoples. For Casas, both divine law and natural law entitled Amerindians to keep their property and natural lords. He was adamant that the Spaniards' inhumane behavior set a wrong example of Christianity, one native peoples would come to abhor and that would go against his approach of a gentle method of evangelization and teaching by example.

Licenciado Francisco Falcón, a Spanish scholar who wrote the "Representación de los daños y molestias que se hacen a los Indios"—an important treatise for the second Limeño Council of the Church in 1567—followed Casas by denying that a true conquest had ever taken place. Amerindians had willingly subjected themselves to Spanish rule. They did not understand the meaning of the *requerimiento* (a customary admonition of invaders, in Spanish, prompting Indians to surrender to Christianity) because of the language barrier. Instead of the *requerimiento*, native peoples witnessed conquistadors' violent invasion: "And, to the contrary, what they [Indians] saw was that [Spaniards] entered killing, stealing, and committing other crimes."[23] As a result, Falcón proposed that native Andeans were neither warned to abandon "idolatry" nor advised that Spaniards had come to put an end to it. Likewise, Garcilaso de la Vega, in his *Comentarios reales de los Incas* (1609), proposed that Andeans had surrendered peacefully to Pizarro and willingly accepted Spanish rule and Christianity. Guamán Poma de Ayala, Garcilaso's contemporary, also denied that any true Spanish conquest had taken place.[24] For Falcón, Pope Alexander VI's bull gave the crown the religious responsibility for converting Indians but no rights to expropriate their lands and exert political power. Because the Spanish crown had no legitimate right of *señorío*, the restitution of native Andeans' lands, resources, and political power was in order. Falcón went into great detail to demonstrate that the foundation of colonialism was illegal, and he implicitly proposed a negotiation with the king.

Native Andeans would accept Spanish rule as long as the tribute and *mita* systems were adjusted to closely resemble the preexisting Inca systems. While he used the Scholastic debate to turn against the legitimacy of Spanish rule, he sought to reestablish the Inca forms of social organization, which he considered fair.

The debate over the legitimacy of Spanish rule lost most of its impetus with Casas's death in 1566, the Indians' demographic decline, and the end of the missionary dream. The Spanish jurist Juan de Solórzano mediated and seemingly closed the debate in the seventeenth century, asserting that the 1493 bull gave Spain no rights of dominion. But since the Catholic kings were unaware of this ruling and acted in "good faith," assuming their invasion of America was legitimate, then it was so. According to Roman law, it was ultimately Spain's consistent presence in America over such a long period that in fact came to bestow the right of *dominium*.[25] Thus, Solórzano finally upheld legal Roman precepts over the 1493 papal bull.

THE DEBATE AMONG ANDEAN SCHOLARS

The historiography of the debates over just titles and Spain's right to remain in the Americas and rule the people there focused on the Spanish scholars' side of the debate. Some scholars even assumed that after the Toledan reforms the Spanish right of *dominium* was no longer questioned and that even those who supported Indian rights accepted the "just titles."[26] However, Andean scholars from the time of Guamán Poma de Ayala continued to dispute the legitimacy of Spanish rule as a result of implementation of the Toledan reforms. This section examines Andean scholarly discussions of the legitimacy of Spanish rule in the years following the Toledan reforms and throughout the eighteenth-century Bourbon reforms. As native structures of authority and the Indians' social condition were challenged in specific ways by both sets of reforms, Indian and mestizo writers revisited the debate over just titles to reinterpret and redefine their place in society.

Almost a century after Bartolomé de las Casas's campaign had gained momentum and while Viceroy Toledo's political and social reforms were still in full sway, a group of native and mestizo writers revived the dispute over Spain's right to conquer and colonize, particularly its right to displace Amerindian authorities from their positions of power and to appropriate lands, community labor, and other communal assets crucial for Amerindians' sustenance.[27] Andean intellectuals understood that their positions as the natural rulers of their indigenous constituencies would be most persuasively validated through Europeans' own notions of political legitimacy. In other words, they deliberately selected ideas and terms such as just war, natural law, divine law, and common good to validate their rights before the Spanish king. In the process, however, they displaced these concepts to a critical territory that not only de-legitimized the

Spanish conquest and its aftermath but also undermined the political purposes of the Toledan reforms.

Garcilaso de la Vega was probably the first Andean scholar to use the notion of natural law to legitimize the rule of the Inca, along with the argument that the Inca had been monotheistic before the Spanish arrival.[28] After Garcilaso, Don Felipe Guamán Poma de Ayala, in his *Nueva corónica y buen gobierno*, elaborated on divine law and natural law. He stated that the whole world belonged to God, but, within it, Castile belonged to Castilians as much as the Indies belonged to Indians and Guinea, in Africa, to blacks. In the Indies, Guamán Poma maintained, Castilians were foreigners, or *mitmaqs* in Quechua, and only the Indians were the "natural owners of this kingdom" (*propietarios naturales de este reino*). Guamán Poma developed his rationale by proposing that it was not the mandates of the king or the pope's bull that legitimized this design:

> Each one in his/her own kingdom is the legitimate proprietor, possessor, not by the king but by God and for the justice of God.... Thus, even if [the king] grants *merced* [awards] to the priest or a Spaniard who obtains *composiciones* [amended land titles], he is not the right proprietor[s]. Thus, they must pay obedience to the principal lords and justices who are the legitimate proprietors of the lands, be they lords or ladies. And all Spaniards, mestizos and mulattoes should honor them.... Thus, consider this, once for all: There is no [*encomendero*] or lord of the land but only us; we are the legitimate proprietors of the land by the law of God and by justice and laws.[29]

Guamán Poma masterfully maneuvered the issue of evangelization to delegitimize the plundering of Andean wealth and the abuses of *encomenderos* and miners. He denied that a conquest had taken place because Atahualpa did not resist the Spanish invasion and accepted Pizarro peacefully; therefore, native Andeans were not subjects because they had never been made subject to any conquest: "Atahualpa and Chalco Chima Quizo Yupanki died in the hands of the Christians of Don Francisco Pizarro ... the ambassadors ... of the conquest, sent by your majesty Don Carlos, and so, in the right time, the Christians charged, and the Indians did not defend themselves, and then they gave themselves in to your Majesty."[30] In other words, Andeans had obeyed the customary "Requerimiento." Guamán Poma reiterated the same point in different forms according to the various themes he addressed. When elaborating on the *encomenderos*, for example, he stated: "The said [*encomenderos*] should not be called [*encomenderos*] of Indians or conquistadors by a just right because they did not conquer the Indians. Rather, the Indians willingly and peacefully yielded to the crown."[31] Before Guamán Poma, both Casas and Mendieta had argued along the same lines in favor of the restitution of Indian *señoríos* and property.

In another instance, Guamán Poma maintained that when the Spanish "ambassadors" of the king (Pizarro and Almagro) arrived in Tumbes, Huascar sent

Guamán Poma's grandfather, Guamán Malque de Ayala, to make peace with them.[32] These ideas are consistent with his point that the discoverer of America was Saint Bartolomé, one of the apostles, who came from Jerusalem, had been preaching in the Andes before the Spaniards arrived, and returned during the time of Synchi Roca's rule over Cusco and Collao.[33] Thus, the Andeans already knew Christianity, since they had converted well in advance of Pizarro's arrival; therefore, they offered no resistance to Pizarro, and there was no need for conquest. Without questioning the king's right to rule, he charged that conquistadors had no right to subject Andeans to their control and that, therefore, the restitution of their stolen property was in order. Guamán Poma not only used a unique rendition of "divine law" to defend restitution, but he also denied the medieval principle of "just war" as applied to Andeans and categorized them as "old Christians," thus debunking the stereotype of Andeans as heathens. Sometime around 1667, Jerónimo Lorenzo Limaylla offered a similar rendition: "[B]ecause [the Indians] converted freely and spontaneously and without violence, they received willingly the faith."[34]

In the late seventeenth century, the mestizo and *cura doctrinero* Juan de Cuevas Herrera supported Guamán Poma's idea that there had been no conquest by reinterpreting the history of the Spanish conquest to empower the Inca religious tradition. Cuevas Herrera argued that rather than Pope Alexander VI's 1493 bull, there was a more solid foundation that legitimized Spain's just titles in the Americas. In an interesting adaptation of the Quetzalcoatl myth, he argued that through a revelation to the "Inca Viracocha," Pachacamac, the demiurge, prophesied the coming of the bearded, white, and blond people. Because they were allegedly bringing the "true religion," Pachacamac prompted the Andeans to surrender. Thus, the new kingdom of Peru was given to Castile by the "divine will" of Pachacamac: "The Inca left saying that doubtless it was the will of Pachacamac that these kingdoms were passed on to the Spaniards, and instructed his people to adjust to heaven's design."[35] By equating the "will of Pachacamac" with the "will of God," the writer ended up legitimizing Spanish rule in the Andes, saying it was God himself who gave the Spaniards these kingdoms "from [his] own hands."[36] At the same time, Cuevas Herrera tried to uplift Inca mythical stories and give them as much power as Christianity possessed. His narrative implicitly gives Pachacamac, the world maker, the same status as the Christian God, in spite of his Christian training as a *doctrinero*.

While these Andean intellectuals disputed the Spanish stories of just war and the legitimacy of Spain's takeover of the New World by denying that a conquest had taken place, others reelaborated the concept of natural law or natural rights to fight for the restitution of *cacicazgos* lost as a result of the conquest and consolidation of Spanish rule. The discussion that follows explicates the tenets of this debate, which gave theoretical strength to the formation of Andean discourses of ethnic autonomy under colonial rule.

THE "NATURAL RIGHT" TO ANDEAN SELF-GOVERNMENT

Perhaps the most developed contestation of Spanish rule is the thorough exposé of political autonomy that constitutes the core of the Andean Jerónimo Lorenzo Limaylla's texts. In his 1667 "Representación," late-medieval theological discourses were turned into rhetorical tools to reset the limits on native authority imposed by Toledo and to neutralize the wider effects of his reforms. This use of medieval theology as a salient feature of colonial Andean scholarship also informed the "Cinco memoriales" of Juan de Cuevas Herrera and served as the theoretical grounds of the "Representación verdadera" in 1749–1750. Even the edicts of Túpac Amaru in 1780–1781 and letters by *caciques principales* from different areas who struggled to validate their authority in the new era resorted frequently to such categories to legitimize their claims, as I have established. Each of the writers, however, used these tenets to promote different agendas that responded to the different times in which they lived.

Through a discussion of both natural and divine law, Limaylla intended to demonstrate that during the seventeenth century, the disenfranchisement of Indian authorities and the political subordination of native Andeans more generally were illicit. Following Francisco de Vitoria, Limaylla maintained that God created all people (not just Christians) in his image, giving them the power to rule over all other creatures who lacked reason; in this, God makes no distinction between believers and infidels. Therefore, all people have a "natural right" to all things on earth that emanated from "divine power"—including the right to rule, the ultimate expression of justice. Limaylla redefined this natural right as "a divine gift given to all men, both believer and infidel, because God did not distinguish between them. Thus, it is illicit to take away this natural right from anyone, even from the infidel, without just cause.... No ruler with a good sense of power and political authority may commit such injustice, breaking neither natural nor [d]ivine law without incurring in a crime and sin opposed to the virtue of justice."[37] By unproblematically equating Andeans with infidels, Limaylla implied that in taking away the Andeans' *cacicazgos*, Spaniards were committing a double transgression: they were infringing on human law and committing a sin against divine law. Therefore, in this estimation the conquest becomes both illegal and sinful.[38]

Limaylla "taught" the king a lesson in Scholastic political theology on the origin and legitimacy of rule. For him, government emanated from natural rights, an organizing principle that, through laws, moves everyone to prioritize the *bien común* (common good) over private interests. Displacing the notion of the natural right to rule from the original European context to the Andean peoples' struggles against the Toledan reforms, the writer directly empowered Andean natural lords: "Thus, both infidels and believers have jurisdiction over their subjects and peoples ... because both of them naturally formed congregations and cities. Therefore, just as it is natural for the believers to subject themselves to their superiors, it is the natural right of the infidel[s] to constitute, uphold, and give jurisdiction to their rectors, kings, and caciques to govern them, directing their actions to the common good. Because the natural right is common . . . the rights of the people are universal for all [n]ations."[39] By extending the natural law to the "republic" of the Indians, Limaylla invalidated the political displacement of the Andean lords, which intensified in the Toledan era: "Naturally, God has given Andeans the right to rule and freedom: All [n]ations and peoples, even the infidels, who possess lands and kingdoms . . . have the right to their freedom, and their kings and princes have the power given by their subjects . . . and their princes and lords are also free to govern them, preserving the precious immunity of their subjects' freedom and also their assets."[40] Andean *kurakas*, like European princes and infidel lords, had a legitimate right to rule their own communities. This natural right of Andeans to self-rule and to retain their assets offered further justification for the many petitions for restitution of community lands and *cacicazgos* and abolition of the *mita* that flooded the Council of the Indies, particularly during the seventeenth century.

To demonstrate that Andean lords were fully entitled to their *señorío*, it was also necessary to establish that they were not barbarians—namely, that reason guided their actions according to medieval Scholastic tenets. Entitlement to lordship within the confines of the Spanish empire was only accorded to Christian rulers; Limaylla understood the link between reason and Christianity at the time as extending this natural right:

> [Andeans] are rational men who have rational souls redeemed with Christ's blood; and God created them with special providence so that [they] may achieve this [spiritual] principal goal and thus be governed at the temporal and political level[s], directing the regime to their benefit. Because these [n]ations are free and they did not recognize lords and superior authorities other than those that, as lords, governed them, and because they converted freely and spontaneously without violence . . . [t]herefore, it is the obligation of the Spanish kings to seek the well-being of those who recognized them as kings, treating them as they would do with the rest of their vassals, preserving their life and freedom, without taking away their chiefdoms and their communal and personal property.[41]

Andeans were rational and Christian by their own free will, not by conquest. This rationality not only validated Andean lords' right to self-rule but also sustained their condition as free subjects and contested the harshness of the *mita*, an important issue in Limaylla's texts. The "peaceful and spontaneous conversion"—a recurrent argument in Casas, Guamán Poma, and other Andean writings—reappears here, denying the conquest and Andeans' condition as "colonized" and suggesting a subtext of Andean elites' political autonomy in their own social and territorial spaces.

In the colonial situation in the Andes in the late seventeenth century, conversion to Christianity appears in Limaylla's texts as a case of negotiated reciprocal benefits—a colonial resignification of the Andean *mañay*—between the Spanish colonizers and Andean lords that would guarantee the latter the possibility of continuing to rule their ethnic communities, the chance to recover their lands and communal assets, and access to prestigious organizations in return for their acceptance of Christianity. More specifically, the notion of reciprocity that Andeans advanced in colonial times, although within a hierarchical framework, accepted colonial obligations in exchange for access to certain basic rights that secured an expected level of cultural and social community reproduction through increased population and other factors, as well as access to the legal system that protected those rights. The unevenness of the reciprocal arrangement was not the key issue because Andeans had been used to such an arrangement since Inca times.[42] For Limaylla, the abusive intrusion of Spanish officials and priests, who took over Indian labor and lands and attempted to replace ethnic chiefs with handpicked ones, was a violation of this reciprocal agreement by the Spaniards. The ultimate rhetorical strategy in the "Representación" was to stress the effects of such violations by persuading the king of the threat runaways, or *relapsos*, posed to the success of the religious and social control of Andeans:

> The kings of Spain are obligated to preserve [the Indians'] natural lordships and property so that they [the Indians] don't feel the Christian faith and religion to be burdensome, ominous, and horrible, which, in any case, would be the fault of those who turned a law that was based on love and charity into a strenuous law. Therefore, the king should defend them from the extortion, vexations, and humiliations they suffer, by applying justice so that [the Indians] do not slip back into idolatry, out of desperation and for distrust of the remedy, feeling that worshipping false Gods would be better than losing their souls' salvation, thus wasting the purpose of evangelization.[43]

Political displacement would cause the Andeans to revert back to idolatry, putting the entire evangelization effort at risk. Thus, the call was for the king to reestablish balance through justice.

Andean perceptions of colonialism and the relationships between the king and his native subjects in Peru were also informed by European history and political culture. Fray Calixto de San José Túpac Inca and his coauthors in 1749–1750 discussed at length the discrimination against Andeans in the major colonial institutions. They uncovered the workings of colonial discriminatory attitudes toward Andeans by casting Spanish rule as an essentially Machiavellian, exclusionary regime: "Is this not a practice of Machiavellianism, this policy that the Spanish Catholic government has insensibly introduced, whose slogan is 'the [s]overeigns who pretend the absolute rule of their domains should exclude the original dwellers from offices, titles, and power positions,' and if they show sentiments for this affront, the sovereigns must destroy them and sweep them all away?"[44] The Andean friar infers here that Machiavelli's practice of fomenting factionalism within the Roman Empire inspired Spaniards to introduce odious distinctions among Spaniards, creoles, native Andeans, and mestizos—thus promoting enmity, disunity, and social inequality. Behind using allegories to Machiavelli to represent Spanish rule is an understanding of that rule as tyranny, a disruption of the kingdom's natural order of social balance. Such a rendition of social harmony between the king and his subjects was usually represented by the Aristotelian idea, further developed in medieval times, that the state is an "organic" *corpus politicum mysticum*. By naturalizing the social order and sustaining the status quo, the idea of the organic body politic is that, as with the human body, the kingdom is an integrated whole in which all the parts are equally necessary and naturally bonded; the ruler (the head) and the subjects (the limbs) are bound together by nature because without any of them the kingdom is neither healthy nor functional. Likewise, when problems emerge, the body of the kingdom needs a "medico," usually the ruler, who can cure the malaise.

In colonial Andean writing, however, the metaphor of the body politic was reframed to represent the fracture of reciprocity and the social disharmony within the kingdom and to subtly point to the responsibility of the king:

> The oldest disease of the body politic has occurred when the truth does not find its way to the head. [In this case, the head] rarely knows even the basics ... and this piece of the gigantic body of the empire ... is so in pain, that I think it is sick and in grave danger, and if prompt and effective remedy is not applied, chances are the malaise will become incurable.... [Ultimately] this body is so sick that it is imperative to sever and cut off its individual pieces to cure it, reform it, and heal it.[45]

Limaylla's "Representación" echoes Cuevas Herrera's claim, prompting the king: "It is not possible that as they represent the disease to you, you fail to cure it, as the medico that you are; and as a father, you are supposed to defend their rights. ... [I]t is worthless to know the power of the medicine ... if it is not applied individually to the sick. Thus, the sick lose their lives and he who was supposed to be the medico and to heal the sick body ... himself turns out to be the murderer."[46] This language subtly merges a critique of the colonial officials with a critique of the king himself as the "head" of the kingdom and the authority ultimately responsible for the situation of Andean subjects, the sick "limbs" of the empire.

The "Machiavellian" officials constituted the tyrannical anomaly of the body politic. The representation of Spanish rule as tyranny is one of the connecting threads in all of the Andean discursive production beginning in the 1600s with

Guamán Poma, Cuevas Herrera, and Limaylla and extending through Vélez de Córdoba, Fray Calixto, Atahualpa, and Túpac Amaru II in the eighteenth century. As a generic image of Spanish rule, tyranny was directed by Andeans—in different ways according to the different conjunctures of each period—against *curas*, prelates, officials, and Spanish elites as violators of accepted norms of reciprocity, which measured their notion of justice.

CONCLUSION

Andean discussions of the nature of Spanish rule and their relationship with the king and his representatives were rooted in late-medieval political theologies. They further developed such theories to strengthen the political and moral foundations of an Andean discourse of justice. However, Andean scholars framed these principles in terms of their traditional notions of reciprocity, which guaranteed them access to certain rights and opportunities as they adopted the notions of European culture. By defining that Andeans had natural rights to self-rule and to own property, by prompting the king to enforce these universal principles to maintain the common good, by constructing Andeans as people of reason and rationality, and by translating divine law as revelations to "the" Inca god, an implicit cultural negotiation is presented in which European theologies and notions of rule are used to support Andean agendas of self-rule. This construction allowed the intellectuals under study to question the foundational acts of Spanish rule in America and its religious and juridical justification. Thus, the reworking of these Scholastic and Neo-Scholastic tenets also gave theological, ethical, and political force to Indian authorities' struggles for the restoration of *cacicazgos* and community property, which would secure the survival of their world. In employing such concepts, these colonial Andean writers argued that Spanish rule in the Andes was illegitimate and that the Toledan reforms were illicit because they violated fundamental natural rights that should be restored by the king to remedy the tyrannical nature of his rule. Such rights were the reciprocal benefit Andeans deserved for having accepted the rule of Christian kings and officials along with their religious demands, a kind of reformulated, pre-colonial *mañay* in colonial times.

The redeployment of European theological and legal ideas by these Andean intellectuals renders their scholarship an intriguing form of trans-culturation that reflects the productive trans-Atlantic and cultural interaction of which Indian and mestizo ladinos from Peru were part and parcel during the mid- and late-colonial years. Beyond their contribution to the development of Scholastic ideas from an Andean point of view, these thinkers destabilized ("subverted them from within") such concepts even as they used them to unveil the illegitimacy of the Spanish practices of rule that challenged Andeans' condition as free subjects of the empire and sought to strip from them their traditional political authority. As represented in Andean writings, these practices excluded or "severed" native Andeans from the kingdom's "body" and left them outside the colonial "reciprocal" bond between the king and his subjects.

As Andean intellectuals contested the obliteration of Andean power and community organization by the Toledan policies, the scholarly elaboration discussed in this chapter also contributed to the formation of an Andean discourse of ethnic autonomy. This elaboration also sought to legitimate the recurrent critiques of colonial injustice that enriched a preexisting tradition of protest in colonial Peru. To grasp the richness and cultural agency of Andean protest discourses, the motives, rhetorical strategies, and intertextuality behind the critiques of the colonial legal system are discussed in Chapter 5.

NOTES

1. Ortiz, "Contrapunto cubano del tabaco y el azúcar."

2. Pratt, *Imperial Eyes*, 6.

3. Certeau, *The Practice of Everyday Life*, 31–32.

4. The general review of ideas that follows is by no means an in-depth rendition or discussion of the ideological corpus in question or the debates in which such theories were embedded, nor does it attempt to present a history of those schools of thought. In this brief introduction to the tenets of these philosophies, only the concepts relevant to the discussions of the colonial Andean texts under consideration will be outlined.

5. Aquinas, "On Law and Natural Law," 616. Aquinas believed, however, that toleration of tyranny was less dangerous than opposition or rebellion. Reijo, *Social and Political Theory of Francisco Suárez*, 12.

6. Aquinas, "On Law and Natural Law," 614–615.

7. Ibid., 621.

8. Reijo, *Social and Political Theory of Francisco Suárez*, 7–18, 29.

9. Barreda Laos, *Vida Intelectual del Perú*, 89.

10. On the social and cultural implications of the colonial definition of indigenous individuals as minors of age within Spanish patriarchal relationships in colonial Peru, see Premo, *Children of the Father King*, 19–42, 92–97.

11. "Representación verdadera," 157. In Roman law, the foundation of Spanish laws, "reason" was the basis of natural rights, and only civilized people were defined as people of reason. Thus, only civilized peoples were entitled to political and social rights.

12. Barreda Laos, *Vida Intelectual del Perú*, 14, 18, 37–38, 52, 80–86.

13. Ibid., 95.

14. The contours of this debate are described here following Pagden, *El imperialismo español y la imaginación política,* chapter 1, "Desposeer al bárbaro: Derechos y propiedad en la América española." The work of Vitoria is also interspersed; Vitoria, *Reflecciones sobre los indios.*

15. Mignolo, *The Idea of Latin America*, 17–20.

16. Pagden, *El imperialismo español y la imaginación política*, 36.

17. Vitoria, *Reflecciones sobre los indios*, 80.

18. Pagden, *El imperialismo español y la imaginación política*, 42.

19. Vitoria, *Reflecciones sobre los indios*, 73.

20. Pagden, *El imperialismo español y la imaginación política*, 44.

21. Phelan, *Millennial Kingdom of the Franciscans in the New World*, 98–100. Mendieta was probably one of the first writers to compare the image of the Jews' slavery under the Egyptians with the oppression of Indians, an image that permeated virtually all of the Andean texts studied in this book.

22. Pagden, *El imperialismo español y la imaginación política*, 50.

23. BNM [ca. 1567], Falcón, "Representación de los daños y molestias que se hacen a los Indios," 220–237v.

24. "Unlike the first Spaniards . . . [they were] conquered neither with weapons nor with bloodshed or effort." Guamán Poma de Ayala, *Nueva corónica y buen gobierno*, 167, 395[397]; also in 358, 386[388].

25. Pagden, *El imperialismo español y la imaginación política*, 62.

26. Estenssoro Fuchs, *Del paganismo a la santidad*, 463.

27. Adorno's assertion that Guamán Poma was one of the few Andeans who took part in the debates about the conquest and colonization and left a written record (Adorno, "Felipe Guamán Poma de Ayala," 86) should be reconsidered. As discussed in this chapter, several known Andean intellectuals, including Cuevas Herrera and Limaylla in the 1650s–1660s and Fray Calixto de San José Túpac Inca in 1749–1750, among others, engaged in written discussions of the "just titles" and questioned the legitimacy of the Spanish presence in the Americas.

28. Vega, *Comentarios reales de los Incas*, 60–62.

29. Guamán Poma de Ayala, *Nueva corónica y buen gobierno*, 857–858, 894, 915[929], 958[972].

30. Ibid., 141, 162[164].

31. Ibid., 520–521, 550[564].

32. Ibid., 894, 957[971].

33. Ibid., 342, 368[370].

34. Limaylla, "Representación," 224.

35. Cuevas Herrera, "Cinco memoriales," 219–219v.

36. Ibid.

37. Limaylla, "Representación," 214v–215.

38. Similar elaboration of these "natural rights" to self-rule appeared in letters from *caciques principales* from La Paz, contemporaries of Limaylla, who confronted the functionaries of the Audiencia of La Plata and the provincial government in 1650 over the dispossession of Andeans through dubious *composiciones de tierras*. *Caciques* and *gobernadores* Don Cristóbal Nina, Don Pedro Santos, and Don Juan Quispe claimed that their rights to *dominium* were part of the natural rights pertaining to "all men of the world, either the believers or the infidel, friends or enemies, vassals of Christian princes or pagan ones, Catholics or otherwise." AGI, "Escrito de los Indios de la Paz," Marzo 30, 1650.

39. Limaylla, "Representación," 217–218.

40. Ibid., 219v–220.

41. Ibid., 223v.

42. Stavig, *The World of Túpac Amaru*, xxvii.
43. Limaylla, "Representación," 225.
44. "Representación verdadera," 164.
45. Cuevas Herrera, "Cinco memoriales," 267, 269.
46. Limaylla, "Representación," 238v–239.

❧ 5 ❧

ANDEAN DISCOURSES OF JUSTICE

The Colonial Judicial System under Scrutiny

For modern scholars, the work of Felipe Guamán Poma de Ayala and the increasing amount of Indian litigation in the royal courts initiated the tradition of social criticism by colonized subjects in the Andes. This tradition continued and was developed beyond Guamán Poma's time by the mid- and late-colonial scholars studied in this book. The textual work of these later Andean authors is permeated by recurrent critiques of key aspects of Spanish rule, which express their understanding of the colonial crisis in the seventeenth century and the impact of the changes introduced in the eighteenth century to resolve it. The critiques appear in their texts often as a prelude to the enunciation of specific changes or reforms they deemed necessary to restore social balance, a format similar to the *memoriales* of Fray Bartolomé de las Casas in the first half of the sixteenth century.[1] The critical approaches of these writers delve into the continued ineffectiveness of the justice system and provide a record of the conflicting relationships of Indians vis-à-vis colonial authorities and the church from the perspective of Andeans themselves.

This chapter focuses on the discursive construction of Andean critiques of the colonial system, from approximately 1650 to the 1780s, which centered in the institution of *corregidores*, the *mita* system, and the colonial church.[2] Since Andean scholarship did not exist in an isolated discursive circuit but instead formed part of a wider, usually subtle intellectual dialogue (intertextuality) among creole, clerical, and enlightened discourses in the Viceroyalty of Peru, the chapter's last section reviews the main lines along which such dialogue occurred. Andean scholars selected models of criticism embedded in the writings of Fray Bartolomé de las Casas and missional narratives, which used biblical images and, most commonly, the "Lamentations" of the prophet Jeremiah as persuasive rhetoric to prompt the king to reverse the social imbalance in the Andes. The trope of *agravios y vejaciones* (offenses and hardships) inflicted upon "defenseless" Indians thus became a staple in the narratives used to criticize the colonial justice system. Andean intellectuals, however, used such models to support an agenda that diverged from that of Casas, the ecclesiastical missionaries, and Guamán Poma, stressing instead the need to empower Andean nobles socially. During the colonial period, creoles, "enlightened" officials, and ecclesiastic *letrados* criticized the state with a similar rhetoric while seeking to revamp the evangelization project, support state reform, and, most important, strengthen the empire. As this almost inadvertent dialogue took place, the *letrados* occasionally appropriated Andean knowledge and experience to construct discourses in support of societal reforms that differed from Andeans' goals, thus partaking in the subtle relationships of power that took place in the "lettered city," a space intellectual Andeans accessed in rather contentious ways. A sector of local creoles did occasionally support Andean agendas and ally with Andeans politically. Thus, their texts are more closely linked to Andean scholarship.

CRITIQUE OF THE *CORREGIDOR*

One of the major transformative events in the relationship between Spaniards and Indians occurred with the introduction of the *corregidor* in the second half of the sixteenth century, a royal effort to curtail the power of *encomenderos*. The relationship between Spanish *corregidores* and Andeans was the epitome of the multifarious conflicts arising from the everyday reenactment of colonialism. The networks of colonial power that linked *corregidores*, lieutenant *corregidores*, miners, *hacendados*, merchants, *obraje* owners, priests, and even *caciques* and *protectores de naturales* appeared within the field of Andean political awareness and became the target of criticism in Andeans' texts.[3]

A few decades after Guamán Poma's work and more concerned with the failure of evangelization in Charcas, Juan de Cuevas Herrera carried on this critical tradition toward the mid- and late seventeenth century, representing abusive and corrupt *corregidores* as "non-Christian" and "enemies of God," the king, and the royal treasury. But most important, he regarded these officials as a plague who threatened the stability of the empire:

> Corregidores are a pest that consume Indians and won't stop until they finish them all . . . and Y. M. [Your Majesty] sustains these kind of judges at the expense of thousands of your royal treasury. They are declared enemies of God, Y. M., disguised as ministers, [enemies of] your royal treasury, and the preservation of this kingdom. . . . They are people who enter their posts through the door of sacrilege and exit through that of [a]theism.[4]

The mestizo parish priest directly questioned the king about wasting money on sustaining "anti-Christian" *corregidores*. Cuevas Herrera devoted one of his five *memoriales* to a description of the malfeasance of *corregidores*, emphasizing defrauds of the royal treasury, violence against Indians in the collection of tribute, and, most important, the illegal introduction of *repartos* in Chuquisaca in the late seventeenth century and the series of abuses that accompanied it—all of which gave Andeans an inaccurate image of Christians and their religious ways.[5]

The practice of *repartos* was consolidated in the Andes in the eighteenth century, and another Andean scholar from Lambayeque, the *cacique* and *procurador de naturales* Don Vicente Morachimo, directed the thrust of his reports toward the evils of the *corregidores* and their *repartos*. He asserted that *corregidores* charged excessive fees for goods detrimental to the Indians' health. He also denounced the practices of *corregidores* and their lieutenants from the Province of Collao in the 1730s—who compelled *caciques* to pay overdue fees for the *repartos*, confiscated their property, and jailed them—while forcing numerous Indians to transport merchandise long distances without paying the appropriate costs.[6] During the extirpation campaigns, Cuevas Herrera accused *corregidores* of being indirectly responsible for the failure of evangelization, whereas Morachimo associated the weakness of Indians' conversion to Catholicism with the violence of the system of *repartos* in the first decades of the 1700s:

> I consider that the Indians are annihilated because of the harsh treatment of corregidores. Without exception, all [c]orregidores put out at the very least between a hundred thousand to two hundred thousand pesos in repartos in the small provinces every two years. . . . From this, one infers, Lord, this is the end for the Indians. They [the Indians] get inebriated . . . and do other things and even if they do not lack knowledge of our holy Catholic faith, they can always quit it because they are not treated like fellow-creatures and they experience the opposite to what is taught to them, and all goes here against the holy commands, laws and ordinances on this matter.[7]

The corroboration of the manifold corruption among *corregidores* in different periods substantiated the Andean critique of colonial institutions of justice more generally. The focus on the ways official corruption often resulted in violence, defrauding the royal treasury and causing Indians to escape to the mountains and relapse to idolatry, strengthened Andeans' claim that the position of *corregidor* should be abolished. *Corregidores* were accused of transferring tribute funds to cover unpaid *repartos*, and the Andean authorities who denounced these crimes lost their chiefdoms, as *corregidores* replaced them or even sent them to jail. For example, Morachimo denounced the imprisonment of the *kuraka* Joseph Chuquiguanca, from the Azángaro *repartimiento*, for opposing abuses by the local *corregidor* and the imprisonment of Marcos Javier Copacondori, *cacique* from the town of Asillo, and a *cacique* from Carabaya Province for similar reasons.[8]

Andean writers indicated that *corregidores* directed their violence toward the more vulnerable social groups, such as indigenous women, elders, widows, young girls, and particularly the poor. They explained how women were forced to work in *obrajes* and Spanish households, which prevented them from taking care of their own households and plots. Juan de Cuevas Herrera in particular provided abundant denunciations regarding women forced into concubinage by *corregidores* and lieutenant *corregidores*, who took advantage of their position to sexually abuse and deprive these women of their small assets and resources. When widows and other poor women appealed for justice, *corregidores* often deceived and mistreated them because they were mostly illiterate, poor, and perceived as weak.[9]

The writers understood that official corruption undermined the social and economic interests of Andean communities, attacking the collusion among judges, *visitadores, corregidores*, viceroys, and other elite Spaniards. According to Morachimo's accusations, for example, these networks covered up violations of royal laws mandating the good treatment of Indians and obstructed the upper levels of justice by *oidores* (*audiencia* judges) and viceroys in the 1730s. Morachimo explained in detail the various transgressions of individual laws by these officials and substantiated them with concrete cases he knew from regions such as the Chicama Valley (Trujillo), Guacho (Chancay), El Cercado (Lima), Potosí (Charcas), Chiclayo (Piura), Asillo (Azángaro), Langasica (Huarochirí), Carabaya, Chachapoyas, and Huancavelica.[10] Thus, given the nature of his job as *procurador de naturales* and his concern with the plight of Indians, Morachimo had a wider view of the anomalies within the colonial justice system.

The increasing replacement of hereditary lords with *caciques* who more readily acquiesced to the *corregidores'* demands led to a deterioration of ethnic authority and was still a critical issue in the late seventeenth century. By then, critiques of these colonial *caciques*, perceived as little more than members of the colonial state, showed up frequently in Andean texts. Juan de Cuevas Herrera's "Cinco memoriales" launched the harshest critiques against nonhereditary *caciques* in Charcas Province. They were invariably represented as "a necessary evil."[11] *Caciques* and *kurakas* added to the Indians' *agravios y vejaciones*: "Kurakas are the domestic enemies from the day the Indian is born until he dies: they are one enemy that comprises three: world, devil, and flesh."[12] This description followed the general tone of the critique of *corregidores* and delved into a series of similar accusations. To highlight the decadence of the *caciques* of his time, Cuevas Herrera exalted the virtues of the old native chieftains: "The old caciques were men of authority, capacity and Christianity ... versed in the Spanish language and Latin, beautiful musicians, escribanos, and accountants ... and above all they were very zealous of the [d]ivine [c]ult."[13] The mestizo scholar constructed the Indian past as a seamless, harmonic time, with no conflicts between Indian authorities and their constituencies. These disparate images of Indian authorities attest to the changes Spanish colonialism introduced in the Andean communities in the Province of Charcas, where Cuevas Herrera served as a *doctrinero*, and also speak to Cuevas Herrera's internalization of colonial culture, as well as his longing for peaceful coexistence between Spaniards and Andeans.

In the first decades of the eighteenth century, as litigation against the abusive *repartimiento de comercio* increased, attacks on the colonial judicial system focused on the inefficiency of the crown's mechanisms to oversee the conduct of the judges and *corregidores* most responsible for the failure of law enforcement. Morachimo explained, for example, that the 1722 royal decree, intended to end such abuses by *corregidores*, in reality only submitted them to a formal *residencia* (review of office), itself plagued by corruption in the form of a colluding alliance of inspectors and *corregidores*.[14] To substantiate his indictment of the justice system, Morachimo cited each law violated as supporting evidence of the social unrest generated by abusive colonial officials, especially judges and *visitadores*.[15]

The list of law violations that generated violence and protest, according to Morachimo's "Manifiesto," was rather long, but only a few instances suffice to give a sense of the range of issues he chose to illustrate the ineffectual nature of colonial justice for Andeans. An ordinance of the *real audiencia* from May 20, 1722, approved the free use of the main square by Indians so they could participate in Lima's market. According to the Andean *procurador*, since 1730, Andeans had been forced to pay two silver reales a day to use those spaces.[16] The following decade problems reached a critical point as the Bourbons sought to rationalize and regulate the use of urban public spaces; as a result, Indian vendors were banned from such spaces.[17] Morachimo also denounced a second *ordenanza* (ordinance), contained in Book 2[6], Title 18[12] on personal service (from the "Recopilación"), that prohibited the use of Indian labor in sugar mills and textile workshops and also went unenforced: "In spite of the prohibition, the corregidores pressure caciques to send Indians to the obrajes where they are paid in food and cloth, thus the Indians remain in a status of perpetual slavery."[18]

Morachimo and Fray Calixto de San José Túpac Inca denounced the same alleged violations of laws by *corregidores*, including the exemption of Andeans from the *alcabala*, payment of travel expenses for those serving the mining *mita*, the prohibition against assigning *mita* workers to *corregidores* and other ministers, legislation outlawing physical punishment and torture in *obrajes*, and legal enforcement of the *arancel* (legal wage for *mita* workers). Exhaustive discussions of the failure of the colonial judicial system and the inefficacy of government authorities eventually led to attacks on the king for his "tyranny" and negligence. As explained in Chapter 3, the social critique of Spanish government in the "Representación verdadera" appears enveloped in the sophisticated rhetoric of the prophet Jeremiah's "Lamentations," clearly conveyed in this passage:

> But, what a disgrace!, my lord, that the doors of justice are closed for us, and we find your justice neither in you or your ministers nor in your bishops or pastors, who are there only to impede that our lamentations and complaints reach you.... The crown has fallen down from our heads.... Jeremiah cried as though saying: for our sins we are in such devastation that it seems we do not have a king. And your vassals the Indians cry the same thing, lord, because even though we have a pious, Spanish and Christian Catholic king, we are treated as though we had none, and [as though] there was no king for them [the Indians] because they cannot see him, neither talk to him.... Therefore, what we experience is a violent, hard, cruel and tyrant government, which the king's ministers have invented, and very different from what has been practiced in all Catholic kingdoms and from the honest intention of the king.[19]

The use of Jeremiah here softens the criticism of the monarch for overlooking the plight of his Indian subjects. Since the king and his officials failed to provide the expected protection to Andean subjects, they behaved as tyrants. Andean writers, however, were usually cautious and launched subtle attacks against a distant crown, only to follow them with anxious insistence that he was not responsible for the "tyranny" of his representatives in Peru. In the face of officials' protracted negligence and the inefficient system of law, Andean scholars presented themselves as the true guardians of justice in the kingdom by reclaiming the freedom to travel to Spain to inform the king about the state of law enforcement.[20] This concern is consistent with the previously mentioned efforts to have Indians appointed as *protectores de naturales* and *escribanos*.

The social crisis generated by the *repartos* escalated with the reforms of Charles III in the 1760s, particularly the fiscal reforms, making the limits of colonial justice for Andean subjects abundantly clear. Thus, the boundaries between peace and war in the Andes became rather thin. When peaceful efforts fell short of obtaining justice, upheavals erupted in pursuit of aims virtually identical to those Andean scholars attempted through petitions and critiques. Several times during the seventeenth century, Andeans attempted rebellions to put an end to the *mita* system, and more consistent rebellions in the late eighteenth century were focused on rejecting the *reparto* system and the Bourbon reform efforts. In the midst of the most violent challenge to Spanish rule, in 1780–1781, José Gabriel Condorcanqui Túpac Amaru II's discourses of social justice (protest against the *agravios y vejaciones* inflicted upon Andeans) drew upon the social and political subordination of common Andeans to advance a wider program of Andean power. His Inca messianism served as a rallying ideology that helped create a multi-ethnic alliance for rebellion. The fact that other Andeans had voiced most of Túpac Amaru's ideas prior to 1780 does not undermine the importance of his discourses of anti-colonial rebellion. The rebel leader and scholar placed previous Andean discourses within the framework of open rebellion against colonial injustice—a textual synthesis conveyed in the language of force that encompassed not only the 1781 upheaval but also the wave of localized uprisings, conspiracies, and rebellions that preceded it.

The opposition to *corregidores* and the textual representation of these colonial officials' evil nature were unanimous among leaders of the Great Rebellion, who used canonical texts to advance their social critiques and views of change. Túpac Amaru's brother Diego Cristóbal, for example, reiterated in his letters that *corregidores* abused Indians, forcing upon them the *repartimiento* of useless items at exorbitant prices. *Repartos* never did conform to the official rates or to the correct quantity or quality. Diego Cristóbal announced that "the covetousness of corregidores and other *mandones* [imposed *caciques*, amenable to *corregidores'* will] was so blind and disproportionate that they had no other interest than their personal benefit, thus forfeiting entirely the conversion, conservation, and good treatment of the *naturales*." He proposed instead that the best strategy for social justice, "the spiritual and temporal conservation of the subjects," was a "pacific and gentle treatment," which had been advised since the times of Roman figures such as Tito Libio and Seneca. According to Diego Cristóbal, Saint Paul had also warned that "covetousness was the devil's lure, which unleashes harmful desires and is the root of all evil.... The main harvest that should be collected from Indians must be their conversion, teaching, and conservation, since that is why the special providence of God entrusted Indians to the protection of the faithful, Christian, and Catholic monarchs from Spain."[21]

Thus, in moments of deep social unrest, scholars and rebels shared similar views of the colonial establishment and seem to have been grounded in similar rhetorical strategies. The use of canonical literature and legal discourses and the rejection of abusive colonial practices help us understand the links between Andean scholarship and rebellion in the eighteenth-century conjunctures of social crisis. It then becomes understandable why political aims that most believe were first voiced during the Túpac Amaru Rebellion, such as the abolition of Spanish *corregidores* and their replacement by Indian judges, originated much earlier, as will be explained in more detail in Chapter 6.

ANDEAN CRITIQUES OF THE COLONIAL CHURCH

The fact that most of the Andean writers under study were members of the lower church in different capacities makes the pattern of textual critiques of such an institution more striking or perhaps most understandable. One of the most intriguing features of these critical narratives is the coexistence of Christian and anti-clerical discourses and these scholars' ability to question the evangelization strategy without compromising their claim for inclusion in the church. The purpose of this criticism was to expose how the behavior of corrupt and abusive church members contradicted their spiritual mission. The writers sought to prove that deviant *doctrineros*' and prelates' wrongdoings further perpetuated the subordination and degradation of Andean women and men. The critique of colonial Christianity explained later foregrounds the racial issues underlying the social practices of ecclesiastic members in the New World, as seen by colonial Andean writers. In their eyes, the Roman Catholic Church became a colonial institution rather than one that truly promoted spirituality and equality for Andeans. In the end, Andean scholars defined the decadence of church officials in Peru as the major cause of the evangelization project's failure: Indians' running away to the "montaña," at the margins of the Christian world, to get away from social injustice is a common theme in Andean writings throughout the colonial period and across different regions of the Viceroyalty of Peru.

Among the leading scholars who articulated the most thorough and complex criticism of the church, Juan de Cuevas Herrera composed his works primarily in Charcas Province toward the end of his long service as a *doctrinero*, in the years following the major extirpation campaigns of the seventeenth century in the Archbishopric of Lima, when the failure of these campaigns to uproot Andean "idolatry" was more apparent. Cuevas Herrara called attention to the relaxation of moral behavior within the church and warned about the impending danger this represented for sustaining the program to Christianize Indians.

In discussing the extirpation officials' misbehavior, church historian Kenneth Mills described how the moral orientation of the Council of Trent found expression in the process of extirpation of idolatries in the Lima archdiocese. He argued that ecclesiastic officials' questionable morality debilitated the structure of a purification program whose foundations lay in the moral superiority of the church ideology and ministers. Mills highlighted the fact that prominent church figures were aware of this misbehavior and the problems it posed for the success of Indian conversion.[22] Juan de Cuevas Herrera, a lower church figure, seems to have been well aware of this anomaly, as he partook in the criticism of *curas doctrineros*' and extirpation officials' misconduct. As opposed to Mills's thesis, however, Cuevas Herrera, a *cura doctrinero* himself, did not ultimately place the blame on Andeans' "errors." In Cuevas Herrera's narrative, the actual "bad Christians" were the Spanish priests and officials rather than Andeans; his "Cinco memoriales" endeavored to demonstrate that responsibility for the hurdles in the evangelization process in seventeenth-century Charcas lay in the ways of the church itself. In line with Mills's thesis, nevertheless, this section demonstrates that Cuevas Herrera's texts represent the conscious effort of Andeans from within the lower church to fight back against the Lima church's moralizing campaign by "redeploying" Christian morality. Cuevas Herrera essentially put the magistrates of the sacred in front of their own "mirrors" of morality, which the Tridentine church had deployed upon them and the faithful.[23] He recast *curas doctrineros* and inspectors of idolatry as "sinners" in need of reformation and, in turn, called for a figurative purification campaign against them to regenerate the kingdom: "[Ultimately], this body [kingdom] is so sick that it is imperative to sever and cut its individual pieces to cure it, reform it, and heal it."[24] As opposed to the corrupt church officials, Cuevas Herrera presented himself as the true model of virtue and restraint; overall, he upheld Andeans as morally superior to Spanish clerics and other officials.

Cuevas Herrera's work discusses the crisis of evangelization, which he referred to as the "mortal accidents of this kingdom" or the "impediments for the full conversion of Indians" in the subtitle of "Cinco memoriales."[25] The *doctrinero* argued that the conversion program was doomed by its own structural weaknesses and those of the colonial system more generally: the negligence and inefficiency of the high prelates in charge of overseeing conversion, coupled with the ineptitude of *curas doctrineros*, the excesses of *corregidores*, and the overexploitation of *mitayos*, yielded a thin "harvest" of true Christian souls among Andeans.

The first of his five *memoriales* was intended to demonstrate that most *curas doctrineros* had not met the qualifications required or fulfilled their duties correctly as "fathers, pastors, masters, tutors, and defenders." He was adamant that *doctrineros* must be primarily men of letters and proficient in the language of the Indians.[26] Cuevas Herrera questioned the irregular methods used in the selection of *curas doctrineros* and linked the "bad administration of the gospel" to the damage caused to the Indians' souls and salvation. He tried to move the king to action: "Oh great lord! Oh Catholic monarch! Oh pious king! How harmful it is for the good administration of the gospel in these kingdoms the great distance that there is from those [the king's] eyes to these abated feet." Cuevas Herrera proposed that *curas* who did not know the Indian language should not be paid and should be forced to return the salary they had unjustifiably earned to the royal treasury.[27]

Cuevas Herrera used this criticism not only to question the church's management but also to empower Andeans as more apt candidates for the priesthood.[28] But he also advocated for the replacement of secular *doctrineros* by Jesuit priests, whom he portrayed as champions of the cause of Indian justice and true missionaries who were "born in this world to illuminate it, carrying the sun's light of Christ's justice all around it."[29] Cuevas Herrera's claim that the Jesuits should take over the Indian parishes echoed a similar, wider campaign in the mid-seventeenth century, launched by different authorities who proposed that a few or at least one parish in each province should be reassigned to the Jesuits.[30] In 1649 Archbishop Pedro de Villagómez launched the second major extirpation-of-idolatry campaign in the Archbishopric of Lima, which was opposed by *caciques* and commoners alike because of the ineffectiveness of the previous campaigns and the many complaints of excesses committed by the secular clergy.

Cuevas Herrera contributed to these denunciations, stressing church ministers' departure from spiritual aims in favor of more worldly business interests. Colonial priests and prelates, according to him, busied themselves conducting and managing commerce, *obrajes*, and estates. Presenting himself as a witness to the abuses he denounced, he provided examples of the moral turpitude of *visitadores de idolatrías* (inspectors of idolatry) who allegedly obtained money from *curas* under extortion and were far more concerned with collecting *curas'* dues than with the spiritual care of their parishioners. The Andean *doctrinero* opposed this practice, arguing that the state of poverty in the Province of Charcas made it difficult, if not impossible, for poor parishes to pay the customary fees to ecclesiastical inspectors; he rejected the methods for collecting *curas'* dues employed by these *visitadores*. In reference to abuses by the inspectors of idolatry, Cuevas Herrera declared: "To send out one of these inspectors amounts to release [of] one of the four devils, who are tied up in the Eufrates. Because they are men whose only God is money. This prompts them to honor the rich and unworthy, while they affront the virtuous for being poor."[31] Cuevas Herrera charged that bishops and archbishops, with their retainers, overburdened parish priests with excessive demands that were ultimately paid by the poor parishioners who provided the labor and products demanded for prelates' prolonged visits to Indian towns.[32]

During the first decades of the eighteenth century, in the Provinces of Lima, Huarochirí, Trujillo, and Piura, the results of evangelization and the behavior of *doctrineros* seemed to have improved little, according to the reports of Indian officials. Introducing complaints similar to those articulated by Cuevas Herrera, Procurador and Diputado General de Naturales Vicente Morachimo documented thoroughly his own critique of the church. But as opposed to Cuevas Herrera, whose charges were barely substantiated with proper names and locations, Morachimo denounced the *curas doctrineros'* lack of commitment and their ambition and covetousness. He also pointed to *curas'* mismanagement of Indian communal and *cofradía* assets, overcharges of tithes and other ecclesiastical fees to Indians, and disobedience of royal laws mandating the foundation of schools in *doctrinas*.[33] Both Cuevas Herrera and Morachimo stressed that *curas doctrineros* forced Indian women to perform domestic service, weaving, and carrying wood and water, among other activities, in which they underpaid them or did not pay them at all. In addition, the two scholars denounced *doctrineros* for seizing properties of deceased Indians and widows and sexually abusing Indian women, as Guamán Poma had questioned earlier, in approximately 1615.[34]

This set of writings constitutes a rich record of Andean scholars' views of Indian subordination by the church. Even though infused by the writers' political interests and biases, the accounts offer a rare glimpse into the conflicting relationships of Andean peoples with the colonial ecclesiastical institution, through Andeans' own words.[35] Cuevas Herrera in particular represented a critical voice from within the lower echelons of the church and offered a rendition of the practices that eroded the church's legitimacy as a spiritual force among Indians and mestizos in the post-extirpation period of the seventeenth century. As a writer, a *cura doctrinero*, and a mestizo descended from the Inca, Cuevas Herrera offered a view of church politics at the local level and endeavored to find experiential common ground with the impoverished, women, and the illiterate—subjects relegated to the margins of the colonial world. To be sure, his proposals reinforced the ecclesiastical discourse that supported the aims of evangelization and the legitimacy of the king as the purveyor of justice for Indians.

Morachimo, a solitary voice within the judicial system advocating for Indian justice in the 1730s, viewed these irregularities as a reflection of the crisis of the colonial legal system, from which the church did not escape; he used the force of legal discourse to underscore the social disorder that stemmed from the consistent violation of laws. Like Cuevas Herrera, Morachimo believed Indians' running away from the church to resume their idolatrous practices and the losses to the royal treasury as a result of the decreased tributary population in Indian towns were just some expressions of this crisis of justice. His petitions reinforced the role of law in social order, the aims of evangelization, the legitimacy of the king as the supreme purveyor of justice for Indians, and, thereby, the hegemony of the Spanish empire. He expected the king to issue "the prompt mandates he deems appropriate to curtail such prominent harms."[36]

Perhaps the most powerful indictment against the church in the eighteenth century is found in the "Representación verdadera," in which Fray Calixto and other Andeans discussed the exclusionary approach of the church vis-à-vis Indians in the priesthood. The key argument was that the church had systematically denied Indians full membership in the Catholic Church as priests and higher ecclesiastical authorities, even after centuries of conversion to Christianity. In addressing the king on the subject, the "Representación verdadera" stated:

> Our and your churches in America are like widows because they do not have
> even one natural Indian of theirs as a pastor, a vicar of a parish, or a prelate,
> in spite of the many laws of the Holy Mother and Roman Catholic Church,
> mandating that Indians be chosen among the capable ones. The Church is a
> widow because Spanish men have taken most of its dignities. They have sepa-
> rated from us and don't see us as pastors. They use those positions as renters who

join them for pure temporal convenience and benefit. The Church is a widow and we, her children, are starving without the spiritual bread. . . . Oh Lord, Oh King, Oh father of ours, in what a nation is this happening?[37]

In the friar's eyes, the American church was incomplete (like widows), as it was in his time. The statement reframes the Catholic theology that represented the priesthood as a mystical marriage of the priest to the church or of nuns to Christ. Andeans would marry the church if they were not prevented from performing as ecclesiastical authorities and functionaries. The conflicting relationship between Indians and the church is represented as a marriage truncated by the Spanish, who monopolized the ecclesiastical positions of power in the church and considered Christian Indians unable to perform as priests—thereby denying them the opportunities and recognition they would otherwise enjoy as priests, prelates, or missionaries. Indian women were equally excluded from opportunities for social ascent and spiritual improvement. Fray Calixto stressed the obstacles for Indian women in the church and in society:

> In the ecclesiastical and religious state and in the secular nobility, Indian and mestizo women, even though they have sharp minds, face the same unhappy death [as] Indian men, and even more so for them since they are a weaker and less robust sex. Because it is hard to see our daughters being made servants and slaves of Spanish women, who are arrogant, haughty, and disdainful. They all believe they are far superior [to] the miserable Indian woman who serves them humbly. . . . And they have nowhere to advance themselves spiritually. Is there any [worse] oppression than ours, Lord, that in more than 200 years there has not been even one nunnery founded for Indian women, because the Spaniards have usurped all the existent ones?[38]

This passage makes evident not only Andean scholars' conscious effort to emphasize the colonial church's discriminatory policies against Indian women but also their perception of the power dynamics among women across ethnic lines. The intellectual Andeans speaking in this text also appeared to have internalized colonial gender views, perceiving Indian women as more fragile than men and stressing the subordination of Indian women in Spanish convents:

> Lord, the women and virgins in Sion and Judá are humiliated, affronted, and lost. [How is it possible] that Indian and mestizo women are not admitted in the convents as nuns or even as lay nuns but only as donadas, like black, mulatto, and zambo women are usually received, [that is], as servants of the Spanish nuns? [How is it possible] that Spaniards have created such a third state of donadas for Indian, mestizo and zambo women without the approval of the church, or any council or the king?[39]

Here, the status of Indian women is symbolized anew by the oppression of the Hebrews under Egyptian rule, while the writers regret the degradation of Indian women in convents as *donadas*—a status that puts them closer to *castas*, looked down upon by Andean nobles. The corollary to Fray Calixto's critique of the church is that Indians were not treated as true members of the church, and their conversion to Christianity was a historical error. The abusive and corrupt practices of members of the upper church, parish priests, and colonial officials more generally created moral devastation and hopelessness that prompted Indians to escape the control of the church and the state. This expedient ultimately explained the failure of Franciscan missionary work following the rebellion of Juan Santos Atahualpa in the Franciscan mission areas of Cerro de la Sal in 1742, which continued later in other frontiers of the viceroyalty. The Huarochirí rebellion in 1750 also articulated the lack of opportunities for recognition of Andean nobles in the priesthood as one of its motives (see Chapter 3).

Even though writers like Cuevas Herrera, Morachimo, and Fray Calixto came from regions as disparate as the Provinces of Charcas, Saña, Tarma, and Lima and wrote at different times, their critical discourses against the church reflect a long pattern of tension and unrest between curates and their Indian parishioners. Their discourses capitalized on the inconsistency between the religious rhetoric of ecclesiastical officials and preachers of the Gospel and the non-Christian behavior of Spanish Christians, which harmed the church's credibility as a spiritual institution among Indians. The incisive criticism of Andean churchmen against the misbehavior of clerical officials was also grounded in awareness of the moral expectations of the church by agents of religious purification, with which these Andeans, as *doctrineros* and mission aides, were well acquainted. Their discussions stressed the failure of *curas*, judges of idolatry, and other prelates to comply with the canonical prescriptive formulas of the post-Tridentine church (after 1563), which admonished ecclesiastics to teach morality by example and to remain "mirrors" of virtue for the Indian parishioners while constantly monitoring themselves for necessary self-correction—all of which was crucial for preservation of the church's religious and social authority.[40] Along with others within the church and the state, those scholars acknowledged that evangelization was far from a successful undertaking. They posed that Andeans found no solace or social justice in the church, and, in response, they opted to run away to the "montaña" (wilderness), a place of refuge in the frontiers of Christianity and civilization where they would be lost to the evangelization enterprise and to institutional mechanisms of social control.[41]

Like Cuevas in the late seventeenth century and Fray Calixto in the mid-eighteenth century, Morachimo led readers to believe that ultimately the very functioning of the colonial society undermined the spiritual justification of the Spanish conquest and settlement of the Andes. He was particularly concerned that the Andeans' abandonment of towns and flight to the montaña constituted the "loss of [both] the spiritual . . . and temporal fruit," which posed a threat to the system: "[P]eople [who become] rooted out from their towns became God's worst enemies. This is harmful for the royal treasury and the well-being of the ones who remain."[42] Instead of placing responsibility for the general failure of evangelization on Andeans' idolatry or superstitions, as most missionaries and extirpators of idolatries had done in the past, Morachimo held corrupt *curas doctrineros, corregidores*, and judges accountable for the failure of the spiritual project of colonialism. Starting in the late seventeenth century, Juan de Cuevas Herrera had proposed that parishioners should not provide for the priest's material needs at the expense of their own spiritual well-being and that no parishes should be assigned to priests who did not meet the language requirements. He demanded the recall of those who enjoyed *doctrinas* without fulfilling the mandatory qualifications and urged the king to have *visitadores* selected by merit as opposed to collusion, as had been the case with Cuevas himself.[43]

In the eighteenth century, when Andean representatives had been struggling for five decades for enforcement of the privileges legally granted by the king in 1697, Morachimo and Fray Calixto insisted that the king should make the enforcement of laws regarding Indian matters a priority and that laws that were no longer effective should be replaced with new, more effective ones. Along with Jerónimo Lorenzo Limaylla around 1677, Morachimo and Fray Calixto favored the creation of a body of Indian priests who, familiar with native languages and cultures, would be in a better position to successfully persuade their fellow Andeans to embrace Christianity. To a large extent, the struggles of Andean elites for access to the priesthood were rooted in a common understanding of the inefficiency of parish priests and their alignment with colonial networks of corruption. Efforts to gain access to positions of power and knowledge within colonial establishments would become the primary goal of a lengthy Andean movement for social inclusion, which started roughly in the late seventeenth century (see Chapter 6).

The tradition of Andean critiques of the church dates back to the *Nueva corónica y buen gobierno* (ca. 1615). In this text, Felipe Guamán Poma de Ayala questioned *curas doctrineros*' behavior, detailing a wide variety of types of mistreatment of Indians—including sexual abuses of native women, exploitation of Indian men and women, and widespread exploitation of indigenous children in ways unknown in the Andes prior to the Spanish invasion.[44] As Cuevas Herrera had tried to state the true duties of *curas* and prelates by illustrating their irregular conduct, Guamán Poma acutely developed his discussion of priests' systematic disregard of the mandates of the Lima provincial councils of the late sixteenth century, even claiming that such abuses deserved scrutiny by the Inquisition. Guamán Poma was one of the earliest Andean scholars to state that priests were responsible for Indians' escaping from the towns and parishes and to construct mestizos in a negative light.[45]

The critique of the church in both the *Nueva corónica* and the later Andean texts under examination accurately represents the tension between a harsh indictment of the secular clergy in rural parishes and overt support of the Jesuit order and, eventually, of members of the high secular clergy. Guamán Poma showed respect for the work of Bishop Cristóbal de Albornoz at the beginning of his journey.[46] Even though Cuevas Herrera also supported and praised the work of the Jesuits—his own mentors—his "Cinco memoriales" seem to have been devised to provide public support for the Jesuits for revamping the evangelization enterprise after the extirpation of idolatry campaigns failed to uproot Andean religious cultures.[47] Unlike Guamán Poma, the Andean mestizo scholars Cuevas Herrera and Fray Calixto spoke from within the lower echelons of the church, and their calls for social change were based on the view that an Indian priesthood would correct the anomalies of church practices in the Andes. The Andean critique did not question the church as a social institution but instead stressed the anti-Christian practices of corrupt and abusive prelates, the debasement of Indians by priests, and the exclusion of native Andeans from the priesthood by the secular church and religious orders—all of which called for an overhaul of the colonial church.

CRITIQUE OF THE POTOSÍ *MITA* SYSTEM

The *mita* system was perhaps the most controversial institution of Spanish colonialism in Peru. Its very existence raised questions about the status of Indians as free subjects. The strain this compulsory draft added to the Indians' demographic decline and to the social and cultural reproduction of Indian communities more generally challenged the legitimacy of Spanish rule and put into question the effectiveness of colonial justice. Intellectual Andeans—including the mestizo and *licenciado* Francisco Falcón, a scholar who partook in the initial discussions of this institution in the late sixteenth century;[48] the Jauja elite Indian Jerónimo Lorenzo Limaylla; and the mestizo curate Juan de Cuevas Herrera—lived in an age and a place where the Potosí and Huancavelica *mitas* loomed large over Indians' social life. Their writings mirrored these realities and offered the harshest critiques of the evils of European colonialism from Andeans' points of view.

Cuevas Herrera in particular offered a firsthand account of the Indians' mining experience in Potosí, where he claimed to have been a miner for a time. His *memoriales* formed part of the ongoing debate over the abolition of the mining *mita* in the seventeenth century, a debate that included the unacknowledged participation of Andean scholars.[49] Cuevas Herrera delved into a description of the types of exhausting labor natives performed in the fields, mines, *obrajes*, estates, and long-distance trade.

The writer set out to deconstruct stereotypes of Indian miners' "laziness," which contributed to justifications for the compulsory *mita*: "Let's destroy once and for all this diabolic argument and reassert that Indians are a working people."[50] Elaborating on Inca traditions of work for the state, Cuevas Herrera argued that in Inca times, idleness was not tolerated and that in Inca societies, even the handicapped were occupied in productive activities.[51] He pointed to the political use of the stereotype: "Indians are hard-working people; what they refuse is to work for free, which is what miners really want them to do."[52] Cuevas Herrera reversed the stereotype against the Spaniards: "They are the real enemies of work because they came to America escaping from it and they never got used to it."[53] Along with *corregidores*, *azogueros* were the main targets of Cuevas Herrera's attacks. He described them as "sinners" who not only committed "injustices and sacrileges" but also engaged in fraudulent activities, such as redeeming the widespread *mita de faltriquera*, which reduced the royal fifth and silver production.

The critique of the strenuous work Indians faced in the mines provided the foundation for Cuevas Herrera's discourse of social justice, which highlighted forced labor as an illegal practice that destroyed indigenous social networks and pre-established forms of reciprocity. Cuevas Herrera stressed that the *mita* imposed travel expenses on *mitayos*, forced them to abandon the household economy, and propitiated the abuse of the absentees' wives by *corregidores*, priests, and other males. He went to great lengths to emphasize the fragile position of native authorities who had to render (*enterar*) the *mita* even when the number of tributary escapees increased. Failure to fulfill the *mita* obligation in its entirety, according to Cuevas Herrera, made these chiefs subject to severe punishment and even execution. The writer highlighted the violent nature of the *mita* and its devastating social effect, indicating that mine workers resorted to suicide as an ultimate, desperate escape when they could tolerate no further oppression by Potosí silver mine owners.[54] This rhetorical strategy also plays out in his discussion of Indians' personal service in Spanish households and haciendas. He charged that not only did they receive no payment for this forced work, but most of the Indians ended up indebted to their "employers" for the value of lost items or because they were victims of deceit or robbery while taking care of Spanish property. In sum, Cuevas Herrera concluded that while they were away rendering personal service, Indians left their homes and possessions unattended, worked for free, lost their freedom, inherited labor debts, and were ultimately subjected to outright slavery.[55]

The corollary concerning the social situation of *mitayos* is that the *mita* system constituted an additional impediment to indigenous Andeans' full Christianization: "While rendering the mita service, they [Indians] don't attend mass, neither [do] they confess themselves, nor [do] they hear sermons or remember God."[56] Thus, Cuevas Herrera pointed to another key contradiction of the colonial system: the need to generate wealth for the empire versus the religious justification of its colonial mission. As a *doctrinero*, he professed to have taken the side of faith in opposition to colonial demands. Along the discursive lines of the biblical "Lamentations" of Jeremiah, in around 1650 Cuevas Herrera compared the situation of Indian workers in the Potosí silver mines, whom he considered to be slaves, to that of the ancient Hebrews under Egyptian rule. Whereas the Hebrews were able to keep their property and live with their families, Indian slaves endured far worse conditions: "They are treated worse than black slaves themselves, because even the lowest of them [blacks] can come and kick a poor Indian a hundred times, and, as Jeremiah predicted, for Indians to eat even black slaves' leftovers should be a great thing."[57]

Although the general tone of the critique is one of bitterness and lamentation, toward the end of his text the author proposed—albeit somewhat pessimistically—new strategies to ameliorate the Andeans' plight. The *mita* should be extended to idle Spaniards, who allegedly introduced robberies and other criminal elements into Indian villages; idle Spaniards should be sent back to Spain, and further Spanish immigration to Peru should be stopped.[58] Although somewhat timidly, Cuevas Herrera suggested that the *mita* system should be abolished and endorsed the incorporation of African slavery into silver mining in Potosí instead, in support of a previous royal decree by Philip III. While rejecting Amerindian slavery as a "sin," an "injustice," and a "sacrilege" by *azogueros*, Cuevas Herrera did not hesitate to endorse the use of African slaves, whom he relegated to the lowest position in colonial society.

In closing his discussion of the social disorder created by the *mita*, the writer's images strikingly resemble those of earlier Andean scholars. The trope of "the world upside down" (*mundo al revés*), found in the *Nueva corónica* and the Spanish literature of the Golden Age, appears here as a metaphorical means of summation to elucidate the corollaries in Cuevas Herrera's text: "Everything collapsed, everything is turned upside down: desolation of Indian towns, destruction of provinces and decimation of Indians.... There is no remedy. I do not know what the remedy is for all these ills."[59] Indeed, the pessimistic feeling that there was no future for Andeans permeated the text and sought to move the king to deliver justice for Indians.

Overall, the colonial critique of justice, the church, and the Potosí *mita* by Andean scholars speaks to both the experience of social hardship by Andean commoners and the exclusion of Andean elites under Spanish rule but also to the political imaginary of Amerindian elites in the mature colonial period. The reiteration of the general ineffectiveness of the system, the overt lack of colonial justice, the social degradation of Indian women and men, and the imminent collapse of Indian authority made evident the deep sense of distrust and frustration among survivors of Andean societies, mostly in the seventeenth century. In the eighteenth century, although these critiques recurred, the discursive and political emphasis seemed to be on how such a state of disorder would and should come to an end through the participation of capable, literate, legitimate, and noble Indians and mestizos in the institutions of government in the colonial society. They engaged in a changing political discourse of justice that revealed their willingness for social change and their ability to manipulate the weapons of the system, including literacy, Christian rhetoric, writing, and litigation, to de-legitimize it—a form of agency one can only perceive through a painstaking textual and discursive analysis of their texts. Thus, Andean critical interpretations of colonialism allow us to question the role of literacy and religious education as weapons of social control by the church and the state. The fact that virtually all the Andean writers studied in this book proclaimed their Catholic affiliation and nearly all were members of the lower church in various capacities makes their criticism of the state and ecclesiastical institutions even more striking.

The Andean scholarly critique of colonialism as a genre was also an intertextual field in which various discursive streams met through a textual dialogue. Yet the voices that questioned the colonial order came from different camps of the Peruvian lettered world and society. As much as Andean scholarship was engaged in a dialogue with European Scholasticism and Neo-Scholasticism, it was also in a dialogical relationship with local creole renditions of the trope *agravios y vejaciones* and critical discourses of reform from enlightened Bourbons. To understand the tone of this dialogue and the disparate agendas it supported, the next section synthesizes other forms of critical narratives of Spanish colonialism and discusses their convergence with, and departure from, the Andean writings with which this study is concerned.

ANDEAN CRITICAL WRITING IN DIALOGUE WITH OTHER COLONIAL DISCOURSES

The genre of colonial criticism in the Viceroyalty of Peru was not only the province of indigenous and mestizo intellectuals. Members of the colonial non-Indian elites wrote critical tracts in which they seemed to share the grievances and indictments raised by Andean intellectuals. Such tracts are found occasionally in the 1650s (peak years of the *mita* abolition movement) and more clearly in the reformist Bourbon era, from the 1730s onward. Either acknowledged or not, a rich dialogue (intertextuality) among critical discourses of protest and reform in creole, peninsular, and Andean writings can be traced. An intertextual exploration is in order to illuminate the dynamics of such a dialogue so we can establish the elements of an intellectual colonial culture of protest and reform in which the discourses of the educated elites of the Spanish and Indian "republics" intertwined, contended, and attempted to affect the order of things for native Andeans. This interaction also exposes the trans-cultural and cross-ethnic nature of the "lettered city" in Peru that at certain conjunctures became an unstated common ground for the social construction of discourses of protest, an important feature of the colonial intellectual culture.[60]

The early sermons of the conquest era brought together two streams of discourse that would become foundational in the formation and transformation of Andean discourses for years to come: religion and justice. Bernardino de Sahagún, Bartolomé de las Casas, and other early missionaries provided the foundations for this discursive confluence in the Americas. But elite Andean scholars moved Casas's discourse to a different arena, advancing an agenda somewhat removed from the ecclesiastical aims of evangelization. They consistently employed the trope of *agravios y vejaciones* as a tool of political and cultural negotiation. Their long narratives describing an array of abuses and affronts eventually became grounds for reclaiming redress in the form of social reforms and noble privileges, and they ultimately fostered the agenda for ethnic autonomy as they—at times directly, at times indirectly—ultimately placed the blame for social injustice on the king himself. This section also highlights the rarely acknowledged contribution of Andean scholars, through letters and *memoriales*, to public debates taking place in royal courts on both sides of the Atlantic regarding the troubling issue of the *mita* system and the campaign for its abolition.

CREOLE WRITINGS AND ANDEAN SCHOLARSHIP

The changing social relations among creole, mestizo, and Indian subjects took place on an everyday basis in Indian villages, rural areas, and colonial cities as indoctrination, racial mixing, market and work relations, and efforts at social control advanced. In rural areas and small towns, it was sometimes difficult to distinguish ethnic boundaries between these groups because creoles also spoke native languages, many Indians and mestizo ladinos spoke Spanish, and color lines tended to blur across the social landscape. Because they often shared a common hostility toward the *corregidor* and other Spanish authorities, it was not uncommon for creoles to seek recognition of leadership among Indian and mestizo peoples. Some creoles sought matrimonial alliances with members of Inca elites to access their wealth, or they rallied Indians for allegiance and support for their own political struggles.[61] As a result of a degree of commonality in their grievances and oppressors or perhaps seeking political dividends, creole lawyers, judges, scribes, priests, petty officials, and some landowners shared sympathy for the Andeans' cause, as they needed their alliance to confront the power of the Spanish authorities or to play off of the rivalry between elite factions. A group of creole advocates of Andeans' causes thus emerged in colonial Peru who engaged in crafting petitions, representing Indian Andeans in litigation, and writing scores of protest discourses that help us understand the formation of a colonial culture of protest as a cross-ethnic and cross-class field.

Juan de Padilla's "Parecer."

The oppressive nature of the *mita* system in colonial Peru engendered an unintended cross-ethnic and cross-class movement for its abolition in the Audiencia of Charcas in the seventeenth century, with its most critical moments in 1656–1666, which involved a legal campaign, Andean activism, and ultimately rebellion. The legal campaign generated a wealth of protest writing by creoles and native Andeans alike. Andean agendas for justice, however, differed from the more institutional aims of the creoles, who cared more about political control and feared Indian rebellion and the relaxation of Catholic values and practices among Andeans.

Juan de Padilla, the prominent creole and *alcalde del crimen* in the Audiencia of Lima introduced in Chapter 2, wrote his incisive "Parecer"[62] on the state of Indian affairs in mid–seventeenth-century Peru, including the *mita*, personal service, and religious indoctrination. Although he advocated redress for the "hard work, affronts, and injustices that native Peruvians suffer at the spiritual and temporal levels"[63] and attacked the behavior of colonial miners, officials, parish priests, and the religious orders, his writing diverges from the tradition of Andean scholarship. Padilla primarily endorsed the imperial project of spiritual conquest, the productivity of mines, and the overall moralization of society through the rule of law.

Among the "temporal" problems, Padilla emphasized the injustices committed within the Potosí *mita* and particularly questioned the *mita de faltriquera*.[64] Padilla stressed that demographic decline redoubled the workload of the surviving indigenous peoples and proposed abolishing the *mita de faltriquera* and maintaining the *mita* only to supply workers for mines that were still active. He also supported the prohibition of Indian forced labor in *obrajes*, particularly child labor in agriculture areas far removed from their homes and shepherding in remote areas. In general, he denounced the excessive tributes and low wages for Indians, as well as the corruption of viceroys and their retainers.[65]

Among the spiritual problems, Padilla was concerned with the poor quality of Indians' indoctrination, the condemnation of many souls that resulted from a lack of ministers, the resilience of "idolatry," *curas doctrineros'* overcharges for religious services, the mistreatment of Andeans, and their abjection in *obrajes* run by priests. Denunciations of *curas doctrineros'* business practices and negligence, as well as the lack of supervision by the prelates of the church, were staples of Padilla's "Parecer." Padilla was clearly voicing the kinds of complaints that were staples of the many *capítulos* Andeans filed against *curas* in the ecclesiastical courts.

Padilla proposed the enforcement of ecclesiastical inspections by able and incorruptible inspectors and the removal of *curas* who did not teach the doctrine, as well as those who ran private businesses in their *doctrinas*. One of the most detrimental evils inflicted upon indigenous peoples, Padilla maintained, was the expropriation of their lands by Spaniards and the religious orders.[66] Padilla asked for enforcement of previous royal decrees that mandated the restitution of these lands and sufficient information and legal assistance for Andeans to ensure the success of their litigation in this matter:

> We can see the justice of God when those treasures get lost in the sea, or when they are enjoyed by the enemies of the faith, or when Indian uprisings jeopardize these kingdoms infested of enemies and earthquakes.... Y. M. [Your Majesty], have pity on your poor and miserable vassals and put remedy to their hardships. But, make your decrees be enforced, and don't content yourself with just issuing commands. I heard the opinion of a kuraka, which I hope won't become true. He said to a cura doctrinero: "See father, how costly it is for us this our [g]ospel; it wouldn't be so if we were to obtain that He, God Our Lord, who sees and doesn't forget their [the Spaniards'] persecutions, raised the lash against the [m]onarchy and restituted it to its old peace and grandeur.[67]

His indictment of the colonial system, prompting the king to take immediate action, made clear Padilla's fear of Indian rebellion. Padilla concluded his "Parecer" by reminding the king that Indian Andeans were the backbone of the kingdom and the ultimate producers of Spain's wealth, for which they had suffered all kinds of *agravios y vejaciones*.

Although evidence of a direct influence in either direction between Padilla and Cuevas Herrera is not available, Padilla's "Parecer" addressed social issues in the Potosí area that Cuevas Herrera had probably voiced earlier and chosen to criticize systematically in his "Cinco memoriales." Cuevas Herrera's critique, as opposed to Padilla's, was supported by his testimonial account based on twenty years of experience as a *doctrinero*. The two texts were produced roughly in the mid-seventeenth century, however, and they reflect the social unrest of those times and the heated debates over the *mita* system in the Audiencia of Charcas (see Chapter 2). Strikingly, they also have a similar structure, with thematic sections that correspond to subdivisions of the text, which Cuevas Herrera designated as "*memorial*" and Padilla called "*punto*." Padilla's "Parecer" drew more public attention than the Andean texts at the time and inspired a heated debate in 1657. As a judge in the Audiencia de Lima, he could be more easily heard by the king; as miners and colonial authorities felt their interests threatened, they also reacted to his accusations and proposals.

Diego de León Pinelo, a Jewish *converso* (convert from Judaism to Christianity) and lawyer who was the *protector de naturales* in Lima in 1657, wrote an extensive response to Padilla—basically restating the existing *reales cédulas* and viceregal decrees issued to remedy each of the irregular situations Padilla denounced. León Pinelo had little to say, however, about the reasons for the long-lasting official disregard for those decrees. Although Padilla appeared to defend Indians' interests, he was more concerned with institutional disorder, such as the corruption of priests and prelates, and with the fiscal impact of the withdrawal of silver mines from production, which the *mita de faltriquera* encouraged. To strengthen the evangelization of Indians at a time when a major extirpation campaign led by Archbishop Pedro de Villagómez of Lima was under way, Padilla strongly recommended assigning one *doctrina* in each *corregimiento* to the Jesuits, as he believed they would render more effective indoctrination. This endorsement was shared by Cuevas Herrera, as documented in the first section of this chapter.

Jerónimo Lorenzo Limaylla's "Representación" was part of Andean *kurakas'* larger effort to end the *mita* imposition in around 1667. His manuscript validated Padilla's "Parecer," as he cited extensively the 1660s royal decree issued in response to it. Limaylla regarded Padilla as "a scrupulous minister."[68] In turn, Padilla's writings used the subordinated condition of indigenous peoples to reinforce his own agenda. The details of the colonial Andean experience listed in Padilla's "Parecer" were widely known to members of the Audiencia of Lima. As an *audiencia* judge, Padilla must have drawn from numerous complaints and appeals *kurakas* and other Andean representatives had brought to the Audiencia of Lima and to the king since the late sixteenth century. Padilla sought to strengthen evangelization through Jesuit missionaries and to oppose the extirpation campaigns of Archbishop Villagómez, which, as indicated earlier, were highly unpopular among *caciques* and other Indians.[69]

In addition to Juan de Cuevas Herrera and Felipe Guamán Poma de Ayala, groups of *caciques* from different areas of Peru—members of the Indian networks who championed the campaigns against the *mita* system—understood the political value of the pronouncement against the *mita* by a prominent creole member of the *audiencia*. They, in turn, used Padilla's "Parecer" to empower their own demands against the *mita* and overtly expressed support for the *alcalde del crimen*. In a *memorial* they sent to the king on November 28, 1662, they voiced their trust of Don Juan de Padilla for his great generosity, expressed as "divine majesty," and for his support of the conservation and well-being of Indian vassals, referred to as "human majesty." They recognized Padilla's actions in favor of the Indians— namely, the "pious letter" or "*memorial*" that caused the king to order, on October 21, 1660, the creation of an ad hoc junta to redress Andeans for the hardships endured in *mitas* and *obrajes* and for the eviction from their lands. Simultaneously, they made clear that two years after the royal order the junta had still not met, in spite of the *caciques'* efforts to bring their grievances to such a committee. In 1662, Don Jerónimo Limaylla was among the signatories supporting Padilla, along with six other Indian authorities from Arequipa, Cusco, Jauja, Vilcashuaman, and Omasuyo.[70] As mentioned in Chapter 2, Don Juan Guaynapiric from Jarama Province was among other *caciques* who formally declared their support for Padilla's *memorial* and actions and his request for the prohibition of the *obrajes* set up by clerics from the Mercedarian orders in his town.[71]

The Oruro "Manifiesto": Creole/Andean Alliance.

As Andean and official efforts—including the viceroy's—to abolish the *mita* largely failed in the 1650s and 1660s, another important critical stream of writing appeared in the 1730s as mounting social unrest led to the beginning of an era of rebellions. We can consider this stream an extension of the tradition of Andean scholarship under discussion. The eighteenth-century rebellions generated a fair amount of writing, which appeared to begin with Juan Vélez de Córdoba, usually identified as creole.[72]

Vélez de Córdoba was one of the most visible leaders of an aborted Indian, mestizo, and creole rebellion against *repartos, mitas*, and tributes that took place in the mining town of Oruro in 1739 and protested royal attempts to exact tribute from creoles and mestizos.[73] Originally from Moquegua, Vélez de Córdoba claimed to be the grandson of an "Inca king." The anonymous "Manifiesto," found in the possession of the mestizo leader Miguel de Castro but attributed to Juan Vélez de Córdoba, bears a striking resemblance in rhetorical style and philosophical background to other Andean texts from that era. The Oruro "Manifiesto" created common ground for a creole-Inca-mestizo alliance within the Oruro movement; these groups were described as the legitimate "lords of the land" and victims of the same "tyranny." Concomitantly, the Oruro "Manifiesto" called for an alternative way out of the "captivity" suffered by Andeans and explored the reasons the participants should "force the will to shake off the yoke of our cervixes."[74]

As a record of a common political culture shared locally by noble Indians, mestizos, and creoles, this is one of the earliest eighteenth-century texts to articulate a utopian discourse in the Andes—an attempt to restore the Inca empire, which promised freedom to creoles, noble Andeans, and their native subjects: "[This is] an heroic act to restore that which is ours [*lo propio*] and liberate the fatherland, purging it from the tyranny of the guampos [Spaniards] who devour us as our ruin grows by the day. . . . My only intention is to reestablish the great empire and monarchy for our ancient kings."[75] The version of the "Inca empire" Vélez de Córdoba envisioned was, in fact, a monarchy headed by an Incan descendant, in keeping with the colonial governing tradition of viceroys and *corregidores*. It was, however, a cross-ethnic project that united Peruvian-born commoner Indians, creoles, *caciques*, and mestizos of the "fatherland," who would "live together like brothers and congregate in a single body, destroying the Europeans."[76]

An alliance had been made with the Incan nobility through the Indian governor Eugenio Pachacnina, whom Vélez de Córdoba presented as the Incan leader representative of the movement: "[He is] one of the royal blood from our Incas of the great Cusco, descendant of the Inca in fifth degree, and with desires to restore his own kingdom and reestablish that monarchy." Speaking on behalf of Pachacnina, Vélez continued: "He implores creoles and caciques and all natives to give him a hand to support this heroic action."[77] This is likely the first rebellion with a clear anti-colonial platform, since the rebels demanded total abolition of tributes, *mitas*, and *repartimientos* and advocated the abolition of *corregidores*, "whose tyrant figure we will try to erase from this republic."[78] The manifesto offered to employ creoles in the offices of the kingdom according to their loyalty to the *caciques* and to honor them as the "Lords of the land." In the new order of things, Andeans would be relieved from tribute and *mita* obligations, and their lands and autonomy would be restored. The Oruro "Manifiesto" ends with a cry of rebellion that stresses the cross-ethnic alliance and the religious identity of its leadership: "Thus, fellow creole brothers, dear caciques, and my beloved natives, hands on to our plan, since we have justice and God Our Lord on our side, and, thus it will protect us in such a just undertaking. May God protect you and give the success and the effort needed."[79]

As with the tradition of Andean writing, the Oruro "Manifiesto" shares the Neo-Scholastic thesis that tyrannical regimes could be legitimately overthrown through rebellion. This served as a moral and theological justification for Andean cross-ethnic rebellion, not only in 1739 Oruro but in the "Great Rebellion" as well. The characterization of the Spanish regime in Peru as a "tyranny" was widely shared among Andean scholars throughout the colonial period, as established in Chapter 4. In the late seventeenth century, Jerónimo Lorenzo Limaylla and Juan de Cuevas Herrera focused on the hardships of the *mita* system in Potosí and Huancavelica as a series of abuses perpetuated by unchecked miners and colonial judicial authorities. Juan Vélez de Córdoba, Fray Calixto de San José Túpac Inca, and Túpac Amaru II, in the eighteenth century, viewed the abusive *repartos* by *corregidores* and the furthering of colonial demands—such as the increasing taxation by the Bourbons and the *mita* itself—as signifying the imbalanced relationship between the rulers and the ruled, which essentially configured a tyranny. Vélez de Córdoba framed the Spanish conquest and its aftermath as the early signs of a tyrannical regime and Spanish encroachment on Indian lands as a destabilizing factor in the effort to Christianize the Indians: "When Spaniards came to America they acted tyrannically, beheading the kings and natural lords of this land. Spaniards usurped their lives, all their assets, and the lands with all their yields and benefits."[80] Vélez de Córdoba demanded the total restitution of chiefdoms and community assets to native lords as a necessary step in the process of evangelization. As opposed to Padilla's "Parecer," the Oruro "Manifiesto" and the rebellion are examples of creole advocacy of Indian causes and cross-ethnic political alliances. In the "Manifiesto," one thus appreciates a stream of creole critical tradition that is inextricably connected to the Andean scholarship analyzed in this book.

Justifying rebellion and defiant actions to put an end to Spanish tyranny seems to have operated not only as a rhetorical tool but also as a political strategy in the mid- and late-colonial Andean rebellions. In the 1730 Cochabamba rebellion, for example, *curas* who supported the movement advised the rebels, who had seized items from Spaniards' shops, that they were not obligated to return anything because their actions were part of a "just war" to defend their freedom.[81] In the same vein, Vélez de Córdoba encouraged natives to "get away with the *repartimiento* items" (*no pagar el repartimiento*), since *corregidores* had "robbed" and "sucked" Indians' labor.[82]

The Oruro "Manifiesto" reached beyond its time, stirring Andean rebellions elsewhere. A copy of the blueprint was confiscated from a rebel participant in the 1750 Huarochirí uprising eleven years later.[83] The mestizo participants Tomás Agudelo and Ramón de Castro distributed the "Manifiesto" in Chayanta and Cochabamba during rebellions in 1780.[84] The circulation of Andean writing followed the regional pattern of the mining economy in Upper Peru—which activated a series of sub-regional economies, markets, and rebellions, linking them with those of Lower Peru in both economic and political terms. Creole and Andean discourses of protest intersected as local creoles and Andeans developed collaborative projects of rebellion and combative writing. These projects were possible in part because the Bourbon attempts to regain political and economic control of Peru in the eighteenth century increasingly separated creoles from opportunities for political, economic, and social advancement, only to push them closer to Andeans than to peninsulars. The fact that the dividing lines between Inca nobles and local creoles were increasingly blurred in rural areas of Upper Peru also facilitated the political alliances.[85]

CLERICAL NARRATIVES AND THE ANDEAN WRITING CULTURE

Starting in the 1540s, cross-currents of native and clerical discourses began to emerge in the colonial world of Peru stemming from the pedagogical relationship between Indian nobility and religious mentors, either individually or in the schools for *caciques*, seminary schools, and mission towns and also in day-to-day contact in churches, *cofradías*, congregations, and other interstitial spaces where trans-culturation took place. Andean discourses borrowed heavily from the literary imagery and narrative styles of the missional epistolary genre to which the writers were exposed, a corpus of writing that emerged from the religious orders' practices of spiritual colonization.

The Franciscan missionary authority Fray Buenaventura de Salinas y Córdoba and other lesser *doctrineros* provided inspiration to the Andean writings of Don Jerónimo Lorenzo Limaylla, the Andean noble from Jauja Province (see Chapter 2),[86] as the Franciscans had been expanding their missions in the Mantaro Valley since 1548.[87] One good example, exhibiting the negative representations of Spaniards also common in Andean texts, came from the town of Mataguasi (Jauja

Province) in 1667, written by its *cura doctrinero* Fray Alonso Zurbano, who wrote in support of Limaylla's petitions to the king. Zurbano considered the Indians predestined for heaven because of the suffering they had endured with "saintly" patience. He condemned the questionable behavior of Spaniards, regarding them as "worse than pagans who are Christians only in name; because even though they have been educated in politics [*política*] and with Christian milk, they become cruel scourges of these poor Indians' innocence."[88] He praised the kings for the great decrees they issued to protect Indians but found that the negligence and carelessness of *corregidores* rendered those laws useless.

Having spent nearly a decade as a Franciscan mission aide in Tarma and Cusco (mid-1720s–mid-1730s), Fray Calixto de San José Túpac Inca's "Representación verdadera" amply expressed this discursive influence in 1749. The letters and reports to his superiors by Fray Juan de San Antonio, the Franciscan vice commissary of the Cerro de la Sal missions during Juan Santos Atahualpa's rebellion in 1742, reveal a rhetorical model similar to that of the "Representación verdadera." In the biblical style of the "Lamentations," Fray San Antonio bewailed that Indians were "the children that claim, as the prophet Jeremiah, for the bread of doctrine and die hungry because there is none who impart it to them."[89] Fray Calixto paraphrased San Antonio's wish for more indoctrination, but he subtly slipped in a demand for education in science and letters for Andean elites, a more secular and modern view: "Lord, as our Father, you disposed that the bread of the Doctrine in science and Letters was imparted to us. . . . Thus, your ancestors commanded that we were admitted in Schools and Literary Lecture Halls. But we are fasting from this bread, because our father the king does not know whether it is imparted to us."[90] Fray San Antonio, along with the authors of the "Representación verdadera" in 1749–1750 and those of the "Planctus indorum" in around 1751, shared a similar understanding of Andeans' relapse into "idolatry." Fray Juan José de San Antonio explained the failure of the Franciscan missions during the Juan Santos Atahualpa rebellion to his superior Fray José Gil Muñoz:

> [B]ecause of the excessive and infernal covetousness, tyranny, cruelty, scandals against Indians, mestizos, and helpless Spaniards in the obrajes, mines, sugar mills, haciendas and cane fields . . . and to free themselves from so much affront and tyranny, they run away to the mountain[s], preferring to join the infidel rather than tolerating the burdens that Spaniards place on them. . . . Tyrannies, cruelties, and idolatries are deeply rooted and the faith is very distorted in many parts of the kingdom . . . because Indians see that what Spaniards do to them is against God's law. Then, they do not believe the doctrine we predicate.[91]

This Scholastic elaboration of "tyranny" and "cruelty" at the hands of Franciscan mission authorities in 1750 explained the destruction of their mission towns and justified the Franciscans' applications for royal funds to rebuild their missions in the Cerro de la Sal area. The redefinition of "tyranny" was introduced during the post-conquest period by Fray Bartolomé de las Casas to strengthen his indictment against Spanish conquistadors and support the abolition of the *encomienda* system.[92] In the mid-eighteenth century, however, intellectual Andeans adopted the same expedient to stress the monopoly of power by Spaniards and to pose a political and moral objection to colonialism (tyrannical Spaniards were not truly Christian).

Fray Calixto's and Juan de San Antonio's approaches differ more clearly. For Fray San Antonio, the solution to the social chaos created by the Spaniards was to reinforce evangelization. For Fray Calixto, the remedy was education for Andean elites in "sciences and letters" and representation in the ecclesiastical and civil positions of government, which, in turn, would effectively free Andeans from colonial tyranny. However, the commonality of language and representations of colonial officials in both the Franciscan and Andean writings reveal a shared religious background, a common missional culture, and the tension between religious orders and the colonial government. Fray Calixto de San José Túpac Inca's style resembles the Franciscan narratives that questioned the cruelty of colonial officials. His use of biblical rhetoric, such as the template of Jeremiah's "Lamentations," and the baroque method of a hypothetical question-and-answer discussion were rhetorical staples of the Franciscan writings of bishops and high missionary officials as well.

Among the papers confiscated from Fray Calixto in his cell the night he was detained in 1756, the authorities found interesting writing material, including a compilation of notes from different writers such as the Franciscan bishop of Quito, Don Alonso de la Peña Montenegro, from 1731. The notes included indictments against colonial abuses and opinions in favor of the admittance of Indians and mestizos into the Catholic priesthood.[93] The manuscript also contained segments of juridical statements in Latin by the well-known Spanish jurist Don Juan de Solórzano regarding the admission of Indians to the priesthood and included other scholars' statements in favor of justice for Indians, probably composed by clerics who also wrote in Latin. A second section was a transcription of a portion of the book *El secular religioso* (The Secular Priest) by Don Juan Bautista del Toro, printed in Madrid in 1721, about the oppression of Indians in New Granada. A question-and-answer section on the central theme of Indian priesthood follows, with new interjections from Bishop Montenegro and Solórzano, introduced by an editor as "Mr. Montenegro asks, in Book 3, Treatise 8, Session 2, Folio 368, if Indians may be ordained without special dispensation. And there he says the following."[94] The "Representación verdadera" incorporated a reworked format of similar question-and-answer discussions of Indian priesthood, the representation of Indian oppression as "slaves of slaves," racist representations of blacks and mulattos as "vile people," and the reiteration of the many laws that supported the Indian cause.[95]

The clerical writings circulated among Andeans as they engaged in missionary work, as they were mentored as *curas* or lay brothers by other ecclesiastics, or as they prepared manuscripts in collaboration with other priests. But from all these texts, Andeans selected the rhetorical elements they deemed useful to buttress the criticism of Spaniards, such as the "Lamentations," notions of Christian justice, and the ecclesiastical epistolary style. Rather than unconditionally endorse the missionary goals and ecclesiastical agendas of the clerical narratives, they fostered their own agenda for a more secularized education and social participation in religious, social, and political offices.

ANDEAN SCHOLARSHIP AND BOURBON IDEOLOGIES

As the Bourbons set out to rationalize and reform the imperial administration, a layer of criticism of the old Habsburg administrative style emerged that incorporated the trope of *agravios y vejaciones* inflicted upon Andeans, together with a critique of the apparent malaise of the empire as evidenced by protracted administrative corruption. Jorge Juan y Santacilia and Antonio de Ulloa's "Discurso y reflexiones políticos sobre el estado presente de los reinos del Perú" exemplifies this trend.[96] Juan and Ulloa were two professional Spanish sailors who traveled to Peru on a scientific expedition in 1736 to work on astronomical measures of the equator and prepare a report. In the "Discurso," they presented an indictment of the state of affairs in Peru that focused on military security in the colony, contraband, the irregular conduct of *corregidores* and the clergy, a general evaluation of colonial functionaries, the rift between creoles and peninsulars, and an assessment of the potential for the Kingdom of Peru's natural resources to increase royal revenue. The policies proposed to solve the perceived irregularities had apparently been in preparation before the sailors even composed the reports, which therefore became "useful" tools to lend credence to the reforms the Bourbon administration had considered beforehand.[97]

Juan and Ulloa incorporated the Andeans' rhetoric of *agravios y vejaciones* and depicted the misbehavior of *corregidores* as "tyranny" by attempting to make a case for extreme administrative disorder.[98] They appeared to be condemning the illegal practices of *repartimiento de comercio* that *corregidores* and their associates conducted against natives and linking them with the causes of Juan Santos Atahualpa's insurrection.[99] The Spanish expeditioners proposed improving the methods of selecting *corregidores* by choosing honest, capable individuals willing and able to treat indigenous peoples respectfully. Among the most salient policies they proposed was the prohibition of all forms of *repartimiento de comercio* and extending indefinitely *corregidores'* terms in office with a salary of no less

than 2,000 pesos.[100] As noted, in 1732 the Bourbon court supported the printing
and distribution of the Indian *procurador* Vicente Morachimo's "Manifiesto de
agravios y vejaciones," which circulated in the royal court of Madrid for more
than a decade before the critical reports of Juan and Ulloa were prepared.[101]

Regardless of whether such claims were based on reliable evidence, Juan
and Ulloa's text exhibited the anti-clerical stand of the Bourbon era, particularly
because of the *agravios y vejaciones* clerics inflicted upon Indians, which allegedly
resulted in their lack of interest in religion and the poor quality of indoctrination. One of the more sensitive issues raised was that of complicity between *curas*
and *corregidores*—specifically, the allegations that *curas* conducted businesses
that diverted them from their indoctrination duties. Juan and Ulloa attacked lay
brotherhoods and their *fiestas de hermandad* (community festivals), which the
authors considered harmful to indigenous communities' finances.[102] The sailors
admonished the secular and the regular clergy overall but were particularly harsh
toward the regular clergy assigned to doctrines. These clergymen were accused of
forcing Andeans to work in their farms and *obrajes* on holidays and during Lent,
forcing concubinage upon indigenous women, and having children with them.[103]
In examining the impact of these transgressions by priests, Juan and Ulloa reiterated an argument already present in Andeans' writings: that misrule and injustice
by *curas* had prompted Indians to run away to the mountains and join the "infidel," thus rendering evangelization a failure.[104]

Most of these accusations had been raised and substantiated in writings
since the seventeenth century, including Juan de Cuevas Herrera's *memoriales*
and Juan de Padilla's "Parecer," and in the eighteenth century in Andean texts of
Vicente Morachimo and Fray Calixto de San José. The use of these arguments
and examples of Andean experience under Spanish rule to advance a modernizing agenda of imperial reform by the Bourbons makes evident the political
appropriation of Andean writing by crown officials, who contributed to build
Bourbon hegemonic ideologies with the purpose of regaining political power
and legitimacy.[105]

CONCLUSION

Colonial Andean scholarly efforts to produce critiques prompt a reconsideration
of the Uruguayan Angel Rama's notion of the *ciudad letrada* as an intellectual and
political space exclusive of creole and peninsular officials and ecclesiastics, who
had privileged access to legal information and its channels of circulation within
the empire. Intellectual Andeans' knowledge, concretized in complex tracts, fed
the circuits of the written word—which, however inadvertently, entered the
colonial *ciudad letrada*. Their writings partook in current debates over justice for
Andeans, challenged the legitimacy of Spanish rule, questioned the church's lack

of moral authority, campaigned against the *mita* system, and proposed reforms of the empire before and during the Bourbon era of imperial reform. Their participation in the colonial realm of the written word also contributed to the early formation of the public sphere in Spanish America, which, even though in a contentious fashion, allowed for the presence of Andean elites' ideas and texts in the royal courts, however narrow those canonical niches may have been.

Andean scholarship contributed to the formation of a colonial culture in the cross-ethnic interstices of the *ciudad letrada*, a trans-cultural contribution that produced a rich written record of colonial critiques by Andean elites in search of social change and by others seeking to sustain or reform the status quo. Educated Andeans endeavored to discern Spanish colonialism, discussed its impact on the lives of Indians and mestizos, selected and reformulated European tenets, and employed existing rhetorical traditions from the ecclesiastical and secular discourses to make their voices heard in the restricted colonial world of letters underlying the justice system. The unstated textual dialogue between Andean and creole writings aligned with Andean agendas reflects their relationship of collaboration. Conversely, a similar dialogue between Andean and "enlightened" creole and peninsular discourses unveils the relationships of power and knowledge that rendered Andean scholarship invisible and mute in official writings, as such discourses utilized Andeans' criticism and the experience of Indian oppression and injustice to empower their own agendas of reform and political control of the empire.

Andean discourses of social justice reinforced the long-standing trope of *agravios y vejaciones*, which was reelaborated throughout the colonial period. It was originally a rhetorical device of Lascasian manufacture in the sixteenth century, which sought to stir up remorse in abusive Spanish Christians and fear that their souls would be condemned as inducements for immediate action by the monarch. Andean scholars resignified the trope during the social crisis of the *mita* in the 1600s to advocate that the institution be abolished and as a "service to the crown" so they would deserve social privileges. This strategy continued throughout the 1700s, when Andean scholars also used the trope in times of social crisis and rebellion—such as 1739, 1750, and 1780–1783—to question the colonial order of things and to carve spaces of Indian autonomy within that order.

As used by "enlightened" Spanish advisers such as Juan and Ulloa, in 1749, the trope evolved into a rhetorical stratagem used to support imperial agendas of reform aimed at restoring social order, economic recovery, and political control. Furthermore, the rhetoric of *agravios y vejaciones* inflicted upon Andeans in the Bourbon discourses discussed here created a power schema that eventually translated into policies that further obliterated the social fabric of Indian societies in the Andes, which, in the end, prompted them to take a radical stand embodied by rebellions in the late eighteenth century.

Various creole and peninsular writings also utilized Amerindian subordination and its textual description to further political agendas that in one way or another diverged from the purposes that had led Andean intellectuals to write their own discourses of social justice. We can trace the pattern of appropriation of Andeans' social circumstances and discourses of protest by members of the colonial establishment back to the founders of the controlling leitmotiv of *agravios y vejaciones de los indios*—such as Fray Bartolomé de las Casas, Antonio de Montesinos, Domingo de Santo Tomás, and Pedro de Gante, among others—in the early days of Spanish colonialism in the Americas. In their discourses, virtually all of these scholars articulated the oppression of Amerindians in *encomiendas* and mines to justify an imperial project of evangelization that sought to uproot indigenous religions rather than to achieve Andeans' general well-being.

Within Andean discussions of justice in a colonial situation, a pattern of argumentation appeared along an axis that extended from Felipe Guamán Poma de Ayala, Inca Garcilaso de la Vega, Juan de Cuevas Herrera, Jerónimo Lorenzo Limaylla, Juan Núñez Vela de Rivera, Vicente Morachimo, and Fray Calixto de San José Túpac Inca to the Túpac Amaru writings. The specific political and social conjunctures each of these writers confronted varied throughout the colonial period, and their interpretations of social justice changed accordingly. But the continuity in rhetorical style and the convergence of discursive streams are remarkable. The rhetoric of *agravios y vejaciones*, the description of Spanish rule as a form of "tyranny," the denunciation of social injustice within *mitas*, and the abusive *corregidores* and *curas* seemed to emerge on a recurrent basis whenever Andeans' political, cultural, and social survival appeared highly compromised. As opposed to their early Andean counterparts, such as Guamán Poma de Ayala and Garcilaso de la Vega, among others, Andean intellectuals of the late seventeenth and eighteenth centuries integrated their scholarship into a wider practice of ethnic activism for social change—undertaken through collective networks of writing, trans-Atlantic travel, and political action in Spain to produce legislation in favor of Indians. When those efforts proved insufficient, the later intellectuals supported massive rebellion, at times less visibly than at others.

The critical voices of Andean intellectuals show that they were aware of the limited ability of colonial justice to include Andeans in the empire effectively, in spite of the legal discourse of the crown contained in the many royal decrees—issued but seldom enforced—to castigate abuse and protect the kingdom's "labor force." This failure, in turn, made it possible for Andean officials and lettered subjects to create a legal counter-discourse that substantiated the king's continued negligence in enforcing his own laws, thus allowing Andean leaders to project themselves as the grantors of justice for Indians and to continue to fight for that justice. By calling for the election of Indian judges and *protectores de naturales*, Andeans were subverting the racialized nature of colonial justice from within—

an unintended aim of colonial rule and the use of its own discourse in a different register.[106]

Finally, the discourses of social justice by intellectual eighteenth-century Andeans reveal their adherence to colonial legal codes and their recognition of the king as the supreme legal authority. Why did Andean scholars and authorities vehemently stick to colonial laws even when judicial authorities, the king included, appeared perpetually and systematically unwilling to enforce them? How did Andean elites understand their places in society, and what were their long-term goals to alter the social confines to which they were relegated? A close analysis of Andean struggles for social inclusion as part of their impetus for social autonomy allows us to approach initial answers to such questions.

NOTES

1. Casas, *Brevísima relación de la destrucción de las Indias*.

2. The exposé of Andean scholarship in this and the remaining chapters follows the chronology of the texts under study, indicated earlier, although occasional references to relevant sixteenth- and early–seventeenth-century antecedents are introduced as necessary.

3. The pattern of Andean criticism of *corregidores*, and of the system of justice more generally, began to take shape in the work of Guamán de Poma de Ayala in approximately 1615. Aware of the effect of Toledo's policies, Guamán Poma devoted many pages to the *corregidores'* detrimental effect on the lives of Indian women and men. He attacked the colonial networks of collusion and enrichment that bound colonial officials and other prominent Spaniards. A few of the many examples of this pattern are found in Guamán Poma de Ayala, *Nueva corónica*, 487[491]–518[522].

4. Cuevas Herrera, "Cinco memoriales," 238, 239v.

5. Ibid., 238–251v.

6. AGI, Lima, 422, Morachimo, "Manifiesto de los Agravios," 2–3v.

7. Ibid., 1–1v.

8. Ibid., 2–3v.

9. Cuevas Herrera, "Cinco memoriales," 242–243, 245–245v, 259–260. Similar criticisms had been advanced in Guamán Poma de Ayala, *Nueva corónica*, 564[578]–569[583].

10. Morachimo, "Manifiesto de los Agravios," 5v–11v. Morachimo lists, for example, abuses in the collection of the *alcabala*; delayed and underpaid salaries, as well as poor working conditions, in *obrajes*, haciendas, and mines; assaults of Amerindian traders on the road by those who worked for *corregidores*; underpayment for Indian products in the markets by Spaniards and lay priests; *encomenderos'* and *curas doctrineros'* encroachments on Indian lands, followed by *composiciones de tierras*, which eventually turned into expropriation; excessive demands for gratuitous Indian labor; and mismanagement of *cofradías'* assets by priests, as well as their poor ecclesiastical service and ambition—all of which, Morachimo claimed, caused Indians to abandon their towns and relapse into idolatry.

11. Cuevas Herrera, "Cinco memoriales," 251v.

12. Ibid., 252.

13. Ibid. Other characterizations of *caciques* as "alcoholics," "anti-Christian," "corrupt," and ultimately the worst exploiters of their communities are listed in ibid., 252–255.

14. "Sir, this measure would be great if only the ministries in charge of the residencia were honest, conscious, and zealous of God's and Y. M.'s [Your Majesty's] work. But, what has been seen here is that most appointed judges are the servants of the same corregidores and what they seek is two hundred or three hundred pesos. Then, Y. M., what kind of review could they conduct? . . . It is frequent that, bribing the [*residencia*] judge with six hundred or seven hundred pesos, they give a good review, and the crimes the official committed go unpunished, and justice for Indians is not served." Morachimo, "Manifiesto de los Agravios," 2.

15. One case serves to emblematize the ways indigenous peoples had to finance judges' salaries: "Law 46, Book 11, Title 33 and 34 of visitadores, folio 299 [from the *Recopilación de leyes de las Indias*], establishes that the salaries of the judges appointed for settling tax issues be paid from the funds of *acaldías mayores* [highest local government office]; and that such judges pay for their personal expenses, so that this burden does not fall onto Indians. . . . However, Sir, Indians have always paid at least four hundred and fifty pesos for the judges' and their servants' salaries and expenses. And if they do not do that, they are imprisoned and mistreated. To avoid such pain, these miserable Indians have to do whatever the judges want." Morachimo, "Manifiesto de los Agravios," 4.

16. Ibid.

17. In approximately 1749–1750, Fray Calixto denounced the violence of Lima's *alcalde ordinario*, who evicted an Indian noblewoman from the central plaza. "Representación verdadera," 125.

18. Morachimo, "Manifiesto de los Agravios," 5v.

19. "Representación verdadera," 126–127.

20. Ibid., 128v–130v.

21. Diego Túpac Amaru, "Copia de la carta que el rebelde Diego Túpac Amaru respondió a la que le escribió el señor obispo del Cusco," 150–151.

22. Mills, "Bad Christians in Colonial Peru," 185–190.

23. Ibid., 186.

24. Cuevas Herrera, "Cinco memoriales," 267, 269.

25. Ibid., 218, 220v.

26. Ibid., 221–221v.

27. Ibid., 221–224, 238. Starting in the sixteenth century, criticism of the *doctrineros'* lack of language skills had been raised even by the Jesuit José de Acosta; it was criticized by Guamán Poma and others in the seventeenth century.

28. Ibid., 222v–224, 238.

29. To illustrate the "exceptional" cases of virtuous prelates and missionaries he claimed to know, he praised "exemplary" Jesuits such as the Cusco bishop Fernando de Mendoza (1609–1618) and the missionary Juan de Arroyo. Ibid., 220v (quotation), 222–222v, 225v. Cuevas Herrera offers further apologetic representations of the Jesuits and support for their missionary work in 222v, 227v, 239, 252, 255.

30. Among others, these authorities were the Viceroy Principe Don Francisco de Borja y Aragón Principe de Esquilache, Viceroy Conde de Alba de Aliste, Fiscal Protector de Naturales Francisco Valenzuela in 1654, Audiencia of Lima judges Don Juan de Padilla and Bernardo Iturrizarra along with Protector de Naturales Diego León Pinelo in 1657, and in 1663 Viceroy Conde de Santiesteban. García Cabrera, *Ofensas a Dios*, 55–63. García Cabrera argued that this proposal was an alternative to, and a rejection of, the extirpation of idolatries by Villagómez. The Jesuits did not accept this role since they supported Villagómez, although apparently lukewarmly.

31. Cuevas Herrera, "Cinco memoriales," 233v–235.

32. Ibid., 234v. *Visitadores* remained in the towns longer than necessary, since their expenses were paid by the Indian towns. This practice led to frequent complaints and discontent. García Cabrera, *Ofensas a Dios,* 61.

33. Morachimo, "Manifiesto de Agravios," 9v–13. Complaints about excessive ecclesiastical fees continued well through the late eighteenth century. See Stavig, *The World of Túpac Amaru,* 191; O'Phelan, *Rebellions and Revolts,* 144–148.

34. Cuevas Herrera, "Cinco memoriales," 223–224v, 226v–227, 232v–233; Morachimo, "Manifiesto de los Agravios," 9v, 10, 10v–13v. Guamán Poma at times blamed the Indian women for such abuses, calling them *"putas"*; for the most part, though, he acknowledged that they were forced into such acts by oppressive *curas, encomenderos, corregidores,* and others. Guamán Poma de Ayala, *Nueva corónica y buen gobierno,* 529[543], 539[553], 541[555], 563[577], 824[838], among others.

35. Cuevas Herrera hoped to be rewarded at the end of his life with a prelateship as *ecclesiastical visitador* or inspector. After Cuevas Herrera, Juan Núñez Vela de Rivera petitioned and successfully obtained a post as the *racionero* of the Arequipa cathedral. For an assessment of conflicts between the church and the Indians during late-colonial rebellions in Upper Peru, see Robins, *Priest-Indian Conflict in Upper Peru.*

36. Morachimo, "Manifiesto de los Agravios," 13v.

37. "Representación verdadera," 120. A more systematic discussion of the defense of Andeans' right to the priesthood is developed in Chapter 6.

38. Ibid., 122.

39. Ibid., 122v–123.

40. Mills, "Bad Christians in Colonial Peru," 183.

41. Cuevas Herrera, "Cinco memoriales," 240; Morachimo, "Manifiesto de los Agravios," 8v; "Representación verdadera," 124.

42. Morachimo, "Manifiesto de los Agravios," 3.

43. "Visitadores [should not be chosen from among] the relatives of prelates ... or the favorites of judges and other prominent characters." Cuevas Herrera, "Cinco memoriales," 238.

44. The critique of the padres (fathers) is only a portion (approximately 100 folios long) of a complete section Guamán Poma devoted to criticizing the entire structure of the church and to offering his "remedies." Guamán Poma de Ayala, *Nueva corónica y buen gobierno,* 561[575]–657[671].

45. Ibid., 560[575]–570[584]. Guamán Poma argued that the sexual abuse of indigenous women by priests was producing a growing number of mestizos and recommended that Indian men and women avoid attending the doctrine: "It is very just, and in the honor

of God, that children and adults don't go to the doctrine and neither [that] women go to his house [the priest's]. Thus, Indians' [population] in this realm will augment and the towns won't be deserted" (575[589]).

46. Ibid., 676[690].

47. Cuevas Herrera, "Cinco memoriales," 220v–221.

48. Falcón, "Representación de los daños y molestias que se hacen a los Indios," 220–237v.

49. "To be able to speak satisfactorily on this matter, without adding anything . . . I became a miner in Potosí for some time. The abundance of what has to be said is such that it impoverishes my discourse." Cuevas Herrera, "Cinco memoriales," 255v. For a more detailed presentation of the contours of the debate on the *mita* system, see Cole, *Potosí Mita*, 46–61.

50. Cuevas Herrera, "Cinco memoriales," 257.

51. Ibid., 256. "In Inca times . . . even the blind, the limpy, the one-handed, and the handicapped worked in whatever they could."

52. Ibid., 257.

53. Ibid., 256v.

54. Ibid., 225–264.

55. Ibid., 265.

56. Ibid., 262v.

57. Ibid., 263. See other quotes from Jeremiah's "Lamentations" in ibid., 231.

58. Ibid., 256v, 268v.

59. Ibid., 252–254.

60. In presenting these ideas, only the main lines of non-Andean discourses that underlay Andean protest scholarship in mid- and late-colonial Peru will be identified; the exposition of such ideas, therefore, is by no means exhaustive.

61. O'Phelan, "El mito de la independencia concedida," 67, 73. In the Andes, even wandering peninsulars were proclaiming themselves Inca descendants and leading rebellions against Spanish rule. One of the more striking examples is Pedro Bohorques, a poor Andalucian conquistador in search of the elusive El Dorado in the mythical Paititi in the 1630s. He eventually proclaimed himself to be Apo Inka and led the rebellion of the Colchaquies, only to be executed because he was accused of instigating the Lima rebellion by the *kurakas* in 1666. Lorandi, *Spanish King of the Incas*. For a discussion of interracial relationships between creole and Inca elites in late-colonial Cusco, see O'Phelan, *Rebellions and Revolts*; Garrett, *Shadows of Empire*; Cahill, "Liminal Nobility."

62. Pareceres were common in colonial administrative writing. They were part of officials' duty to inform the king about the state of affairs; on critical issues, the king would also request opinions from specialists and suggestions of possible lines of action. Padilla sent his "Parecer" to the king on July 20, 1657.

63. Torre Villar, *Los pareceres de Don Juan de Padilla*, 107.

64. Prior to this arrangement, Padilla continued, Indians had only received wages worth twenty reales per week (a peso was typically worth eight reales). Miners profited from the low risk and the quick cash they received from Indian captains of the *mita* and the *caciques* through the *mita de faltriquera*; mine owners were paid seven pesos for each Indian's week of work. Ibid., 113.

65. Ibid., 113–114, 119–125.

66. Ibid., 115–116. Encroachments on Indian lands and the corresponding lawsuits would continue well through the late eighteenth century. See Stavig, *The World of Túpac Amaru*, 111–128.

67. Ibid., 125.

68. Limaylla, "Representación," 239–240.

69. García Cabrera, *Ofensas a Dios pleitos e injurias*, 55–63.

70. AGI, Lima, 15, Noviembre 28, 1662. Limaylla was preparing to visit the royal court for the second time that same year and was requesting permission to travel to Spain, which the king granted.

71. AGI, Lima, 17, Don Juan Guaynapiric, Lima, Noviembre 29, 1662.

72. Rowe, "Movimiento Nacional Inca del siglo XVIII," 18. Rowe identified Vélez de Córdoba as a mestizo.

73. For analyses of this conspiracy, see O'Phelan, *Rebellions and Revolts*, 86–97; Thomson, *We Alone Rule*, 163, 170, 177–178, 325–326.

74. AGI, Charcas, 363, "Manifiesto," 9v.

75. Ibid., 10, 11–11v.

76. Cited in Thomson, *We Alone Rule*, 170–171. Vélez de Córdoba apparently coordinated efforts with *caciques* from coastal Peru and Cochabamba. Ibid., 325.

77. AGI, Charcas, 363, "Manifiesto," 11.

78. Ibid.

79. Ibid., 12v.

80. Ibid.

81. O'Phelan, *Un siglo de rebeliones anticoloniales*, 96.

82. AGI, Charcas, 363, 11.

83. O'Phelan, *Rebellions and Revolts*, 96. The "Manifiesto" must have circulated during the Huarochirí rebellion along with the "Representación verdadera," among other Andean texts.

84. AGI, Lima, 363, 9v–11v.

85. O'Phelan, "El mito de la independencia concedida," 67, 73; Thomson, *We Alone Rule*; Stern, *Resistance, Rebellion, and Consciousness*; Cahill, "Liminal Nobility."

86. Salinas Córdoba wrote the *Memorial de las historias del Nuevo Mundo Pirú* in 1653, a model of Franciscan missionary writing and criticism of the abuse of Indians under colonial rule. Salinas y Córdoba, *Memorial de las historias*.

87. Heras, *Aporte de los franciscanos*, 51.

88. AGI, Indiferente General, 640, Fray Alonso Zurbano, "Carta del R. P. Predicador," Mataguaci, Febrero 12, 1667.

89. AGI, Lima, 541, Fray Juan de San Antonio, July 11, 1750, 8.

90. "Representación verdadera," 119v.

91. AGI, Lima, 541, Letter from Fray Juan de San Antonio to Fray José Gil Muñoz, 1750, 9v.

92. Casas, *Brevísima relación de la destrucción de las Indias*.

93. AGI, Lima, 988, Bishop Alonso de la Peña Montenegro, "Agravios que continuamente se hacen a los indios" (ca. 1731), 1–12. The notes from Montenegro include quotations from the Bishop of Chiapas, Fray Bartolomé de las Casas, about the deci-

mation of the Caribbean Indian population at the hands of cruel conquistadors in the 1490s.

94. Ibid., 10.

95. Ibid., 1v, 4v.

96. Juan and Ulloa's report was embedded within the larger discourse of the *criticista* and *proyectista* literature of the time, which also utilized the trope of *agravios y vejaciones* coupled with extensive critiques of official corruption and urged that the empire be overhauled to curtail the power of local administrators and strengthen the economy according to the needs of eighteenth-century European capitalism. Partaking in the principles of English liberalism, the two men attacked the unproductive work of the clergy, called for the formation of industries, and demanded an end to the Catholic Church's monopoly over economic resources. Examples of *criticista* literature in colonial Peru were Viceroy Marquéz de Castelfuerte's "Relación de gobierno" (1724–1736) and the creole Victorino Montero's "Estado político del Peru" (1742).

97. Juan and Ulloa, *Noticias secretas de América*, 85.

98. Ibid., 232, 236–237.

99. Ibid., 244–250. The evidence the sailors used, however, has been questioned as consisting of exaggerated, sweeping statements, some of which the expeditioners could not possibly have witnessed as they claimed. Andrien, "*Noticias secretas de América*," 178–179.

100. Juan and Ulloa, *Noticias secretas de América*, 254–259.

101. Andrien, "*Noticias secretas de América*."

102. Juan and Ulloa, *Noticias secretas de América*, 265–266, 284–286.

103. Ibid., 272–274, 279–281.

104. Ibid., 274–275.

105. Andrien, "*Noticias secretas de América*," 186. Along with Andean discourses of protest, Andrien identifies the conflicting discourses of reform by colonial elites and the approaches to imperial reform rooted in the Spanish Enlightenment proper. Ibid., 177.

106. Certeau, *Practice of Everyday Life*, 31–32.

❧ 6 ❧

The Political Culture of Andean Elites

Social Inclusion and Ethnic Autonomy

ANDEAN ELITES AVIDLY SEARCHED for avenues of social recognition within the colonial world and viewed such spaces as niches from which to reassert their sense of nobility in a world that increasingly denied them the opportunities and rights to which they felt entitled. In her intriguing discussion of the links between *pureza de sangre* and religion, María Elena Martínez maintained that the incorporation of the Castilian notion of purity of blood had implications for the definition of Indian corporate rights and that the royal recognition of Indian purity introduced concerns about blood, genealogy, dynastic histories, and race among the native elites of Mexico.[1]

Underlying the recurring critique of colonial rule by Andeans is the idea that Spanish rule introduced ethnic discrimination in the Andes—a practice foreign to Andeans—in which only Spanish Christians received ecclesiastical and secular honorific positions. Ladino scholars articulated this position in their indictments of the Spanish monopoly over positions of power, although at times they voiced a longing for the Spaniards' love and respect. Eventually, they expressed their position as part of a hope that Spaniards and Andeans could live together as Christians without conflict, merging fully "in body and soul." Alongside their discursive criticism of Spanish discrimination, then, since the late seventeenth century, Andeans had supported a coherent agenda of social inclusion that developed further in the eighteenth century, including access to positions of power they were denied given their status as "newly" Christian Indians.

This chapter explores the ways Andean intellectuals justified these inclusionist positions. Why were Andeans so eager to join the priesthood and other colonial institutions of power in spite of their criticism of these institutions? The complexity of Andeans' political and intellectual practices emerges in the textual and political history of their campaigns for Indian priesthood and education, reconstructed in this chapter, against the backdrop of their understanding of prevalent notions of purity of blood that presented a barrier to the fulfillment of their entitlement to such opportunities. The point of departure is the 1697 royal decree, known as the *cédula de honores*, and Andeans' struggles to secure its enforcement. The *cédula de honores* became a cornerstone for Andean legal and political activism in the decades to follow, at least until Charles III issued a decree in 1776 that recognized the *cédula de honores* and began to enforce it. This chapter examines the discursive underpinnings of the campaigns, offering a linguistic analysis that is contextualized in both their history and results and in contemporary discussions of the cultural transformation of the Indian elite class in the mid- and late colonial period.

The Andean proposals for social change demonstrate the transformation of educated Andeans into a group of politicized agents, aware of their ability to participate in the process of social and cultural change. This period saw the consolidation of a colonial regime that shifted from the paternalistic Habsburg rule to the more pragmatic and modernizing Bourbons. Both dynasties, however, were almost equally dismissive of the royal *cédulas* of 1697 and 1725 and the later reissuing of these two rulings that acknowledged native elites' political and social privileges. Colonial authorities remained largely negligent regarding native Andean claims for social justice, as market forces and rising colonial demands for Andean labor and goods increasingly undermined Andeans' notions of authority and introduced deep social divides within the "republic of Indians."[2] Both the secularization of Indian parishes in 1750 (see Chapter 3) and the 1776 royal decree enforcing social privileges for Indian elites allowed Andeans access to a few lower positions in the secular clergy, but not before the aftermath of the Túpac Amaru Rebellion, which did little to modify the dominant trend of excluding indigenous peoples from positions of power in colonial society.

Writing was paramount in the discursive articulation of intellectual Andeans' campaigns for social inclusion, a cultural practice that enabled their search for social equality and autonomy through questioning colonialism's hierarchical order and redefining elite Andeans' place in the changing colonial world. While seeking social recognition, Andean elites struggled to access a world of social opportunity akin to that of the colonial nobility and to enjoy the relative freedom it entailed. They endeavored to participate in institutions of power and knowledge, but although sanctioned by royal decrees, admission to convents and schools and to positions in the judicial system proved beyond the reach of most. On the other hand, these Andeans' political and social imaginaries remained within the confines of a hierarchical view of the Indian world. Their social and political goals were geared toward elite Indians and mestizos only, leaving little or no room for a more extensive egalitarian notion of Andean rights that would bridge the social distance between elites and commoners within the Indian republic.

Colonial *kurakas* and other lettered Andeans seized every opportunity to belong to prestigious institutions equivalent to those of the Spanish nobility. Very important, they also struggled to be recognized as full members of the church, asserting their ability to act as priests, missionaries, bishops, and prelates; they even campaigned for the beatification and canonization of members of their own communities, qualifications that would allow them into spaces of the utmost sanctity in the afterlife. Along with their desire to belong to religious institutions, Indian and mestizo scholars viewed secular education as a way out of their historical subordination and sought access to schools for *caciques*, seminary schools of the religious orders, and universities. They empowered themselves by locating their discourses in the gap between the potentially favorable mandates of the monarch and the systematic disregard of such laws by the colonial church and authorities in Peru.

HISTORY OF THE LEGAL
CAMPAIGNS FOR ANDEAN NOBLE PRIVILEGES

Although the crown had sanctioned certain religious prerogatives for noble Indians and their descendants in the sixteenth century,[3] these mandates remained dormant; in practice, the crown had only sporadically granted exemptions to noble Indians in the first two and a half centuries of colonial rule. In the late 1600s, intellectual Andeans began to advance a legal campaign to have the crown recognize their social standing and the opportunities attached to it in the colonial world of Peru. Such efforts may have been in part a response to the social unrest created by official attempts, or rumors about such attempts, to hold mestizos liable to *mita* and tribute obligations. Attaining recognition of noble privileges would likely deter such attempts by reasserting the mestizos' elite status.

As a result of Juan Núñez Vela de Rivera's lobbying in Madrid, on March 26, 1697, the king issued a new royal decree resanctioning noble privileges for Indian elites and their mestizo descendants. The ruling established that they should receive "all the preeminence and honors, both ecclesiastical and civil, that is [*sic*] customary to confer to the noble [h]idalgos of Castile, so that they can participate in any community that requires stature of nobility, because it is clear that they were noble even in their former state of *gentilismo* [gentiles' standing before conversion], and their subordinates paid vassalage and tribute to them."[4] The ruling is important not only because it explicitly acknowledges new avenues of social inclusion and power for Andeans but also because it implicitly invalidates neophytism as a reason to deny Indians and mestizos access to key social institutions that required purity of blood for admission. The struggles over the enforcement of this ruling, however, have a history of their own, a long legal and textual battle for social inclusion waged by Andean scholars in the royal courts. The campaigns unveiled the impossibility for the Habsburgs and, later, for most of the Bourbon administration to sustain an inclusive discourse of empire vis-à-vis their Indian subjects.

Individual and collective efforts by Andean elites to obtain privileges and restitution of their *cacicazgos* and lands through litigation had started in the sixteenth century. Since then, Andeans had been aware of Spanish laws and used them to support their claims at both the rhetorical and practical levels. A more concerted effort to advance a comprehensive agenda for social inclusion, however, can be identified as beginning in the late seventeenth century. A key intellectual figure in these struggles was Juan Núñez Vela de Rivera, the mestizo *racionero* (prebendary) from the Arequipa cathedral in 1691 and one of the exceptional Andeans who accessed ecclesiastical positions in that century. While residing temporarily in the royal court in Madrid, he articulated *memoriales* that offered different arguments for the recognition of Andeans as *cristianos viejos,* or old Christians, in support of Andean demands for expansion of their rights within ecclesiastical, secular, and social organizations more generally. In 1693, for example, Núñez Vela de Rivera obtained a decree from King Charles II declaring Indians and mestizos eligible for appointments to the Inquisition Tribunal.[5] That recognition seemed to allow for exceptions to Andeans' automatic status as *neófitos* (neophytes) and idolaters. Historian Juan Carlos Estenssoro Fuchs also stressed that this change implied the recognition of *pureza de sangre* for Andeans. After returning to Lima in 1695, Núñez Vela de Rivera continued his activism for Indian autonomy, becoming chaplain of the recently founded Copacabana *beaterio* and church and supporting with *memoriales* the canonization process of the Indian Nicolás de Dios.[6]

Prior to the royal decree of March 26, 1697, the key textual evidence in the legal campaign for Indian privileges was a *memorial* from 1691 written by Núñez Vela de Rivera. This text became the legal cornerstone that supported claims for the social inclusion of Andeans in the church, schools, and military orders. The ensuing 1697 mandate further mobilized *kurakas* from various regions of the viceroyalty to cross the Atlantic to the royal court in what became a long campaign for its legal enforcement.

Núñez Vela de Rivera's text also links most of the Andean writings analyzed in this chapter. All of the texts and authors discussed sought social mobility for elite Andeans by using the paths available within the colonial system in an effort to attain social equality between the nobles of the two "republics," as subjects of the same king. Along with the other writers, Núñez Vela de Rivera used the rhetoric of evangelization to validate the status of Andeans as old Christians, individuals who had long ago renounced their status as gentiles and "idolaters." Núñez Vela de Rivera's *memorial* stands out for its construction of social and religious identity. Introducing himself as a descendant of Synchi Roca and Spanish knights, he identified himself as a mestizo, a "descendant of gentile Indians, Christian primitives" of the Peruvian kingdom, and a "most faithful son of the Roman Catholic Church."[7] Throughout the text he speaks in the first-person plural, referring to "we" the Indians, and he consistently claims privileges and social honors for noble Andeans, himself included. Unlike all other Andean intellectuals, Núñez Vela de Rivera chose to identify himself as a descendant of the "gentiles" rather than denying his "idolatrous" past, as Jerónimo Lorenzo Limaylla, Juan de Cuevas Herrera, and Fray Calixto de San José Túpac Inca did. Núñez Vela de Rivera validated an indigenous past in which he de-stigmatized Andeans' condition as "primitive gentiles" because of their Christian conversion at the time of the conquest. Thus, he "erased" the stigma attached to being a gentile, which was usually regarded as "idolatrous," and identified himself as a descendant of primitive Christians because doing so allowed him to position himself within the religious framework of his royal audience and to show the evangelization project's effectiveness.

Núñez Vela de Rivera's *memorial* reminded the king of his commitment to equalize Andeans' status with that of Spaniards and demanded a wide range of noble privileges for Andeans.[8] To support his demand, the mestizo from Arequipa used the text of the *Instrucción* (instruction) the Catholic kings had given Christopher Columbus in 1492. He interpreted the *Instrucción* as a reciprocal arrangement between the crown and Andeans, in which the latter would accept Christianity and vassalage to the king in exchange for privileges and treatment akin to those accorded all Spanish subjects. Inspired by the *Instrucción*, Núñez Vela de Rivera remarked about the Catholic kings' interest in officially recognizing the *pureza de sangre* of Andeans and their nobility:

> Since, as a father and protector . . . Y. M. [Your Majesty] is obligated in conscience to look after us and defend our honor, you should command that the pristine blood of Indians will not be an obstacle, impediment, or restriction to obtaining ecclesiastical dignities, even the bishopric; neither will it prevent them from entering schools, churches, chairs, universities, chaplaincies, military offices [including military orders], and all which is related to the service of Y. M., and which may require purity of blood to access, because this is totally present in the Indians, the most faithful vassals of Y. M.[9]

Núñez Vela de Rivera redefined the colonial notion of purity of blood to include Andeans in the category of *cristianos viejos*. His peculiar rendition of the Spanish notion of *pureza de sangre* is based on descent from gentile idolaters, thus validating the Andeans' "idolatrous" past while equating it with European Catholics' own past: "And, since the foundation of honor rests upon purity of blood, and Indians certainly have it in excessive and noticeable amounts, therefore, on the surface of the earth, there is no other nation that exceeds the Indian in purity of blood. Because they [native Andeans] bring their genes from gentile idolaters like all the ones who now profess the [R]oman [Ca]tholic religion."[10]

Rather than their inherited nobility, previously recognized in Spanish law, what accorded the status of *pureza de sangre* to Andeans was the fact that they had descended from "gentiles and idolaters" who later converted to the Roman Catholic religion, just as all Spaniards from pagan roots had converted in the early times of the church and were now officially considered *cristianos viejos*. Thus, he metaphorically "cleansed" the Andean past and constructed a new ground of social equality between Andeans and Spaniards, both of whom shared a gentile past. Núñez Vela de Rivera's reformulation of the Andean past as gentile validates the evangelization project of his day while opening an avenue for broader advancement of his fellow Andeans. In sum, Núñez Vela de Rivera argued that conversion to Christianity should suffice for the recognition of Andeans as nobles. Since conversion also entailed *vivir en policía* (living like "rational" people gathered in towns), he understood that it was necessary to receive the same honors and recognition as those given to civilized Europeans.

To further reinforce these claims, Núñez Vela de Rivera used the foundational text of the *Instruccion* to remind the king of his debt of reciprocity to his indigenous subjects in the late seventeenth century. He supported Andeans' right of nobility on a clause in the *Instruccion* in which the Catholic kings ordered Christopher Columbus "to give gifts and donations to the Indians and to honor them substantially," hoping that the mandates of Charles II's ancestors would still have authoritative power two centuries later. He appealed to "the compact that at the beginning of those conquests the king made with his natives, in which he promised that if Indians accepted subjection and received the sacred gospel, he would honor them as he did the rest of his vassals."[11] Núñez Vela de Rivera attempted to negotiate reciprocity with the king. The appeal to the *Instrucción* and its implicit compact was also a rhetorical strategy to articulate reciprocity in the language of the colonizer in an effort to achieve an Andean agenda, aimed at reasserting the noble status of Indian elites and their mestizo relatives and at preventing royal attempts to downgrade their standing and make them liable to colonial obligations akin to those of commoners.

This reference to a "compact" reveals that Núñez Vela de Rivera's ideas were infused with Scholastic notions of the kingdom as an organic whole, a *corpus politicum mysticum*, prevalent in late-medieval Spain and influential in Limaylla's and Fray Calixto's writings. Núñez Vela de Rivera's representation of the king as a "father," "protector," and "the only hope of the Indians" reflected the trans-culturation of European philosophies in the colonial Andes and his self-perception as a subject bound to the king by reciprocity. The Andean author thus implied that the king, as the foremost legal protector of the Indians, had the responsibility to enforce for Andeans the right to join the priesthood, to receive education in *colegios mayores* and universities, to be granted professorships in universities, to found chaplaincies or *capellanías*, and to hold military positions: "Y. M. and your supreme ministers are obligated in conscience to look after our honor and defend us from all those who want to calumniate our pristine blood.... God chose Y. M. as our father for our protection."[12]

The famous *cédula de honores* issued on March 26, 1697, in Madrid[13] recognized Andeans' status of nobility equal to that of Spaniards and ratified privileges King Charles II had recognized in 1588, granting Amerindian and mestizo women and men admission to religious institutions and the right to hold positions in the political government and the military.[14] The privileges of nobility thus given to Andeans on the basis of their allegiance to the king and colonial values naturally strengthened royal authority. For Andeans, however, this may also have amounted to a partial political victory. After all, the decree opened the way for an ethnic space within traditional colonial institutions of power and began to break through, at least at the legal level, seemingly insurmountable racial barriers. Although the 1697 *real cédula* remained unenforced for years, it was a crucial achievement for Andeans at the symbolic level, representing that writing and lobbying in the royal court could be factors in the negotiation of beneficial laws.

Within the political and scholarly culture of elite Andeans, Núñez Vela de Rivera's *memorial* constituted a crucial point in the systematic incorporation of legal discourses into Andean scholarship and became a vital tool in the campaigns for social inclusion in the eighteenth century. Although Andean authorities had systematically used litigation and legal discourses since the sixteenth century, Indian visitors, with their *memoriales*, showed up more frequently in the royal court in the years following the 1697 royal decree, giving special vitality to a trans-Atlantic movement of protest writing and constructions of identity that brought members of the Amerindian elite simultaneously closer to and farther from the apex of the empire. With the ascent of the Bourbons to the head of the Spanish empire, changes occurred in which colonial demands on Andeans tightened, the illegal practice of *repartimiento de comercio* intensified, and tensions between local officials and Andeans increased. Social unrest and rebellions characterized the eighteenth century, in which some of the goals of the campaigns for social inclusion were articulated anew, particularly in the Huarochirí and Túpac Amaru rebellions. Toward the end of the century, particularly after 1783, the crown began to enforce the right to join the priesthood only for *caciques* and elite Incas who had fought against Túpac Amaru, although they were ordained only as secular priests.

The struggles for enforcement of the 1697 royal policy involved further writing, traveling, and negotiation with viceregal and royal authorities. Don Francisco Saba Capac Inga and Don Joseph de Castro, Indian nobles from Lima and leading figures within Lima's Indian networks, initiated this phase of the legal campaign, which extended for approximately the next seventy years. They put together *memoriales* and letters and sent them to the Viceroys Diego Ladrón de Guevara, Diego Morcillo Rubio de Auñón, and Marqués de Castelfuerte and to Kings Philip V and Louis I in 1711, 1722, 1724, and 1726. They demanded that the *cédula de honores* finally be published and circulated, since ecclesiastical and state authorities in Peru were systematically ignoring it.[15] An intertwined exchange of correspondence among different levels of the colonial administration followed the Indian petitions. The king invariably issued new *cédulas* reinstating the purpose of the previous ones but did little more than warn officials in Peru of the gravity of their negligence, and the petitions languished in this endless bureaucratic inertia.[16] In 1732 Procurador de Naturales Vicente Morachimo joined this legal campaign, and Fray Calixto did so in 1749. One of the main reforms he demanded was the abolition of innocuous laws and the issuing of new ones, responding to the new realities of Christian Andeans who had come of age and were ready to act as ambassadors of God on earth.[17] Not until September 11, 1766, was a royal decree issued by Charles III, along with a confirmation by Pope Gregorio XIII, that reiterated and reinstated the contents of the 1697 and 1725 royal decrees.[18]

INTELLECTUAL BATTLES FOR THE ANDEAN PRIESTHOOD

Before the Europeans arrived in the Andes, Andean and Inca lords exerted power over the almost inseparable realms of the sacred and the mundane. After the Spanish invasion, *kurakas'* ability to act within these spheres was constrained by the new colonial arrangement.[19] In an effort to continue to legitimate the sacred character of their authority within the colonial situation, *kurakas* and other members of the Andean elite strove to occupy spaces within the colonial sacred sphere, increasingly dominated by the Catholic Church. Andean elites' struggles to enter the priesthood can be understood, then, as an effort to access the newly redefined realm of spiritual power in society.

Sakari Sariola interpreted Fray Calixto's claims for the priesthood in the "Representación verdadera" as an expression of the Andean intelligentsia's desire to participate in the creation of spiritual symbols and in forms of "spiritual self-organization" within the colonial situation. Andeans perceived that the Catholic priesthood was an avenue to spiritual power and sometimes even an opportunity for social advancement. This strategy would enable them to forge ethnic identities and spaces in which Christianity would attempt to replace preexisting indigenous beliefs. Sharing the "divine principle" would function as a "protective and life-giving symbol instead of a threatening *memento mori*."[20] Sariola's interpretation usefully acknowledges the politics of spirituality in the colonial situation and the motivations of subordinate Andeans when participating consciously in the religious realm of the colonizer, an empowering space to counter social exclusion in the name of Christianity.

After studying the Indian campaigns for sainthood and the priesthood in colonial Peru as expressions of Indian Catholic virtuosity, Juan Carlos Estenssoro Fuchs argued that colonial Andeans sought acceptance into Catholicism to fully partake in its "symbolic and institutional reproduction," which also revealed Andeans' impetus to preserve their autonomy within the colonial society.[21] Estenssoro Fuchs interpreted the church's systematic opposition to the admission of Indians and mestizos into the priesthood as an acknowledgment of the danger implicit in their full inclusion. The admission of Andeans into the priesthood, a profession allowed only to Spaniards and creoles, threatened to blur racial barriers the church had upheld for centuries. Rather than reflecting Andeans' desire to assimilate into Catholicism, their struggles for recognition as Christians were dangerous weapons that threatened to erase well-entrenched colonial hierarchies.[22]

This interpretation helps us make sense of Andeans' stubbornness in pursuing the priesthood, even after many years of continuous ecclesiastical disregard for the crown's policies in favor of Andean social privileges. Estenssoro Fuch's interpretation is important for understanding Andeans' struggles to equalize their status with that of Spanish nobles as a form of anticolonial struggle that reveals Andean intellectuals as deconstructors of the colonial social order through their canny use of its own legal and religious discourses.[23] The 1677–1716 Indian campaign for access to heaven was an important movement that made evident the social activism of the Lima network of Andeans and their drive for ethnic autonomy at the spiritual level.

The desire to join the priesthood and share ecclesiastical positions with creoles and Spaniards represented a way for Indian nobles to participate simultaneously in colonial public life and the spiritual realm of power within colonial society. In pre-Columbian societies Andean authorities had led the sacred and the profane, but in the colonial situation they struggled to maintain a spiritual presence in the public arenas. Even within the constraints of the hierarchical colonial order, they still sought openings of power for themselves, mostly at the local and lower levels of society. As most spheres of life were socially and politically defined, in the colonial setting the sacred was a realm of power and exclusion that mirrored the contending forces and attitudes prevalent in the larger society. Andean struggles for access to the priesthood also had an autonomous impetus, however. The recruitment of Indian missionaries and native teachers for Indian communities, the insistence on the need to preach in the native language, and the campaigns for Indian priesthood all reflected the desire of *caciques* and mestizo leaders to control Andeans' religious realm.

The Catholic Church in America had to grapple with the inherent contradiction of a Christian institution engaged in spiritual conquest and the inconsistency between the Christian promise of human equality and the racial basis of the colonial project with which the church was deeply associated. Concerns for Andean inclusion in religious institutions of power conjured up long-standing ecclesiastical notions of purity. In *Genealogical Fictions*, María Elena Martínez established that since the late fifteenth century in Iberia, ecclesiastical statutes of *pureza de sangre* had functioned to preserve the purity of religious and social institutions by excluding new Christian converts of Jewish and Muslim origin. She also argued that similar statutes were brought to America and shaped Indians' perceptions of themselves. The Indian nobility became invested in the writings of their ancestry and concerned with the notion of purity, as the crown recognized Indian purity and entitlement to noble privileges.[24] Fray Calixto and Núñez Vela de Rivera were well aware of this royal jurisprudence, as they exposed the legitimacy of their claims for inclusion on the grounds of their purity of blood and their condition as old Christians. Thus, Fray Calixto delved into a full deconstruction of neophytism as a barrier of Spanish ecclesiastical manufacture and strove to demonstrate Andeans' identity and status as *cristianos viejos*, overtly denouncing the racial differences introduced by Spaniards into the Andean world: "After the conquest of the West Indies, the Spanish founded a monarchy different from any other [monarchy] ... with that differentiation of Spaniards and Indians, so absurd, absolute and tyrannical ... and which turns even harder by the day."[25] In justifying his claims for the creation of an Indian noble knightly order, Limaylla made it clear that the order would help elevate elite Indians' dignity "so Spaniards would have them [Indian nobles] in high regard, and would hesitate to oppress them."[26]

Among the body of Andean writings in the late colonial period, the "Representación verdadera" stands out as the foremost rendition of Andeans' will to participate in the realm of Catholic priesthood and presents the most complex discussion of the institutional and theological obstacles that systematically prevented Indian subjects from being accepted as intermediaries between humans and God. The text capitalized on an apparent opposition: on the one hand, the crown's endorsement, but non-enforcement, of the admission of capable Indians to the priesthood, which would have allowed Andeans to mediate between the people and God, and, on the other, their systematic exclusion from ecclesiastical spheres of power by the Peruvian church, mostly the religious orders. The idea of purity of blood and the assumption that Andeans had never stopped being neophytes kept them from being fully acknowledged as mature Christians by the church.

The campaign for Indian and mestizo participation in the priesthood developed at the intellectual and legal levels during the years preceding the 1750 Huarochirí rebellion and the Lima conspiracy—mostly in the Lima area, with a clear locus in the Cercado *cabildo*. Not only the illegal *repartos* and increasing tribute in the mid-eighteenth century but also the lack of enforcement of the 1697 *cédula de honores* increased the frustration of Andean communities and leaders, who usually gathered at the seat of the *audiencia* to publicize their grievances and organize movements against these irregularities.

The "Representación verdadera" in particular represented the main locus of a complex argument that advocated noble Andeans' right to enter the priesthood. Its discussion intertwined knowledge of the history of the early Catholic Church, theological debates in the Scholastic style, and the contribution of Andean experiential knowledge and intellectual agency. The text ultimately demonstrated the inconsistency of ecclesiastical policies regarding native participation in the church across time and space. Fray Calixto sought to debunk the reasons the ecclesiastic councils of the sixteenth century, still prevalent in the eighteenth century, denied native applications to the priesthood. Thus, the "Representación verdadera" disputed ecclesiastical assumptions of Indians' religious status as "gentiles," "neophytes," and "idolaters" and the construction of Indians as alcoholics, promiscuous, and savage—300 years after the evangelization programs had begun.

The textual validation of the campaign for the Andean priesthood gravitated around juridical expedients, theological debates, redefinitions of Indians' social status, and discussions of native Andeans' ability to act as priests. Andean scholars seemed to invoke no spiritual reasons to support their desire to become "magistrates of the sacred." The underlying argument is political at the same time that it is revealing of the politics of religion within the colonial context.

The dossier entitled "Breve y compendiosa satisfacción,"[27] an entire subsection of the "Representación verdadera," engaged in a counterpoint with ecclesiastical views to construct a critique of the church's social discrimination against Indians. The text used authoritative canonical sources, including Saint Paul's epistles and opinions of other founding figures of the early church in Rome, the mandates of the Church Councils of Nicea and Trent, and the writings of Chiapas's Bishop Fray Bartolomé de las Casas—all of which provided theological and theoretical support for the Andean claims for recognition as *cristianos viejos*. Aside from these more Western sources, the "Breve y compendiosa satisfacción" also incorporated rhetorical strategies and examples from Inca Garcilaso de la Vega's *Comentarios reales de los Incas*, since its elaboration of Inca religion reinforced Andeans' arguments in favor of a Catholic Indian priesthood. The text develops

an imaginary counterpoint between the supporters of natives and mestizos joining the priesthood and the church councils' and Episcopal views on the issue,
which were fundamental in defining Andeans as gentiles and neophytes and constructed stereotypes that identified them as alcoholics and illiterate.

ANDEAN DECONSTRUCTION OF
THE ECCLESIASTICAL EXCLUSION

The discussion of Andeans' ability and entitlement to mediate between God and
Indian congregants was a political battle against the power of colonial ecclesiastics and their discourses to "fix" Amerindian identities through ethnic stereotypes. This constituted the "colonial difference,"[28] which justified the exclusion
of Andeans from the church on the basis of their ethnic otherness. The overall
argument of Andean scholars was directed toward the Episcopal authorities in
Lima, who perpetuated the views of the sixteenth-century Lima church councils. In Archbishop Pedro de Villagómez's pastoral letter from 1649 and in his
response to Juan de Padilla's "Parecer" in a letter to King Philip IV (July 21,
1657), Villagómez expressed more vocally how difficult it was to uproot idolatry.
Among other reasons, he believed this difficulty stemmed from

> the cunningness of the devil and the rusticity and small capability of the
> Indians, and also from the fact that they were *ab initio* children of idolaters,
> given to customary drunkenness, and most importantly [because] they imitate
> their ancestors in this issue of idolatry . . . and also given the diligence that the
> ministers of idolatry put toward their own preservation, as well as the disposi-
> tion of their towns and the fact [that] they are inevitably surrounded by the
> objects they use to worship.[29]

Archbishop Villagómez conducted extirpation campaigns in the Lima diocese during the years 1641–1671, with particular emphasis in 1649–1670, and
his views seem to have prevailed in the Peruvian church until the mid-eighteenth
century. Andean scholars waged a discursive war against the stereotypes highlighted in the statement just cited.

In terms of religious maturity, the church councils regarded indigenous peoples as gentiles and idolaters because of their descent from non-Christian forebears, a perceived inferior status that in the eighteenth century still had a powerful discriminatory force. In this view, *gentilismo* "handicapped" Andeans. Their
ancestors' paganism made them prone to misunderstand Christianity and relapse
into idolatry. Thus, the ecclesiastic discourse of the Lima church forced Andean
intellectuals to separate themselves from their forebears and profess: "Our forefathers the Inca kings and other gentiles sinned indeed . . . for their prolonged and
multiplied idolatry, it is true; but they are no longer our fathers, though they and
we still bear their iniquities. Are not thou, Lord, our Father, our Lord and our

King? For how long should we be held responsible for someone else's idolatry, bearing such an affront upon us?"[30] The statement evidently constructs Andeans' religious identity as old Christians.

Fray Calixto debunked the notion of *gentilismo*, arguing that it lay at the very inception of the Catholic Church in the Old World: "It was from gentile converts that the [p]ontiffs, [b]ishops, [p]resbyters, deacons, nuns, and monks, from Pope Saint Lino to the present, originated; [a]nd the Catholic Church is made up of that gentilismo, later converted to Christ by [b]aptism."[31] Andeans reminded Spaniards that idolatry had existed in Spain and all of Europe, Africa, and Asia since antiquity and had coexisted with Christianity since the Middle Ages. Therefore, early Andean religious customs did not make Andeans any worse than European Christians: "In the thirteenth century, in Poland and in the surrounding kingdoms of Germany, Christians were still living like gentiles, worshipping leafy trees, stones, and snakes ... and all throughout Europe even today, there are superstitions and omens among Christians, who maintain the names of gentility."[32]

Episcopal authorities also categorized Indians as neophytes. As newly converted people, Indians were viewed as incomplete Christians, unable to comprehend the canon or to minister as competently as Spanish priests and prelates. Aided by a letter from Saint Paul and the theses of the Council of Nice, Fray Calixto argued that by the eighteenth century, Indians were no longer *neófitos*. According to the credited sources, ten years after being baptized, gentiles ceased to be gentiles and became eligible for ecclesiastical preferment. Therefore, Peruvian and Mexican Indians could not be considered neophytes, since they had been baptized and Christianized about three centuries earlier: "These American [I]ndians from Peru and Mexico entered the Church and have been baptized for more than two hundred years, and they are now twenty or thirty generations farther from gentilidad and still they cannot find a way out of it."[33] The writers are thus aware of the inconsistencies of the church's stances regarding neophytism, as applied to Indians and mestizos.

The discussion in the "Representación verdadera" then turns to the idea that while the early church in Europe incorporated colonized peoples, the Peruvian church marginalized Andeans and obstructed their attempts to become full Christians. According to Andean scholars, Jewish converts and former slaves were elevated to high ecclesiastical positions in the early period, whereas the Peruvian church denied the positions to Andeans, even those legally defined as free subjects and despite their "willing" conversion to Christianity. The text's examples extend to the early Roman Empire, arguing that gentiles of Greek origin later became knights in the Roman Empire. The Romans did not simply impose their religion on the vanquished, but to bring about social peace they also incorporated the gods of the vanquished into their own pantheon.

Almost equating the Roman and Inca approaches to empire, the text points out that the Romans "received their conquered's idols, religions, ceremonies, and their 'wandering gods,' thus integrating them happily and agreeably."[34] The text continues: "And thus the Romans conquered all [of] the world. And they made knights out of the nobles from all the conquered nations, who enjoyed privileges, immunities, and respect. . . . Also, the noble and plebeian Moors that remained in Spain became Spanish."[35] What the Andeans did not discuss was the different phases in the long history of the church. During its early times, it needed to gain adherents and supporters to grow, although in the eighteenth century, as a hegemonic and powerful institution, it reproduced the racial barriers prevalent in the larger colonial society to maintain its power and differentiation. Similarly, the text contested accusations that Indians were drunkards, retorting that drinking was a European practice and the consequence of the abusive *repartos*.[36]

The writers proposed a political and cultural negotiation to the king: conversion would more effectively preserve Christendom and monarchical authority if missionaries were Indians. Their relatives and friends would listen to them, and Indian and mestizo friars and clergy would be less costly than Spanish friars.[37] If allowed into the priesthood and ecclesiastical positions, the argument went, Indians and mestizos would be more effective missionaries in areas where Spanish missionaries had met fierce resistance. The manuscript tacitly alluded to the viceregal army's failed attempts to extinguish Juan Santos Atahualpa's rebellion in Cerro de la Sal, which had broken out six years earlier, in 1742, stressing the need to send Indian and mestizo missionaries to support the conversion of those who had "retreated to the mountains" in resisting the efforts of the church. Spanish missionaries had been, and would continue to be, unable to reach out if they proved unable or unwilling to incorporate Andeans as missionaries: "Spaniards are unable to reach so many of the gentiles because of the natural horror, aversion and fear that they, themselves, rouse in the Indians and because they know that Spaniards intend to enslave them instead of treat them with love for their souls. Thus, it is useless that Y. M. keeps sending costly armies of missionaries to the area because the more they come, the less successful they will be."[38]

The mestizo and *doctrinero* Juan de Cuevas Herrera sought to empower Andeans who were proficient in both European and Amerindian languages, suggesting that they were more competent to act as missionaries and priests than their Spanish counterparts. What the text proposed was based on placing value on the Andean experience, and the offer to collaborate in the civilizing mission was more complex than mere acceptance of the colonizers' religious projects. This effort had the potential to situate Andean missionaries and the Andean faithful in a more favorable position to compete with Spaniards for key positions of spiritual and social control in their communities. In support of this right, Andeans such as Fray Calixto later claimed, for example, that since the Congregation of

Propaganda Fide in China ordained native Chinese as missionaries, Andeans should be allowed to benefit from similar ecclesiastical policies in the Andes.[39]

In deconstructing the ecclesiastical discourse regarding impediments to the creation of a sanctioned Andean priesthood, the authors contrasted racial discrimination in the colonial church with the ethnic diversity of the institution in its formative stages in Mediterranean Europe:

> Thus, one sees that among Spaniards, the French are admitted to the priesthood and so the Spaniards are admitted to the priesthood among the French, and both of them [enjoy that right] among Italians, and all of them [enjoy that right] in their own and foreign regions only because the Holy Mother Catholic Church receives every man, her children, in the universal embrace of her love, and she doesn't want Zion's roads to the priesthood to be closed for them to ascend to perfection. Because if her husband, and head, who is Christ . . . serves everyone, why has this Church been closed to Indians and only to them, when it was not closed to the [b]arbarian gentile sects, the serfs, and the free? If [Indians] are already Christians, why not [let them also be] priests? . . . There are no laws, neither [n]atural, written nor [d]ivine [g]race, neither positive nor humane, and neither ecclesiastical nor royal laws that oppose it. There is only a tyrannical error practiced by the capricious Spanish vanity. . . . Why is it that only in the Indies are Indians not received into the orders and dignities?[40]

The intellectuals who crafted this text suggested that the church of Christ had stopped serving everyone and turned against Andean believers, clearly exposing the church's disparate positions. The difference between being an Andean Christian in Peru in the eighteenth century and a European Christian in the early church would then be the "colonial difference," which deemed the European faithful superior to Andeans because of the latter's perceived lower ethnic status. Unlike the gentiles in the early Mediterranean church, Andeans in late-colonial Peru saw their potential for full membership in the church reduced to that of the faithful with duties (e.g., paying tithes and abusive ecclesiastical fees, attending mass, confessing) rather than entitlement to minister in positions of power, as the Spanish Christians did. More clearly, the text denounces colonial discrimination against indigenous prospects:

> And since antiquity, it has been seen that there have been a handful of secular Indian presbyters both in Peru and New Spain, although this has created contempt and repugnance among Spaniards. . . . [The Spaniards] have become the sole masters and possessors of all that is spiritual, eternal, and temporal. . . . [A]nd just because candidates [to the priesthood] are white and Spaniards, they are easily admitted, and, with no hesitation, the habits are granted to these unworthy, ignorant, vicious, illegitimate, adulterous, and sacrilegious [men]. Thus, the orders are crowded with disgusting and illegitimate children.[41]

By seeking admission to the priesthood, Andeans were attempting to break the racial monopoly of the sacred space, to create an opening into the spiritual realm of power of the colonial society, a crack through which Andean scholars were able to situate their claims for religious inclusion. The consistent postponement of recognition of Indians and mestizos as full Christians reveals one of the prominent dimensions of the church as a colonial institution that deliberately turned evangelization—a temporary tool—into a permanent undertaking.[42] Because the colonial church largely failed to grant Indians access to the priesthood, the Andean nobility undertook the task of advancing its own campaign to make the institution consistent with the Christian discourse of social inclusion and to actualize the Habsburg promise of granting privileges to Indian elites, which seemed available only to a select few. A brief history of Andeans in the priesthood will historically contextualize the scholarly discussion that ultimately turned a seemingly religious campaign into a political battle over Christian exclusion and ethnic empowerment.

THOSE WHO MADE IT: A BRIEF HISTORY OF ANDEANS IN THE COLONIAL PRIESTHOOD

Only a handful of Andeans managed to join the priesthood prior to the late eighteenth century, and they remained rare exceptions.[43] In a way, the history of colonial Andeans in the priesthood is the history of a spiritual impossibility that reveals more about the institutional hurdles Andeans faced in their attempt to join religious orders and the secular clergy. But even an examination of these obstacles is significant because it tells us much about the politics of spirituality in a colonial setting and the ways Indian subjects attempted to negotiate them.

The ecclesiastical councils in the sixteenth century had the power to define the guidelines for eligibility for the priesthood, even though the religious orders themselves eventually exerted a measure of freedom of interpretation. The 1552 church council in Lima opposed the ordination of Indians, arguing that they were neophytes and therefore prone to misinterpret the divine mysteries. Given the scarcity of *curas doctrineros* in Peru, the second church council in 1567 considered allowing mestizos, fit and proficient in native languages, to be ordained into the sacred orders, although they would not be given the opportunity to hold *beneficios* (parishes). The council did not take serious steps to implement this policy, however, and in practice the Lima church precluded Indians and mestizos from ordination and confined them to serving only in the roles of sacristans and altar boys. Indians thus remained excluded from the priesthood because of their neophytism and impurity of blood.[44] The third council added that mestizos ordained *ad titulum indorum* could be assigned to *doctrinas* following their ordination.[45] Finally, in 1682 a Limeño provincial council of the church approved the ordination of native Andeans and mestizos provided they were legitimate and fit for the priesthood.[46] It seems, however, that in practice secular authorities were reluctant to implement this policy. For its part, the Mexican church's policies were little different. The 1555 Mexican council expressly prohibited the ordination of Indians, mestizos, and blacks. Both the Franciscan and Dominican orders adopted the same policy in 1576.[47]

High-ranking members of the church in Rome, by contrast, seemed to have more consistently favored the admission of Indians to the priesthood. In 1586, as a result of a petition circulated by mestizos, Pope Gregorio XIII sanctioned the ordination of mestizos by the bull *Nuper ad Nos* and provided a special dispensation for illegitimacy. He also authorized that legitimate Indians could be ordained as priests, provided they fulfilled the conditions of competence and other virtues previously mandated by the Council of Trent. The cardinals' college at the Vatican rejected the exclusion of Indians from a priestly career in 1631, concluding that Indians' ordination was consistent with royal policies on the matter and was only at odds with the dispositions of the American episcopate. Francesco Ingoli, secretary of the Propaganda Fide congregation in Rome, warned in 1638 that the American church would remain weak and incomplete if it did not ordain Indian priests.[48]

The Spanish crown also exhibited an ambiguous attitude toward the ordination of nonwhites in America. During the second half of the sixteenth century, the crown reprimanded secular authorities for allowing mestizos into the priesthood in Mexico (1550), Quito (1568, 1575), New Granada (1576), Lima (1578), and Santiago de Chile (1588) and ordered the immediate suspension of new ordinations. In 1588, a new royal decree abolished previous decrees and allowed mestizos and mestizas to join religious orders and nunneries.[49]

The royal attitude began to change as a result of new petitions filed by mestizos in the late seventeenth century. Although King Charles II, in 1691, and King Philip V, in 1725, issued royal decrees that allowed Andeans to enter both the priesthood and the *colegios mayores* (religious colleges), the secular and regular clergy largely disregarded the decrees. In 1726, *kurakas* from Lima were still petitioning for this right and asking the *real audiencia* to make public the royal decree of 1725.[50] Not until 1776 was the ruling on Andean priesthood amply diffused in Peru. This change had to do with Pope Clemente XIII's brief to America the same year, prompting the admission of Andean elites to *colegios mayores* and religious orders "according to their capacity." Shortly thereafter, Charles III likewise issued a royal decree that restated the previous mandates.[51] The opinions and attitudes of the Peruvian church diverged from the will of the kings and the pope for a long period, as these decrees and statements illustrate. In practice, a dispensation from the bishop—seldom granted—was mandatory to ordain individual Indians and mestizos. Moreover, in most religious orders' statutes the ideal of *pureza de sangre*, which excluded those considered neophytes, remained a major hurdle to Andeans' ability to join the priesthood. Only in exceptional cases did secular authorities diverge from the institutional requirement of purity.

Around 1731, Quito bishop Alonso de la Peña Montenegro, whose writings inspired Fray Calixto's advocacy of the priesthood, maintained that Andeans did not lose their right to join the priesthood because of their origin and nature. As long as they were apt and capable, he maintained, they might be admitted into the church "to its service and holy ministries." The bishop, however, adhered to the early mandates of the Council of Trent that state that only legitimate Christians are eligible for the priesthood, and "Indians could lose this right for their vices, bad customs and life."[52] In other words, it would be up to the ecclesiastical authorities, Spanish and creole, to individually determine native Andeans' eligibility. The extent to which cultural differences and racial origin would be associated with vices and bad customs was an issue with which Andeans always had to contend. The disparate opinions over the position of Indians in the church held by authorities in Spain and Rome, on the one hand, and the Peruvian episcopate and religious orders, on the other, reveal a long-lasting rift within the power institutions of colonialism—one Andean scholars would seize in every possible way to empower their struggles for social inclusion in the institution that controlled spiritual power in the realm.

Over the years, Andeans who managed to enter convents and monasteries did so mostly in marginal positions—either as *donados* (servants), mission aides, or lay priests—and were seldom ordained as priests with full capability to administer the sacraments. Andeans thus entered the religious orders in a subordinate capacity, in which they were regarded as secondary members of the order; they could wear habits but were not allowed to take vows.[53] *Donados*, however, did receive religious instruction and training in Latin, Spanish, and native languages. Because of their cultural and linguistic background, many performed missionary work, serving as *predicadores* (preachers) and aides to facilitate the introduction of new prospective indigenous groups into the evangelization campaigns.[54] Fray Calixto de San José Túpac Inca, discussed earlier, had joined the Franciscan convent of Santa Rosa de Ocopa in Tarma as a *donado* and served there for years, probably starting in the late 1730s. Later, in 1750, after he entered the Franciscan seminary in Valencia (Spain), he was able to be ordained, but only as a lay brother.[55]

The Indian enrollment situation slowly began to change in the late eighteenth century when the number of Indian priests seems to have increased as the age of Bourbon secularization progressed and concerns about *pureza de sangre* waned, even though they still played a role in the evaluation of Andeans' applications to the priesthood. Changes in the church's attitude toward Amerindian Christianization, now less associated with concerns about idolatry, allowed more

Amerindians to be ordained as priests.[56] Scarlett O'Phelan has maintained that the secularization of the *curatos de indios* along with the *cédula de honores* facilitated the admission of Indians and mestizos to the clergy. She only identified a few Indian priests before the Great Rebellion, however, and most of them served as secular priests in the minor orders, with a number proceeding from the Cusco area.[57] The available evidence predominantly suggests that the number of ordained Indian priests, even following the 1766 royal decree by Charles III, remained rather low in spite of unsupported affirmations to the contrary.[58] Most mestizos and Indians ordained in the late eighteenth century were in the minor orders, were stationed in remote posts, and served only as assistants.[59] Only after the Great Rebellion do the numbers show some improvement, although ordinations remained largely circumscribed to the Cusco area and among such prominent Inca lineages as the Carlos Inga, the Choquehuanca, the Sahuaraura, the Tito Atauche, and the Pumacahua. Such promotions were granted as rewards for support of the colonial establishment during the Great Rebellion.[60] David Garrett maintained that in 1792, at most 5 percent of the priests in the regular orders of the Cusco Bishopric were noble Indian men.[61] Other sources have maintained, without sufficient empirical support, that by the end of the eighteenth century, Indian priests had been appointed in all of the ecclesiastic *cabildos* in New Spain and Peru, in areas densely populated by Indians. Hans-Jürgen Prien maintained that Indian priests were numerous, although they were classified as minor clerics, with little possibility for promotion.[62] Overall, the available evidence supports a very modest degree of Indian ordination toward the end of the eighteenth century.

Regardless of the actual numbers of Andeans admitted to the priesthood, it seems clear that—although belated and reiterative—the 1769 and 1776 royal mandates by King Charles III, along with the bull of Pope Gregorio VIII, represented a response to Andean struggles for the priesthood. They were particularly a response to the trans-Atlantic activism of Fray Calixto de San José Túpac Inca and the comprehensive set of proposals raised in the "Representación verdadera" and the "Planctus indorum," copies of which were sent to the pope in 1751 and may have reached him. The decree benefited Andean elites from Cusco more than those from the Audiencia of Lima area, whose *caciques* and mestizo relatives had been more actively engaged in the campaign for these opportunities.

Beyond directly critiquing ecclesiastical regulations, however, Andean aspirants to the priesthood had been using creative ways to access religious positions. *Caciques* became involved in the foundation of *capellanías* and other pious organizations to secure posts as chaplains for family members, endow applicants to the priesthood, and enhance their institutions' prestige.[63] O'Phelan described this strategy by Andean and mestizo applicants to the higher orders, along with their self-empowerment as native speakers of indigenous languages.[64] In some areas of New Spain, possessing a *capellanía* was a sine qua non for entering the priesthood.[65] Andean lords' daughters entered nunneries earlier than Indian men were able to obtain access to the priesthood.[66] Although such cases were rare, they likely occurred because in the predominantly male-oriented ecclesiastic power structure, even white Spanish nuns had long been excluded from the wide range of power roles performed by priests in the Catholic Church, not to mention from higher positions.

Overall, the key question remains: why did the Peruvian church—particularly the regular orders such as the Jesuits, Franciscans, and others—so consistently deny Andeans the priesthood and so confidently disregard royal and papal mandates on the matter? In attempting to answer such questions, we must remember that the colonial church had to come to terms with its own contradictions. The raison d'être of the church in America was to evangelize and convert; granting the priesthood to indigenous peoples would seem to have been a natural result of a successful missionary enterprise. The church embraced Indian converts through sacraments such as baptism, confession, matrimony, and eventually communion and extreme unction. Yet when good converts were ready to administer the sacraments and spirituality more generally, the church turned its back on them with the typical inclusion/exclusion ambiguity that characterized its approach to Amerindian religiosity. This ambiguity sustained or justified Indian nobles' ongoing effort to become fully recognized as *cristianos viejos* and therefore eligible to participate in the divine realm, mediating between mortals and God.

Francesco Ingoli concluded in 1638 that Spanish American ecclesiastical authorities had actively prevented the ordination and education of native Andeans, not because they were incapable or alcoholic by nature but rather to facilitate their continued subordination. The most important cause of the stagnation of missionary work in the seventeenth century, Ingoli maintained, was the exclusion of Indians from the clergy, combined with the association of evangelization with their dispossession and enslavement. Indians were intelligent, capable, disciplined, and fast learners and were often superior to Europeans in their devotion and moral values. In fact, Ingoli proposed, admitting Indians to the priesthood would eliminate the linguistic ignorance of bishops and foreign missionaries and the need for Spanish missionaries, who used evangelization as a pretext to carry on their own business affairs and intrigues rather than to assist native Andeans spiritually.[67] In the seventeenth century, Ingoli was already aware of the colonial interests of the church, a structural rather than a theological reason for excluding Indians from the priesthood.

In interpreting the ecclesiastical attitude toward Indian priesthood, Venezuelan historian F. Eduardo Osorio maintained that the rejection was a response to the system of racial hierarchies prevalent within the larger colonial society, which also permeated the ecclesiastical institution. Allowing Indians into the priesthood would unsettle the ideological hegemony that supported colonial domination by leveling off racial differences at the religious level, which could jeopardize the social dominance of whites.[68] The de facto recognition of Indians as full Christians (no longer neophytes in need of conversion) eligible for the priesthood would render void the role of the church in the New World, since its presence was justified on the grounds of bringing Christianity to infidel Indians. Once these Indians had reached the status of *cristianos viejos* and were able to minister as priests and nuns, the evangelization project and the presence of the Spanish church would no longer be necessary, at least in theory. But, obviously, the church's scaffolding was well entrenched within the structures of colonial society and had vested interests that diverted to a wider field of power.

Along similar lines, Estenssoro Fuchs posited that an "Indian priest" would have been a contradiction in itself, from the point of view of the colonial rationale, because recognition of Christian Indians' coming-of-age would mean they were no longer Indians; ordaining Indian priests would thus amount to doing away with the category "Indian" altogether, with the consequent disappearance of colonial ethnic hierarchies such neophytism endorsed.[69] As minors in the process of Christianization, neophytes needed protection, guidance, and mentorship. Once the ecclesiastical institution was well established in America, these were no longer treated as temporary stages in a conversion process but instead as a permanent state that would secure the continuity of the ecclesiastical institution. The church had thus become a colonial institution that perpetuated the racial hierarchies of both the larger colonial world and itself as a hegemonic institution within that world.

These challenges to the church's ability to control Indians underlay its negative responses to the claims for Indian access to the regular and secular orders. Those responses stemmed from the recognition of the power Indian parish priests could exert in their communities and the potential remote parishes in particular would represent to the achievement of Indian autonomy. The danger that religious Andeans would support Indian rebellions, for example, became particularly clear in 1757, when Fray Calixto was condemned to life in exile and seclusion for his political activism before and after the rebellion in Huarochirí.[70]

In the colonial situation, Indian priesthood was a double-edged sword. Indian priesthood had the potential to serve an agenda for ethnic autonomy, as was the case in the social movements led by Juan Núñez Vela de Rivera, Jerónimo Lorenzo Limaylla, Vicente Morachimo, and Fray Calixto. On the other hand, Indian priesthood could also function as a legitimizing tool for Christianity among Indian subjects, institutionalizing Indian priests within the state's and the church's larger civilizing and political mission. In fact, a vocal and enthusiastic group of Indian priests bitterly opposed the Túpac Amaru upheaval and the rebel leader in particular and stood out as ideological strongholds of the dominant church and the crown in the Cusco area in the 1780s.[71] A more inclusive church could have granted Indians access to the priesthood and worked to win them over to its agenda of social control, as Secretary of the Propaganda Fide Ingoli had early envisioned, without jeopardizing the interests of the Franciscan institution he represented in Rome. Obviously, the results of these positions were unpredictable, as was the colonial project of Indian education, which similarly served opposite purposes simultaneously. The textual campaigns for the Indian priesthood overall reveal Andeans' political awareness of those realities and the way struggles for the priesthood constituted just one piece of the Andean agenda for ethnic self-assertiveness as a tool of Indian resistance under Spanish rule.

EDUCATION FOR ANDEANS IN SCIENCE AND LETTERS

In spite of the 1697 *cédula de honores*, educational opportunities for Indians proved elusive. Only two *colegios* for *caciques* operated in Lima and Cusco, each with a long history of financial problems. Such schools seemed to fade away as the eighteenth century approached, receiving a final blow with the expulsion of the Jesuits in 1767. Beyond that, opportunities for Andeans in the *colegios mayores* and universities appeared less accessible; only a handful of elite Indians and mestizos managed to enter those establishments. Following a long history of Andean petitions and lobbying for admission to schools, a more clearly articulated claim for Andean education appeared in the "Representación verdadera" in ca. 1749–1750.

The condition of illiteracy was used to characterize and then to ostracize natives and mestizos from positions within the Catholic Church, and educated Andeans were well aware of the political and social value of literacy and education—especially in the late colonial period, when European enlightened culture had high regard for education and progress. Indian illiteracy, as viewed by the church and colonial officials, became a stereotype that naturalized Andeans' mental and intellectual inferiority, another expression of the "colonial difference." To rebut the assumption that Indians were mentally unable to learn how to read and write, let alone to become more broadly educated, the "Breve y compendiosa satisfacción" developed four arguments that concisely addressed the politics of literacy and education in the colonial situation.

First, by "remaining brute and illiterate,"[72] Fray Calixto maintained, Indians were unable to defend themselves in the Spanish world. In all business matters, they had to deal with Spanish functionaries (judges, lawyers, attorneys, and scribes) who were prejudiced and less than impartial. Second, because of native Andeans' illiteracy, ecclesiastical and administrative positions were given to Spaniards, even those that involved the administration of Indian hospitals. For the same reason, Spaniards were free to monopolize the religious orders, even if they were not the best candidates for priestly service. Third, Spaniards did not care about educating themselves because their social and racial status, "the superiority of being a Spaniard," was sufficient for them to access ecclesiastical positions and privileges.[73] Finally, by keeping Indians illiterate, lower-status Spaniards who had been shepherds, *gayanes* (laborers), or *oficiales* (workers) back in Spain were able to behave like "knights" in Peru. Spaniards could remain idle while enjoying administrative positions and social privileges, a situation that would continue as long as Andeans remained illiterate.[74]

Ultimately, Andean intellectuals were aware of the political connotations of illiteracy under colonialism. The "Representación verdadera" thus deploys a rather "enlightened" defense of education:

> Although among Spaniards it is seen as a sign of vileness . . . illiteracy is not a fault among Indians because it is involuntary. They would love to learn how to read and write and advance in Latin and literature, but it is not possible because Spaniards overload them with work and obstruct all their ways to obtain learning. Spaniards think that teaching an Indian is a waste of time because he will be a nobody and all he would do is sue them; then, when the Indian complains and defends himself, that is an offense [for Spaniards]; learning is an atrocious crime; and [an] Indian's ignorance is the greatest virtue, achievement, and convenience for the Spaniard. . . . Such ineptitude is not natural or permanent. Quite the contrary, it is seen that they [Indians] are very quick and smart, and they have an acute comprehension and tenacious memory.[75]

This passage reflects the more secular nature of the education Andeans pursued in the eighteenth century, as well as the political advantages Spaniards derived from keeping Indians ignorant. Illiteracy was not "natural" but political. It was their subordinate position in the colonial society that separated Indians from the world of letters.

But Andeans were also well aware of the importance of education in achieving social mobility and political autonomy. They not only reclaimed access to educational opportunities but also insisted on running the educational establishments created for young members of the indigenous elite, as becomes clear in this passage from the "Breve y compendiosa satisfacción":

> It is said that it is easy to remove and remedy this irregularity [illiteracy] in Indians . . . by letting them learn freely the letters and study in universities like Spaniards and even mulattos . . . and they should be allowed to possess the schools and study houses they have in Lima, in El Cercado, in the San Martin school, in Cusco and in all other seminary schools of the [b]ishoprics in the Indies; and by opening schools in all Indian towns, so they can learn how to read and write as it has been commanded by the Lords Kings of Spain, this

situation would be remedied. But what happens instead is that, against all reason and deceiving Y. M, the corregidores usurp all the salaries that Y. M. disposed to pay for schoolteachers.[76]

Ethnic autonomy in Indian schools was a shared goal among members of the Lima Indian network in 1755. One of those members, Don Felipe Tacuri Mena, an Indian representative, wrote from Madrid to the Cercado *cabildo* in Lima, advocating for self-run Indian schools. His letter illuminates that education and autonomy were linked in the minds of late-colonial Andean elites and scholars. Writing from Madrid, Tacuri Mena informed the Cercado *cabildo* about a petition granted to the Tlaxcala Indian *presbítero* (presbyter) Don Julián Cirilo y Castilla for the creation of a school for the children of *caciques* in Mexico, to be run only by Indian *presbíteros* without the intervention of Spaniards or creole priests and with the full financial support of the crown. He urged the Lima *caciques* to find the most apt subject to raise a similar petition and stressed that "if the petitioner is a presbítero, I have no doubts the petition will be granted as we desire. This said gentleman [Cirilo y Castilla] says that the perdition of our nation is to remain together with these ravens, and that with this separation, it will be seen who will gain."[77] Cirilo y Castilla had, in turn, addressed his "Papel político legal" (legal and political paper) to the Council of the Indies sometime around 1753, advocating for the foundation of a school for Indian priests in which the teachers would be Indians, for the purpose of mentoring Indians as parish priests and missionaries so they could indoctrinate other Indians in their native languages. Apparently, Cirilo y Castilla spent the last thirty-five years of his life in Madrid, petitioning and lobbying for the foundation of these schools.[78]

Another interesting aspect of Andeans' views on education is the nature of the knowledge they sought in the eighteenth century. Rather than religious instruction or indoctrination, the writers made clear their desire to advance in literacy, Latin, literature, and the sciences. In the "Representación verdadera," the call is for knowledge in "science and letters," a rather secular approach to education: "Lord, as our Father, you disposed that the bread of the [d]octrine in science and letters be imparted to us. . . . Thus, your ancestors commanded that we were admitted into schools and literary lecture halls. But, we are fasting from this bread, because our father the king does not know whether it is imparted to us."[79] The text equates spiritual food with a more secular knowledge in science and letters, suggesting that Andeans were as avid for knowledge as they were hungry for spiritual bread. To realize their educational goals in science and letters, the Andean authors demanded admission to "royal schools and seminaries," alongside the children of the Spanish and creole elite.[80] The goal in this statement was to enable Andeans to access avenues of knowledge at all levels—including universities—thus enabling them to perform as authorities and agents in the public realm of state and church administration. The statement also mandated that

Andeans' right to education be enforced, subtly reproaching the king for the non-enforcement of his ancestors' stated will (laws) in that regard.

Andeans continued to reclaim educational opportunities throughout the eighteenth and nineteenth centuries and well into the late twentieth century. In Fray Calixto's time, education seems to have been understood only as an instrument for achieving a more expansive role in public life that would enhance Andean nobility and social standing vis-à-vis Spaniards. The "Representación verdadera" also attested to noble Andeans' desire to participate in the lettered world, public offices, and other occupations of noble rank as well as in public spaces, where they sought to become socially visible: "Spaniards do not allow Indians any noble occupations, or other elevated thought, such as devoting themselves to the letters or the study of the liberal arts and sacred theology, as well as becoming members of the militia, governing by themselves the camps and divisions; neither do they want Indians to become judges, lawyers, procuradores, or join other professions where they could be distinguished for their prowess and exploits."[81] This is a significant expression of the modernizing imaginaries of late-colonial Andean thinkers, which contributed from their relatively subordinate positions to the discursive construction of an incipient public sphere inhabited by the upper echelons of the Indian republic in Peru.

Overall, the texts that sustained the campaigns analyzed here constitute an important record of social inclusion that must be regarded as the result of legal battles for ethnic reassertion and the enforcement of early laws that potentially empowered Andean elites. In the process, Andean scholars and activists unmasked the ambiguous approach of the Habsburg monarchs, as well as the Bourbons before 1776, toward Indian elites—an approach that involved simultaneous concessions and neglect.

Along with trans-Atlantic travel and the use of discursive and legal strategies in their efforts to obtain direct justice from the king,[82] the Amerindian battles for social recognition and inclusion were further developed in the Bourbon eighteenth century through visual, oral, and performative devices. These devices included genealogies represented in Inca paintings, such as those of the Cuszqueño school; religious performances, such as the "Corpus Christi" procession in Cusco; dances; wancas, or Quechua theatrical representations of the death of Atahualpa based on oral traditions and texts; and masquerades to celebrate the coronation of Bourbon kings (see Chapter 3).[83] This was also a period in which Inca lords appeared more often in public using traditional Inca paraphernalia (e.g., tunics, textiles, keros [Inca vessels], ritual jewelry, furniture).[84] These practices were institutionally promoted through royal decrees recognizing the noble privileges of those who demonstrated Inca ancestry and were also sought by Indian intellectuals and nobles who believed these legal and cultural practices would foster their struggles for political and cultural survival.

The culminating moment of the legal campaigns for social inclusion and social justice was the explosive outburst of discontent and rebellion in the years 1780–1783 in Upper Peru. The insurrectionary conjuncture opened a space in which Andean rebels attempted to achieve, through violence, a long-anticipated state of social justice they had been unable to attain through legal struggles. The rebels felt they were forced to rebel for the same reasons as those other indigenous intellectuals from the past had denounced and campaigned against. Diego Cristóbal Túpac Amaru explained this to the Bishop of Cusco, as the rebel expressed his doubts about the offer of general pardon by Viceroy Agustín de Jáuregui y Aldecoa in 1781:

> These inhuman men [*corregidores*] have been the cause and the principal axis of this rebellion. Otherwise, these miserable [Indians] could not have possibly shaken off the heavy and unbearable yoke that, against reason and justice, the subaltern ministers had placed upon them, going against the many repeated, wise, and good dispositions that the paternal love of our monarch had issued incessantly to their benefit. But they could not attain anything for their powerlessness and orphaned state. This is why these *naturales* became excited and agitated by themselves, without my brother Joséf Gabriel Túpac Amaru having any influence.[85]

The lines dividing legal and insurrectionary approaches to justice became blurred, as to the end, rebels maintained a willingness to abide by the terms of the colonial compact of justice between king and subjects rather than seek a revolutionary transformation of the colonial society, even if their methods were akin to those of revolutionary movements. Even more specifically, José Gabriel Condorcanqui Túpac Amaru II expressed his adherence to colonial law to Visitador General José Antonio de Areche in 1781, at a peak moment of the insurrection: "I lack the right voice to express the royal greatness of our father and lord. . . . [Y]ou must publish his royal greatness and explain the core of his love: the recopilación de Indias, the ordinances, royal decrees, provisions . . . and other dispositions addressed to all the viceroys, presidents, judges, audiencias, chancellors, archbishops, bishops, priests . . . which I think they all are in favor of these poor neophyte Indians."[86]

In the midst of violent confrontation, the rebel leaders expressed their will to follow royal laws, as other groups did, but they also demonstrated their awareness that full Indian inclusion in the world of the colonizer was impossible to attain. After Andeans' systematic efforts to forge social equality, the colonial subordination of the "republic of Indians" to the "republic of Spaniards" proved resilient. In the long process of campaigning and writing for social inclusion and ethnic autonomy, Andean intellectuals also attempted to bring about social and political change through reforms of the imperial administration, which uncovered another facet of their activism and allows us to further understand the changes in the political and social imaginaries in the Andes near the end of Spanish colonialism.

REFORMATION OF THE EMPIRE

Andean scholars crafted proposals for reform of the colonial administration of the Indian republic consistent with their agenda for social inclusion. The Andean tradition of proposing political and social reforms was not new in mid- to late-colonial Peru. At the turn of the seventeenth century, Don Felipe Guamán Poma de Ayala filled his *Nueva corónica y buen gobierno* with propositions to remedy the manifold ills of the problematic colonial world in which he lived. These reforms reflected his notion of *buen gobierno* (good government) and included a series of urgent steps he believed King Philip III needed to take to restore the balance for Andean societies, which had been lost with the Europeans' disruptive presence since the conquest period. Such "remedies" serve as a record of early attempts by Andean intellectuals to act as political agents in the colonial world.[87] Andean writers of the seventeenth and eighteenth centuries were also concerned with social matters long overdue for immediate action. Their proposals varied from specific requests to broader sweeping reforms, which not only offered a hint of their different interests and views of social change at different times during those centuries but also anticipated the political agenda of the Great Rebellion beginning in 1780.

Aware of the correlation between colonial exploitation and the anomalies of Spanish rule and the troubled evangelization process in the late seventeenth century, the mestizo and *cura doctrinero* Juan de Cuevas Herrera voiced a series of political demands. He sent his petitions to the king, asking for the replacement of *corregidores* and more power for *caciques* in the local administration. For the administration of justice in the provinces, he demanded that a new *alcalde* be elected from among the resident *hacendados*, who would conduct inspection tours and administer justice. Along with the *alcaldes mayores* or *caciques*, this *alcalde* "would collect and render the tribute" to the crown.[88] In the end, Cuevas Herrera suggested that even *alcaldes ordinarios* could easily and cheaply perform the tasks of the *corregidores*, thereby avoiding much harm to the Indians and saving money for the crown.[89] Although it is not clear whether these elected Spanish mayors would be less corrupt or incompetent than the *corregidores*, this is one of the earliest demands by Andeans to remove the entire administrative position of *corregidores*—considerably earlier than a similar claim was articulated by Fray Calixto in 1749 and earlier than the 1780 rebellion, in which Túpac Amaru and Micaela Bastidas "enacted" this demand in a more radical form.

Concomitant with their critiques against the colonial church, Andean scholars proposed a reform of the ecclesiastical administration at the local and episcopal levels. To remedy the protracted abuses and inefficacy of parish priests, Cuevas Herrera asked for a more selective policy of assigning *beneficios* (parishes or benefices) to attract honest persons to this job. Very important, he demanded that *curas* be proficient in native languages, and for those who already held the position without meeting the language requirement, their salaries should be suspended immediately. To secure the transparency and efficiency of pastoral visits, ecclesiastic *visitadores* (inspectors) were to be carefully selected to avoid the conflicts of interests that were common when relatives or associates of *oidores*, prelates, and the reviewed parties were appointed ecclesiastical judges. He recommended that virtuous, mature, and zealous functionaries who spoke Indian languages be selected to conduct these inspections. Cuevas Herrera's proposals echoed some clerics' and particularly the Jesuits' complaints about the poor language training of parish priests and proposed to work toward language training for missionaries to secure delivery of the Christian message to rural Indians. Although Cuevas Herrera's petitions in this regard reflected his support for mission work and Christianity at large, his suggestions offered mechanisms for control of the abuses committed against Amerindian women and men by corrupt and inefficient priests. In many ways this discourse empowered Cuevas Herrera himself as an Andean *doctrinero* who spoke Spanish and Aymara, skills he put at the forefront to support his aspiration to become a prelate.[90] These suggestions attempt overall to bring transparency and efficiency to both the colonial state and church administration without questioning or undermining the meaning and roles of those institutions.

As Cuevas Herrera joined the voices campaigning for the abolition of the *mita* system in the seventeenth century, he agreed that in fairness the Potosí *mita* should be abolished. Nevertheless, he only advocated for lessening the amount of work assigned to *mitayos* "because natural reason demonstrates that it is unfair that just a few [Indians] now have to carry out the amount of work that previously took many of them to complete, and also it is unjust not to reduce their workload as the number of people declined."[91]

With respect to the *mita* issue and other social concerns included within the larger problem of the ineffectiveness of colonial justice for Indians, the most comprehensive set of recommended changes was formulated in the mid-eighteenth century when the "Representación verdadera" appeared amid an insurrectionary conjuncture, intensified by the *repartos* and new threats that mestizos' precarious standing could be downgraded to that of tributaries. The wholesale reforms of the justice system proposed in the text were intended to modify the judicial structure and procedures to achieve effective justice for Indians. Because unruly and corrupt officials had devalued the power of the law, the need for restitution of legal procedures in ecclesiastical and secular matters was reiterated. This restitution involved not only effective enforcement of past laws beneficial to the interests of native Andeans but also the replacement of ineffective laws to create suitable legislation according to contemporary problems. In a way, this proposal accentuated the role of Andeans as legal activists, pressuring for the production and abolition of laws as they saw fit.

The set of petitions for new laws revealed Andean ladinos' new self-perception as de-colonized subjects. They fought for laws that overall reformulated the subordinate status of "Indians" in colonial society. As an example of laws needed urgently, the removal of restrictions that complicated Andeans' free passage to Spain appears as an indicator of the change in the times.[92] In 1749, legal activists such as Fray Calixto questioned the restriction of Andeans' free mobility and the kind of tutelage the crown had exerted over Indians since they were legally constituted as minors. In conquest times, Fray Calixto maintained, laws prohibiting Indians' free passage to Spain made sense for Spaniards. In the current times, however, such laws no longer applied, perpetuating Andeans' lack of freedom: "Is there anything more oppressive than, whereas slaves can get their freedom and move around and travel to Spain, the Indian, even the noble, becomes a tributary and mitayo of your [Spanish] serfs and lacks the free will to choose where to live, or to pass to Spain to meet his king and show him his wounds?"[93] As has been pointed out, Indian authorities and other intellectual ladinos who represented native communities had been traveling to Spain since the late sixteenth century. The claim for free mobility thus evokes the transformation of Indians into more autonomous, cosmopolitan subjects who deemed themselves entitled to present their complaints directly to the king and were concerned with enforcing, by practical means, their right to use the legal system. Andean ladinos were well aware of the existing legislation that allowed *kurakas* in particular to seek justice directly with the *audiencias*[94] and wanted to expand those rights to other elite Andeans so they could bring their cases to the king.

Along the same lines, Andeans reclaimed the freedom to own their community assets, to manage them by themselves, and to be able to dispose of them so they could conduct businesses autonomously; they claimed their right to manage their own haciendas, Indian hospitals, brotherhoods, and community funds, "just as the Spanish administer theirs."[95] In colonial Peru, the administration of the *colegios de caciques*, Indian hospitals, *cajas de comunidad* (a safe or box containing community documents and cash) and Indian *cofradías* was supervised by Spanish and ecclesiastical authorities. These proposals sought to debunk the idea that native Andeans were legally minors and needed supervision and tutelage in their own social organizations. The writers felt Andeans "were subjects of trust, reason, honesty, and credit."[96] Furthermore, this reform included the prohibition against renting the community's and Indian hospitals' assets to Spaniards and mulattoes, since this practice left the funds exhausted and with unpayable debts. Aware of the opportunities and the need to engage in the market economy,

Andeans demanded freedom to participate in that economy (*tratar y contratar*) without being hampered by the *alcabala*, which was illegally levied on Indian merchandise—further burdening Indians already overwhelmed with personal service, the *mita*, and the *repartimiento de comercio*.[97]

Because access to the priesthood was a crucial aspect of the Andean vision of social inclusion in the public domain of society, Andean scholars articulated this demand in ways that reflected their understanding of social equality among Spanish and Indian women: "[And that] according to merit, legitimacy, sufficiency, and virtue, [Andeans] be admitted in the sacred orders and the ecclesiastic beneficios. Likewise, competent Indian and mestizo women should be allowed to possess the black and white veil as *monjas profesas* [nuns taking vows] either in the Indian nunneries founded for them or elsewhere."[98] The proposal was tailored to the requirements the Council of Trent had set for candidates applying to the priesthood and for women seeking admission to nunneries, requirements that referred mostly to competence, virtue, and legitimacy.

This Andean proposal also contained limits to gender equality, however. Although women were included in the full agenda to enter religious institutions, the "Representación verdadera" made no claims for Indian women to be eligible to perform in an equal capacity as priests, nor did it question the gender hierarchies of power within ecclesiastical institutions—a level of gender consciousness that even today is largely absent from the Catholic Church. Social equality and Indian political participation featured prominently in the political imaginaries of colonial Andeans, who deemed themselves capable and willing to perform in positions of power within both the church and the state administration.

In this regard, both the desire to expand public spaces of power for elite Indians and the limitations of their views on gender equality become more apparent: "And [we ask] that those Indios who will be mentored in the future and those who are at present being mentored (because there are some now) be designated for the ecclesiastical and secular dignities; and that bishoprics and canonries be conferred to them as well as they be appointed as ministers of the Holy tribunal [of the Inquisition], consultants, *garnachas* [judges] in the audiencias, and especially that the fiscal protector and the two procuradores be Indians."[99] Such a comprehensive reform would have substantially altered the ethnic composition of the secular and ecclesiastical administrations. These suggestions bring to the surface the range of roles intellectual ladinos attempted to play in the public domain of colonial society, none of which appeared open for Indian women. Definitions of the category "Indian" thus underwent significant reformulation by late-colonial Andeans who sought political power within the most prominent institutions of government, in the process undoing their status as Indians and minors—considered both political and social "handicaps" in Spanish law and colonial practice.

This proposal echoed the comprehensive range of rights reclaimed by Andean elites since the 1697 *cédula de honores*, still unenforced in Fray Calixto's time. Likewise, these reforms spoke to a movement conducted by the indigenous Cercado *cabildo* to eliminate the legal tutelage of Spanish *protectores de naturales*, widely criticized since the seventeenth century for their inefficiency and corruption and their inability to support the enforcement of the *cédula de honores*. In the decades preceding the composition of the "Representación verdadera," the Indian *cabildo* had set out to request that the position of *procuradores de naturales* be redefined to make qualified Indians eligible to hold the post. Through the *diputado de los indios* (deputy for the Indians) Pedro Nieto de Vargas, they finally obtained a royal *cédula* on July 1, 1735, that granted the posts of *protectores* and *diputados generales* to competent Indians.[100]

In around 1749–1750, the "Representación verdadera" insisted on the matter because the decree was not enforced, as the Spanish *procuradores* Conde de Villanueva, Jerónimo de Portalanza, and Manuel Soriano, among others, remained in those positions for about thirty years after the decree was issued. After a long legal battle for enforcement of the 1735 royal decree by the Cercado *cabildo* and its two officials, Alberto Chosop and Joseph Santiago Ruiz Túpac Amaru Inca, they obtained final approval from the Audiencia of Lima to act as *procuradores de naturales*—a position long held by Spaniards, although intended to defend Indian legal rights. As an example of the wider struggles to seat Indian secular and ecclesiastical judges, the "Representación verdadera" articulated this claim:

> But what a disgrace, my lord, that the doors of justice are closed for us, and we find your justice neither in you nor your ministers nor in your bishops or pastors, who are there only to impede our lamentations and complaints from reaching you. Because there is no secular or ecclesiastical judge from our nation . . . neither [do we] have a procurador of ours. . . . And despite the fact that King Dn. Felipe V, our glorious father, has commanded through a royal decree from 173[5] that we had two Indians as our procuradores in each audiencia, and that also Indians were to act as protectores in the cities of the kingdom, nothing has been done about it, because when laws benefit Indians either they are not enforced or they are turned against us.[101]

Andeans' struggles to have their own *protectores de naturales* were the result of their long experience with a decadent judicial system in which non-enforcement of laws for the preservation of Indian labor and Indian noble privileges was an institutionalized pattern. Holding the office of *protectores de naturales* would have allowed Indian officials the freedom to travel to Spain and to periodically inform the king and the Council of the Indies about the state of Indian judicial matters—law enforcement—in the colonies. Indian *procuradores* could also have defended their cases in the regional *audiencias* and influenced their judicial decisions, which might otherwise have reflected only the interests of the most powerful groups. Of course, there was also the incentive of a position endowed with a salary and that entailed a measure of social prestige, as the holder was usually knowledgeable about the law, if not a lawyer himself, and a noble of pure blood. Chosop and Ruiz Túpac Amaru Inca faced the opposition of a well-entrenched bureaucracy of mostly corrupt Spanish lawyers who had held the position since the post-conquest era and whose most vocal member in 1734 was the former Spanish *protector de naturales* Don Juan de Portalanza. Chosop and Ruiz Túpac Amaru Inca led the legal struggle for enforcement in the 1760s, finally obtaining the recognition of the *real audiencia* on October 1, 1763.

Doubtless, the most radical proposition of the "Representación verdadera" was to abolish the post of *corregidor* and replace it with Andean administrators or judges. This idea attempted to redefine the boundaries of colonial and Andean authority and revealed Andeans' concern about political autonomy: "And [we ask] that the Spanish corregidores ... must be removed absolutely and totally; and judges, or Indian corregidores for Indians, should be appointed who govern them appropriately; and that Indians only be subject to Y. M. and to the viceroy for temporal matters, and to the bishop for spiritual ones ... and that Indians be governed by Indians themselves, and that they are their own corregidores, and that Spaniards do not have anything to do with them."[102] Thus, the new line of authority would bypass the provincial government, and its functions would now fall under the purview of the *caciques*. Tribute collection would be rendered promptly to the king by Indian *corregidores*, since they would not have the financial obligations of the Spanish *corregidores*, which usually delayed the remission of tribute moneys to the crown. Most important, this proposal would be a "detour" that included the abolition of the hated *repartimiento de comercio*, an abusive practice conducted by *corregidores*: "repartimientos will cease."[103] *Caciques* would not purchase their posts, so they would not face the ensuing debt burden. Also, unlike Spanish *corregidores*, Andeans were parsimonious in their consumption, so it would be relatively inexpensive for the king to replace Spanish *corregidores* with Andean judges. Thus, the king would save the money he was spending on salaries for ineffective officials, and, as a bonus, many gentiles would stop practicing idolatry and convert to Christianity.[104] Early-modern Andean scholars thus expressed a pragmatic understanding of imperial finances at the time of the Bourbon reforms while using their suggestions to advance their own interests so they could remain outside Spanish purview.

The proposed set of sweeping reforms to state administration involving Indian participation ended with key changes to the judicial system: "It would be good that a new tribunal be set up ... that depended directly on Y. M., and that [the tribunal] be made up of one, two or more bishops and other noble people . . . very respectful of God and faithful servants of your Majesty, along with Indian nobles and mestizos, the knights of the Spanish and Indian Nation."[105] This authority structure would put an end to the non-enforcement of laws benefiting Andeans and would advise the king about detrimental laws that should be eliminated. The prohibition on Indian travel to Spain and the laws endorsing the *mita* system were among those to be abolished, while the said tribunal of justice could address an effective, practical execution of the privileges and *fueros de indios* for noble Indians. The tribunal would last only until Indian men and women were admitted to the religious orders and noble Andeans were granted admission to royal schools, seminaries, and universities throughout the kingdom. These mandates were to be obeyed by all *audiencias*, bishops, and officials, who were to facilitate the documents required for Andeans to travel to Spain to assure the king that his laws were duly enforced.[106]

These reforms attest to the ways Andeans envisioned their political participation in the achievement of social justice: a structure of justice tied directly to the king, in which representatives of Spaniards, Indians, mestizos, and the church would share judicial power in a tribunal specially designed for Indian matters. This proposal for participation by noble Andeans in a special tribunal of justice, away from the regular colonial justice system, was the culmination of Andeans' long search for justice directly from the king to circumvent the protracted neglect of previous laws for the social empowerment of the Andean elite. Elsewhere in the "Representación verdadera," a variant of the proposal was raised to the king: "You should rule that other judges elected by us be appointed along with caciques, principal Indians, and that all of them carry out your royal will."[107] Thus, these thinkers contested the protracted malfunctioning of a colonial justice system plagued by corruption, exclusionary practices, and systematic noncompliance with sanctioned royal mandates in favor of Indians—themselves the result of the consistent intervention of Andean authorities in *audiencias* and the royal court in Madrid. Perhaps they exposed too blatantly the contradictions between the religious foundations of Spanish rule and the political practices of the secular and clerical states inherent in the colonial situation.

Given the stratified and segregated nature of colonial society, this sharing of judicial power between colonial elites and a group of subaltern subjects was a proposal too challenging to be considered by the crown and its advisory council. After receiving the manuscript from the Franciscans Fray Calixto de San José Túpac Inca and Fray Isidoro de Cala in 1750, King Ferdinand VI commanded Viceroy Conde de Superunda to investigate the denunciations that preceded the proposals. The viceroy, with the support of the king, ordered the banishment and seclusion of Fray Calixto, whom the viceroy ultimately held responsible for the "Representación verdadera" and the social activism the manifesto helped support.

The composition of the proposed tribunal of justice indicates that Andean elites were, in theory, willing to share judicial power with Spaniards and the church. These proposals, however, acknowledged no place or representation for the large sectors of elite women and non-elite Indian women and men, let alone the vast sector of black and mulatto women and men, whom Fray Calixto perceived as inferior to the Indians. None of these groups were included as eligible representatives in the proposed tribunal of justice, which shows the internalization of the notions of purity of blood and exclusion in these Indian-mestizo discourses of Andean power.

Overall, the reform proposals questioned the concentration of power by Spaniards, and the spirit was to end the subordination of the "republic of Indians" by the "republic of Spaniards": "With this [reform], we all will be saved, and everyone, both Spaniards and Indians, will have peace, Spaniards governing Spaniards and Indians governing Indians."[108] This reassertion of Indian self-government harkened back to the Habsburg attempts to separate Indians from Spaniards in two different administrative republics. But these intellectual Andeans envisioned an Indian republic in which Indian commoners would be governed autonomously by members of the Andean elite who, empowered by privileges akin to those of the colonial nobility (education, priesthood, social recognition), would administer justice for Indians and ensure fulfillment of the colonial demands on their own.

The proposals outlined here imagined various degrees of Indian autonomy as a way to deny Indians' subordinate condition as legal minors and ultimately to do away with the sanctioned category of "Indians" for elite Andeans. In various ways, the proposals reflect the fact that these late-colonial Andeans envisioned themselves as cosmopolitan subjects, aware of the political rights that would define them as autonomous, de-colonizing ethnic subjects and free them from the constraints of colonial impositions. The reforms also reflect Andean intellectuals' willingness to participate as free subjects in the economy and as capable and knowledgeable candidates for political participation in the state administration, which would enable them to engage in political self-government.[109]

A comparative analysis of different reform efforts by mid- and late-colonial Andeans reveals that the demands raised during the rebellion of Túpac Amaru denote the reformist aspect of the insurrection and the fact that its demands had been articulated earlier in the proposals examined here, in spite of Túpac Amaru's advocacy of violent social change.[110] Along similar lines, in 1780 Túpac Amaru proposed the creation of *reales audiencias*, presided over by a viceroy, located close to Indian towns for prompt administration of Indian justice.[111] Although none of the writers discussed here placed the abolition of tribute at the head of their agenda, perhaps because they understood tribute as Andeans' contribution to the reciprocal compact in exchange for the conditions necessary to secure their social and cultural reproduction under Spanish rule, Túpac Amaru's vision of an upcoming Inca rule in the Andes through a revolution and with no place for Spaniards in the new society stands out as more radically anti-colonial than the vision of any previous Andean leader.

Beyond the feasibility of these reforms and regardless of whether Andeans were successful in their attempts to reform the empire's administration, the nature of the proposals is important in its own right, as they represent a common political culture of Andean elites under Spanish rule—more clearly articulated in the 1700s in the decades before the Great Rebellion. That is, their impetus was to carve a more autonomous space within colonial society in the face of the failed arrangement of the "two republics," which Andeans regarded as an opportunity to redefine their own place in society rather than as a serious empowering policy. The overall aim of the proposals for social reform was to achieve justice for Indians at different levels and to hold Spaniards accountable for the one-sided, nonreciprocal relationships they had established with Andeans.

As a political undertone and a driving force in colonial Andean scholarship, ethnic autonomy mirrors a long-standing tradition of political and cultural battles by Indian authorities to organize their lives somewhat independently of the colonial authorities. The history of these battles is extensive and mostly unwritten, but as an illustration of such an impetus, a few references suffice here. In 1623 the Chicho Indians from the Valley of Tarija (Province of Charcas) demanded that the Spanish administrators of the *censos* (Indian lands rented out to non-community members) and *cajas de comunidad* cease having control over the communities' assets. They asked the crown to replace these officials with the *kurakas*.[112] Another episode illustrates the impetus for religious autonomy. Indian devotees of the Virgin of Copacabana in Lima took it upon themselves to petition for and follow up on the construction of a chapel for the virgin in the San Lázaro neighborhood, where they felt they belonged and where the virgin was originally lodged before the town's Indians were forcefully relocated to El Cercado in 1591.[113] They campaigned for about thirty years, obtained the funds needed, and were finally allowed to build the chapel in 1633. At that time they applied for construction of an Indian *beaterio*, which they obtained and built themselves. They reclaimed the right to choose the chaplain and to manage the *cofradía* and *beaterio* as patrons of the church. They also complained that the designated priest did not know Quechua, the language they wanted for the religious services. Finally, in 1704 the Indians were allowed to choose their own chaplain and were considered the legitimate founders of their chapel and *beaterio*.

Even within the framework of colonial Christianity, Andeans felt entitled to control the religious organizations of which they were a part and in which they had invested community funds. This expression was as much religious as it was political, and it had to do with a strong sense of ethnic self-assertion under

Spanish rule rather than a revival of Inca ways or the search for Inca identity per se, in the case of their complaint about the lack of prayers in Quechua.

CONCLUSION

As colonial pressures mounted following the Toledan reforms—threatening the survival of Indian life and structures of government—Andean authorities, writers, and legal representatives advanced a social and political movement to access the honor, political authority, and symbols and institutions of social prestige accorded to them. This movement had started in the early seventeenth century, but it became broader and more coordinated in the late 1600s. The attempt was less about seeking full assimilation into Spanish society than about the realization of an autonomous and reformulated "republic of Indians." In such an ethnic niche, Andeans imagined having their own priesthood and ecclesiastical authorities, Indian and mestizo representatives in the secular government, and school system. In addition, they would partake in the performance of power practices, such as belonging to knightly orders, *cofradías, capellanías*, and similar groups. Those who perceived themselves as legitimate heirs to chiefdoms and as old Christians of pure blood needed not only the political but also the social recognition attached to power in the colonial society, a necessary step to be considered by Spaniards as valid interlocutors and recipients of authority and thereby to maintain their power structures in the new colonial era.[114] Inasmuch as these prominent Andeans struggled to erase the hierarchical relationship between the two "republics," their texts betray the elitist biases of their social agendas. Those eligible for participation in the aforementioned institutions included only noble Indians and their mestizo descendants, excluding the lower echelons of the "Indian republic" from such opportunities.

The Andean discourses created in the search for social equality revealed the cultural negotiation of Andeans' reciprocal expectations between ethnic autonomy and obedience to imperial rule. They questioned the injustice of colonialism and advocated Indian autonomous organizations while playing the role of ideal colonial subjects, endorsing the goals of empire to stress their allegiance. Understanding these negotiations of rule and identity helps us to visualize the interstices in Andean discourses at which departures from the colonial agenda emerge. They allow us to question assessments of these Andean practices as forms of plain "cultural assimilation" or as mere co-optation or corruption of Indian authorities and elites.

Limaylla's petitions to both the *cacicazgo* of Luringuanca and the knightly orders on behalf of noble Indians were denied, as the king and the Council of the Indies considered him incapable of producing complex *memoriales* and because granting these honors would inconveniently motivate other Indians to petition and travel to the royal court. Although the 1697 *cédula de honores* granted elite Indians and their mestizo descendants the right to access schools, the reality was that during the eighteenth century the schools for *caciques* languished, and Andeans' participation in *colegios mayores* was marginal. By far the most contentious issue in the efforts for social inclusion proved to be the admission of noble Indians to the priesthood, since even after two centuries of evangelization the Peruvian church did not feel Indians were sufficiently Christianized to perform key roles in the colonial realm of the sacred. Even though a few more Indians were admitted to the priesthood after 1776, only a few had been admitted after the secularization in 1750, and for the rest of the colonial period they remained largely excluded from holy orders. The reforms of the colonial administration of justice proposed in the "Representación verdadera" were largely disregarded in the royal and viceregal spheres after Fray Calixto was exiled and secluded in a remote Spanish monastery in Ormus (Valencia) in 1756, where he likely died. Andean intellectual and political battles to join the colonial spheres of power demonstrated that the hierarchical divisions of race and ethnicity in colonial Peru tended to prevail over paternalistic laws that promised, and rarely delivered, inclusion of Andeans in the social world of the ruling elite.

The Andean proposals of reform in particular placed indigenous and mestizo intellectuals at the forefront of a de-colonizing movement that promoted forms of political participation in institutions of justice, knowledge, and spirituality. By reclaiming the freedom to travel to Spain, informing the king, and actively seeking enforcement of what they perceived as empowering laws, they attempted to scrutinize the performance of judicial and ecclesiastical officials. The mid-eighteenth-century impetus to have Indians appointed as *corregidores, protectores de naturales, escribanos*, and elected judges in a special tribunal for Indian justice challenged the colonial justice system's protracted inability to deliver on the colonial discourse of making Indians true members of the kingdom's body politic and on the fictional discourse of social equality between the nobles of the two republics. In striving to self-manage their social organizations and communities, opening avenues for participation in the market economy, and reclaiming their right to own and manage property, Andeans sought to advance their social condition as mature and autonomous subjects of the empire. They effected a deconstruction of their imposed colonial identity as "Indians" and rid themselves of the subordinate status of legal and social minors.

Through their critiques, proposals, and trans-Atlantic travels, Indian scholars acted as indirect lawmakers and law enforcers. These roles placed them and the Indian networks they were part of within the nascent public arena of the colonial judicial system. Even in the midst of the late-colonial Great Rebellion, they used the discourse of law as a referent to justify their struggle; their proposals, in turn, attempted to change the legal basis of imperial administration to measures that facilitated the avoidance of Spanish rule in the Andes, even if they continued to pledge allegiance to the king—an uncertain and distant "head" of the dislocated body politic.

Simultaneously a by-product and a rhetorical tool of the political and social activism of Andean educated leaders, a consistent endeavor to redefine the identities of colonial Indians and mestizos underlies the texts under study. Their attitudes, values, and discussions of religiosity also add a textual layer to ethnic self-perception and the campaigns for social inclusion. Along those two themes, Chapter 7 approaches the politics of identity formation in Andean scholarship to further discern changes in Andean culture under colonial rule.

NOTES

1. Martínez, *Genealogical Fictions*, 112–122.

2. Glave, "The 'Republic of Indians' in Revolt," 514–515.

3. On August 31, 1588, King Charles II had ordered archbishops and bishops to ordain mestizos who met the necessary sufficiencies and "*calidades.*" Mestizo women who likewise qualified were to be admitted to nunneries. *Recopilación de leyes de las Indias*, tomo 2, libro 1, título 7, ley 7. Available at http://www.congreso.gob.pe/ntley/LeyIndiaP.htm. Individual efforts to acquire prestigious social distinctions had been advanced prior to 1697 by elite Andeans seeking access to *cacicazgos* and exemption from tribute and *mita* obligations. An intriguing case was the request for the creation of a knightly order for the "Incas and Montezumas," advanced in approximately 1677 by the Jauja noble Don Jerónimo Lorenzo Limaylla, one of the Andean writers studied in this book and introduced in Chapter 2. He argued that as subjects of the same king, Andean and Spanish nobles were socially equal and therefore entitled to the same privileges. He wanted to associate the order with Santa Rosa, a patron saint dear to Andeans and creoles alike. Limaylla, "Memorial."

4. "R. C. que se considere a los descendientes de caciques como nobles en su raza," Madrid, Marzo 26, 1697. Transcribed in Konetzke, *Colección de documentos*, vol. 3, part 1, 67.

5. Estenssoro Fuchs, *Del paganismo a la santidad*, 495. See also Chapter 2, note 73.

6. Ibid., 497.

7. AGI, Indiferente General, 648, Juan Núñez Vela de Rivera; AGI, Lima, 19, Juan Núñez Vela de Rivera, 1690.

8. Among other things, Núñez Vela de Rivera demanded that noble Indians and mestizos be admitted as knights in military orders, including the prestigious Toyson de oro Order, and admitted as bishops and cardinals in the Holy Church of Rome. Buntix and Wuffarden, "Incas y reyes españoles," 164.

9. AGI, Indiferente General, 648, Juan Núñez Vela de Rivera, 1.

10. Ibid.

11. Ibid.

12. Ibid. On May 30, 1691, the king had approved a *real cédula* commanding that schools of Castilian language be founded in Peru and New Spain as a first step toward enabling Indian nobles to occupy public positions. AGI, Lima, 22.

13. "R. C. que se considere a los descendientes de caciques como nobles en su raza," Madrid, Marzo 26, 1697. Transcribed in Konetzke, *Colección de documentos*, vol. 3, part 1, 66–67.

14. *Recopilación de leyes de las Indias,* libro 1, título 7, ley 7, *reales cédulas* of August 31 and September 28, 1588, by Felipe II. Available at http://www.congreso.gob.pe/ntley/LeyIndiaP.htm.

15. AGI, Audiencia de Lima, 495, Lima, Octubre 26, 1711; Lima, Abril 1, 1722; Lima, Junio 27, 1724; Lima, Mayo 13, 1726. Thirty-one *caciques* and Indian nobles signed the *memoriales*; regions represented included Pachacama and Lurin, Jaen de Bracamoros (Chachapoyas), La Magdalena (Lima), Miraflores, Andahuailas, Cusco, San Bartolomé of Guánuco, and Manta in southern Ecuador.

16. AGI, Lima, 495, Buen Retiro, Marzo 31, 1722; AGI, Lima, 22, Cuadernos nos. 1–3. The Indian memorialists responded with more writing and travel and this time demanded that the text of the 1697 *cédula* be engraved on bronze plaques and posted in the major plazas of the *real audiencia*'s principal cities. AGI, Audiencia de Lima, 495, Lima, Mayo 13, 1726.

17. "Representación verdadera," 145v–146.

18. "Real cédula para que los indios sean admitidos en las religiones, educados en los colegios y promovidos, según su mérito y capacidad, a dignidades y oficios públicos," San Ildefonso, Septiembre 11, 1766. Transcribed in Konetzke, *Colección de documentos*, vol. 3, part 1, 333–334. AGI, Lima, 495, Buen Retiro, Marzo 31, 1722. For the papal confirmation, see AGI, Lima, 22, Cuadernos nos. 1–3. The royal decree was finally promulgated in Lima and Callao, by order of Viceroy Don Manuel de Amat, on June 10, 1767, and was posted as a public edict and promulgated by public crier by the Protectores de Naturales Don Alberto Chosop and Don Joséph Santiago Ruiz. Paz y Guiní, *Guerra Separatista*, 281–286.

19. See Ramírez, "Cosmological Basis of Local Power in the Andes."

20. Sariola, *Power and Resistance*, 183.

21. Estenssoro Fuchs, *Del paganismo a la santidad.*

22. Ibid., 26, 78.

23. Estenssoro Fuchs discussed the religious practices of virtuous Indians in colonial Peru and examined at length the particular case of the Indian Nicolás Ayllón's canonization process (1677–1716). Even though this case proceeded successfully to the point of receiving recognition of sanctity by Rome, it was delayed and finally frustrated by the Inquisition in 1716. Even though unacknowledged by the Inquisition, Estenssoro Fuchs argued, the reasons for the denial were the inconsistency inherent in the identity of an Indian saint and the enforced status of Indians as permanent neophytes. Ibid., 468–493. For Estenssoro Fuchs, the "Representación verdadera" represented a "culminating moment" in Indians' long pursuit of incorporation into Catholicism, a step closer to achieving religious autonomy.

24. Martínez, *Genealogical Fictions*, 112–122. Martínez also argues that Spanish notions of purity were redeployed in the New World against people of African descent. Indeed, Fray Calixto's negative perceptions of blacks reflect such a bias (see Chapter 7), while he also used the notion to empower Andeans.

25. "Representación verdadera," 146.

26. Limaylla, "Memorial," 207.

27. The dossier's full title is "Brief and compendious rendition of the reasons that the Spanish nation holds for the erroneous practice of rejecting the admission of the very pristine and very noble Nation of American Indians and the mestizos and descendants from the Indians in the religious orders of friars and nuns and to the ecclesiastical dignities."

28. Mignolo, *Local Histories/Global Designs*, 13.

29. AGI, Lima, 59, cited in Marzal, *La transformación religiosa peruana*, 139; Villagómez, *Carta pastoral*.

30. "Representación verdadera," 120v.

31. Ibid., 133v.

32. Ibid., 131.

33. Ibid., 134.

34. Ibid., 146v.

35. Ibid., 147.

36. Ibid., 137–137v.

37. Ibid., 157v.

38. Ibid., 153v.

39. Ibid., 157.

40. Ibid., 142–142v.

41. Ibid., 143, 144v.

42. Estenssoro Fuchs, *Del paganismo a la santidad*, 27.

43. Among them were most of the Andean scholars whose writings constitute the core of this book, including Cuevas Herrera and Núñez Vela de Rivera. Fray Calixto attained the status of lay brother, and José Rafael Sahuaraura was appointed a *cura doctrinero* in 1784. A few others were also known in 1751, including Cirilo y Castilla. Proficiency in native languages as well as Castilian and Latin seemed to have helped Cuevas Herrera enjoy an appointment as *cura doctrinero* in various towns of the Charcas Province for most of the seventeenth century, and in the mid-eighteenth century Fray Calixto became a mission aide and ecclesiastical functionary.

44. Vargas Ugarte, *Concilios Limenses*.

45. AGI, Lima, 988.

46. Vargas Ugarte, *Concilios Limenses*, 46.

47. Ricard, *La conquista espiritual*, 349.

48. Prien, *La historia del cristianismo*, 244; Osorio, *Clamor de los Indios Americanos*, 29.

49. *Recopilación de Leyes de las Indias*, libro 1, título 7, ley 7, *reales cédulas* from August 31 and September 28, 1588, by King Philip II. Available at http://www.congreso.gob.pe/ntley/LeyIndiaP.htm.

50. AGI, Lima, 495, 9–9v.

51. Olaechea, "Los indios en las órdenes religiosas," 256; Konetzke, *Colección de documentos*, vol. 3, part 1, 333.

52. AGI, Lima, 988.

53. As a result, religious orders customarily received not only native Andeans but also occasionally mulattoes and blacks as *donados*, although the church tried to prevent this practice several times. Olaechea, "Los indios en las órdenes religiosas," 242. It seems

that the number of *donados* was significant at times. The San Francisco de Jesus convent in Lima had no fewer than forty during the seventeenth century. Although they remained excluded from the priesthood for many decades, it seems that as the eighteenth century neared, a few were allowed to officiate as priests. In New Spain, *donados* apparently came to be highly regarded for their moral virtues and spiritual achievements. Some were reported to be able to perform miracles and become saints. Torquemada, *Monarquía Indiana*, Libro 18, Cap. 11, 111, 237, cited in Olaechea, "Los indios en las órdenes religiosas," 245.

54. Olaechea, "Los indios en las órdenes religiosas," 244.

55. Ibid., 252.

56. Figuera, *La formación del clero indígena*, 384.

57. O'Phelan, *La gran rebelión*, 56, and "Ascender al estado eclesiástico." O'Phelan cited six Indian postulants to the major orders, some from areas outside Cusco: Manuel de Avalos and Ramón Charhuacondori in 1755; Joseph Antonio Montes, 1756; Marcos Caballero de los Reyes, 1759; Nicholas Zevallos (n.d.); and Gregorio Aguilar de Vergara, 1757; as well as the mestizos Luis de Averza and Francisco Mariaca. Most of these Indian and mestizo priests had been ordained in the minor orders and were seeking promotion to the major orders. O'Phelan lists these ordained Incas: Antonio de Bustamante Carlos Inga, parish priest of the Guaripaca Doctrine, Cusco, as apparently in 1760 he was already functioning in that capacity; Gregorio Choquehuanca, interim parish priest, was promoted after the Great Rebellion; Manuel Chirinos y Cabrera, brother-in-law of Don Juan de Bustamante Carlos Inga, applied in 1754 for an ecclesiastical post at the Cusco cathedral and was reluctantly admitted; and Don Francisco Javier Carlos y Antequera (no date of appointment given), son of Joséph de Antequera, in turn parish priest of Guallatas (Cotabambas) in 1765. O'Phelan, *La gran rebelión*, 59, 60, 66.

58. In 1772 the Holy Office worried that there were "numerous Indian priests ordained in Peru." Archivo Histórico Nacional (AHN), Legajo 2212, Expediente 1, Carta del tribunal de Lima, 10-1-1772, cited in Estenssoro Fuchs, *Del paganismo a la santidad*, 514. The numbers of ordained Indians and mestizos remained low in spite of a 1769 dispatch from Charles III commanding the foundation of seminaries in which at least a third or a fourth of those admitted were Indians or mestizos. Cited in O'Phelan, "Ascender al estado eclesiástico," 323.

59. Brading, "Tridentine Catholicism," cited in O'Phelan, *La gran rebelión*, 58.

60. The members of Cusco's prominent Inca lineages in the priesthood prior to the Great Rebellion were Rafael José Jiménez de Cisneros Sahuaraura Tito Atauche, a presbyter in the Cusco diocese; Sixto Sahuaraura Tito Atauche and Leandro Jiménez de Cisneros Sahuaraura Tito Atauche, the latter also a presbyter in the same jurisdiction; and Fernando Ramos Tito Atauche, curate from the town of Umachari. Among the royalist Incas ordained as priests as a reward for their roles in fighting the Great Rebellion were Don Pedro Solís Quivimasa, Don Antonio Solís Quivimasa, and Diego Chuqicallata. In 1784 Don Gregorio Choquehuanca was promoted to *racionero* of the La Plata cathedral; he had been an interpreter for the colonial authorities during the Great Rebellion and donated cattle to the royal troops. The children of Don Pedro Sahuaraura, who was killed in battle fighting against Túpac Amaru in Sangarará, became eligible for the priesthood and were offered a paid *congrua* (entrance fee), royal scholarships to enter the school of *caciques* in San Borja, and *capellanías* in which they would minister as chaplains. Durand,

Colección documental de la independencia del Perú, 226. José Rafael Sahuaraura, the writer of the "Estado del Perú" and brother of Don Pedro Sahuaraura, was given the Juliaca doctrine in propriety in 1784. Don Leandro Sahuaraura, brother of the previous two men, was a lieutenant priest in the town of Nuñoa. Ibid., 247. Fernando Ramos Tito Atauche, their uncle, received the title of chaplain of the *cacique* Don Pedro Justo Sahuaraura's troops and a scholarship to study in the Cusco seminaries; he was ordained by the archbishop. He also became an interim *doctrinero* in Carabayas; in 1809 he was promoted to the Soraya and Angaraes doctrines and was nominated as an ecclesiastical judge and *vicar foráneo*. O'Phelan, *La gran rebelión*, 67. A daughter of Mateo Pumacahua's was temporarily accepted to the creole monastery of Santa Clara in Cusco.

61. Garrett, *Shadows of Empire*, 144.

62. Prien, *La historia del cristianismo*, 247.

63. Such a practice is richly documented in the Archivo Arzobispal del Cusco (AAC). (To mention a few cases, AAC, Caja 66, Paquete 3, Expediente 68, ff. 1–5, 1–11, 1–31, 1739; Caja 2, Paquete 4, Expediente 71, f. 5, 1814. See also Archivo Departmental del Cusco, Notarial, Juan Bautista Gamarra, Leg. 133, 1746–1781.) For a discussion of the financial and political implications of Indian chaplaincies and benefices in the Cusco area, see Garrett, *Shadows of Empire*, 144–145.

64. O'Phelan, "Ascender al estado eclesiástico," 316–325.

65. Gruzinski, *La colonización de lo imaginario*, 261.

66. Burns, "Nuns, Kurakas, and Credit," 56–57.

67. Ingoli cited in Prien, *La historia del cristianismo*, 245.

68. Osorio, *Clamor de los Indios Americanos*, 27.

69. Estenssoro Fuchs, *Del paganismo a la santidad*, 514.

70. See the discussion of Fray Calixto's activism in Lima in Chapter 3.

71. In 1784 the Inca noble and priest José Rafael Sahuaraura, an ardent supporter of the ecclesiastical institution and the Cusco bishop Don Juan Manuel Moscoso y Peralta, adopted the position of the Spanish administration in de-legitimizing the Great Rebellion and its leader and also in favoring the hard-line militaristic approach against the rebels. Sahuaraura also represented the most conservative ecclesiastical discourse of the time, endorsing an inquisitorial approach toward participants in the rebellion and toward the social control of Andean survivors more generally. Sahuaraura Tito Atauche, "Estado del Perú."

72. "Representación verdadera," 139.

73. Ibid.

74. Ibid., 139–139v.

75. Ibid., 136v–137.

76. Ibid.

77. Quoted in Loayza, *Fray Calixto Túpac Inca*, 81.

78. Tanck de Estrada, *Pueblos de indios*, 165.

79. "Representación verdadera," 119v–120. Simultaneously, in the late eighteenth century the enlightened bishop of Trujillo, Baltazar Martínez Compañón, promoted the foundation of elementary and boarding schools for native boys and girls, with an emphasis on literacy, religion, and useful trades, to Hispanicize and neutralize contemporary native rebels and turn them into "loyal, productive and Christian citizens." Ramírez, "To Serve God and King," 74.

80. "Representación verdadera," 167.

81. Ibid., 135v.

82. Virtually all of the Andean scholars and activists who led the campaigns made their way to Madrid with their petitions and sought audiences with the king, including Limaylla, Núñez Vela de Rivera, Morachimo, and Fray Calixto.

83. On the use of genealogies and paintings, see Gisbert and José de Mesa, *Historia de la pintura cuzqueña*. On the performance of Inca nobility and also the use of paintings, see Dean, *Inca Bodies*. On the use of Inca choreographic dancing, theatrical representation, and Inca portraits, see Estenssoro Fuchs, *Del paganismo a la santidad*, 498–508.

84. Szemiński, "The Last Time the Inca Came Back," 284–285. Szemiński follows John Rowe's notion of an "Inca nationalist movement" (explained in Chapter 2) and views these cultural expressions as part of that movement, maintaining that "Inca nationalism" involved the participation of both Inca nobles and commoners and was based on a resignification of "ancient religious precepts." Both the participation of commoners and the redefinition of the Inca or pre-conquest Andean religion, however, are unclear in this notion of "Inca nationalism" before the rebellion of Túpac Amaru and after the writings of Garcilaso de la Vega and Guamán Poma de Ayala.

85. Valcárcel, *Colección documental de la independencia del Perú,* 151.

86. Túpac Amaru II, 1781, reproduced in Durand, *Colección documental del bicentenario*, 204–222, 212.

87. As previously stated, Guamán Poma de Ayala was probably the first Andean intellectual to articulate a discourse of justice against the *encomienda* system, the institution of *corregidores*, and the legitimacy of the Spanish conquest and rule. Likewise, he first demanded the restitution of Amerindian lands to their legitimate owners following the pillage of the Spanish conquest, along with a series of changes to the colonial administration and the church. Some of these demands were inspired by the earlier writings of the Dominicans Fray Bartolomé de las Casas and Fray Domingo de Santo Tomás, as well as, more closely, the benevolent practices of Bishop Jerónimo de Loayza toward native Andeans. Adorno, *Cronista y príncipe*, 33–35.

88. Cuevas Herrera, "Cinco memoriales," 247v.

89. Ibid., 251v.

90. Ibid., 237v–238. Cuevas Herrera was apparently seeking an appointment as a prelate or an ecclesiastical *visitador*.

91. Ibid., 264.

92. *Recopilación de leyes de las Indias,* libro 6, título 7, ley 17, Madrid, December 10, 1576. *Real cédula* prohibiting *caciques* and *indios principales* from visiting the court without royal license.

93. "Representación verdadera," 121–121v.

94. *Recopilación de leyes de las Indias,* libro 6, título 7, ley 1a, Valladolid, Febrero 26, 1557. *Real cédula* ordering the *audiencias* to hear cases involving Indians on their *cacicazgos*. While Fray Calixto led a struggle in search of justice directly from the king, other contemporary Andeans in the town of Andagua resisted payments of overdue tribute by rejecting the authority of the *corregidor* and acknowledging the jurisdiction of the viceroy only for Indian matters. Salomon, "Ancestor Cults and Resistance," 151, 155.

95. "Representación verdadera," 166v.

96. Ibid.

97. Ibid., 166v.

98. Ibid., 167.

99. Ibid.

100. On July 10, 1735, a royal decree stipulated that capable Indians could in effect be elected by the Indian *cabildo* to perform as *procuradores de naturales.* Alberto Chosop and Joseph Santiago Ruiz Túpac Amaru Inca finally attained appointments as principal and substitute *procuradores de naturales,* respectively, in 1763 and performed as such well into the late 1780s. AGN, Derecho Indígena [hereafter DI], Leg. 18, Cuad. 311, ff. 8–12, 22–23, 38–39v, 57–59, 60–68.

101. "Representación verdadera," 126.

102. Ibid., 167v.

103. Ibid., 168.

104. Ibid., 167v–168.

105. Ibid., 168v–169.

106. Ibid., 169.

107. Ibid., 128.

108. Ibid., 168.

109. David Cahill spoke about the "constitutional activism" of the twenty-four Inca electors in Alférez Real, Cusco, during the 1814 "Revolución de la Patria," Cahill, "Liminal Nobility," 178. This was perhaps an expression of Andean elites' willingness to participate in the political conduct of society, already articulated in the mid-eighteenth century by Andean intellectuals and activists such as Fray Calixto.

110. See discussion in Chapter 3, "José Gabriel Condorcanqui Túpac Amaru II."

111. AGI, Lima, 1039, 29–29v.

112. AGI, Charcas, 53.

113. For detailed accounts of the Indians' removal from the San Lázaro neighborhood to El Cercado in 1591 and the history of the miraculous Virgin of Copacabana, see Lowry, *Forging an Indian Nation,* 51; Estenssoro Fuchs, *Del paganismo a la santidad,* 458, 497. Estenssoro Fuchs maintained that the Andean scholar Juan Núñez Vela de Rivera, the key figure behind the *cédula de honores* and the proceedings for the canonization of Ayllón, was chosen as chaplain of the Copacabana chapel after his return from Spain in 1695. For an extensive presentation of the founding of the Cercado Indian town, see Lowry, *Forging an Indian Nation.* For more details on this subject and the intra-elite and internal ecclesiastical tensions underlying the removal of the San Lázaro Indians, see Coello de la Rosa, *Espacios de exclusión.*

114. Pease, *Perú Hombre e Historia,* 312.

❧ 7 ❧

THE POLITICS OF IDENTITY FORMATION IN
COLONIAL ANDEAN SCHOLARSHIP

COLONIAL ANDEAN TEXTS become key windows for studying the discursive formation of identities and the politics that underlie them, since in writing, Indian and mestizo intellectuals found a crucial tool to convey their social and political aspirations and worldviews. The process of identity formation is an important aspect of colonial ethno-genesis, which also involves the conscious efforts of the colonized to redefine themselves and their "others" in situations of social distress and upheaval. Karen Powers's notion of ethno-genesis as a constant re-creation of ethnicity helps us understand changes in group and individual identity. In the Andean context, the interethnic encounters Spanish colonialism provoked through migration produced such a re-creation, a process of contention in which the disparate forces of the colonized and the colonizers gave birth to a distinctive society in which Andeans "reinvented themselves as a culture."[1]

In colonial Peru, interethnic encounters took place in different regions but mostly in Lima, a unique cosmopolitan city in the viceroyalty. Uprooted Indian immigrants (*mitayos*, artisans, *yanaconas* [native retainer subject to a colonial overlord]) of different ethnicities from the highlands, the coast, and perhaps from the Amazon rainforest had come to reside and sojourn in the "city of Kings," as had a significant portion of Afro Peruvians. In these diverse communities, Spaniards, Indians, and other castes came to coexist in places such as the segregated Indian town of El Cercado and other Indian neighborhoods, including San Lázaro, La Magdalena, and Santa Ana.[2] Lima was especially a meeting place for native authorities from the Audiencia of Lima, who converged on the royal court while carrying through judicial appeals—a task that usually resulted in prolonged sojourns in the city.

As the general interplay between native Andeans and Spanish peoples deepened with the implementation of the Toledan reforms in the late sixteenth and seventeenth centuries, a constant redefinition of Indian authority and identity boundaries transpired that took on renewed impetus as the Bourbon policies advanced in the eighteenth century. Andean writers reconstructed the images of themselves and their colonial "others" as native authorities were stripped of political power in their communities, losing control over the communal means of life and ultimately becoming the target of a systemic attack on indigenous culture that took on racial connotations.

While images of the self and the colonial "others" featured prominently in Andean texts, the practices of writing to top authorities in the kingdom and visiting the court in Spain were also a performance of identity and power that allowed for the contestation of colonial stereotypical constructions of the colonized and the redefinition of identities in ways that strengthened Andeans' struggles for social and political empowerment. Andean intellectuals presented themselves as capable and legitimate noble subjects, envisioning themselves as members of knightly orders, wearing Spanish clothing, and carrying weapons. As knights of the Indian republic, they "naturally" sought admission to the priesthood, schools, and universities and ultimately would crown themselves as alternative kings.

Constructing identities of the self and the colonial "others" through discourse was a political as much as a cultural process, a discursive and communicative operation that seems to have functioned as a cultural negotiation with the Spanish value system, intended to gain the acquiescence of the royal interlocutor and the rights Andean elites felt entitled to as a result of having accepted Christianity and provided tribute and service to the crown. Functioning as a sort of inverted Andean *mañay* (a religious compromise between conquerors and conquered to achieve social peace in pre-colonial times), Andean intellectuals adopted such Iberian notions and symbols as *pureza de sangre* and expected to be entitled to social privileges. Thus, the ideas of membership in the Catholic priesthood, access to Western education, and belonging to knightly orders make sense—less as unproblematic acculturation than as a strategic response to pressing historical and political needs. The way intellectual Andeans used these values and symbols, however, differed from that of Spanish authors. For Andeans, these were struggles to shed the imposed identity of "Indians" and perpetual pupils and neophytes and to become "old Christians," less in the spiritual regard than as an avenue for social self-assertion and eventually ethnic autonomy under Spanish rule.

The process of identity formation was a contested one in which political and religious imaginaries were inextricably connected. The ways the Christian language and concepts were used reveal Andean scholars' awareness of the politics of religion in a colonial setting, which reverberates in every folio of their manuscripts. They wrestled to define themselves as the most devoted and oldest Christians in the land, an anxious trope that unveils spirituality as a highly contentious field in which Andean intellectuals' political understanding of Christianity featured prominently. The political needs of an "Indian nation" (Indian nobles of different ethnicities and their mestizo relatives), struggling to redefine the republic of Indians as equivalent in all respects to its Spanish counterparts, led Andeans to fight over the meaning of Christianity and the power to minister it in the Andes. Educated Indians and mestizos launched legal and textual battles that generated a rich record for the study of colonial ethno-genesis: the colonized's social and discursive strategies to forge and refashion religious and political identities to overcome the rigid colonial social and ethnic hierarchies and emerge as a unified non-Spanish ethnic body (Indian nation) entitled to remain distinctive in times of deepening social unrest.

This chapter addresses the Andean discursive formation of identity in a three-fold manner. First, it describes the self-construction of Andeans as nobles, as they simultaneously moved closer to and departed from a European understanding of social differences and allegiance to the king. Because Andeans also constructed their identities in a relational and oppositional manner, with the point of reference always the Spaniards' religious, social, and political identification, they portrayed themselves as the Spaniards' opposites. Second, the chapter examines the construction of colonial subalternity in Andean scholarship—elite Andeans' perceptions of Indian commoners and other colonial subordinates, such as women, blacks, and other *castas*. Third, Andean writers consistently commented on the colonizer's behavior and nature, which configured their construction of oppositional identities. The second half of the chapter discusses at length the more salient discursive aspects of Andean religiosity through the ways Christianity was articulated and religious identities were defined.

TRANSFORMING INDIAN ELITES INTO COLONIAL NOBLES

The legal and discursive campaigns by Andean intellectual and leaders for social reaffirmation and the many individual petitions by *caciques* seeking to partake in the public performance of power were also struggles for the redefinition of their identities. At stake was the representation of Indian elites as an Indian nation of

noble subjects, shedding the status of "Indians" to wrestle respect from the colonizers and create a niche for themselves. These efforts brought Andeans closer to
colonial power standards and cultural values as they strove to actualize a reciprocal relationship with the king. Requests for *mercedes* (public favors adapted
as forms of attaining justice), for example, entailed a kind of writing that situated the petitioner within the space of the colonizer's culture, and they allow a
glimpse of the politics of Indian identity formation. Without overtly questioning
the colonial ascription of "indios," the writers proclaimed that they were first and
foremost Christians and loyal vassals of the king, a first step toward an exposé of
their "good service." This language constitutes the Andean bid to share the religious and political universe of the European colonizer.

In approximately 1677, Jerónimo Lorenzo Limaylla advanced a rendition of
the Indian "good service" theme in his "Memorial" to petition for the creation of
a Santa Rosa knight order for Indian nobles. Claiming to be speaking on behalf
of the *caciques principales* and governors from the entire kingdom of Peru, "all
those Nations," Limaylla attempted a negotiation of the noble privilege: "The
Indians from the kingdom do not lack [merits] because they have been serving
Y. M. [Your Majesty] for hundreds of years ... paying tributes and rates as well
as the caciques and governors attending to their obligations, thus showing their
love for Y. M."[3] He subtly altered the notion of good service, however, by drawing
attention to the key role of elite and non-elite Andeans in sustaining the empire.
This understanding of good service empowered the work of native commoners
and Indian authorities as a service that secured the empire's financial strength. If
the ideas of colonial subjection of commoners as tributaries and the condition of
elites as the enforcers of such subjection were accepted, Limaylla and the nobles
of "all those Nations" should have been entitled to become knights of the Indian
republic.

In his "Memorial," Limaylla appeared to be supporting the Toledan project
of Indian *reducciones* and the ecclesiastical extirpation effort. Yet the eligibility
for noble privileges he proposed reveals more clearly the contrast between the
apparent and subliminal agendas for nobility Andeans sought in the years around
1677. In his proposal, the requested preeminences should only be given to virtuous descendants of *caciques* who, "since the moment we received our holy apostolic law, had not relapsed into idolatry, superstition, or other sins that stain its
stability."[4] But the purpose of the preeminences was, more clearly, that "caciques
should have some estates and the necessary distinction ... so that they are better
appreciated by Spaniards because only with such wealth would they [Spaniards]
hesitate to oppress them [Indians] and, in turn, they [Indians] would communicate with them [Spaniards] with more love and less fear. Thus, there would be
more stability in those empires and it would be a great pleasure to be the vassals
of Y. M."[5]

This passage supports a notion of honor that involves Spaniards viewing Andeans with dignity and respect as opposed to simply mimicking the colonial notion of honor, which sought to distinguish Spanish nobles as socially superior. Clearly, Limaylla sought social empowerment and equality between the nobles of the "two republics" in return for Andeans' good service and even viewed this social balance as the key to Spanish hegemony.

Limaylla's counterparts in the 1720s refashioned their past to validate the good service they contributed in this strategy of negotiating rules by redefining the Andean *mañay* in colonial times. They invoked deeds of their ancestors, which at the time of the Spanish conquest and early-colonial years may have established new arrangements of reciprocity, as evidence of their ancestors' good service to portray themselves as loyal subjects. Among the members of the Lima network of *kurakas* in 1724, the descendants of the sixteenth-century Apoalaya—a powerful Indian lineage from the Mantaro Valley in central Peru—attempted to establish their good service through evidence of their ancestors' "collaborative" deeds during the Spanish conquest. In the eighteenth century, the *kurakas* sought to be recognized for their loyalty as an extension of the loyalty of their Apoalaya forebear, allegedly a general of the Inca army who was able "to reconcile his obligation [to the Inca] with the great service he rendered to the [Spanish] crown."[6] Apoalaya, a military chief of the Huanca, allied with Pizarro to counteract the Inca invasion of the Mantaro Valley in the conquest years. Such examples of collaboration reflected customary pre-colonial forms of reciprocity between conquerors and conquered.[7]

The same document from 1724 refers to Don Francisco Saba Capac Inga Yupanqui, another member of the network, who, along with twelve other native nobles from the Province of Lima and other regions, identified themselves as members of a collective "Indian nation, descendent from Inca emperors." They advocated for the enforcement of the 1697 *cédula de honores* and for other social justice issues they had been raising since 1711. Inga Yupanqui empowered himself before the king through the good service of his ancestors starting in 1640, specifically Maestre de Campo Don Jerónimo Paulli Chumbi Saba Capac Yupanqui Inga, *cacique* and *gobernador* of the Pachacama Valley and the Port of Lurin. Paulli Chumbi led 200 Indian soldiers to help the viceregal forces fight enemy pirates on the Barlovento coast and continued to collaborate in similar enterprises until late in his life.[8] In 1724 his descendant Don Francisco used the same expedient as a credential for his own fidelity to the king.

The validation of their service might imply that *kurakas* and other elite Andeans appear to have been endorsing the imperial aims of the Spanish crown, such as conquest of the Inca and the defense of the empire against other European powers, as well as supporting colonial notions of nobility and distinction. In this particular case, the *kurakas* were protesting a *bando* that prohibited mulattoes, blacks, and Indians from wearing Spanish clothes, and they were petitioning to be clearly distinguished from such groups and to be entitled to dress in Spanish garb like the nobles they were. Even more intriguing is the reelaboration of their historical good service as part of their construction of ethnicity in the eighteenth century.

The network of *kurakas* from different areas of the Audiencia of Lima and officers of the Lima Indian Battalion who signed the *memorial* not only proclaimed themselves as an Indian nation of descendants of the Inca emperor but expected to be recognized for good service offered during the early collaboration between the colonizers and the Huanca in the Mantaro Valley, to conquer the Inca. They also claimed to have helped the ethnic lords of the Pachacamac Valley in 1640 and the viceregal armies fight other rivals of Spain in Europe. The ethnic lines within this diverse group of Andeans are redefined and seemingly blurred, and their past rivalries seem to fade away; the notion of an "Indian nation" is subtly introduced as a conglomeration of undifferentiated ethnicities from different regions of the viceroyalty, sharing a common history devoid of interethnic contention. Although applied to the Túpac Amaru Rebellion, Charles Walker's idea that the Inca symbols were part of an "invented tradition" from colonial times as opposed to a "primordial memory"[9] is pertinent here as well—perhaps even more so than in the case of the Cusco people, since the ethnic Andeans writing from Lima who represented themselves as an Indian nation were from various regions of the Viceroyalty of Peru.

The Indian memorialists from 1724 also brought religious expedients to bear when substantiating their loyalty. They identified themselves with Indian, mestizo, and creole figures—known in Lima as models of virtue and mystical qualities—in their effort to be seen as good Christians and therefore deserving of ecclesiastical distinctions. In their gallery of Indian "exemplary lives," they exhibited the names of the "venerable" Nicolás de Dios, founder of the congregation "Casa de Jesús, María, and José," who after his death came close to becoming the first Andean saint in colonial Peru. The list of virtuous Indians and mestizo men and women in the early eighteenth century included Brother Francisco de San Antonio from the Recoleta of Santo Domingo; Brothers Antonio Barreto and Juan Cordero, the latter of whom was the "great pious founder of the Convalescencia de los Naturales [Indian hospital] in Lima"; Sister Inés de Jesús María from the Encarnación nunnery; Sister Catalina; Sister Magdalena de Jesus, "of outstanding and continuous prayer"; and Sister Francisca Anchipula, "venerable founder of the noble Indian women's convent Nuestra Señora de Copacabana." Past *caciques* of exemplary life and noble blood, such as Don Juan Ucho Inga Tito Yupanqui, *cacique principal* and *encomendero* from the Querocotilla *repartimiento* (Chachapoyas), completed the long list of honorable and loyal Christian figures.[10] Andeans strove to be models of spiritual purity, but not only for religious reasons. They also presented their virtuous deeds and descent as entitlement to *mercedes* for their good religious service to the evangelization enterprise, for which stressing their identity as noble and honorable colonial subjects on an equal footing with Spaniards was crucial.

The list of revered Indians and mestizos deserves attention, as some of these "virtuous lives" were also associated with other, more earthly underground currents of protest and rebellion in seventeenth-century Lima. In 1650, the canonization of Nicolás de Dios was the target of an Andean movement sustained by a network of *caciques* and mestizos such as Don Juan Núñez Vela de Rivera and other creole sympathizers in Lima, discussed in Chapter 6. Don Juan Ucho Inga Tito Yupanqui was one of the participants in the movement for enforcement of the 1697 *cédula de honores* during the first decades of the 1700s. While the figures of the past may have indeed been pious individuals, these Christian models of virtue were also Indian and mestizo members of the church who in one way or another engaged in activism for Andean religious autonomy—the founding of convents for Indian nuns, advocacy of Indian sainthood, the founding of Indian confraternities, and similar activities—rather than exhibiting an unproblematic identification with Christianity. Ultimately, this group of Indian authorities turned the basic condition of colonial subordination, that of tributary Indians and *mitayos*, not only into a sign of loyalty and a rendering of good service but also into an empowering symbol on which the entire empire depended:

> And if all those [names] referred to above, without mentioning others who have not manifested themselves because of their poverty, have not displayed the greatness that God gave them . . . we should explain that even though they are not nobles, in their own sphere they contribute equally to Y. M. with their tribute and personal services, which are some of the most useful services to your crown, because thanks to their continuous work and their judicious response to the mitas, they work the mines, the treasures of the kingdom fructify, and they [tributary Indians] are in every way the ones more devoted to such work.[11]

This rendition of Indians' good service in 1724 echoes the one by Limaylla in his 1677 "Memorial," mentioned earlier. Later Andeans, such as Fray Calixto in 1749–1750, also felt compelled to use the legal content of the *cédula de honores* as a legitimate frame to define Andeans as noble subjects. Not only did the mandate recognize that descent from gentiles did not bar Andeans from access to the priesthood, but it also stated clearly that colonial authorities should reward them with the same preeminences accorded to Spanish nobles. Fray Calixto thus argued that Andean and Spanish nobles were social equals, as they were both subjects of the same king—a key argument echoing Limaylla's assertion of nobility. The "Representación verdadera" contributed substantially to create the notion of an Indian nation. Its introductory page expresses the text's nature as a lamentation from "the entire Indian Nation" spoken on behalf of the "Indios Americanos" (American Indians), regardless of social or ethnic differences.[12] Andeans' perception of themselves as nobles of the Indian nation served as a weapon to fight their way into spaces of social advancement and autonomy rather than as a tool for simplistic and opportunistic social climbing that emulated the noble Spaniard. This would be, in practice, a way to erase the racial difference that forced Indians to remain at the lower echelons of colonial society. Overall, Andean scholarship reinterpreted the "merits" necessary for *mercedes* in a wider sense than the colonial notion of good service and used them as negotiating instruments to attain a reciprocal arrangement in which members of the Indian nation could empower themselves as a group of ethnic counterparts of the Spanish nobles and thus fight colonial racial assumptions and Spanish prejudiced attitudes toward Andean elites.

IMAGES OF *INDIOS NATURALES* AND THE SUBALTERN "OTHER" IN ANDEAN TEXTS

While Andean scholars framed their own identities as noble Christians and loyal subjects of the Indian nation, they also generated images of *indios naturales*, or common Indians, in a relational and somewhat oppositional pattern. The tensions that emerge in Andean intellectuals' perceptions of tributary Indians inadvertently emphasized the subordination of Indian commoners at large. Whereas educated Indian elites described themselves as capable and deserving of their autonomy and power, they portrayed their "fellow" Indian commoners for the most part as weak and inferior and projected onto them the colonial perceptions of the state and the church vis-à-vis Indians at large as wholesale minors in need of paternalistic protection. These perceptions could also be the legacy of precolonial hierarchies.

Exposure to ecclesiastical literature, which played a key role in the mentoring of Indian intellectuals throughout the colonial period, contributed to the dissemination of images of native Andeans as "docile," "rational," capable of understanding godly matters, but also "naive," "weak," and "miserable."[13] In the late seventeenth century, Juan de Cuevas Herrera expressed his internalization of such descriptions, as he deplored the poor state of evangelization in the parishes of Charcas Province. He represented Amerindian commoners as "poor victims" and distanced himself by designating them using the third-person plural "they": "[T]hey are helpless, convulsed and humiliated, as Isaiah would call them. They are pupils lacking a spiritual father."[14] Cuevas Herrera, a parish priest, shared Spanish legal definitions of indigenous peoples as minors and the connotations of inferiority attached to them: "I say that these unhappy [Indians] are pupils and the priest must be their tutor ... as though it was written in a testament.

... I say it should be this way, out of Christian piety, because of their imbecility, ineptitude, and narrow minds."[15] As a parish priest, Cuevas Herrera felt it was his duty to protect his flock by stressing their helplessness before the kingdom's patriarch.

Likewise, Cuevas Herrera's contemporary in Jauja, Jerónimo Lorenzo Limaylla, consistently maintained a third-person plural ("they") narrative voice when referring to non-elite natives as "infidels" and "idolaters." Exhibiting a biblical-sounding narrative style, Limaylla portrayed Andean commoners as "sheep ... poor lambs ... oppressed as the Hebrew under the barbarian yoke of the Egyptians" in an effort to emphasize their helplessness and the need for protection and to draw the king's attention to their plight.[16] While depicting them as "weak" and "inferior," Limaylla slipped in an interesting suggestion that the Indians' weakness was a result of their history: "[T]hey [the Indians] are naturally fragile, and weaker of force and energy than they were during their *gentilismo* [condition of gentiles], when they were among the more bellicose and strong of the region, like the other [n]ations of the world."[17] Inadvertently, the writer implies that Christianization made Andeans weaker, even though this might also imply that they had become more "civilized."

Like *indios naturales*, Indian noblewomen were portrayed with a similarly patronizing view. In defending female Indians' right to enter religious orders in 1749, Fray Calixto and his cowriters represented indigenous women as "pure," "docile," and potential models of spiritual perfection. This perception, along with their view of single mothers as potential or real threats to the social order, attested to the European mores already settled into the imaginary of late-colonial Andeans.[18] These writers, however, claimed the right to join religious orders for noblewomen and mestizas as well. Overall, while indigenous and mestizo scholars sought to empower themselves as capable, rational, noble, and loyal subjects, they inadvertently prolonged the subordination of female and male *indios naturales* by continuing to describe them as ethnic inferiors.

In the process of constructing Andean elites as colonial nobles, Andean writers inadvertently took part in another creative operation. Implicit in the dialectic dynamics of marking social distinction and privilege is the existence of an "other," the reverse image of the noble, the underprivileged without whom Andean elite individuals could not exist. In this sense, Andean writing inadvertently helped strengthen the colonial creation of ethnic and racial difference. Because the struggles for Andean social recognition—both textual and legal—implied an empathy with the notion of hierarchies and distinctions, the acceptance of Iberian notions of purity of blood, Andeans contributed consciously or unconsciously to marking hierarchical boundaries among their fellow subordinate subjects and other castes of the colonial society based on the perceived superiority of Andean nobles. Andean scholarship thus produced a record of identity construction in which Spanish values and understanding of social order entered the world of the Andean elite, marked interethnic and racial boundaries, and defined more clearly their sense of superiority within the subordinate colonial community.

This creationist process reveals itself in the complaints of the Lima network of *kurakas* in 1724, at a time when Viceroy Castelfuerte was attempting to hold mestizos liable for *mita* and tribute. The viceroy had lumped Indian nobles and mestizos with the group of other *castas* who were prohibited to wear Spanish-style clothing. This is a case of the Andean elite's desired performance of identity and concerns about drawing lines of difference among the colonized to realize the legal promise of social equality between the nobles of the two "republics": "We supplicate Your Excellence to issue a provision . . . declaring that Indians and mestizos must not be included in the prohibition on [wearing Spanish] dress, along with blacks, mulattoes, and zamboes, and instead, they must be understood as and comprise one whole body with the Spaniards and hope to receive this merced in all justice."[19] The symbolic representation of social status through clothing worn in public spaces would distinguish noble Andeans from groups that, in their minds and according to the larger Spanish society, were considered inferior. Thus, the nobles of the Indian nation still retained a hierarchical view of society, particularly during their struggles to leverage their rights as nobles in equal standing with Spaniards.[20]

A similar construction of subalternity emerged in 1749–1750 when, claiming the right for noble Indians to travel freely to Spain, the "Representación verdadera" identified African immigration to the Andes as "harmful" and referred to Africans in these words:

> Is there more oppression for us, that a generation so strange and servile stands in a better position than Indians, and that black slaves are set free to move around and may pass freely to Spain, whereas the Indian, even the noble, has to pay taxes and render the mita? Oh God! Is it possible that even your own slaves can become our masters that mistreat us and persecute us, and your powerful hand does not move to redeem us? . . .
> All that has been done so far is that the kingdom gets crowded with strangers from [E]thiopia, blacks, mulattoes and zambos . . . those atrocious, indomitable swine and outrageous people that have brought vices, evil, sodomy and continuous burglary.[21]

In this passage the hostile tone in reference to other subordinate subjects is used to deplore what the writers perceived as the fact that Andean Indians had less freedom and status than blacks, thereby implying that, among all colonial subjects, noble Andeans deserved a higher status. While the writers seem to have internalized racist biases against blacks and mulattoes, they also express a more general identification with colonial notions of hierarchy and distinction.[22]

CONSTRUCTING THE COLONIZER:
IMAGES OF THE COLONIAL "OTHER"

Andean scholars effected a construction of the colonizers' identities as deviant and opposed to those of Andeans. They depicted Spanish authorities and priests in images that stressed their "non-Christian" and "evil" nature as a way to contest charges of idolatry and other negative identities imposed upon Andeans by ecclesiastical discourses and colonial authorities' narratives in chronicles, reports, laws, and pronouncements in court. Bartolomé de las Casas had contributed to this form of identity construction in the 1540s by adopting biblical metaphors to cast *cristianos* (Spaniards) as "very cruel and ravenous wolves, tigers, and lions."[23] These biblical and Lascasian images continued to provide tropes for Andeans' construction of the colonizers' identity as the natural opposite of the allegedly weak and naive Andeans. In accusing *corregidores* of deterring Indians from conversion, Cuevas Herrera later maintained that "corregidores are pests," "they are the enemies of God," and "they are men whose only God is money." Likewise, Cuevas Herrera often referred to abusive *hacendados* in very negative terms, as "[T]urks or [M]oors with neither God nor law,"[24] revealing the extent to which Spanish conquest ideologies also permeated educated Andeans' minds.

In the mid-eighteenth century, as they protested against racial exclusion by the church, Fray Calixto and the unknown coauthors of the "Representación verdadera" used all possible adjectives that denote social transgression to depict the colonizers, contesting similar representations of Andeans by clerics and officials: "[T]hey have taken over [everything] temporal, spiritual, and eternal ... and everything is justified on the account that the candidates [for the priesthood] are white and Spaniards, and thus they are admitted although they are unworthy, ignorant, vicious, illegitimate, adulterous, and sacrilegious. Thus, the [religious] orders are infested with lowly born people."[25] Virtually all the texts under consideration portrayed colonial officials in unequivocally negative terms, equating them with the most vicious animals and deadly diseases and highlighting their corrupt, violent, and non-Christian behavior—casting them as "sinners." Similar representations of Spanish officials are also found in the creole/mestizo writings that worked for common cause with Andeans, such as the "Manifiesto de Oruro" (1739). Juan Vélez de Córdoba described colonial authorities as "thieves," "tyrants," and ultimately "vampires who sucked our blood, leaving us so depleted that only our mouths are left for us to complain."[26] In this regard, there had been little change in Andeans' perceptions of Spaniards from the early writings of Guamán Poma de Ayala, in the seventeenth century, to the late eighteenth century.

Indian scholars' discursive construction of their own identities and those of the Spaniards gravitated around a binomial opposition between colonized and colonizers and simultaneously contested the colonial rhetoric that contributed to producing racial stereotypes. The rhetorical strategies surrounding identity formation revealed educated Andeans' use of foundational biblical images and ecclesiastical discourses in the Americas. On the other hand, their discourses revealed that Andeans, especially in times of upheaval, negotiated identities by rejecting certain images and stereotypes imposed upon them by the colonizers while redeploying those definitions against their perceived "others," according to the political needs of the struggles and criticisms they were conducting at any given time.

This shifting and negotiation of identities, which may appear as ambivalence to non-Indian contemporaries, were part of the traditional practice of the pre-colonial *mañay* and came to be visually and performatively represented in the public rituals of the age-old urban baroque culture in colonial cities and towns of the Spanish empire.[27] Andean nobles' participation in pageantry, for example, was part of the construction of their political identity through public performance in the colonial city. In a parade in Lima in 1748 as part of the viceregal celebrations of the new Bourbon king Ferdinand VI's coronation, the *cabildo* of El Cercado led a masquerade of eleven Inca kings, their *coyas* (Inca queens), and cheerful dancers lavishly dressed. The pageant closed with a banner that read "Long live the Catholic monarch Don Ferdinand VI, King of Spain and Emperor of the Indies," with the last cart pulled by eight horses and displaying the royal coat of arms—the "imperial eagle of Lima grasping a flag with the cross and the Indians with their plumes and flutes and whistles underneath, celebrating happily their subjection."[28]

These overt signs of allegiance and surrender should not be taken at face value, however. Behind the baroque signs of Indian allegiance and political subordination to the empire was a silent parade of rebellion, a layer of radical resistance to colonial rule. The same Indian entity that organized the parade, El Cercado *cabildo*, was also behind the rebellions planned to take place in Lima and throughout the areas surrounding the viceregal capital sometime after 1748, which eventually broke out in 1750.[29]

In the public ceremonial life of Lima and Cusco, Indians wanted to represent their loyalty as subjects of the king, but this overt demonstration was only one aspect of a more complex political culture. While for some it may have been seen as a genuine gesture, for others it was only one side of the way Indians perceived their relationship with the king, particularly in times of social upheaval. Although informed by the asymmetrical relationships of colonialism, Andean reciprocity continued to define relationships between *kurakas* and their constituencies for centuries. Similarly, *caciques* and other native authorities perceived and represented their relationship with the king in a reciprocal manner (*mañay*). After all, a measure of reciprocity, real or imagined, between the king and his subjects was implicit in the European notion of the state as a *corpus politicum mysticum*.

By displaying their allegiance, the noble Indian performers were also sending a message of unfulfilled reciprocity. In 1748–1749, El Cercado *cabildo* was still demanding the enforcement of the *cédula de honores* and the abolition of the *repartimiento de comercio*, just when a new *arancel* practically legalized the latter, and the "Representación verdadera" was being prepared with demands for sweeping reforms of the empire's administration, with Indian participation. The nobles within the Indian network centered at El Cercado *cabildo* participated in the parade to express their role in the *mañay*, often a compact of reciprocity frustrated by the Spanish king, which Indian leaders were resolved to enforce either through law or rebellion—both possibilities were represented and subtly present in the parade. The parade, some would say, was a demonstration of Inca revivalism. Most noble Indians in the parade were not of Inca descent, yet they seemed to have shared the urgency to redefine themselves as a unique ethnic group—a redefined Incan-ness—in late-colonial times, an Indian nation that would include members of various ethnic groups and regions, not strictly ethnic Incas. These were, after all, times in which the powerful effect of market forces, social divides, migration, and closer interethnic relations in cities tended to erase ethnic lines in favor of a more "generic Indianness."[30]

Interpreting the complex nature of Indian and mestizo political culture, particularly Andean scholars' construction of identities in the colonial period, involves an understanding of the dialectical dynamics of allegiance/rebellion—a reminder that allegiance could also be just one aspect of Indian resistance under colonial rule. Constructions of Andean identity embodied the tension between the loyal Indian and the rebel. After all, Andeans may not have quickly forgotten their traditional *mañay* under Inca rule. Their practices of resistance and mediating constructions of identity suggest ongoing redefinitions of the political *mañay* in late-colonial times.

IDENTITY AND RELIGIOSITY: THE VERY NOBLE AND VERY BEST CHRISTIANS OF THE INDIAN NATION

The manipulation of religious categories, identities, and discourses was central to the cultural expression of mestizo and Indian educated elites, and their texts serve as unique windows into the changing religious culture in the mid- and late-colonial Andes. Overt expressions of pious Catholic devotion and reiterated proclamations of Christian identity were staples of the Andean writings under study, but the pattern was also present in Guamán Poma's *Nueva corónica y buen gobierno* (ca. 1615). How are we to interpret these expressions of Christian identity by ethnic elites in a colonial situation, and to what extent did they pertain solely or at all to the realm of spirituality? Further, what meaning should be ascribed to Andean Christianity, as publicly articulated in mid- and late-colonial Andean writings? After long exposure to Christian indoctrination and the workings of the church, colonial Andean intellectuals probably well understood the less spiritual undertones of Christianity and the social and political power wielded by the "magistrates of the sacred."[31] The wealth of information on Andean religiosity contained in the Andean texts reviewed here begins to indicate alternative functions of Christianity, such as language and Christian discourses, in the context of Andeans' struggles for greater participation in the sphere of the sacred.

By exploring Andean writers' production of religious meaning through their discursive practices, we can understand why they were invested in presenting themselves as the "true" Christians of the land and exactly what being Christian meant in the late colonial era for subordinated ethnic subjects endeavoring to participate in the institutions of social and political life. An analysis of the politics of these Andeans' religious discourse and identity serves as a window onto the larger issue of Andean religiosity in the public realm of writing and social participation in the sacred sphere. This section sheds light on the ways an important segment of Andean society expressed their views of colonial Christianity and defined both their and the colonizers' identities along religious and ethnic lines.

In understanding educated Andeans' expressions of Christianity, Kenneth Mills has suggested that seventeenth-century Christian Andeans constantly reformulated Christian codes and that they had "consciously or unconsciously 'changed' in order to meet the new pressures on their own terms instead of being only shaped by them."[32] More broadly, I maintain that instead of an unquestioned identification with Catholicism, Andean scholars subtly redefined Christian dogma and discourse to fight ethnic discrimination and colonial oppression and used such redefinitions to empower their struggles for ethnic autonomy starting in the late seventeenth century. They used images from the Bible, and Christian canonical rhetoric in general, as pragmatic tools to pave their way into the colonial fields of power and prestige usually denied to Indians and ultimately to fight for social equality by moving away from colonial definitions of who they were.

The literature on colonial Andean religion has largely remained centered on the sixteenth and seventeenth centuries. The focus of these studies has gravitated around the early evangelization efforts, the subsequent campaigns of extirpation, and the changes introduced in the three church councils of Lima—namely, the new strategies for religious conversion through purification of the Christian message and the cultural transformation of native Andeans more generally.[33] Scholars have questioned notions such as "acculturation," "conversion," and total rejection of Christianity—commonly used to explain Amerindian religious changes after the Spanish conquest—interpreting them as homogenizing categories that dismiss native agency, nuance, patterns of religious variation, and the reciprocal influence between Christianity and indigenous religious systems.[34] Colonial Andean religion has been viewed as a blending of the pre-Hispanic and Catholic religious systems toward a new rendition referred to as syncretism and the crystallization of Andean Christianity.[35]

In subsequent decades scholars criticized this interpretation of syncretism, mainly for its assumption that this was a completed religious synthesis between the two systems that remained unchanged after the mid-seventeenth century.[36] Syncretism also denies indigenous peoples the ability to select and synthesize elements from both Christianity and their own religious beliefs and practices and to rework those elements in the process. Both religious conquest and complete Indian rejection of Christianity were rather exceptional occurrences in the entire process of religious change in the Andes following the Spanish invasion. Scholars now tend to agree instead that the relationships between Indian and Spanish religious cultures ran the gamut of complex forms of mutual interaction, from adaptation to a complete reworking of both Andean and Christian practices and beliefs. These relationships did not necessarily represent an equal exchange and varied across time and space depending on myriad political, social, and cultural-historical factors.[37]

In understanding Andean religiosity in the late 1600s and the 1700s, this section moves beyond discussions of syncretism by discerning Andean elites' deployment of religious discourse in their search for social autonomous spaces as an important dimension of religious change. Although commentaries on the persistence of Amerindian religious rites and beliefs (usually a diverse and changing combination of pre-Hispanic and Catholic practices) continued to appear in the eighteenth century, it seems that by then the bulk of the Amerindian population subscribed, at least publicly, to a distinguishable set of Catholic symbolic practices, which formed an important part of the varied Andean religious cultures. By the late colonial period, questions about conversion and idolatry seemed to have been less of a concern of the church and the state, at least in the central areas of Peru, although they are reiterated in Andean writings as a shield to advance an agenda of inclusion in church institutions. By then, more widespread literacy and social activism by Andean scholars had defined new territory for the expression of their religious thought and political culture, producing new discursive forms that demanded new ways to read native religiosity. Concomitant with the use of Inca symbols of authority in painting, genealogies, public ceremonial life, and Indian writings for recognition of their nobility in the seventeenth and eighteenth centuries, the Indian and mestizo writers under study articulated expressions of religiosity in complex *memoriales* and representations to the king and the viceregal authorities. These sources opened a new venue for today's analysts to reexplore the more worldly functions of colonial Andeans' religion, the undertones of anxious identification with Christianity, their insistence on becoming full members of the church, and other expressions of deep piety and devotion that have led some to believe Indians were completely Christianized.

Beyond social and individual spiritual practices (e.g., rites, customs, inner experiences, indoctrination), the study of the discursive formation of religious ideas by a group of Christianized Andeans shows that Indian and mestizo religiosity appeared within a highly politicized field in which thinkers systematically redefined Christian principles to defy the practices of the Peruvian church and to question the behavior of Spanish practitioners of Catholicism. Rather than representing digressions on purely spiritual matters, their comments on religion are infused with political undertones, as the contradictions within Spanish colonialism gave them a strong rhetorical impetus: the gap between an empire sustained by universalizing Christian principles and the exclusionary practices of its ecclesiastical and governmental institutions. The writers used these conditions as tools to empower Andeans as the kingdom's moral capital and to diminish Spaniards as anti-Christian and morally unauthorized to rule.

THE WORLDLY POWER OF DIVINE WILL

The political deployment of religious concepts featured prominently in Andean discussions of the legitimacy of Spanish rule, as discussed in Chapter 4. The notion of "divine will" in particular was redefined to both accept and problematize Spanish justifications of the conquest while upholding Inca religious history as the supreme spiritual symbol and wresting legitimizing power from Christianity. In discussing the legitimacy of the Spanish presence in the Andes, Juan de Cuevas Herrera reformulated the myth of Viracocha to explain the defeat of the last Inca ruler in Vilcabamba and reworked the notion of divine will, not with Scholastic arguments but through a "prophecy" by Viracocha:

> Viracocha . . . banished by his [f]ather Yavarvacac Inca to the Chita place, near Cusco, saw a thing, not a human vision or corporeal representation, but the figure of a white and blond man with a beard similar to ours: [t]his figure spoke clearly to him that in forthcoming times, some people like him would come bringing the true religion, one better than the one they then professed, and that it was the will of Pachacamac, the world maker, that Indians become their subjects, receive it [the new religion] and pay allegiance to the newcomers. This prophecy was repeated among them from generation to generation and Guayna Capac, the oldest of the Incas, repeated it again, warning that the moment was arriving in which the men foreseen by Viracocha would come and then they [Andeans] should receive them, obey them, and pay service to them, just as Viracocha had commanded and he [Guayna Capac] was commanding again. . . . Thus, Atahualpa Inca, the son of Guayna Capac himself, received our fellows [Spaniards] with the customary love and friendliness. . . . Finally, Fuanso [*sic*] Inca, Guayna Capac's legitimate heir, coming out from the Vilcabamba [M]ountains with more than 200 D [thousand] warriors, seized the city of Cusco, where only 150 Spaniards had been left. By an evident

miracle, God Our Lord saved them from such a multitude, like the gospel's seed. They [the Inca] thus believed the truthfulness of his ancestors' predictions. Addressing his people, he said that undoubtedly it was Pachacamac's will that these kingdoms must become the Spaniards'. He tenderly asked his people to obey heaven's design and turned back to his refuge, where the ingratitude and unkindness of a Spaniard, whose life he had graciously and kindly spared, paid him back with death. . . . Therefore, my conclusion is, my Lord and [C]atholic King, that God, the [s]overeign King, gave these kingdoms of Peru to the House of Castile.[38]

More than a century earlier, Spanish chroniclers and conquerors had contributed to the creation of the Quetzalcoatl myth in Mexico. Similar versions of Viracocha's myth and the miracle of the apostle Santiago saving the Spaniards from the Inca army in Cajamarca also appeared during the conquest of the Inca. To deny the Spanish conquest and the justice of their invasion, Guamán Poma had written in approximately 1615 about the presence in the Andes of Saint Bartolomé, missionizing before the arrival of the Spanish conquistadors.[39]

Reformulating the legitimacy of Spanish rule by invoking the myth of Viracocha may also have facilitated the acceptance of Catholicism and the Spanish presence among Andeans. In the late seventeenth century, Cuevas Herrera's rendition of the myth contributed to the re-creation of the story of Spanish conquistadors being perceived as envoys of the ancestral gods. Beyond the historical accuracy of the events he related, however, the choice of validating divine will through an Inca prophecy that allegedly took place in pre-Christian times is intriguing. Cuevas Herrera's projection of notions of divine law onto the Inca past reveals his religious creativity and reminds us of Mills's reiteration that for Andeans the two religious traditions were usually complementary rather than contradictory and changed over time according to different understandings of those traditions.[40]

While Cuevas Herrera set out to demonstrate that the Americas were "given" to the Spaniards by divine will, he did so through a particular rendition of the Viracocha myth—possibly mediated by the Spanish chroniclers—and an allegory for the orality of pre-colonial cultures: the phrase "by the mouth of God." More important, "heaven's design" and "Pachacamac's will" both function as legitimizing agents in the text, although emphasis seems to lean toward the latter.

Thus, Cuevas Herrera's rendition of Viracocha as God's interlocutor can be seen as part of what Peter Gose considers the Spanish attempt to "reconcile the discovery of America with a Christian universalizing history."[41] By casting the defeat of the last Inca rebellion in Vilcabamba as a sign of divine will or the fulfillment of Viracocha's prediction, however, Cuevas Herrera admitted that the Inca god was able to communicate directly with the Christian God and that Andeans could also be the people "chosen" by God. In this way, while the writer legitimized Spanish rule, he empowered the Inca religion and Andeans as people able to elevate their thinking to godly matters—a capability some missionaries, including Jose de Acosta, denied them. By presenting Viracocha as the recipient of God's revelation ("by the mouth of God"), Cuevas Herrera undermined the relevance of the 1493 bull by Pope Alexander VI as a legitimizing tool of the Spanish spiritual conquest and rule. Simultaneously, as he merged the prophecy of Viracocha into a historical justification of Spanish rule, Cuevas Herrera validated Inca history as part and predecessor of Western history.

This narrative operation links Cuevas Herrera's rendition of the past with similar discursive proclamations from earlier in the century. Inca Garcilaso de la Vega's rhetorical strategy in his *Comentarios reales de los Incas* (1609) sought to change the image of the Inca society in Europe by reconciling Inca and European historical traditions and, thus, to conflate aspects of the Christian and Inca religions.[42] In fact, in the introduction to the "Cinco memoriales," Cuevas Herrera made explicit that Garcilaso de la Vega was part of his intellectual inspiration:

> [He is] an author free from any suspicion, Garcilaso de la Vega, an excellent elder of the pure royal blood from the Inca kings. And, if you don't believe him, come, communicate, and ask the few remaining branches [heirs] of the royal trunk.... I, as one of them, since I am the fourth grandson of Don Christobal Paullu, son of the Great Guayna Capac, third brother of the two Incas Huascar and Mancolo, I have researched very well that these my ancestors' kingdoms ... have come to be very justly Y. M.'s, may God keep them prosperous as I wish.[43]

Cuevas Herrera's identity in this passage follows the pattern of cultural negotiation explained in the previous section. He projected himself as a member of the Spanish church, a Christian, and a loyal subject who recognized the legitimacy of Spanish rule. From that standpoint he spoke of the colonizers as "our fellows" when relating Atahualpa's encounter with Pizarro. Simultaneously, he empowered himself as a direct descendant of the Incas from Cusco and authorized his discourse by acknowledging the inspiration of Garcilaso de la Vega, whom Cuevas Herrera identified strategically as an elder "of the pure royal blood from the Inca kings." Alternating these two forms of identity—a cultured Inca noble and a devout Christian and subject of a Spanish king—these Andeans dwelt in a liminal space, a threshold between the Spanish and Andean worlds, from which Cuevas Herrera sought justice for his native fellows, however unstable such a place may have been.

Garcilaso de la Vega's *Comentarios reales de los incas* constituted a seminal work in the reconstructions of Inca history and memories in mid- and late-colonial Andean scholarship.[44] In 1749 the Andean composers of the "Representación verdadera" developed the most complex elaboration of Andean religion to dispute the ecclesiastical stereotyping of Andeans as idolatrous. The manuscript's subsection "Breve y compendiosa satisfacción" clearly drew on Garcilaso de la Vega's thesis that Andeans had already been monotheistic before the Spanish invasion:[45]

> The Peruvian Indians from the kingdom of Cuzco were gentiles and less idolatrous and superstitious than the Roman, Spanish, European and Greek gentiles, because they did not worship a superior deity other than *Pachacamac*, which means the demiurgic, the one who animates everything, and the Sun, whom they believed to be their lieutenant and the [f]ather of their Inca kings. They did not have thirty thousand gods like the Roman and European gentiles of the [O]ld [W]orld, but only the Sun, whom they worshipped with external and visible adoration, and thus, they painted it and built its temple; whereas to *Pachacamac* they did not paint or create an idol, but they worshipped it with inner and spiritual veneration, stating that he was invisible and immense.... Thus, wisely ignorant, they worshipped in Pachacamac the true God, creator and life giver of heavens and earth, whom they did not know as one and trine and by revelation and faith infused in baptism, but they knew it by the natural reason that dictated to them that God was one, unique, and omnipotent.[46] (original emphasis)

In a similar manner, Garcilaso de la Vega claimed that the Inca "held Pachacamac in higher and more sincere veneration than the sun" and that Pachacamac was the unknown maker of the world.[47] Using the same translation as, and reinterpretation by, Garcilaso de la Vega effected more than a hundred years earlier, the "Breve y compendiosa satisfacción" cast the Andean past as "less idolatrous" than the Christian European past. The text slightly modified Garcilaso's elaboration of how Andeans knew about God prior to Christianity. For Garcilaso de la Vega, Andeans worshipped a variety of gods, emphasizing the predominance of the Sun and Pachacamac.[48] The "Breve y compendiosa satisfacción," in contrast, simply erased the polytheistic nature of Andean religions in an effort to equate their cults of the Sun and Pachacamac with the Christian monotheistic ideal. Assuming that only the Inca religion had existed in the Andes prior to the European invasion, the text conflated Pachacamac—a pre-Inca deity of the northern coastal peoples of ancient Peru—with the Sun as one god. This monotheism, however, was nuanced with dualistic tones. Pachacamac and the Sun had "invisible" and "interior" as well as "visible" and "exterior" manifestations. Thus, this monotheization or Christianization was informed by the dualism of Andean gods (God/human) but presented in a different fashion to fit the needs of the argument (invisible/visible).

Just as Garcilaso de la Vega attempted to rectify the historical record of Inca culture for Europeans,[49] the "Breve y compendiosa satisfacción" occasionally attempted to "straighten out" errors in the Spanish understanding of Andean religion, such as the meaning of *huacas* (Andean sacred entities or objects and places of reverence). Through a discussion of the various meanings of the word, the text contests the ecclesiastical accusation that *huacas* were idols Andeans worshipped. As opposed to Garcilaso de la Vega's explanation of the manifold connotations of *huacas*, however, the "Breve y compendiosa satisfacción" chose only a few and emphasized that *huacas* were a type of Amerindian art object rather than idols: "Ancient Indians would mold and work those figures to imitate nature in all they would see . . . and with them they had so much fun in the feasts they made to their Inca kings . . . and they would offer these figures to them as if they had brought them to life. . . . Thus, those things were not idols that the ancestors worshipped but figures with which they brought nature to life through imitation."[50] Basically, Andeans were not idolaters but figurative artists, perhaps in the best tradition of the Spanish Renaissance.

COLONIAL "SIN" AND DIVINE JUSTICE

Reelaborations of Christian notions of sin, punishment, and divine justice appeared prominently in Andean writings that questioned the behavior of Spanish rulers. As he rejected the corruption of *corregidores* and *curas*, Fray Calixto maintained that there would be divine punishment for Spanish officials and priests not only after death but also in this life, in reparation for the violence and expropriation they inflicted upon Indians: "And since God is an honest and just judge, he will punish them here, apart from the punishment that in the other life, precisely, awaits them for the atrocious and inhuman crimes . . . that people subjugated by other nations have suffered."[51] Colonial oppression was framed as a "sin" and colonial officials as "sinners" who deserved double punishment; thus, Indians would be redressed through this kind of divine justice. This reformulation of punishment for "colonial sin" had significant antecedents in the writings of Indian authorities and contemporaries of Cuevas Herrera, also residents of Charcas Province. Earlier in 1650 the *caciques principales* from the Bishopric of La Paz—Don Cristóbal Nina, Don Juan Quispe, and Don Pedro Larua—members of a large social network of native authorities in southern Peru, while reclaiming restitution of encroached communal lands, had launched an apocalyptic rendition of the "divine punishment" that as a damnation awaited colluding Spanish officials and colonists:

> [I]n terms of the Sacred Scriptures, and therefore of the Catholic faith, God
> will switch kingdoms, from one people to another, because the powerful
> commit injustices and slander, injure, mistreat, and deceive the helpless poor
> in various forms. And as the miserable Indians have suffered so many harms
> under the powerful Spanish since they became rulers, so much that the loss of
> their lands was the ultimate aggravation . . . God has made as his just design

the inescapable execution of his punishment for all. So many iniquities have irritated and armed his hands for the vengeance.[52]

The wrath of God would fall upon colonial sinners as the ultimate redress for the expropriation of native Andeans' lands and other injustices. But this rendition of divine justice had a distinctive political undertone: the end of Spanish rule and the advent of a new kingdom ruled by other people. Divine justice forecast the finite character of Spanish rule, the beginning of the end, when Spaniards would lose their "right" to *dominium*. Ultimately, the death of the empire would be the divine punishment for colonial sins.

THE POLITICS OF RELIGIOUS IDENTIFICATION: THE ZAPA INCA VERSUS THE POPE

The power confrontations involved in Andean struggles for social justice permeated their religious reworkings and definitions of religious identity. Andean scholars and social activists were aware of the political power of colonial religion and ecclesiastical authorities and effected a repositioning of the Inca past to accommodate the political needs of their colonial present. In a discursive move that would challenge contemporary ideas about the Andean utopia and the revival of Inca symbols, Andean leaders detached themselves from their Inca roots and customs to displace their identities to the sanctioned territory of Christianity and purity of blood and ultimately to obtain justice in times of colonial expropriation of their communal lands and chiefdoms.

The campaigns for the defense of their lands in the southern Andean region in the mid-seventeenth century led by the *caciques principales* and *gobernadores* Nina, Larua, and Quispe—the authors of the passage just cited and contemporaries of Cuevas Herrera and Limaylla—provide an illuminating construction of Christian identity by Andeans. A cunning argument by the Audiencia of Lima was used against these Indian litigants, which posed that by endorsing *composiciones de tierras* in favor of Spaniards, the king was merely following *"el derecho del Inga"* (Inca law). Since the Inca had allegedly deprived his subjects of ownership of and dominion over lands, by ruling against the Indian litigants the Spanish king Philip would merely be continuing the Inca tradition. What is more intriguing is the *kurakas'* response to such judgment by the fiscal of the Audiencia of Lima in 1650. They claimed that if the king denied Andeans their legitimate land rights, he would be acting

[a]s if for [himself], such a pious and Catholic [m]onarch, the barbarous tyranny of a gentile Indian king [the Zapa Inca] was more important than the just and right decision of a high pontiff of the [c]hurch, the saintly and wise successor of Saint Peter and the vicar of Jesus Christ, supreme sovereign of

heaven and earth, who commended the [k]ing to take care of this [c]hurch of new Christians ... [and help them] to enjoy the freedom of being God's children, governed in peace and justice: not by the laws of gentiles and barbarians, who have expired along with their empire, but by the law of rational peoples, the very sacred, just, royal, and very holy pontifical laws. ... And thus treated, these new converts may understand that, if the gospel was so beneficial for them at the spiritual level, at the temporal level it also improved their situation at the time of Philip, who recognized [Indians] as the owners of the lands because of their being Christians, whereas at the time of the Inca they could not own [the said lands] for having being gentiles, or at least they could not have in usufruct all the ones they needed but which were in effect available.[53]

In 1650 these prominent Andean leaders from La Paz no longer saw themselves as Incas in custom or vassalage but rather as "rational people" and Christian subjects of the church, a new identity that, beyond the spiritual meaning, functioned as a passport to retain their property. They would have no major difficulty detaching themselves from the Inca, their old rivals anyway, who were now viewed as barbarous tyrants—reminiscent of Andeans using descriptions of the Inca created in the Toledan era.

But inasmuch as Andeans tried to be included in the community of old Christians and to gain access to justice, the Christian promise of redemption did not come true. The text next moves into a territory of frustration and distrust:

Not even their [Indians'] venerable condition as new Christians served them well. From their freedom as gentiles, they converted to our Catholic obedience, trusting the security that old Christians promised them, on behalf of God and the [k]ing, that they would be treated, governed, and protected in our Christian discipline much better than they were in their barbarous gentilismo. But, caring only for their personal interests, the ministers of this despicable dispossession regarded Spaniards, mestizos, suspicious mulattoes, the Portuguese, dubious Catalans, and even the French and the Dutch, their enemies, as people of higher status and more capable to own their lands than the Indians. And they deprived [Indians] of the lands that God, nature, and the Catholic [k]ings and the just viceroys had given them. ... For the Indians ... the many and constant prayers, penitence, masses, and prerogatives that they and other good people elevated to God, asking to redress them for so much harm[,] were to no avail either.[54]

The net result of the Indian conversion was the loss of freedom and assets they had enjoyed while they were gentiles. Behaving like a true Christian was to no avail; instead, they became aware of the ethnic biases of the colonial state and the church, which were unable to deliver the promised social justice for native Andeans. The new Christians became quickly disappointed with the colonial pact they had entered into as a result of the conquest; this identification was fractured from the outset. In their new state, Andeans found themselves in a kind of abject liminality: they were no longer Incas, whose empire and customs had "expired" anyway, but they were not true Christians either, since the reasons they had accepted this affiliation never came to fruition. Thus, their outward profession of Christianity was at odds with their inner feelings of frustration and discontent.

The same ambivalence emerged in the mid-eighteenth century when Fray Calixto and his cowriters struggled to debunk ecclesiastical arguments against Indian priesthood. They admitted that their ancestors had "sinned" by practicing idolatry. However, to elude charges of idolatry in their own time, which would have strengthened the definition of Andean prospects as neophytes, the writers detached themselves from their Inca ancestors altogether and professed a new Christian affiliation. They seemed to reject their Inca identities to position themselves as old Christian subjects, pure of blood and eligible for the priesthood.[55] To shed neophytism, the mark of exclusion from religious organizations, Andeans struggled in unpredictable ways throughout the colonial period. Fray Calixto was aware of a *real cédula* by Charles II on April 16, 1693, that granted Indians and mestizos eligibility for positions in the Holy Office Tribunal as "[m]inisters, calificadores, and consultants ... [and] they only have to prove on both [maternal and paternal] lines of descent two Christian grandparents."[56] This decree was the result of Andean scholar Juan Núñez Vela de Rivera's writings and leadership in Peru and Spain.[57]

Although it may sound paradoxical, for Andean activists fighting for social inclusion in the church, being appointed members of the Holy Office was crucial for their identification as old Christians: "Indians would very gladly ... subject themselves to fasting ... and to observance of all the holidays of the [c]hurch by attending mass, and they would willingly subject themselves to the Holy Tribunal [of the Inquisition] in exchange for being honored with [d]ignities, [p]riesthood, and the religious orders, like the rest of Catholics."[58] Thus, they would be considered old Christians, no longer neophytes, and would be able to act as ethnic magistrates of the sacred. Not surprisingly, the 1693 decree apparently did not go into effect, since both the "Representación verdadera" in 1749–1750 and the "Planctus indorum" in approximately 1751 reiterated the same demand. The "Planctus indorum" asserted that Indians had no impediment to being ordained as priests or becoming bishops, since "they are old [C]hristians, after two centuries of being born by [C]atholic parents; and ... the Indians that commit crimes against the faith should be brought to the inquisition, since the immunity against the inquisition has been unduly fomented by Spaniards to prove Indians' condition of neophytes."[59] Again, rather than the actual religious meaning of this statement, it is the political implication of holding positions in the Inquisition Tribunal so Andeans would enjoy the status of old Christians that gives force to the discursive strategy.

"MORE CHRISTIAN AND CATHOLIC THAN SPANIARDS"

Following the same rhetorical line, throughout the colonial period Andean scholars insisted, sometimes to the point of exhaustion, that they were not only Christian but also the true Christians of the land. In fact, they exceeded Spaniards in their devotion. One might wonder, however, why Andeans were still so anxious to reassert their Christian affiliation in the late colonial period. What was behind this discursive gesture of cultural approval for the colonizers' religious practices? Here is just one example of how Fray Calixto defined Andean religiosity in 1749, when he led the written debate over Andeans' perpetual status as neophytes: "With respect to Spaniards, Indians appear more Christian and Catholic and may raise the banner of those utterly Christian and very Catholic, since thousands of them abundantly joined the [c]hurch and received baptism, very quickly and almost without miracles, and despite the many examples of tyranny, cruelty, covetousness and horrendous crimes that they saw in Spaniards . . . and in spite of all this, they converted and still are devoted Christians."[60] Andeans became Christians in spite of Christians, the writer suggested, while Spaniards appeared in reality the antithesis of Christian role models.

Andean scholars who outwardly professed Christianity were also concerned with values such as *pureza de sangre* and supported mission projects, presenting themselves as perfect, loyal subjects of the king. Unconditional adhesion to Catholicism, however, might be seen as an anomaly that fulfilled other important functions. As in Spain, in Spanish American societies the statute of *pureza de sangre* and recognition as an old Christian amounted to being deemed rational and socially acceptable (Spaniards were generically referred to as "*cristianos*") and to having the right to gain access to a number of opportunities, such as admission to the priesthood.[61] Reasserting a Christian identity, then, had important political implications for Indians and mestizos, who still remained excluded from the church in the late stages of colonialism in the Andes.

Rather than indisputable signs of spiritual assimilation with Catholicism, anxieties about Christian identity functioned as a political weapon in a society in which mestizos and *indios ladinos* had become aware of the barriers to their social advancement and the need for ethnic survival. Their accreditation of *pureza de sangre* was also the rhetorical and social device needed to construct genealogies that tied them to the old Incas to support their claims to chiefdoms (in Limaylla's and many other cases) and to free themselves from tribute and *mita* obligations, but at the same time it proved their long-standing conversion to Catholicism and access to a measure of social power that secured ethnic survival—even if that purity of blood was mostly fictional and often deliberately constructed. A redefinition of religious identity was imperative if they were to fight their way into the church; such a resignification unveiled the political and colonial dimensions of Christianity and attempted to fight Andeans' subordinate status as Christian minors and neophytes who would never be Christian enough to minister between humans and God.

In constructing Andeans' religious and political identity, the Andean scholarship discussed here should be distinguished from the notions of Andean utopia and Inca messianism examined by John Rowe, Alberto Flores Galindo, Manuel Burga, and Jan Szemiński, among others, and analyzed later in this chapter—even though both traditions may have overlapped chronologically, especially in the eighteenth century. In their excess of Christianity, Andeans appeared as a unique kind of "good Christians," detached from their Inca past as much as from the Spanish model of Christianity in their time. Spanish officials were clearly un-Christian role models, but the "good" Spanish missionaries were long gone: "Indians were very good Christians and Catholics, because they were such a kind of men who, in spite of what they have seen from the time of the conquest, remained in the faith that the Spaniards founded with such a bad example. This does not deny the saintly examples of early apostolic men of respectability, missionaries, and bishops . . . but they are all gone."[62]

What was being fought in these debates, in the end, was a political rather than a spiritual battle to define who had the power and the moral strength to bear the banner of Christianity and teach the Christian doctrine in the Andes. It was a struggle in which the colonized seized the religious discourse and symbols of the colonizer and exhausted their possibilities to win a space for Andean religiosity over colonial Christianity. Rather than claiming the return of the Inca, as seemed to be the case with the Oruro rebel Juan Vélez de Córdoba in 1739 and Túpac Amaru II in 1780–1781, Andean writers longed for a utopian Christianity that would grant Andeans full membership in the church but would also enable them to demonstrate, with their own pristine example, who the true Christians in the Andes were.

It is also important to recognize, however, the power dimension inherent in the fight for the priesthood and the historical nature of colonial Catholicism. Rather than seeking full inclusion in the Catholic Church per se, Andeans mostly sought to participate in the power spheres of Catholicism because it was *the* predominant form of religion in colonial Peru, a colonial imposition of the spiritual and political powers of the period. The barriers of difference the church had upheld for centuries would have threatened to become blurred if Andeans had been admitted into the priesthood, as Spaniards and, later, creoles had been admitted during the colonial era. Estenssoro Fuchs interpreted the church's systematic opposition to accept Andeans as priests as an acknowledgment of the danger implicit in full inclusion. In other words, rather than simply reflecting Andeans' desire to assimilate to Catholicism, recognition of Andeans as full Christians functioned as a dangerous weapon that threatened to unsettle the hierarchical edifice that sustained colonial institutions.[63] Thus, the public expression of Andean religiosity in writing became highly political, a contestation and a reflection of colonial religion's political nature.

Incorporating Indians and mestizos into the priesthood, however, also had the potential to strengthen the church as an inclusive institution and Christian principles as spiritual guides, thereby buttressing the hegemony of both Christianity and the church. But the church was probably not yet ready to see such an opening; by continuing to limit Indians' access to the realm of the sacred, it would actually intensify their struggle for ethnic autonomy.

AN ALTERNATIVE UTOPIA: "ONE GOD, ONE LAW, ONE KING"

The Andean activists who gathered around El Cercado *cabildo* in the late 1740s and discussed their social and political agenda imagined various alternative ways to escape colonial discrimination. They considered rebellions to defend themselves against the harms of the *repartos* and the Bourbon attempts to downgrade mestizos and Indian authorities. As opposed to the Incan utopian ideas prevalent in different insurrectionary contexts in the 1700s, leaders in the mid-1700s also envisioned the coming of a "true" Christianity—perhaps a long-term social and cultural goal of a more cross-ethnic nature—in which the spiritual equality among humans bound by Christian love would ease the social tensions and redress Andeans from colonial injustice. Summed up as loving each other as one Christian nation, this doctrine had a salient political connotation, however, as an attempt to bridge the distance between Spaniards and Andeans. Fray Calixto expressed the hope that

> [a]ll this [discord] will cease if Spaniards and Indians united and all together became one, and loved each other, marrying among themselves and becoming one whole people and one nation, as though they were vassals of the same master, ruled by the same laws, as though noble Indians were equal to noble Spaniards, and commoner Indians equal to their Spanish counterparts. And being all one single people, merit only would place them in the ecclesiastical and secular dignities: [t]hat way, women would have men to marry and would live honestly and in Christianity, thus avoiding so many spurious children, lowly born, mulattoes, vicious, and born from incontinence. Thus, most children would be legitimate, as they commonly are in Spain where this distinction or discord [mestizos/whites] does not exist, and as they are also among Indians, who bear mostly legitimate children. The kingdom would then be populated by strong and politically united people under one [n]ation, one law, and one [k]ing.[64]

Andeans here envisioned a Christian love of a utopian kind that would make Spaniards love Indians and unite with them (avoiding racial mixing with "lower" castes), embracing Catholic marriage, legitimacy, and colonial law. If Spaniards were able to see themselves as "one" with Indians and, overcoming their racial and ethnic biases, were to legally marry Indian women, a world of social harmony would emerge in which noble Indians would be recognized for their status and be admitted to the priesthood; many single Indian women would find suitable Spanish husbands and would be "restrained" and populate the land with legitimate children.

This love, sealing the union of the "two republics," would represent the dissolution of the Habsburg plan for segregation. The utopian world thus represented, however, endorsed the colonial hierarchical division between nobles and commoners of the "two republics." This utopia was also the dream of an "ideal" society in which the values of the colonizers and the imaginary of the colonized would come together peacefully in a heaven of social harmony, where love would erase discrimination and all subjects would agreeably accept Spanish rule, Christianity, and colonial laws. This notion of love is utopian as much as it is utterly political. It sought to obliterate colonial power relationships through "Christian love," a kind of love and unity that more than 200 years of colonial Christianity in the Andes had failed to achieve. Very important, nevertheless, is the underlying critique of colonial discrimination that emerged from Andeans' utopian dreams of social harmony in the last stages of Spanish rule in the Andes. A utopian realm of Christian harmony was a last hope to counter colonial injustice in the face of protracted exclusion and the ineffectiveness of long-standing royal protective policies.

The prevalence of this political interpretation of Christianity in the writings of Andean scholars studied in this book and in the writings of dozens of other *kurakas* and mestizos must be accounted for as an important layer of Andean thought when assessing the thesis of Inca revivalism in late-colonial Peru. The political substratum of these Christian notions of love and social harmony unveils a different utopia, one enveloped in discourses laden with excessive professions of Christianity. Concealed behind these expressions was a major critique of the realm's major spiritual institutions and the ways Christianity had become a tool of colonialism. This political culture was clear later, in 1780–1781, in Túpac Amaru's religious expression—which appeared to be simultaneously the embodiment of Inca revivalism, Spanish Christian thinking, and support for the church as an institution. As opposed to Fray Calixto's dream, however, Túpac Amaru's dream was to create one nation of Indian, mestizo, creole, and *casta* brothers by killing all Europeans.[65]

ANDEAN REBEL CATHOLICISM?

The political undertone of Andean religion becomes more apparent closer to the rebel conjunctures of the late 1700s and their discursive production. As with the opposing political forces on the ground, the tensions between royal discourses and colonial policies exploded, and Andean thinkers situated their voices and rhetorical weapons in the vacuum left by those tensions. The rebellions in Cusco and La Paz (1780–1783) were both an opportunity and a battle for discursive production, leaving a rich record of Andean rebels' religious and political ideas.[66] In his letters and edicts, Túpac Amaru professed a rather pious Catholicism and overall promised respect for clerics and the church. In his envisioned Inca rule, ecclesiastics would continue to receive tithes and other fees.[67] Nevertheless, he resignified medieval theological notions of "just war" and "divine justice" in ways that subverted conventional interpretations of those Christian precepts. As opposed to the various Andean writings analyzed in this book, Túpac Amaru advocated violence on behalf of Christianity, God, and the church. In spite of his Christian and devotional rhetoric, the Cusco bishop Juan Manuel Moscoso excommunicated Túpac Amaru, probably for good reasons. In line with the Andean scholars studied here, however, leaders of the 1780–1783 rebellions brought to a heightened moment the preexisting colonial critiques, their political use of Christian discourses, and their proposals for reform.

For Túpac Amaru, the rebellion was a "just, defensive war" that had to be waged on the *corregidores* and other colonial oppressors in the Cusco *cabildo* for their long exploitation and abuse of Andeans.[68] After many decades of petitioning and advocating for the enforcement of justice for Andeans, killing tyrannical rulers seemed just. Túpac Amaru had been educated in the school of *caciques* in Cusco by Jesuit mentors and must have been familiar with the Neo-Scholastic tenets that legitimized rebellion when rulers stopped protecting and reciprocating their subjects. The insurrectionary leader presented the killing of Spaniards as a case of divine justice, which amounted to enforcing the laws against abuses by colonial authorities who for around three centuries had gone unpunished. On January 3, 1781, as he was planning to take over Cusco, Túpac Amaru justified the killing of the Tinta *corregidor* José de Arriaga on November 10, 1780, as an exemplary punishment for his alleged actions against the church:

> Corregidores and other people insensitive to all acts of charity have covered up all these extortions against the law of God. . . . Because it has caused me so much pain that this city [Cusco's *cabildo*] has committed so much horror, beheading several of my people without granting them the last confession and dragging others, I must summon this illustrious cabildo to stop the excesses against the townspeople and grant me the entrance to the city. If this is not done immediately . . . I will force my entrance with fire and blood, at the discretion of my troops, without making any distinction among the people there. . . . A situation as important as this demands the surrender of all weapons, regardless of the immunity of those who carry them. Otherwise everybody would have to face the rigor of a just defensive war. . . . [A]nd they would experience all the rigor that divine justice demands.[69]

The execution of rebels without administering the sacrament of confession before death convinced the leader of the *corregidores*' anti-Christian nature. In the aftermath of the Sangarará victory, Túpac Amaru described the anti-Christian behavior of the colonial authorities to the visiting inspector José Antonio de Areche:

> They beheaded women while the Very Holy Sacrament was exposed in the holy [c]hurch of Sangarará, and that immediately unleashed God's wrath: because they did not worship the [s]acred, neither [did] the [s]acred help them; and as the aggravators of priests they died without their help. I sent out a couple of youngsters to preach to them in the streets so that they were treated as Christians (since I did not want to kill them but only to gather them, explain my reasons, and put them in the path of salvation), but heaven's high judgment sent them away, and they gave themselves to death, thus beginning their unhappy destiny. Is this the way to invite us to peace and subjection to the crown, by killing us like dogs without the necessary holy sacraments, as though we were not Christians, by throwing our corpses to the fields so the vultures make a feast out of them ... [and] by killing our women?[70]

Túpac Amaru's violence was, then, a "just, defensive war" against the sacrilegious vicegeral army and Cusco's *cabildo* officials, who unleashed God's wrath and did not listen to his "missional envoys."[71] The rebel leader impersonated a divine judge, crowning himself "Don José I for the grace of God, Inca King of Peru," and proclaiming to be the "dispenser of the divine justice" who would deliver Andeans from Spanish slavery.[72] Thus, the rebellion was conducted in the name of God, but it was also a sort of Andean counter-crusade against the Spanish "Christian infidels" and for the defense of the "sacred Catholic religion":

> [*Corregidores*] are apostates because they disregard the ten commandments. They know that there is one God but do not believe he is rewarding and just, and his own works stand for that. They despise the precepts of the [c]hurch, vilipending the ecclesiastic discipline and punishment, because they learn them as mere ceremonies or fantastic fiction. They never confess themselves because there is no priest [who] would possibly absolve them.[73]

Túpac Amaru's "crusade" was certainly at odds with the kind of Spanish Christianity endorsed by the church, and his writing did not lack determination to make the case that the rebellion was a morally justified "holy war" against non-Christian *corregidores*.

The rebel Catholicism during the upheavals of the period 1780–1783 was a discourse supported by armed action and a series of acts of power that implemented some measures Andean scholars and others had long demanded from the church and never obtained. The rebel leader appointed chaplains for his troops, as some *curas doctrineros* and local *caciques* joined the rebellion. It is also well-known, however, that other priests led troops against the rebels.[74] Túpac Amaru commanded Quechua-speaking priests to serve as his emissaries and to conduct communications and negotiations with the authorities of the Cusco *cabildo* on his behalf. Diego Cristóbal Túpac Amaru, another leader and the brother of José Gabriel Condorcanqui Túpac Amaru II, acted as a bishop during the rebellion, appointing *curas doctrineros* in curacies that had long remained without one. In his words, "[B]ecause I found some curates completely abandoned, I provided these ecclesiastics myself so that the [Indian] souls do not lack the spiritual food and other succor they need. And it would be very appropriate that Your Excellence enabled them with the necessary licenses."[75] Diego Cristóbal felt that his actions still needed the endorsement of Bishop Moscoso to be fully effective.

For his part, Julián Apasa Túpac Katari, the rebel Indian leader in Upper Peru who also adhered to Christianity, performed roles as an ecclesiastic authority. He took over some chapels and summoned ecclesiastics of his choice, while others were "elected" by the *común* (Indian town council) to offer religious services. In the midst of the rebellion, priests such as Don Isidro Escobar, Don Julián Bustillos, and Don Cayetano Torres performed mass and administered the sacraments to the rebels. Katari set up chapels in San Pedro and Pampajasi, outside the city of La Paz, and had weddings consecrated by unauthorized clerics. Ultimately, the judicial authorities accused the rebels of having conducted an "ecclesiastic insurrection" and committing crimes against the "[d]ivine and [h]uman [m]ajesty."[76]

The parabolic language of the Bible, characteristic of the "Cinco memoriales" and the "Representación verdadera," was also present in the rebel's papers. Túpac Amaru's edicts encapsulated religious imaginaries and textual devices known in the Andes since the times of Guamán Poma, Cuevas Herrera, Limaylla, and Fray Calixto. As in the "Representación verdadera" and the "Planctus indorum" three decades earlier, Túpac Amaru equated imperial Spain with ancient Egypt and its pharaohs, the later Goliath with the colonial authorities, and the ancient Hebrews with the Andean peoples.[77] He proclaimed himself the last descendant of the Inca rulers of Tawantinsuyo and the Andean equivalent of the Hebrew prophet Moses and King David, leading the Andeans to true knowledge of God, a sort of promised land where he would be the sole provider of divine justice.

Along similar rhetorical lines, Diego Cristóbal Túpac Amaru used biblical images to link Spanish tyranny with Indian rejection of Christianity when he addressed Moscoso in 1781, arguing that the insurrection was the natural outcome of the cruel and inhuman way *corregidores*, *caciques*, and *mandones* treated Indians. Because they were deaf to the Indians' pleas for justice, Indians could only "clamor like the Hebrew to shake off the oppression of so many pharaohs, and they were forced to fast from the spiritual food like the mass, the word of God, the holy sacraments . . . because they feared that upon their coming to the town . . . such judges . . . and ogres would be ready to demand and collect dues."[78] Oppressed Andeans, like the Hebrews, had to sacrifice their "spiritual food" and rebel to be delivered from colonial rule. Rebellion was thus forced on Andeans so they could live like "good Christians."

IDENTITY AND THE POLITICS OF RELIGIOUS "EXCESS": CONCLUSIONS

The analysis of identity formation in this chapter highlights the views and constructed images of Andeans and their colonial others in light of their own discourses, which expand our understanding of their intellectual creativity and political agency. Rather than simple and homogeneous, Andeans' identities involved a complex of interrelated layers, which, after all, characterizes human consciousness more generally. Andean intellectuals viewed themselves as the moral opposites of, and superior to, Spanish Christians, while they felt socially of a higher class than blacks and mulattoes. In line with the social agenda of ethnic self-empowerment they developed in the late seventeenth and eighteenth centuries, these writers strove to demonstrate that they were capable old Christians as well as social co-equals with the colonial Spanish nobles. As such, educated Andean nobles naturally felt entitled to the priesthood, education in schools and universities, and civil service and to be allowed to perform their nobility publicly through Spanish dress and membership in prestigious social orders.

The textual analysis in this chapter reveals Andeans' political culture of reciprocity and cultural negotiation with the colonizer in the mature stages of Spanish rule. As in their pre-colonial *mañay*, they adopted some of the colonizer's cultural institutions. They used *pureza de sangre* to define their standing as old Christians and nobility as well as their entitlement. These scholars brought to bear their ancestors' willing acceptance of Christianity and rendering of tribute as signals of their compromise with Spaniards' social values, the expectation being that as an "Indian nation," the king would guarantee the means for their social and cultural survival. But Andeans did not simply accept the colonizer's culture at face value; as they wrote their ideas, they redefined the meaning of nobility and purity. Their discussions of neophytism and their defense of access to social opportunities were also political battles over the definition of their identities. They sought to deconstruct the colonial definition of Andeans as Indians who were in a perpetual state of legal minors and fought to shake off the day-to-day tutelage and social control of Spaniards.

From the late 1600s through the late 1700s, *caciques* and other participants in Andean networks from different regions of Peru referred to themselves as an "Indian nation," a homogeneous, ethnic denominator for native elites and their mestizo relatives. This identification was articulated mostly by elite Andeans who strove to equate their social status with that of the Spanish nobles and also deployed it to distinguish themselves from Spaniards and to stress their autonomous agenda. By erasing ethnic boundaries and intra- and internal ethnic conflicts (probably overshadowed by interaction in the city among Andean immigrants from diverse regions) and unproblematically mixing ethnic groups' disparate pasts, the "Indian nation" appeared as a homogeneous front, a redefined group identity used to negotiate opportunities for social advancement by Andean leaders that expressed itself both textually and through political activism in Lima and Madrid. In the area of identity formation, Indian elites, their mestizo relatives, and eventually local pro-Indian creoles shared a common ground, which challenges the contemporary understanding of these groups and their worlds as separate, with mestizos and creoles equally interested in disassociating themselves from Indians.

In describing their religiosity, Andean scholars perceived themselves as more devout Catholics and more loyal subjects than Spaniards; they willingly "surrendered" to Catholicism and filled their texts with a language of piety, devotion, and moral perfection. The discursive presence of this excess and the anxiety over their Christianity, however, prompt us to question the ulterior factors and ambiguity behind their rhetoric, which belies a kind of religiosity somewhat removed from the ideal of the church. Henry Ward's opinion that "the forms of Indian Christianity were more orthodox than the content" could also be applied to Andeans' religiosity in the last stages of Spanish colonialism, as seen in their written texts.[79] A careful analysis of their writings allows other subtexts to appear, a more political layer of discourse that unveils a certain pragmatism: the use of religious rhetoric for political and social empowerment, often expressed in complex strategies for asserting a religious identity that fostered their larger agenda. While stressing their own virtuous and pious Catholicism vis-à-vis non-Christian Spaniards, Andeans rejected the degrading identity of idolaters—which the colonial church had long imposed upon them—and blamed Spaniards' unjust rule for the Indians having run away from the mission towns to the montaña to resume their former religious traditions. In doing so, however, they acknowledged the resilience of native religions as challenging forces even in the late-colonial years.

Andean authors also reaffirmed their longtime conversion to Christianity and "resilient" Catholicism for more than purely spiritual reasons. They constructed their identities as rational and old Christians to establish their eligibility for the priesthood, education, and membership in prestigious organizations. They appealed to a notion of Christian love (*amor al prójimo*) to find a bridge between the Indian and Spanish worlds in their effort to avoid discrimination and attain social equality among the strata of the "two republics." Self-professing their Christian identities allowed Andean intellectuals to speak their truths as rational subjects, "willingly" associated with the dominant spiritual project.

Although Christians, however, Andeans presented themselves as anti-colonial Christians who believed that only the creation of an Indian priesthood and prelatehood would bring true Christianity and social harmony into existence. Their Christianity sought to accomplish the anti-colonial aim of erasing the colonial difference that made them inferior to Spaniards and kept them from self-rule and spiritual and social power. Confirming the creativity of mid-colonial Andean religiosity established by present-day scholars, the writers under study legitimized Spanish rule through the divine power of Viracocha's predictions—thereby diminishing the power of the papal bulls—and Christianized the Andean past as a dyadic monotheism. But they also Europeanized the definition of *huacas* to debunk Andeans' essentializing identity as idolaters. In different instances they detached themselves from their Inca past to identify as rational, less idolatrous Christians.

The religiosity of Andean scholars differed in various ways from the ideal model of Catholicism as preached and practiced by the church and other Spaniards in the Indies. Notions of "sin," "love," "divine justice," and "Christianity" were defined mostly in political terms and related to issues of injustice in this world. Justice, as understood by native and mestizo intellectuals, was the "true" Christianity, which would come about only when Andeans were able to have their own judges, educators, *procuradores*, managers of their organizations' funds, and priests. Ultimately, Andean intellectuals' Christianity played a political function in support of their agenda for ethnic self-assertion under colonial rule, even if that agenda was occasionally nuanced by long-term Christian utopias with cross-ethnic undertones. Their writing unmasked the political nature of the church as a colonial institution in which social and ethnic differences mattered as much as they did in any other non-spiritual organization of colonial society. In all of these forms, Andean religious cultures changed as they faced the colonial everyday encounter with European Christians, no less than Christianity itself was transformed as it was perceived, articulated, and actively reformulated by mid- and late-colonial educated Andeans.

NOTES

1. Powers, *Andean Journeys*, 11.
2. For a historical reconstruction of the formation of the Indian town El Cercado, see Lowry, *Forging an Indian Nation*; Coello de la Rosa, *Espacios de exclusión*.
3. Limaylla, "Memorial," 207v.
4. Ibid., 207.
5. Ibid., 207–207v.
6. AGI, Lima, 495, Abril 1, 1724.
7. Pease, *Perú Hombre e Historia*.
8. AGI, Lima, 495, Abril 1, 1724.

9. Walker, *Smoldering Ashes*, 51.

10. Ibid.

11. Ibid.

12. "Representación verdadera," 118.

13. Casas, *Brevísima relación de la destrucción de las Indias*, 72.

14. Cuevas Herrera, "Cinco memoriales," 219–220.

15. Ibid., 227.

16. Limaylla, "Representacion," 234.

17. Limaylla, "Memorial," 206.

18. "Representación verdadera," 122v, 160v–161.

19. AGI, Lima, 495, Octubre 26, 1724.

20. Similar complaints had been raised in the past by Garcilaso de la Vega, Guamán Poma de Ayala, and other Indian nobles. The *caciques* in 1724, however, were acting collectively to construct their identity, and they did so within the general struggle for more social and political space for Andeans in the late colonial period.

21. "Representación verdadera," 121v, 162–162v.

22. This perception also reveals the extent to which Spanish notions of purity shaped the Indians' mentality and were turned against African Andeans. Martínez, *Genealogical Fictions*, 121.

23. Casas, *Brevísima relación de la destrucción de las Indias*, 72.

24. Cuevas Herrera, "Cinco memoriales," 229, 235, 238, 262v.

25. "Representación verdadera," 143–144v.

26. AGI, Charcas, 363, 10–10v.

27. On earlier Andean performances of social difference and identity through Inca participation in Cusco's ceremonial life, see Dean, *Inca Bodies*.

28. "El día de Lima," 1748, 268.

29. I discussed in Chapter 3 the roles of individual rebel leaders in the parade and the activities of some of the other performers in the legal battles for enforcement of the *cédula de honores* in the eighteenth century and their support of Andean campaigns for the priesthood.

30. Glave, "The 'Republic of Indians' in Revolt," 507, 514.

31. Taylor, *Magistrates of the Sacred*.

32. Mills, "Bad Christians in Colonial Peru," 186.

33. For studies focusing on Andean religion in the sixteenth and seventeenth centuries, see, among others, Marzal, *La transformación religiosa peruana*; McCormack, *Religion in the Andes*; Mills, "Evil Lost to View," "Bad Christians in Colonial Peru," and *Idolatry and Its Enemies*; Griffiths, *The Cross and the Serpent*; Duviols, *La destrucción de las religiones andina*; Griffiths and Cervantes, *Spiritual Encounters*; Cahill, "The Virgin and the Inca." For Andean religion in eighteenth-century Cusco, see Szemiński, "Why Kill the Spaniard?" and "The Last Time the Inca Came Back."

34. Griffiths and Cervantes, *Spiritual Encounters*.

35. Ibid., 286; Marzal, *La transformación religiosa peruana*.

36. Taylor, *Magistrates of the Sacred*, 59.

37. Mills, "Evil Lost to View," 11–12, and *Idolatry and Its Enemies*; Griffiths and Cervantes, *Spiritual Encounters*.

38. Cuevas Herrera, "Cinco memoriales," 219–219v.

39. Peter Gose has proposed that Viracocha, the singular form of a former group of Inca and Andean ancestral deities, was thus redefined and presented by Spanish missionaries as a "wandering apostle" who had conducted early evangelization in the Andes. Gose, "Converting the Ancestors: Indirect Rule, Settlement Consolidation, and the Struggle over Burial in Colonial Peru, 1532–1614," in *Conversion: Old Worlds and New*, edited by Kenneth Mills and Anthony Grafton, Rochester: University of Rochester Press, 2003, 142.

40. Mills, "Evil Lost to View" and *Idolatry and Its Enemies*.

41. Gose, "Indirect Rule," 142–143.

42. In the first book, Garcilaso devoted himself to straightening out Spanish historians' common mistakes about the Inca religion in an effort to find similarities between it and Christianity (i.e., monotheism, the soul's immortality, the cross, and the final judgment). In the prologue, Garcilaso manifested his interest in revising the history of the Inca as rendered by Spanish historians by commenting and glossing their versions. In chapter 19, Garcilaso states that he supplemented the histories with information missing in the Spanish accounts and corrected false information the Spaniards had provided because they ignored the native languages. Vega, *Comentarios reales de los incas*, 6, 46.

43. Cuevas Herrera, "Cinco memoriales," 220.

44. A resurgence of interest in Garcilaso de la Vega's writings among later Andean scholars seemed to have occurred after publication of the second edition of his *Comentarios reales de los incas* in 1723. Osorio, *Clamor de los Indios Americanos*, 14.

45. In the second book of the *Comentarios reales de los incas*, Garcilaso de la Vega presents a history of religion that explains "idolatry" and also traces the origins of monotheism among the Inca: "[The Inca] had no other gods than the Sun, whom they worshipped for its natural benefits and excellence, as they were people more civilized and political than their ancestors." Vega, *Comentarios reales de los incas*, 60.

46. "Representación verdadera," 140.

47. Vega, *Comentarios reales de los incas*, 62.

48. Ibid., 59–64.

49. Ibid., 66–70.

50. "Representación verdadera," 140v–141.

51. Ibid., 165.

52. AGI, Indiferente General, 1660.

53. Ibid.

54. Ibid.

55. "Representación verdadera," 120v. See Chapter 6.

56. Ibid., 150v.

57. AGI, Lima, 19, 20, and 22, cited in Estenssoro Fuchs, *Del paganismo a la santidad*, 493. Estenssoro Fuchs maintained that the ecclesiastical recognition of the canonization of Nicolás Ayllón amounted to a challenge to the customary status of neophytes accorded to Andeans; hence, the intervention of the Lima Inquisition to avoid continuation of the proceedings. On the other hand, the strategy of Andeans' seeking appointments as Inquisition Tribunal officers so they could attain recognition as old Christians is reiterated in the "Planctus indorum" in 1750. Navarro, *Una denuncia profética* ["Planctus indorum"], 20[122], 470.

58. "Representación verdadera," 152.

59. Navarro, *Una denuncia profética* ["Planctus indorum"], 20[122], 470. Likewise, Fray Calixto asked for positions for noble Andeans in the Holy Office. "Representación verdadera," 167.

60. "Representación verdadera," 138v.

61. See previous discussion in Chapter 6, "History of the Legal Campaigns for Andean Noble Privileges." For further discussion of the notion of purity of blood, its original links to religion and racial connotations in Iberian societies, and how the concept evolved in Spanish America and among Indian elites, see Martínez, *Genealogical Fictions*.

62. "Representación verdadera," 158.

63. Estenssoro Fuchs, *Del paganismo a la santidad*, 441.

64. "Representación verdadera," 160–161v.

65. To "live together like brothers and congregated in a single body, destroying the Europeans." Lewin, *La rebelión de Tupac Amaru*, 367, 398, cited in Thomson, *We Alone Rule*, 171.

66. A rich scholarly literature has examined Inca utopianism in the rebellions and their more specific religious substratum. See, among others, Stern, *Resistance, Rebellion, and Consciousness*, particularly these essays in parts 1 and 2: Stern, "The Age of Andean Insurrection"; Mörner and Trelles, "A Test of Causal Interpretations"; Campbell, "Ideology and Factionalismo"; Salomon, "Ancestor Cults and Resistance to the State"; Szemiński, "Why Kill the Spaniard?" and Flores Galindo, "In Search of an Inca." See also Szemiński, *La utopía tupamarista*; Flores Galindo, "La nación como utopía"; Walker, *Smoldering Ashes*; Thomson, *We Alone Rule*.

67. Thomson, *We Alone Rule,* 170. On several occasions he manifested that his project was a Catholic one: "[Our goal] is to preserve the faith and the precepts of our [h]oly [m]other [c]hurch, and to enlarge it." He was stern with ecclesiastics who opposed the rebellion, although he asked them to pray for him in their masses and to commend him to the "divine majesty" for the success of his "enterprise." AGI, Lima, 1039, Enero 3, 1781, 4.

68. Alternative interpretations of the rebels' violence against Spaniards can be found in Szemiński, "Why Kill the Spaniard?" 167. Szemiński discusses the rebels' various perceptions of Spaniards, including that of Spaniards as heretics, which adds to my analysis of Spaniards as anti-Christians, or "untrue" Christians, more generally. Insurrectionists used the idea that Túpac Amaru would end the offenses against the church and the tyranny of *corregidores* to justify their actions with arguments suitable to the dominant colonial regime. Thomson, *We Alone Rule*, 169.

69. AGI, Lima, 1039, Enero 3, 1781, 29.

70. Ibid., 214.

71. Alternative interpretations of the "God" the rebels referred to suggest that this call for violence against Spaniards had a more traditionally Inca meaning. In his analysis of Andean belief systems in the Great Rebellion, Leon Campbell refers to an Andean belief that the Inca creator god, Viracocha, aware of the critical times Andeans lived in, had prompted Andeans to act against those he saw as immoral figures who were going against God. Campbell, "Ideology and Factionalismo," 117.

72. Túpac Amaru, "El Bando de Coronación," 1780, reproduced in Durand Flores, *Independencia e integración*, 173.

73. Túpac Amaru, 780, reproduced in Durand Flores, *Colección documental del bicentenario*, 215.

74. O'Phelan, "El mito de la independencia concedida"; Campbell, "Ideology and Factionalismo"; Valcárcel, *Rebeliones coloniales sudamericanas*, 78; Thomson, *We Alone Rule*, 169.

75. "Copia de la carta que el rebelde Diego Túpac Amaru respondió a la que le escribió el Señor Obispo del Cuzco, sobre su rendimiento." Azángaro, Noviembre 5, 1781, reproduced in Valcárcel, *Colección documental de la independencia del Perú*, 153.

76. "Testimonio de la confesión del reo Julián Apaza, alias Tupa-Catary y de la sentenzia que se dio y ejecutó en su persona," Febrero 20, 1782, reproduced in ibid., 177, 183–184. For further analysis of Túpac Katari's religious beliefs, religious/political dynamics, and symbolic performance of spiritual authority, see Thomson, *We Alone Rule*, esp. chapters 5 and 6.

77. "Maybe the cause of our temporal and spiritual devastation is that the pharaoh that harasses us and mistreats us is not just one but many outsider [*forasteros*] pharaohs, so iniquitous and perverted like the corregidores, their lieutenants . . . and collectors; them being certainly so diabolical and perverse that I presume they were born out of an infernal chaos, impious, cruel and tyrannical." Durand Flores, *Colección documental del bicentenario*, 206.

78. "Copia de la carta que el rebelde Diego Túpac Amaru respondió," 150.

79. Cited in Taylor, *Magistrates of the Sacred*, 61.

⊁ 8 ⊰

CONCLUSION

A SUBTLE CURRENT OF RESISTANCE to the effects of Spanish colonialism in
the lives of Indian elites and their mestizo kin developed in the areas hardest
hit by the impact of both the Toledan and the Bourbon reforms in the seventeenth and eighteenth centuries, respectively. The social movement thus generated articulated a social and intellectual leadership through Andeans' writing,
petitioning in the royal courts, and traveling across the Atlantic to negotiate their
agenda with the kingdom's top authorities and further the enforcement of justice.
They struggled for repositioning as ethnic elites in a colonial society whose rulers
implemented policies that undermined Indian authority and downgraded mestizos, intensified racial discrimination, and altered the fabric of Andean societies
in different but drastic ways; eventually, the most dramatic result was widespread
rebellion. Andean intellectuals contributed extensively to the writing of colonial
critiques and advocated for imperial reform and social change. Thus, their changing political and religious cultures emerged almost naturally as the salient themes
of this history.

As opposed to their earlier counterparts, Andean scholars from the mid-
1600s through the late 1700s expanded their scholarly work to take in a wider

field of political and collective endeavors for social change that included the community of *kurakas*, their mestizo relatives, and eventually creole supporters. With the support of members of the lower church and other non-Indian sympathizers, some of the manuscripts were authored collectively; the writers delivered the manuscripts across the Atlantic and directly addressed the king and royal authorities with their discourses of social justice and imperial reform. Their travels and writings helped prompt the production of a body of royal laws that, although barely enforced, still gave Andean leaders a rhetorical tool to demonstrate the ineffectiveness of the justice system and thereby the dubious effects of the hegemonic attempts by the Habsburg and early Bourbon authorities to include Andean elites in the process of governance and leadership through laws and noble privileges. These writers and rebels expressed their concern about ethnic autonomy, advocating for Andean elites' reconstitution from various regions of the Viceroyalty of Peru as a singular constituency (the "Indian nation") while textually seeking to liberate themselves from the predefined colonial stereotypes of Indians as minors, neophytes, and dependents on state and ecclesiastical tutelage.

These Andean elites constructed a discourse of justice based on a critique of the colonial institutions that loomed large in Andeans' lives, such as the *mita* system, *obrajes*, the colonial judicial system of *corregidores* and *audiencia* judges, and the church. A strong indictment against abuses of Indians and the corruption and incompetence of officials and priests, as well as ethnic discrimination within social institutions, characterized Andean narratives of justice while the writers solidified their critiques with their own philosophical and theological interpretations of European notions of natural right, common good, divine justice, and tyranny. They used these frameworks to demand justice and empower their claims for full participation in the church, *cacicazgos*, schools, and knightly orders and showed concern about the preservation of their political autonomy.

In writing and delivering their proposals for social change, Andean intellectuals joined the efforts of informal networks of *kurakas*, sympathetic clerics, and mestizo sympathizers who—perhaps inadvertently—were beginning to create a public space for the expression of Andean views and imaginaries. The demands and cosmopolitanism of these networks reveal that elite Indian and mestizo leaders were evolving into subjects who struggled for incipient forms of enfranchisement, particularly during the mid- and late eighteenth century. Within these networks, participants appeared to reclaim freedom of movement across the Atlantic to actualize their condition as free subjects. Such freedom would also enable them to own property and participate in market transactions with no obstacles, as well as to reclaim management of their own communal assets and funds. As de-colonizing agents, Andeans demanded secular education, civil service, and equal access to social institutions of power with keen awareness of their ethnic autonomy.

The networks that supported these progressive efforts operated through trans-Atlantic and provincial travel, legal representation, protest writing, and negotiations of proposals for social change. Ultimately, the convergence point of these networks, the seat of the Audiencia of Lima and the Audiencia of Charcas, reflected the structure of the colonial justice system and the regional scope of the social unrest caused by the wholesale reforms that consolidated and restructured the colonial system. Occasionally, members of these networks also supported, directly and indirectly, more radical struggles—including the frustrated rebellions in Lima in 1666 and 1750, the Oruro rebellion in 1739, and the Huarochirí rebellion in 1750. The hypothesis regarding the trans-Atlantic networks needs more testing. The full range of roles of this interconnected activism, as well as the history of the formation, change, and continuity of the networks in these and other regions of the Viceroyalty of Peru, deserve further research.

The writings of mid- and late-colonial Indian elites and mestizos were important sites of identity formation, a highly political endeavor in their contemporary lettered culture. Educated Andeans presented themselves as unquestionably loyal subjects of the king while actually subverting the colonial hierarchical order by seeking equality with the Spanish nobility. They were concerned with asserting their "rational" and "civilized" condition as good old Christians while strategically veiling undertones of Andean identity politics. Their constructions of identity also illustrate the extent to which Spanish social and gender norms shaped these scholars' mental world. While they wrote in part to contest colonial exclusionary practices, their writings also reflected their own internalization of racial biases against blacks and other *castas* in Peru, as well as their shared views of women as pure, naive, and docile. Similarly, they perceived Indian commoners as helpless (*miserables*), passive creatures and assumed that, along with women, Indians needed guidance.

Even though most of the Andean texts studied in this book coexisted with the cultural and political expressions of the "Andean Utopia," starting in the seventeenth century, or with the Inca "revivalism" or "Inca nationalist movement" in the eighteenth century, they offer little association with such trends beyond the self-fashioning heirs of Inca rulers. In the minds of the scholarly Andeans examined in this book, there seemed to be no contradiction among their genealogy as Inca descendants, membership in a homogeneous "Indian nation," and the overt ruptures with their Inca past that were sometimes needed to reassert their present identities as Christians. Beyond the occasional use of Inca names and symbols and the self-representation as an "Indian nation" lies a consistent agenda for Andean ethnic autonomy under Spanish rule, legitimized with a variety of symbols. This agenda would have empowered elite Indians and mestizos as a group culturally and historically distinct from Spaniards and other *castas* and, most important, one entitled to justice and to political and social self-determination.

In the case of Túpac Amaru II, for example, by crowning himself the "Inca king" and writing edicts and *reales cédulas*, he was enacting Andean power by using colonial symbols. Although he protested the burden of tribute, he did not advocate its abolition; further, he did not question Christianity. Perhaps these colonial institutions were accepted as the Andean "contribution" to the colonial pact of reciprocity. The rebel leader's agenda of Inca rule follows almost naturally the historical tradition of earlier Indian elites who sought noble privileges to defend their positions as *caciques* or to gain *mercedes*, which in the Inca past had functioned as customary forms of reciprocity between new rulers and conquered peoples. Túpac Amaru wanted to create an autonomous "republic" of Indians, along with creoles and blacks, rather than an anachronistic return to the Inca society of the past. Andean scholars' long legal and textual battles and their journeys to Spain to demonstrate direct descent from the Inca and negotiate social privileges seem to have less to do with Inca or, more generally, Andean pre-Hispanic customs than with following Spanish law. Theirs was a struggle for ethnic autonomy within the colonial world, aided by the legal weapons the colonial system made available. When those weapons did not work, as usually happened, Andeans used the weapon of rebellion, but in both scenarios what was at stake was autonomy rather than the revival of the Inca past.

For some Andean writers in the mid-1700s—although none from Cusco Province—the Inca past was long gone, but its symbols were still productive. They had the potential to create a sense of collective identity, a memory Inca and non-Inca Andeans from different regions used in the colonial present to empower and distinguish themselves from Spaniards but equally entitled to social and cultural autonomy within a hierarchical and racialized society. In fact, since the late 1500s, most claimants of Inca descent who sought social or political recognition had been redefining their ethnic identity. Resorting to Inca symbols, they applied for *mercedes*, aware that the crown recognized the Inca as purebloods and the "natural" lords of the land. Proving Inca descent, then, was the gate to attain noble privileges and, in many cases, to retain or even access for the first time political rights to a *cacicazgo*. Thus, the notion of an "Indian nation" in the late stages of Spanish rule goes beyond a revivalist claim to carve a wider social and political space within the colonial society in which Indians, mestizos, and creoles—as proposed by Vélez de Córdoba in 1739 and Túpac Amaru II in 1780–1781—were able to live in harmony and obtain justice, away from the interference and "bad example" of Spaniards. The political imaginaries of Andeans since the times of the *cédula de honores* in 1697 and later, in 1749—with the claims of Fray Calixto for wider participation in the administration of justice, the spiritual realm, education, and the market economy—indicate a new Andean consciousness directed toward the de-colonization of their lives and societies and their cultural and political reaffirmation.

Túpac Amaru's vision of a multi-ethnic nation free from Spanish control had antecedents. Even as some claimed Inca descent, the intellectuals from the Andes studied in this work were pushing earlier for the opening up of the political system to redefine Andeans as autonomous political agents rather than Indians. After all, the use of Inca symbols in late-colonial Andean political culture did not preclude other, more progressive political projects.[1] This book not only decenters and questions the "modern" subject in the Andes by stressing the ways Andean scholars went about de-colonizing through ethnic autonomy but also reassesses its own chronology.

The inextricable relationship between colonial Andean scholarship and religion reveals Andeans' contribution to unique developments of Christian discourse and theology in Spanish America. They used Christian ethics as the yardstick to criticize the church—which led them to reformulate notions of "sin," "neophytism," "idolatry," and "divine will"—along with raising their voices against the prevalence of old dictates from the late 1500s' Lima church councils in the management of the priesthood by Peruvian religious orders through the late colonial period. The politicized Christian identity and notions of justice in the scholarship of low-ranking religious men, such as Fray Calixto, Juan de Cuevas Herrera, and Juan Núñez Vela de Rivera, demonstrate that the colonial church was far from homogeneous and that Andean colonial religion cannot be understood without acknowledging the use of Christian discourse to buttress social and political struggles, which unveils Andeans' wider understanding of spirituality.

Although they professed a Christian religious identity in their writings, their renditions usually diverted from the Spanish church's ideal of Christianity and seemed to emphasize Andeans' spiritual and moral superiority vis-à-vis the colonizers and their dubious Christian practices. Becoming a *kuraka* or a *cacique*, a priest, a missionary, or an Indian judge or being appointed to a secular position within the local government was not only a means to attain social prestige in colonial Peru but was also a crucial platform for Andeans to participate in the redistribution of justice they felt was necessary to confront colonial racism. Participation in the spiritual realm of colonial society seemed crucial to counteract the general disenfranchisement of Indian and mestizo subordinates connatural to Spanish colonialism. In the end, native resistance to colonialism was exacerbated by the colonial church's systematic opposition to the legitimate aspirations of longtime converts to partake in the power realm of the sacred, which even royal laws and the disposition of higher political and religious authorities outside Peru seemed to support, at least in their legal discourse.

Wrapped in Catholic devotional phraseology, the recurrence of statements about Indians' and mestizos' just right to join the priesthood unveils a political agenda of native power. They not only understood the symbolic power of religious spaces, positions, and rituals but were also well aware of the actual political power held by priests and church officials in Spanish America. In battling their way into the convent, Andeans learned, among other things, that the realm of spiritual power in a colonial domain was highly contentious—as mediation between humans and God was restricted to a select minority of Spaniards and creoles—and that the colonial church in Peru left only a narrow place, if any, for native Andeans, even as they strove to present themselves as utterly devoted and mature Christians. This recurrence, and the anxiety over access to religious spaces, made evident the colonial church's failure to include Andeans as Christian equals and made Andeans' claims to full membership in the Catholic Church a spiritual impossibility as well as a persistent political goal.

The Andean writers encountered in this book pushed the limits of the Habsburgs' state-crafted segregationist policies to realize a colonial impossibility: Andeans' almost complete autonomy within the "republic of Indians," in a realm with no colonial intermediaries between them and the king and no Spanish or non-Andean ecclesiastic emissaries to mediate their connection with God. In addition, Spanish judges, *corregidores, protectores de indios*, priests, bishops, and *doctrineros* would not be needed. This political/religious imaginary found initial support in the Habsburg principle of equal entitlement to nobility for the elite Indians and Spaniards of the realm, which expressed itself in a long history of unenforced royal laws and a de facto denial of Indian nobles' access to key spheres of spiritual and social power. Thus, Indians painfully realized that beyond the legal discourse of the "two republics," justice in the kingdom was ultimately a means to enforce racial and ethnic inequality.

Andean legal activism sought to secure both the enforcement of previous ineffective laws and the issuing of new *cédulas* to address the social crisis that had driven Indians into social decline. While the recourse to direct justice from the king in an effort to secure the enforcement and production of laws implied recognition of his ultimate authority, Andean intellectuals and activists also found other ways to influence royal policies, and they indirectly produced a record of colonial laws for their advancement under colonial rule. Thus, they and activists from the Indian networks became visible political agents in colonial judicial life. The turn to legal discourse empowered their petitions and at the same time moved the petitioners to explain the history of judicial negligence through their own accounts, as well as their reflections on the behavior of colonial officials. Thus, the non-enforcement of royal laws represented an avenue to question colonial justice while providing an entry point for the production of critical texts that sought the creation of new laws to correct injustices. Most important, Andean scholarship and political action contributed to legal reformulations of the status of Indian and mestizo elites as subordinate groups in Spanish American societies.

The participation of Andean scholars in the realm of the written word in Peru and Spain—with their ideas, styles of argumentation, experience, trans-Atlantic travels, and political strategies—problematizes the notion of the *ciudad letrada* put forth by Angel Rama, who saw it as a domain only for the expressions of colonial Spanish and creole elites. This book has demonstrated that elite Indians and mestizos made inroads into that sphere—however contentiously—by making their voices heard in the *audiencias*, the royal courts of Madrid, and the ecclesiastical councils and even attempting to reach the Vatican. The intertextual relationship between Andean discourses and European Scholastic traditions of political theology along with the common trope of *agravios y vejaciones*, in both Andean scholarship and the discourses of creoles and Bourbon administrators, also prompts Andeanists to expand Mary Louis Pratt's notion of the "Contact Zone" (see Chapter 1) to allow for the joined textual production and intellectual and political collaboration/contention among educated Andeans, creoles, Spaniards, and ecclesiastics.

Simultaneously, the examination of Andean intellectual culture calls us to further identify cultural and intellectual bridges between the two "republics." The use of the term "Andean" in this work speaks to the recognition of the increasing presence of mestizos and some creole supporters in the world of Andean elites as colonial times moved forward and also problematizes a common assumption that mestizos sought unproblematically to separate themselves from the Indian world. The mestizo writers studied here—including Fray Calixto, Cuevas Herrera, and Núñez Vela de Rivera—strove to present themselves as legitimate members of the Indian world, as nobles of the "Indian nation" and descendants of the "gentiles," and their proposals spoke as much in favor of the native elites as they did of their mestizo descendants. In short, educated mestizos were in truth colonial Andean actors who presented themselves as both "Indian" and "Christian." In particular, Fray Calixto's claims for nobility and access to religious power for Indians and mestizos revealed the historical changes in, and expansion of, the Indian world in the late colonial period. Likewise, the increasing visibility of intellectual Andeans in a social sphere in which colonial codes and power practices were exercised and disputed by Andeans and Europeans alike prompts us to recognize a new form of intercultural exchange that characterized colonial culture—one that challenges common understandings of colonial and Andean elites as operating in separate spheres, never to engage in a dialogic relationship or share intellectual interests and practices. This study has also demonstrated how indigenous and mestizo ladinos, with their critical texts and proposals, helped question the analytical value of the Habsburg notion of two separate republics, since their intellectual and social activism not only bridged the "two" worlds but also highlighted the power relationships that held them together and in which Andean leaders struggled to reconstitute their new sense of an ethnic community. This refashioning of ethnicity stimulates further research on, and problematization of, the meaning of "indigenous" in the late colonial period.

The various intersections and disjunctions between Andean and other colonial discursive streams attest to the ways Andean intellectuals engaged the institutional discourses of the colonial lettered world, while such discourses, in turn, appropriated Andeans' knowledge to advance their institutional goals. Likewise, the intertextual relationships among Andean discourses from the early seventeenth century and those that constitute the focus of this work reveal the appropriation of early Andean scholars' discursive elaborations by their later counterparts, as they resituated Inca Garcilaso de la Vega's rendition of Inca history to support the idea of the common past of the "Indian nation." The writings examined in this book attest to the circulation of Garcilaso de la Vega's *Comentarios reales de los Incas* in Andean intellectual circles for nearly two centuries after its publication. Limaylla, Cuevas Herrera, and Fray Calixto adopted and reformulated Garcilaso de la Vega's rendition of the Incan past to reconstruct a common historical memory, cultural identity, and Andean religiosity as the "Indian nation" entered postcolonial times in the Andes. Garcilaso de la Vega's efforts to establish parallels between Incan religion and European Christianity were echoed, with variations, by Cuevas Herrera, Juan Santos Atahualpa, and Fray Calixto. Late-colonial Andean scholars were proud of Garcilaso de la Vega's scholarly achievements and prestige and did not hesitate to cite him extensively. Although taken only fragmentarily, Garcilaso de la Vega's scholarly work functioned as an authoritative source of Andean collective memory beyond the confines of the Cusco area and was used to empower the common cultural identity of Andeans of various ethnicities in the mid- and late years of Spanish colonialism in the Andes.

Thus, the *ciudad letrada* in colonial Peru was not only the chorus of colonial elites' harmonic voices. It was also a multi-vocal space in which the voices of intellectual Indian elites, mestizos, and Africans from various regions of the Viceroyalty of Peru disputed their own places to introduce a necessary counterpoint or dissonance in the midst of otherwise apparently undisputed colonial relationships of power.

NOTE

1. Walker, *Smoldering Ashes*, 51. Walker highlights the importance of pluralizing the subject of nationalism and accounting for its multiple layers in light of Túpac Amaru's political approach.

Epilogue

A T THE CLOSE OF THIS JOURNEY through the lettered cultures of mid- and late-colonial Andeans, it is important to summarily highlight the continuity and change in Andean discursive production and social activism into postcolonial times. In the early nineteenth century, Andean writing reappeared, echoing the aftermath of the social upheavals of the late colonial era from the perspectives of both supporters and opponents.[1] In the subsequent decades, a prevalent genre of Indian memoirs and autobiographies—oral, written, dictated, or a combination of these forms—is found, which became rather prolific in the twentieth century. The post-independence period in Andean Peru brought little change to the deteriorating social situation of indigenous peoples; according to their writings, we might think that the advent of capitalism only deepened their marginalization more generally. Indian *memoriales* abound in postcolonial times, exposing the depth of violence against Andeans in the Peruvian countryside as agrarian capitalism made inroads in the first decades of the twentieth century. The validation of oral history in late–twentieth-century academia has made texts by contemporary indigenous scholars and representatives of communities in the public sphere accessible to wider audiences. Native scholars re-created discourses of protest that also proceed from within community struggles with capitalism in the countryside and in mining and industrial areas.[2]

A prime example of this pattern of legal struggles conducted through extensive networks of Indian legal representatives and large-scale social mobilization into the postcolonial years can be found in Bolivia. During these years, Andean networks of *caciques apoderados* were constituted mostly of traditional indigenous authorities and came to represent communities from around the country in their struggle to recover communal lands and *cacicazgos*. Indian legal representatives, however, no longer traveled to the royal court in Madrid but instead went to the national courts in La Paz; rather than clerics as companions, they were accompanied by their lawyers, in search of social justice from the nation-state.[3]

Even though there are no known extant records of colonial indigenous women's discursive and textual production, in the twentieth century the remarkable participation of indigenous women in the production of oral narratives and the reconstruction of their community struggles through memory reminds us of women's involvement in the social and legal struggles, written documents, and direct negotiation with top authorities for the defense of community land rights—a culture inherited from the colonial Andean scholars and social activists studied in previous chapters.[4]

In the last fifty years, the intersection of religion and popular politics has been central to the social and political struggles of different groups of Latin American poor. What developed in the twentieth century as "liberation theology" bears an unmistakable similarity to the ideas and discursive strategies of the colonial Andean intellectuals studied in this book, although it is usually acknowledged to have begun only in the 1950s–1960s. As opposed to Andean scholarship, liberation theology's tenets are broadly inspired by the modern values of the French Revolution and some Marxist tenets.[5] Liberation theology became the religious doctrinal expression of some Latin American social movements in the 1960s—mostly in Brazil, Peru, Chile, Argentina, Ecuador, Colombia, and Central America—which included key groups within the lower church and a few in the upper church (priests, missionaries, bishops, and lay religious organizations) and an array of social groups and organizations, including women, peasants, workers, and civic communities.[6]

Among liberation theology's central tenets, the reformulation of biblical books such as Exodus as "the paradigm of enslaved people's struggle for liberation"[7] speaks directly to colonial Andean scholars' discursive strategies. As established in Chapter 3, the "Representación verdadera" is a lamentation that paraphrases the words of the prophet Jeremiah on the captivity and oppression of the Hebrews by the Egyptians—a passage Andeans used to protest the hardship they experienced under Spanish rule and as a call for ethnic liberation. Late-colonial Andean leader José Gabriel Condorcanqui Túpac Amaru II also drew a parallel between the oppression of Indians in Peru and the captivity of the Hebrews in Egypt and presented himself as in line with the liberator prophet Moses and the divinely appointed King David.[8]

In most of the writings studied here, Andean scholars offered moral condemnation of colonialism, constructing Spanish rule as inherently sinful (violent, unjust, corrupt, and ultimately non-Christian). Similarly, liberation theology in the second half of the twentieth century advanced a critique of dependent capitalism as an immoral, unfair, and utterly harmful system—ultimately "a form of structural sin."[9] Although indictments of colonialism and the use of the Bible to support ideas of social justice were hardly the exclusive province of the Andean scholars studied in this book, these expedients were part and parcel of the early clerical critiques of Spanish conquistadors, such as those leveled by Fray Bartolomé de las Casas, Fray Domingo de Santo Tomás, and Fray Bernardino de Sahagún in the conquest era. While the specific tenets and agendas of such critiques changed over time, Andean critiques of colonialism through expressions of Christianity have remained a vital and long-lasting feature of Andean political culture. In the process, Christianity and its discursive form have been transformed and reutilized by Andean intellectuals who found no redress for their social marginalization in either the colonial or the national state.

NOTES

1. Sahuaraura Tito Arauchi, "Estado del Perú"; Túpac Amaru J. B., cited in Loayza, *Cuarenta años de cautiverio.*

2. Painemal Huenchal, *Vida de un dirigente Mapuche*; Encinas, *Jinapuni.*

3. Cusicanqui, "Indigenous Women and Community Resistance"; Churi Condori and Ticona Alejo, *Escribano de los Caciques Apoderados.*

4. Cusicanqui, "Indigenous Women and Community Resistance."

5. Löwy, *War of Gods.* Liberation theology also responded to transformations inside the Catholic Church that produced theological reformulations grounded in modern social sciences and philosophy known as "social Christianity," mostly in Germany and France during World War II. The movement attempts to offer a response to the major social, economic, and political changes occurring in Latin America since the 1950s, specifically the widespread phenomenon of poverty in capitalist-dependent societies. See also Klaiber, *La iglesia en el Perú*; Bidegain, *Historia del cristianismo en Colombia.*

6. Löwy, *War of Gods*, 32.

7. Ibid., 34.

8. Durand Flores, *Colección documental del bicentenario*, 206, 237; Szemiński, "The Last Time the Inca Came Back," 287.

9. Löwy, *War of Gods*, 35.

Selected Bibliography

ARCHIVAL SOURCES

AGI   Archivo General de Indians, Seville, Spain
AGN   Archivo General de la Nación
ARSI Archivum Romanum Societatis Iesu, Rome, Italy
BNM   Biblioteca Nacional de Madrid
BRP   Biblioteca Real del Palacio de Madrid, Madrid, Spain

UNPUBLISHED PRIMARY DOCUMENTS (ONLY THE MAJOR TEXTS ANALYZED IN THE BOOK ARE INCLUDED)

AGI, Charcas, 45. Ayavire et al., ca. 1582, 1v–12.
AGI, Charcas, 363. Oruro, "Manifiesto," 9v.
AGI, Indiferente General, 648. Juan Núñez Vela de Rivera.
AGI, Lima, 442. Vicente Morachimo, "Manifiesto de los Agravios, Bexaciones y Molestias, que padecen los indios," 1739, 1–13v.
AGI, Patronato, 171.
AGN, Lima, Escribanía, Siglo XVIII. Protocolo no. 187, Años 1790–1818, 213, 396, 298v.

BNM [ca. 1567], Falcón, "Representación de los daños y molestias que se hacen a los Indios," 220–237v.

BNM, Manuscrito 20193. "Ascendencia de Carlos Inga."

BRP, Madrid, Sign. II/2819. Juan de Cuevas Herrera. "Cinco memoriales en que breve y sucintamente se da noticia de los mayores impedimentos que hay para que estos indios del Perú no acaben de entrar en la ley y costumbres evangélicas. Dirigidos al Rey nuestro señor por el Lizenziado Juan de Cuevas Herrera Cura beneficiado de los Pueblos de Andamarca y Hurinoca en la Provincia de los Carangas, natural de la Ciudad de la Plata en los Carchas." Ca. 1650, 218–269.

BRP, Madrid, Sign. II/2823. "Representación verdadera y exclamación rendida y lamentable, que toda la Nación Indiana hizo a la magestad del Señor Rey de las Españas, y Emperador de las Indias, El Señor Don Fernando VI. Pidiendo los atienda y remedie sacandolos de el afrentoso vituperio y oprobio en que están mas ha de doscientos años. Exclamación de los Indios Americanos, usando para ella de la misma que hizo el profeta Geremias a Dios en el Cap. 5 y últimos de sus Lamentaciones." Ca. 1749–1750, 118–169v.

BRP, Sign. II/2848, Jerónimo Lorenzo Limaylla. "Memorial dado a la Magd. del Sr. Dn. Carlos II. POR Dn. Geronimo Lorenzo Limaylla, Yndio Cazique principal y Governador de la Provincia del Valle de Jauja, del Repartimiento de Lauringunaca en el Reyno del Perú. Suplicando que S. M. se dignase instituir para los Indios Nobles, en quienes concurriesen las calidades expresadas en él, una *Cavallería* ú *Orden* a semejanza de las *Militares*, con que se obviarían los graves inconvenientes que en el día se experimentaban, y sería de alivio honor y reconocimiento para aquellas Naciones, y de gran utilidad al Rl. Erario, por las razones que se refieren." Ca. 1677, 204–210v.

BRP, Sign. II/2848, Jerónimo Lorenzo Limaylla. "Representación hecha al Sr. Rey Dn. Carlos Segundo. POR Dn. Geronimo Lorenzo Limaylla, Yndio Cazique del Repartimiento de Luringuanca Repartimiento, de la Provincia de Jauja, Reyno del Perú, como poder teniente de los demas Caziques Governadores de las demás Provincias del dho. Reyno y como parte principal, y legitima, a quien toca mirara por el alivio y conservación de los Indios *en la cual consiste y estriba* la mayor propagación de la Fe y aumento de la Rl. Hacienda, a fin de que S.M. se dignase dar las providencias convenientes para su ien tratamiento y que no fuesen vejados, ni oprimidos en la dura servidumbre de los españoles." Ca. 1667, 211–247v.

PUBLISHED PRIMARY DOCUMENTS

Acosta, José de, S.J. *De procuranda Indorum salute*, book 5. Madrid: Consejo Superior de Investigaciones Científicas, 1984 [1588].

Alvarez, Bartolomé. *De las costumbres y conversión de los indios del Perú. Memorial a Felipe II, 1588*. Edited by María del Carmen Martí Rubio, Juan J.R. Villarías Robles, and Fermín del Pino Díaz. Madrid: Ediciones Polifemo, 1998.

Arriaga, Pablo Joseph de. *La extirpación de la idolatría en el Pirú*. Estudio preliminar y notas de Henrique Urbano. Cuzco, Peru: Centro de Estudios Regionales "Bartolomé de las Casas," 1999.

Avendaño, Diego de, and Angel Muñoz García. *Thesaurus indicum*. Pamplona: Ediciones Universidad de Navarra, 2001 [1621].

Bandin Hermo, Manuel. "Un descendiente de los Incas, lego Franciscano." *Archivo Ibero-Americano. Estudios históricos sobre la orden franciscana en España y sus misiones* 55 (Enero-Febrero 1923). Año 10, 90–91.

Bernales Ballesteros, Jorge. "Fray Calixto de San José Túpac Inca." *Historia y Cultura* 3 (1969): 5–36.

Casas, Bartolomé de las. *Brevísima relación de la destrucción de las Indias*. Edición de André Saint-Lu. México, D.F.: Rei México, 1988 [1542].

Durand Flores, Guillermo, comp. *Colección documental de la independencia del Perú*, tomo 2, vol. 4. Edited by Carlos Daniel Valcárcel. Lima: Comisión Nacional del Sesquicentenario de la Independencia del Perú, 1971.

Durand Flores, Luis. *Independencia e integración en el Plan Político de Túpac Amaru*. 5 vols. Edited by P. L. Villanueva. Lima: Comisión Nacional del Bicentenario de la Rebelion Emancipadora de Túpac Amaru. 1981–1982.

———. *Colección documental del bicentenario de la revolución emancipadora de Túpac Amaru*, tomo 3. 1981. Lima: Comisión Nacional del Bicentena rio de la Rebelión Emancipadora de Túpac Amaru, 1980.

"El día de Lima. Proclamación realque de el nombre augusto de el supremo señor d. Fernando elvi . . . hizo la muy noble y muy leal ciudad de los reyes Lima fervonzada a influxo del zelo fiel . . ." Jose A. Manso de Velasco. Lima: n.p., 1748, 268–309.

Espinosa Serrano, Waldemar. *El memorial de Charcas. (Crónica inédita de 1582)*. Lima: Ediciones Universidad Nacional de Educación, 1969.

Guamán Poma de Ayala, Felipe. *Nueva corónica y buen gobierno*. Edited by John V. Murra and Rolena Adorno. México, D.F.: Siglo XXI editores, 1980 [ca. 1615].

Inca. "Colegio de Caciques." 1(4) (Octubre–Diciembre 1923): 779–883. Lima: J. C. Tello ed.

Izaguirre, Bernardino de. *Historia de las misiones Franciscanas y narración de los progresos de la geografía en el oriente del Perú. Relatos originales y producciones en lenguas indígenas de varios misioneros*. Lima: Talleres tipográficos de la penitenciaría, 1922 [1870].

Juan, Jorge y Santacilia, and Antonio de Ulloa. *Noticias secretas de América*. Edited by Luis J. Ramos Gómez. Madrid: Historia 16, 1990 [1749].

Konetzke, Richard. *Colección de documentos para la historia de la formación social de Hispanoamérica 1493–1810*, vol. 2, part 1 (1593–1659), part 2 (1660–1690); vol. 3, part 1 (1691–1779). Madrid: Consejo Superior de Investigaciones Científicas, 1958, 1962.

Lewin, Boleslao. *La rebelión de Tupac Amaru y los orígenes de la emancipación americana*. Buenos Aires: Librería Hacehette S.A., 1957.

Lienhard, Martin. *Testimonios, cartas y manifiestos indígenas: Desde la conquista hasta el comienzos del siglo XX*. Caracas: Biblioteca Ayacucho, 1992.

Loayza, Francisco A., ed. *Cuarenta años de cautiverio (Memorias del inca Juan Bautista Túpac Amaru)*. Lima: Pontificia Universidad Católica del Perú, 1941.

———, ed. *Fray Calixto Túpac Inca, Documentos originales y en su mayoría totalmente desconocidos, auténticos, de este apóstol indio, valiente defensor de su raza, desde el año de 1746 a 1760*. Lima: Pontificia Universidad Católica del Perú, 1948.

Lohmann Villena, Guillermo, and Maria Justino Sarabia Viejo. *Francisco de Toledo. Disposiciones gubernativas para el Virreinato del Perú, 1569–1574.* 2 vols. Sevilla: Escuela de Estudios, Hispanoamericanos, Consejo Superior de Investigaciones Científicas, Monte de Piedad, Caja de Ahorros, 1986.

Medina, José Toribio. *La Imprenta en Lima (1584–1824),* tomo 3. Santiago, Chile: Impreso y grabado en casa del autor, 1905.

Mendieta, Jerónimo de, Joaquín García Izcabalceta, and Antonio Rubial García. *Historia eclesiástica Indiana.* Mexico, D.F.: Consejo Nacional para la Cultura y las Artes, 1997.

Montenegro, Alonso de la Peña. *Itinerario para párrocos de indios/Alonso de la Peña Montenegro*; edición crítica por C. Baciero et al., 2 vols. Madrid: Consejo Superior de Investigaciones Científicas, 1995 [1688].

Montero, Victorino. "Estado político del Perú." Madrid, 20 de Abril, 1747. Colección Mata Linares, tomo 78: *Cuarta Parte.* Madrid: Real Academia de Historia, 1970.

Moreno Cebrián, Alfredo, ed. *Relación y documentos de gobierno del virrey del Perú, José A. Manso de Velasco, Conde de Superunda (1745–1761).* Madrid: Consejo Superior de Investigaciones Científicas, 1983.

Navarro, José María. *Una denuncia profética desde el Perú a mediados del siglo XVIII.* Lima: Pontificia Universidad Católica del Perú, Fondo Editorial, 2001.

Nölte, Jurgen. *Repartos y rebeliones: Túpac Amaru y las contradicciones de la economía colonial.* Traducción Carlos Degregori Caso. Lima: Instituto de Estudios Peruanos, 1980.

Polo, José Toribio. "Un libro Raro." *Revista Peruana* 1(8) (1879–1880): 625–634.

Quiroga, Pedro de, and Daisy Ripodas Ardanaz. *Coloquios de la verdad.* Valladolid: Instituto de Cooperación Iberoamericana, Case-Museo de Colón, 1992 [1563].

Recopilación de leyes de las Indias, libro 6, título 6: "Del Servicio Personal"; título 7, ley 17, Madrid, December 10, 1576. *Reales cédulas* from February 1549, December 1563, and November 4, 1601. Available at http://www.congreso.gob.pe/ntley/LeyIndiaP.htm.

Sahuaraura Tito Atauche, José Rafael. "Estado del Perú", AGI, Lima, 76. In *Colección documental de la independencia del Perú,* tomo 2, vol. 1. Edición y prólogo de Carlos Daniel Valcárcel. Lima: Comisión Nacional del Sesquicentenario de la Independencia del Perú, 1992 [1784].

Salinas y Córdoba, Buenaventura de. *Memorial de las historias del Nuevo Mundo Pirú.* Lima: Universidad Mayor de San Marcos, 1957 [1653].

Spalding, Karen. *Royal Commentaries of the Incas and General History of Peru / Garcilaso de la Vega, El Inca.* Translated by Harold V. Livermore, edited with an Introduction by Karen Spalding. Indianapolis: Hackett Publishing, 2006.

Torre Villar, Ernesto de la. *Los pareceres de Don Juan de Padilla and Diego León Pinelo acerca de la enseñanza y buen tratamiento de los indios.* México, D.F.: Universidad Nacional Autónoma de México, 1979.

Valcárcel, Carlos Daniel, ed. *Colección documental de la independencia del Perú,* tomo 2: "La rebelión de Túpac Amaru," vol. 3. Lima: Comisión Nacional del Sesquicentenario de la Independencia del Perú, 1972 [1971].

Vega, Inca Garcilaso de la. *Comentarios reales de los Incas,* tomo 1. Caracas: Biblioteca Ayacucho, 1991 [1609].

Villagómez, Pedro de. *Carta pastoral de instrucción y exhortación contra las idolatrías Exortaciones e instrucción acerca de las idolatrías de los indios del arzobispado de Lima, por el Dr. Don Pedro de Villagómez, arzobispo de Lima; anotaciones y concordancias con las crónicas de Indias.* Edited by Horacio H. Urteaga; noticias biográficas, por Carlos A. Romero. Lima: San Martín, ca. 1919 [1649].

Vitoria, Francisco de. *Relecciones sobre los indios y el derecho de guerra.* Buenos Aires, Mexico: Espasa–Calpe Argentina, S.A., 1946 [1539].

Yupanqui, Diego de Castro Tito Cusi. *History of How the Spaniards Arrived in Peru.* Translated with an introduction by Catherine Julien. Indianapolis: Hackett, 2006 [1565].

SECONDARY SOURCES

Acree, William G., Jr. "Jacinto Ventura de Molina: A Black *Letrado* in a White World of Letters, 1766–1841." *Latin American Research Review* 44(2) (2009): 37–58.

Adorno, Rolena. *From Oral to Written Expression: Native Andean Chronicles from the Early Colonial Period.* Syracuse, N.Y.: Maxwell School of Citizenship and Public Affairs, Syracuse University, 1982.

———. *Writing and Resistance in Colonial Peru.* Austin: University of Texas Press, 1986.

———. "La 'ciudad letrada' y los discursos coloniales." *Hispamerica revista de literatura* 16(48) (1987): 3–24.

———. *Cronista y príncipe. La obra de Don Felipe Guaman Poma de Ayala.* Lima: PUCP, 1989.

———. "Nosotros somos los kurakakuna: Images of Indios Ladinos." In *Transatlantic Encounters.* Edited by Kenneth J. Andrien and Rolena Adorno. Berkeley: University of California Press, 1991.

———. "Felipe Guaman Poma de Ayala: Native Writer and Litigant in Early Colonial Peru." In *The Human Tradition in Colonial Latin America.* Edited by Kenneth J. Andrien. Wilmington, Del.: Scholarly Resources, 2002.

Adorno, Rolena, Pierre Duviols, and Mercedes López-Baralt. *Sobre Wuaman Puma de Ayala.* La Paz: Hisbol, 1987.

Alaperrine-Bouyer, Monique. "Esbozo de una historia del Colegio de San Francisco de Borja de Cuzco." In *Actas de congreso internacional de AHILA (Liverpool 17–22 de Septiembre de 1996).* Edited by John R. Fisher. Liverpool: Asociacion de Historiadores Latinoamericanistas Europeos and Instituto de Estudios Latinoamericanos Universidad de Liverpool, 1996.

———. "Enseignements et Enjeux d'un Héritage Cacical. Le Long Plaidoer de Jerónimo Limaylla, Jauja, 1657–1678." In *Les autorités indigenes entre deux mondes solidarité ethnique et compromission coloniale.* Edited by Bernard Lavallé. Paris: Université de la Sorbonne Nouvelle, París 3, 2004.

———. *La educación de las élites indígenas en el Perú colonial.* Lima: Instituto Francés de Estudios Andinos, Instituto Riva Aguero, Instituto de Estudios Peruanos, 2007.

Amich, José. *Historia de la misiones del convento de Santa Rosa de Ocopa.* Lima: Milla Batres, 1975.

Andrien, Kenneth J. *Crisis and Decline: The Viceroyalty of Peru in the Seventeenth Century.* Albuquerque: University of New Mexico Press, 1985.

———. "The *Noticias secretas de América* and the Construction of a Governing Ideology for the Spanish American Empire." *Colonial Latin American Review* 7(2) (1998): 175–192.

———. "The Coming of Enlightened Reform in Bourbon Peru." In *Enlightened Reform in Southern Europe and Its Atlantic Colonies, c. 1750–1830.* Edited by Gabriel Paquette. Farnham, Surrey, England: Ashgate, 2009.

Aquinas, Thomas. "On Law and Natural Law: Summa Theologiae, First Part of the Second Part, 1–2, 90–94." In *Thomas Aquinas Selected Readings.* Edited and translated with introductory notes by Ralph Mcinery. New York: Penguin Books, 1998.

Bakewell, Peter J. *Miners of the Red Mountain: Indian Labor in Potosí 1545–1650.* Albuquerque: University of New Mexico Press, 1984.

Barreda Laos, Felipe. *Vida intelectual del Perú.* Buenos Aires: Talleres Gráficos Argentinos L. J. Rosso Doblas 951, 1937.

Berquist, Emily. The Science of Empire: Bishop Martínez Compañón and the Enlightenment in Peru. PhD diss., University of Texas at Austin, 2007.

———. "Bishop Martínez Compañón's Practical Utopia in Enlightenment Peru." *The Américas* 64(3) (January 2008): 377–408.

Bidegain, Ana María. *Historia del cristianismo en Colombia: Corrientes y diversidad.* Bogota: Taurus, 2004.

Brading, David A. "Tridentine Catholicism and Enlightened Despotism in Bourbon Mexico." *Journal of Latin American Studies* 15 (1983): 1–22.

———. "The Inca and the Renaissance: The Royal Commentaries of Inca Garcilaso de la Vega." *Journal of Latin American Studies* 18(1) (May 1986): 1–23.

———. *The First America: The Spanish Monarchy, Creole Patriots, and the Liberal State, 1492–1867.* Cambridge: Cambridge University Press, 1991.

Brading, David A., and Harry E. Cross. *Colonial Silver Mining: Mexico and Peru.* Berkeley: Center for Latin American Studies, Institute of International Studies, University of California, 1972.

Buntix, Gustavo, and Luis Eduardo Wuffarden. "Incas y reyes españoles en la pintura colonial peruana: La estela de Garcilaso." *Márgenes* 8 (1991): 151–210.

Burga, Manuel. *El nacimiento de un autopía. Muerte y resurrección de los Incas.* Lima and Guadalajara: Universidad mayor de San Marcos and Universidad de Guadalajara, 2005.

Burns, Kathryn J. *Colonial Habits: Convents and the Spiritual Economy of Cuzco, Peru.* Durham, N.C.: Duke University Press, 1999.

———. "Nuns, Kurakas and Credit: The Spiritual Economy of Seventeenth-Century Cuzco." In *Women and Religion in Old and New Worlds.* Edited by Susan E. Dinan and Debra Meyers. New York: Routledge, 2001.

———. "Notaries, Truth, and Consequences." *American Historical Review* 110(2) (April 2005): 350–379.

Cahill, David. "The Virgin and the Inca: An Incaic Procession in the City of Cuzco in 1692." *Ethnohistory* 49(3) (Summer 2002): 611–649.

———. "A Liminal Nobility: The Incas in the Middle Ground of Late Colonial Peru." In *New World, First Nations: Native Peoples of Mesoamerica and the Andes under*

Colonial Rule. Edited by David Cahill and Blanca Tovías. Portland, Ore.: Sussex Academic Press, 2006.

Campbell, Leon G. "Ideology and Factionalismo during the Great Rebellion, 1780–1782." In *Resistance, Rebellion, and Consciousness in the Andean Peasant World: 18th to 20th Centuries.* Edited by Steven J. Stern. Madison: University of Wisconsin Press, 1997.

Castro-Klaren, Sara. "El orden del sujeto en Guaman Poma." *Revista de crítica literaria latinoamericana* 41 (1995): 121–134.

Certeau, Michel de. *The Practice of Everyday Life.* Translated by Steven Rendall. Berkeley: University of California Press, 1984.

Chang-Rodríguez, Raquel. "Peruvian History and the Relación of Titu Cussi Yupanki." In *From Oral to Written Expression: Native Andean Chronicles of the Early Colonial Period.* Edited by Rolena Adorno. Foreign and Comparative Studies 4. Syracuse, N.Y.: Maxwell School of Citizenship and Public Affairs, Syracuse University, 1982.

Charles, John Duffy. Indios Ladinos: Colonial Andean Testimony and Ecclesiastical Institutions (1583–1650). PhD diss., Yale University, 2003.

Churi Condori, Leandro, and Esteban Ticona Alejo. *Escribano de los Caciques Apoderados. Kasikinakan Purirarunakakn Qillqiripa.* La Paz: Hisbol/The Oral History Workshop, Ediciones Aruwiyiry, 1992.

Coello de la Rosa, Alexandre. *Espacios de exclusión, espacios de poder. El Cercado de Lima colonial (1568–1606).* Lima: Alexandre Coello de la Rosa, IEP Ediciones, Pontificia Universidad Católica del Perú–Fondo Editorial, 2006.

Cole, Jeffrey A. "An Abolitionism Born of Frustration: The Conde de Lemos and the Potosí Mita 1667–1673." *Hispanic American Historical Review* 63(2) (1983): 307–333.

———. *The Potosí Mita, 1573–1700: Compulsory Indian Labor in the Andes.* Stanford, Calif.: Stanford University Press, 1985.

Cook, Noble Davis. *Demographic Collapse: Indian Peru 1520–1620.* Cambridge: Cambridge University Press, 1981.

Cornblit, Oscar. *Power and Violence in the Colonial City: Oruro from the Mining Renaissance to the Rebellion of Túpac Amaru, 1740–1782.* Cambridge: Cambridge University Press, 1995.

Cusicanqui, Silvia Rivera, comp., The Oral History Workshop. "Indigenous Women and Community Resistance." In *History and Memory: Women and Social Change in Latin America.* Edited by Elizabeth Jelin. London: Zed Books, 1992.

Dean, Carolyn. *Inca Bodies and the Body of Christ: Corpus Christi in Colonial Cuzco, Peru.* Durham, N.C.: Duke University Press, 1999.

Dueñas, Alcira. Andean Scholarship and Rebellion: Indigenous and Mestizo Discourses of Power in Mid- and Late Colonial Peru. PhD diss., Ohio State University, 2000.

Durston, Alan. *Pastoral Quechua: The History of Christian Translation in Colonial Peru (1550–1650).* Notre Dame, Ind.: Notre Dame University Press, 2007.

Duviols, Pierre. *La destrucción de las religiones andinas.* México, D.F.: Universidad Nacional Autónoma de Méjico, 1977.

Eguiguren, Luis Antonio. *Diccionario histórico cronológico de la real y pontificia Universidad de San Marcos y sus colegios. Crónica e investigación,* tomo 1. Lima: Imprenta Torres Aguirre, 1949.

Encinas, Enrique. *Jinapuni. Testimonio de un dirigente campesino.* Edited by Fernando Mayorga and Enrique Birhuel. La Paz: HISBOL, 1989.

Estenssoro Fuchs, Juan Carlos. "El simio de Dios. Los indígenas y la iglesia frente a la evangelización del Perú, siglos XVI–XVII." *Bulletin de l'Institut Français d'Études Andines* 30(3) (2001): 455–474.

———. *Del paganismo a la santidad. La incorporación de los indios del Perú al Catolicismo 1532–1750.* Lima: Pontificia Universidad Católica del Perú, Instituto Francés de Estudios Andinos, and Juan Carlos Estenssoro Fuchs, 2003.

Figuera, Guillermo. *La formación del clero indígena en la historia eclesiástica de América 1500–1810.* Caracas: Archivo General de la Nación, 1965.

Fisher, John R., Allan J. Kuethe, and Anthony McFarlane, eds. *Reform and Insurrection in Bourbon New Granada and Peru.* Baton Rouge: Louisiana State University Press, 1990.

Flores Galindo, Alberto. "La nación como utopía: Tupac Amaru 1780." In *La revolución de los Tupac Amaru: Antología.* Edited by Luis Durand Flórez and Carlos Daniel Valcárcel. Lima: Comisión Nacional del Bicentenario de la Revolución Emancipadora de Túpac Amaru, 1981.

———. *Buscando un Inca. Identidad y utopía en los Andes.* Obras Completas, vol. 3. Lima: Sur Casa de Estudios del Socialismo, 2005.

Foucault, Michel. *The Archeology of Knowledge.* Translated from the French by A. M. Sheridan Smith. New York: Pantheon Books, 1972.

García-Bedoya M., Carlos. "Discurso criollo y discurso andino en la literatura peruana colonial." In *Heterogeneidad y literatura en el Perú.* Edited by James Higgins. Lima: Centro de estudios literarios Antonio Cornejo Polar, 2003.

García Cabrera, Juan Carlos. *Ofensas a Dios pleitos e injurias. Causas de Idolatrías y hechicerías. Cajatambo Siglos XVII–XIX.* Cuzco: Centro de Estudios Regionales Andinos "Bartolomé de las Casas" and Juan Carlos García Cabrera, 1994.

Garrett, David. *Shadows of Empire: The Indian Nobility of Cuzco, 1750–1825.* Cambridge: Cambridge University Press, 2005.

Gisbert, Teresa. *Iconografía y mitos indígenas en el arte.* La Paz: Gisbert y Cía. S.A. Libreros Editores, 1980.

Gisbert, Teresa, and José de Mesa. *Historia de la pintura cuzqueña.* Buenos Aires: Domingo E Taladriz, 1962.

Glave, Luis Miguel. *Trajinantes. Caminos indígenas en la sociedad colonial. Siglos XVI/ XVII.* Lima: Instituto de Apoyo Agrario y Luis Miguel Glave, 1989.

———. "The 'Republic of Indians' in Revolt (c. 1680–1790)." In *The Cambridge History of the Native Peoples of the Americas,* vol. 3, part 2. Edited by Frank Salomon and Stuart B. Shwartz. Cambridge: Cambridge University Press, 1996.

———. *De rosa y espinas. Economía, sociedad y mentalidades andinas, siglo XVII.* Lima: Instituto de Estudios Peruanos, Banco Central de Reserva del Perú, Fondo Editorial, 1998.

Gose, Peter. "Converting the Ancestors: Indirect Rule, Settlement Consolidation, and the Struggle over Burial in Colonial Peru, 1532–1614." In *Conversion: Old Worlds and New.* Edited by Kenneth Mills and Anthony Grafton. Rochester, N.Y.: University of Rochester Press, 2003.

Griffiths, Nicholas. *The Cross and the Serpent: Religious Repression and Resurgence in Colonial Peru.* Norman: University of Oklahoma Press, 1996.

Griffiths, Nicholas, and Fernando Cervantes. *Spiritual Encounters: Interactions between Christianity and Native Religions in Colonial America.* Edgbaston: University of Birmingham Press, 1999.

Gruzinski, Serge. *La colonización de lo imaginario. Sociedades indígenas y occidentalización en el México español. Siglos XVI–XVIII.* México, D.F.: Fondo de Cultura Económica, 1991.

Heras, Julián O.F.M. *Aporte de los franciscanos a la evangelización del Perú.* Lima: Provincia Misionera de San Francisco Solano, 1992.

Holbrook, Frank B. *Jeremiah: Faith amid Apostasy.* Boise, Idaho: Pacific Press Publishing Association, 1994.

Jouve Martín, José Ramón. *Esclavos de la ciudad letrada. Esclavitud, escritura, y colonialismo en Lima (1650–1700).* Lima: Instituto de Estudios Peruanos, 2005.

Klaiber, Jeffrey. *La iglesia en el Perú: Su historia social desde la independencia.* Lima: Pontificia Universidad Católica del Perú, 1988.

Lienhard, Martin. *La voz y su huella: Escritura y conflicto étnico-social en América Latina 1492–1988.* Hanover, N.H.: Ediciones del Norte, 1991.

———. "Writing from Within: Indigenous Epistolary Practices in the Colonial Period." In *Oralities and Literacies as Reflexes of Colonization and Resistance: Creating Context in Andean Cultures.* Edited by Rosaleen Howard-Malverde. New York: Oxford University Press, 1997.

Loaiza, Francisco. *Ed. Juan Santos el invencible: Manuscritos del año 1742 al año 1755.* Lima: Imprenta D. Miranda, 1942.

Lorandi, Ana María. *De quimeras rebeliones y utopías.* Lima: Pontificia Universidad Católica del Perú and Fondo Editorial, 1997.

———. *Spanish King of the Incas: The Epic Life of Pedro Bohorques.* Pittsburgh: University of Pittsburgh Press, 2005.

Lowry, Lyn Brandon. Forging an Indian Nation: Urban Indians under Spanish Colonial Control, Lima, Peru, 1535–1765. PhD diss., University of California–Berkeley, 1991.

Löwy, Michael. *The War of Gods: Religion and Politics in Latin America.* London: Verso, 1996.

Macera, Pablo. "Noticias sobre la enseñanza elemental en el Perú durante el siglo XVIII." In *Trabajos de Historia,* tomo 2. Edited by Pablo Macera. Lima: Instituto Nacional de Cultura, 1977.

Mannheim, Bruce. *The Language of the Inca since the European Invasion.* Austin: University of Texas Press, 1991.

Martín, Luis. *The Intellectual Conquest of Peru: The Jesuit College of San Pablo, 1568–1767.* New York: Fordham University Press, 1968.

Martínez, María Elena. *Genealogical Fictions: Limpieza de Sangre, Religion and Gender in Colonial Mexico.* Stanford: University of California Press, 2008.

Marzal, Manuel. *La transformación religiosa peruana.* Lima: Pontificia Universidad Católica del Perú, Fondo Editorial, 1983.

McCormack, Sabine. *Religion in the Andes: Vision and Imagination in Early Colonial Peru*. Princeton, N.J.: Princeton University Press, 1991.

Mignolo, Walter D. "Colonial and Postcolonial Discourse: Cultural Critique or Academic Colonialism?" *Latin American Research Review* 28(3) (1993): 120–134.

———. *Local Histories/Global Designs: Coloniality, Subaltern Knowledges, and Border Thinking*. Princeton, N.J.: Princeton University Press, 2000.

———. *The Idea of Latin America*. Malden, Oxford, Victoria: Blackwell, 2005.

Millones, Luis. *Historia y poder en los Andes*. Madrid: Alianza Editorial, 1987.

Mills, Kenneth. *"An Evil Lost to View": An Investigation on Post-Evangelization Andean Religion in Mid-Colonial Peru*. Liverpool: Institute of Latin American Studies, 1994.

———. "Bad Christians in Colonial Peru." *Colonial Latin American Review* 5(2) (1996): 183–218.

———. *Idolatry and Its Enemies: Colonial Andean Religion and Extirpation, 1640-1750*. Princeton, N.J.: Princeton University Press, 1997.

Olaechea, Juan B. "Los indios en las órdenes religiosas." *Missionalia Hispánica* 86 (1972): 242–252.

O'Phelan, Scarlett. "El mito de la independencia concedida: Los programas políticos del siglo XVIII y del temprano XIX en el Perú y alto Perú (1730–1814)." In *Problemas de la formación del estado y la nación en Hispanoamérica*. Edited by Inge Buisson, Gunter Kahle, Hans-Joachim Konig, and Horst Pietschmann. Bohn: Bohlau Verlag Koln Wien, 1984.

———. *Rebellions and Revolts in Eighteenth Century Peru and Upper Peru*. Berlin: Bohlau Verlag Koln Wien, 1985.

———. *Un siglo de rebeliones anticoloniales: Perú y Bolivia 1700–1783*. Cuzco: Centro de Estudios Regionales Andinos "Bartolomé de las Casas," 1988.

———. *La gran rebelión en los Andes: De Túpac Amaru a Túpac Catari*. Cuzco: Centro de Estudios Regionales Andinos "Bartolomé de las Casas," 1995.

———. *Kurakas sin sucesiones. Del cacique al alcalde de indios Perú y Bolivia 1750–1835*. Cuzco: Centro de Estudios Regionales Andinos "Bartolomé de las Casas," 1997.

———. "Ascender al estado eclesiástico. La ordenación de indios en Lima a mediados del siglo XVIII." In *Incas e Indios Cristianos: Elites indígenas e identidades cristianas en los Andes coloniales*. Edited by Jean-Jacques Decoster. Cuzco and Lima: Centro de Estudios Regionales Bartolomé de las Casas, Asociación Kuraka, and Institut Français d'Études Andines, 2001.

———. "Linaje e Ilustración. Don Manuel Uchu Inca y el real seminario de nobles de Madrid (1725–1808)." In *El hombre y los Andes: Homenaje a Franklin Pease G.Y.* Edited by Rafael Flores Espinosa and Rafael Varón Gabai. Lima: Pontificia Universidad Católica, Instituto Francés de estudios Andinos, 2002.

Ortiz, Fernando. *Contrapunteo cubano del tabaco y el azúcar*. Caracas: Biblioteca Ayacucho, 1978 [1940].

Osorio, F. Eduardo. *Clamor de los Indios Americanos*. Merida, Venezuela: Consejo de Publicaciones de la Universidad de los Andes, 1993.

Pagden, Anthony. *El imperialismo español y la imaginación política. Estudios sobre teoría social y política europea e hispanoamericana (1513–1830)*. Barcelona: Planeta, 1990.

Painemal Huenchal, Martín Segundo. *Vida de un dirigente Mapuche*. Edited by Rolf Foerster. Santiago: Grupo de Investigaciones Agrarias y Academia de Humanismo Cristiano, ca. 1984.

Paz y Guiní, Melchor de. *Guerra separatista. Rebeliones de Indios en Sur América. La sublevación de Tupac Amaru*, vol. 2. Lima: n.p., 1952.

Pease, Franklin. "Kurakas coloniales: Riqueza y actitudes." *Revista de Indias* 48 (Enero-Agosto) (1988): 87–108.

———. *Kurakas, reciprocidad y riqueza*. Lima: Pontificia Universidad Católica del Perú, Fondo Editorial, 1992.

———. *Perú hombre e historia. Entre el siglo XVI y el XVIII*, vol. 2. Lima: Edubanco, 1992.

Peralta, Victor. "Tiranía o buen gobierno. Escolasticismo y criticismo en el Perú del siglo XVIII." In *Entre la retórica y la insurgencia. Las ideas y los movimientos sociales en los Andes siglo XVIII*. Comp. Charles Walker. Cuzco: Centro de Estudios Regionales Andinos "Bartolomé de las Casas," 1996.

Phelan, John Leddy. *The Millennial Kingdom of the Franciscans in the New World*. Berkeley: University of California Press, 1970.

Platt, Tristan, Thérèse Bouysse-Cassagne, and Olivia Harris, eds. *Qaraqara-Charka. Mallku, inka y rey en la provincial de Charcas (siglos XV–XVII). Historia antropológica de una confederación aymara*. Edición documental y ensayos interpretativos. La Paz: Instituto Francés de Estudios Andinos, Plural Editores, University of St. Andrews, University of London, Inter-American Foundation, Fundación Cultural del Banco Central de Bolivia, 2006.

Powers, Karen Vieira. *Andean Journeys: Migration, Ethnogenesis, and State in Colonial Quito*. Albuquerque: University of New Mexico Press, 1995.

Pratt, Mary Louise. *Imperial Eyes: Travel Writing and Acculturation*. New York: Routledge, 1992.

Premo, Bianca. *Children of the Father King: Youth, Authority, and Legal Minority in Colonial Lima*. Chapel Hill: University of North Carolina Press, 2005.

Prien, Hans-Jürgen. *La historia del Cristianismo en América Latina*. Salamanca, Spain: Ediciones Sígueme, 1985.

Puente Luna, José Carlos de la. What's in a Name? An Indian Trickster Travels the Spanish Colonial World. MA thesis, Texas Christian University, 2006.

Quispe-Agnoli, Rocío. *La fé andina en la escritura: Resistencia e identidad en la obra de Guamán Poma de Ayala*. Lima: Universidad Mayor de San Marcos, 2006.

Rama, Angel. *La ciudad letrada*. Hanover, N.H.: Ediciones del Norte, 1984.

Rama, Angel, and John Charles Chasteen. *The Lettered City*. Durham, N.C.: Duke University Press, 1996.

Ramírez, Susan E. *The World Upside Down: Cross-Cultural Conflict in Sixteenth-Century Peru*. Stanford, Calif.: Stanford University Press, 1996.

———. "The Cosmological Basis of Local Power in the Andes during the Sixteenth and the Seventeenth Centuries." In *New World, First Nations: Native Peoples of Mesoamerica and the Andes under Colonial Rule*. Edited by David Cahill and Blanca Tovías. Portland, Ore.: Sussex Academic Press, 2006.

———. "To Serve God and King: The Origins of Public Education in Eighteenth-Century Northern Perú." *Colonial Latin American Review* 17(1) (June 2008): 73–99.

Rappaport, Joanne. *The Politics of Memory: Native Historical Interpretation in the Colombian Andes*. Cambridge: Cambridge University Press, 1990.

———. "Object and Alphabet: Andean Indians and Documents in the Colonial Period." In *Writing without Words: Alternative Literacies in Mesoamerica and the Andes*. Edited by Walter Mignolo and Elizabeth Boone. Durham, N.C.: Duke University Press, 1994.

Recopilación de Leyes de Indias (Libro VI, Título 1, 1.18; Libro 1, Título 13, 1.5). At http://www.congreso.gob.pe/ntley/LeyIndiaP.htm.

Reijo, Wilenius. *The Social and Political Theory of Francisco Suárez*. Helsinki: Societas Philosophica Fennica, 1963.

Ricard, Robert. *La conquista espiritual de México*. Mexico City: Fondo de Cultura Económica, 1995.

Robins, Nicholas A. *Genocide and Millennialism in Upper Peru: The Great Rebellion of 1780–1782*. Westport, Conn.: Praeger, 2002.

———. *Priest-Indian Conflict in Upper Peru: The Generation of Rebellion, 1750–1780*. Syracuse, N.Y.: Syracuse University Press, 2007.

Rowe, John. "Movimiento Nacional Inca del siglo XVIII." *Revista Universitaria del Cuzco* 107(2) (Semestre 1954): 3–33.

Saignes, Thierre. "Algún día todo se andará. Los movimientos étnicos en Charcas (siglo XVIII)." *Revista Andina* 3(2) (1985): 425–450.

———. "Caciques, Tribute and Migration in the Southern Andes." Society and the Seventeenth Century Colonial Order (Audiencia de Charcas). Mimeographed copy, 1995.

Sala I Vila, Nuria. "La rebelion de Huarochirí en 1783." In *Entre la retórica y la insurgencia: Las ideas y los movimientos sociales en los Andes, siglo XVIII*. Edited by Charles Walker. Cuzco: Centro de Estudios Regionales "Bartolomé de las Casas," 1996.

Salcamaygua, Juan de Santacruz Pachacuti Yamqui. *Relación de antigüedades deste reyno del Piru/Juan de Santacruz Pachacuti Yamqui Salcamaygua*, Estudio ethnohistórico y linguistico de Pierre Duviols y César Itier. Lima and Cusco: Institute Français d'Études Andines and Centro de Estudios Regionales Andinos "Bartolomé de las Casas," 1993.

Salomon, Frank. "Chronicles of the Impossible." In *From Oral to Written Expression: Native Andean Chronicles of the Early Colonial Period*. Edited by Rolena Adorno. Foreign and Comparative Studies 4. Syracuse, N.Y.: Maxwell School of Citizenship and Public Affairs, Syracuse University, 1982.

———. "Ancestor Cults and Resistance to the State in Arequipa, ca. 1748–1754." In *Resistance, Rebellion, and Consciousness in the Andean Peasant World: 18th to 20th Centuries*. Edited by Steve J. Stern. Madison: University of Wisconsin Press, 1987.

———. *The Cord Keepers: Khipus and Cultural Life in a Peruvian Village*. Durham, N.C.: Duke University Press, 2004.

Salomon, Frank, and Karen Spalding. "Cartas atadas con quipus: Sebastián Francisco de Melo, María Micaela Chinchanoy y la represión de la rebelión de Huarochirí de 1750." In *El hombre y los Andes. Homenaje a Franklin Pease G.Y.* Edited by Rafael

Flores Espinosa and Rafael Varón Gabai. Lima: Pontificia Universidad Católica del Perú, Instituto Francés de Estudios Andinos, 2002.

Salomon, Frank, and George L. Urioste, trans. *The Huarochirí Manuscript: A Testament of Ancient and Colonial and Andean Religion.* Annotations and introductory essay by Frank Salomon; transcription by George L. Urioste. Austin: University of Texas Press, 1991.

Saphier, William. *The Book of Jeremiah, Including the Lamentations; with Fifteen Drawings in Black and White by William Saphier.* New York: Private printing by N. L. Brown, 1921.

Sariola, Sakari. *Power and Resistance: The Colonial Heritage in Latin America.* Ithaca, N.Y.: Cornell University Press, 1972.

Seed, Patricia. "Colonial and Postcolonial Discourse." *Latin American Research Review* 26(3) (1991): 181–200.

Serulnikov, Sergio. *Subverting Colonial Authority: Challenges to Spanish Rule in the Eighteenth Century Southern Andes.* Durham, N.C.: Duke University Press, 2003.

Sotelo, Hildebrando. *Insurrecciones y levantamientos en Huarochirí y sus factores determinantes.* Lima: Empresa periodística, S.A., 1942.

Spalding, Karen. *Huarochirí: An Andean Society under Inca and Spanish Rule.* Stanford, Calif.: Stanford University Press, 1984.

———. "Social Climbers: Changing Patterns of Mobility among the Indians of Colonial Peru." In *Readings in Latin American History,* vol. 1: The Formative Series. Edited by Peter J. Bakewell, John Johnson, and Meredith D. Dodge. Durham, N.C.: Duke University Press, 1985.

———. "The Crises and Transformations of Invaded Societies: Andean Area (1500–1580)." In *The Cambridge History of the Native Peoples of the Americas,* vol. 3: South America, part 1. Edited by Frank Salomon and Stuart B. Schwartz. Cambridge: Cambridge University Press, 1999.

Stavig, Ward. *The World of Túpac Amaru: Conflict, Community, and Identity in Colonial Perú.* Lincoln: University of Nebraska Press, 1999.

Stavig, Ward, and Ella Schmidt, eds. and trans. *The Tupac Amaru and Catarista Rebellions: An Anthology of Sources.* Indianapolis, Ind.: Hackett, 2008.

Stern, Steven J. *Peru's Indian Peoples and the Challenge of Spanish Conquest: Huamanga to 1640.* Madison: University of Wisconsin Press, 1993.

———, ed. *Resistance, Rebellion, and Consciousness in the Andean Peasant World: 18th to 20th Centuries.* Madison: University of Wisconsin Press, 1987.

Szemiński, Jan. "Why Kill the Spaniard? New Perspectives in Andean Insurrectionary Ideologies in the 18th Century." In *Resistance, Rebellion, and Consciousness in the Andean Peasant World: 18th to 20th Centuries.* Edited by Steven J. Stern. Madison: University of Wisconsin Press, 1987.

———. *La utopía tupamarista.* San Miguel, Lima: Pontificia Universidad Católica del Perú, Fondo Editorial, 1983.

———. "The Last Time the Inca Came Back: Messianism and Nationalism in the Great Rebellion 1780–1783." In *South and Meso-American Native Spirituality: From the Cult of the Feathered Serpent to the Theology of Liberation.* Edited by Gary H. Hossen in collaboration with Miguel-León Portilla. New York: Crossroad, 1993.

Tanck de Estrada, Dorothy. *Pueblos de indios y educación en el México colonial 1750–1821.* México, D.F.: Colegio de México, Centro de Estudios Históricos, 1999.

Taylor, William. *The Magistrates of the Sacred: Priests and Parishioners in Eighteenth Century Mexico.* Stanford, Calif.: Stanford University Press, 1996.

Thomson, Sinclair. *We Alone Rule: Native Andean Politics in the Age of Insurgency.* Madison: University of Wisconsin Press, 2002.

Valcárcel, Carlos Daniel. *Rebeliones coloniales sudamericanas.* México, D.F.: Fondo de Cultura Economica, 1982.

Valle de Siles, María Eugenia del. *Historia de la rebelión de Tupac Catari, 1781–1782.* La Paz, Bolivia: Editorial Don Bosco, 1990.

Varesse, Stefano. *La sal de los cerros. Una aproximación al mundo campa.* Lima: Universidad Peruana di Ciencias y Tecnología, 1973.

Vargas Ugarte, Rubén. *Concilios Limenses (1551–1772),* tomo 2. Lima: Imprimatur Juan Cardenal Guevara, 1956.

———. *Historia del Perú virreinato (Siglo XVIII) 1700–1790.* Lima: Imprimatur: Hernandus Vega Centeno, Vicaris Generalis, 1956.

———. *Historia general del Perú virreinato (1689–1776),* tomo 4. Lima: Editorial Carlos Milla Batres, 1966.

Walker, Charles. *Smoldering Ashes: Cuzco and the Creation of Republican Peru, 1780–1840.* Durham, N.C.: Duke University Press, 1999.

Yannanakis, Yanna. *The Art of Being In-Between: Native Intermediaries, Indian Identity, and Local Rule in Colonial Oaxaca.* Durham, N.C.: Duke University Press, 2008.

Yupanqui, Diego de Castro Titu Cusi. *Instrucción al licenciado Don Lope García de Castro (1570), Inca Titu Cusi*; estudio preliminar y edicción, LiLiana Regaldo de Hurtada; paleografía, Deolinda Villa E; índices Juan Deyo B. Lima: Fondo Editorial, 1992.

Zamora, Marganta. *Language and Authority in the Comentarios Reales de los Incas.* Cambridge: Cambridge University Press, 1990.

Zarzar, Alons. *"Apu Cachauaina Jesús sacramentado" Mito, utopía y milenarismo en el pensamiento de Juan Santos Atahualpa.* Lima: Centro Amazónico de Aplicación Práctica, 1989.

Zavala, Silvio. *El servicio personal de los indios en el Perú (extractos del siglo XVII),* vol. 2. Mexico City: El Colegio de México, 1979.

INDEX